Penguin Handbooks

James Beard's Theory and Practice of Good Cooking

James Beard was born in Portland, Oregon, and it was there that his lifelong love affair with good food started. His first cookbook, *Hors d'Oeuvres and Canapés*, was published in 1940 and since then he has written many bestselling cookery books, including *The James Beard Cookbook*, *James Beard's American Cookery* and *Beard on Bread*. Over twenty years ago Mr Beard started giving cookery classes in what is now the kitchen of the restaurant Lutece, which was the beginning of his famous cookery school, now located in New York's Greenwich Village. Well-known throughout the United States as a cooking authority and demonstrator, Mr Beard travels widely and has taught cooking in many parts of America.

James Beard's Theory and Practice of Good Cooking

In collaboration with
José Wilson

Illustrations by Karl Stuecklen

Penguin Books

Penguin Books Ltd, Harmondsworth, Middlesex, England
Penguin Books, 625 Madison Avenue, New York, New York 10022, U.S.A.
Penguin Books Australia Ltd, Ringwood, Victoria, Australia
Penguin Books Canada Ltd, 2801 John Street, Markham, Ontario, Canada L3R 1B4
Penguin Books (N.Z.) Ltd, 182–190 Wairau Road, Auckland 10, New Zealand

First published in the U.S.A. by Alfred A. Knopf, Inc. 1977
Published in Penguin Books 1981

Phototypeset by Filmtype Services Limited, Scarborough, Yorkshire
Made and printed in Great Britain by
Richard Clay (The Chaucer Press) Ltd, Bungay, Suffolk
Set in Monophoto Photina

Contents

Foreword

Good Cooking Needs Good Tools 9
Boiling 21
Roasting 67
Grilling 103
Braising 133
Sautéing 163
Frying 203
Baking 221
Thickeners and Liaisons 281
Non-cooking 303
Chilling and Freezing 331

Cooking Terms and Methods 355
The Concordance 357
Carving 405
Index 411

Foreword

In my twenty-five years of teaching I have tried to make people realize that cooking is primarily fun and that the more they know about what they are doing, the more fun it is. I love having them ask questions because that's the only way they are going to understand a term or a technique. When I spot a student who is hungry to know all the whys and hows and wherefores, I try to encourage his or her inquisitiveness, knowing that this is the first sign of a creative cook. What is the difference between braising and roasting? Why must you roast a certain cut and braise another? Why do you bake a loaf of bread at a certain temperature and a cake at a different heat? What does 'proving' dough mean? Why is pastry precooked for some tarts, fully cooked for others, and not precooked at all when you bake a pie? Then there are the questions that come up about flavouring and seasoning. Why is it that a touch of nutmeg improves the flavour of a béchamel sauce or a soufflé base? Can you really cook chicken with forty cloves of garlic without the garlic being overpowering? Why are freshly ground black peppercorns preferable to white? Why is it essential to cook prawns in a well-seasoned liquid?

As a student absorbs the answers to all these continual questions, his understanding deepens and is reflected in the more experienced way he uses his cooking hands, can tell by touch when something is done to perfection, can identify flavours and compare dishes, knows exactly what to do at the market. At that point the student is on his own. He no longer needs to follow slavishly a set recipe; he can rely on his own skills – his taste memory, the understanding he has gained of techniques, flavourings, and food combinations – and build on his knowledge.

When you cook, you never stop learning. That's the fascination of it. Within the last year I have been put on a no-salt, low-calorie diet and I'm discovering all kinds of things about flavouring I never knew before. It *is* possible to cook without salt, or without butter and flour, if you understand the principles of seasoning, reducing, and liaisons. I challenge anyone who thinks differently to spot the absence of salt in a dish skilfully seasoned with garlic and herbs. I have not had to give up the principles of good cooking – and neither would you. Don't look on your diet as a deprivation and turn to dreary diet cookbooks, which are generally so depressing. Good food and good cooking will be even more important to you when you have to follow a limited regime, so follow the principles of cooking herein included – eliminating simply what the doctor orders – and the adventure of discovering a new palette of flavours will be a refreshing challenge.

This book, which José Wilson has helped me put together, is designed to bring every one of you to that stage of being a creative, intuitive cook. Over the years, José has worked with me at my cooking school and she knows well our students' needs. We have tried to present the theory and practice of cooking so that you will understand them just as they learned them. We discuss each technique in considerable detail as we would in our class, anticipating the variety of questions all of you might ask if we were there at your side. Then we show how that technique works, demonstrating in very explicit recipes the way it is applied to the various kinds of meat, to fish, to vegetables, to fruits. We compare the different leavening powers of eggs, yeast, baking powder, and we explore the mysteries of thickeners and emulsions. Always there is a recipe to learn by, usually a simple master recipe followed by ones that are a little more complex and demanding. In other words, the recipes are designed to help you build such a solid grounding in every possible area of cooking that you'll be able to tackle anything.

But because the secret to really good cooking starts in the market, we have included a Concordance in this book. It is the Concordance that finally makes everything work because the materials you buy must always *concord* with the techniques you apply to them. You have to know not only what to look for in order to select good produce, but also how *best* to cook what you buy. So in the Concordance we have put down everything we think you ought to know about apples and meat cuts and fish and spices and herbs and grains and dairy products, with dozens of different suggestions as to how to use each product. We hope you'll find there the answers to all your questions about food so that you can shop confidently, imaginatively, and constructively, building your menu in your head as you select what tempts you that day and what is a good bargain. With the aid of the Concordance, you'll be able to determine how best to cook what you bring home. By checking out that particular food, you will be directed to the right technique, then back to the basic recipes of this book to select the appropriate one on which you can, of course, work out your own variations. For, once you have made the lessons in the chapters a part of your cooking knowledge, and with the Concordance to guide you in shopping, you'll be ready to improvise, invent, experiment and, finally, find your own cooking style.

Note. The very explicit, simple master recipes are all marked

Good Cooking Needs Good Tools

Cooking starts with your hands, the most important and basic of all implements. They were the earliest tools for the preparation of food, and they have remained one of the most efficient, sensitive and versatile. Hands can beat, cream, fold, knead, pat, press, form, toss, tear and pound. They are so sensitive that the instant your fingers touch or feel something, they transmit messages to your brain about texture and temperature. Just by touching a grilled steak or a roast, you can learn to tell when the meat is done to your liking. To test the temperature of a sauce, a soup, a stew, or a vegetable purée, just dip your finger in. Then touch your finger to your tongue, and you'll know whether the seasoning and flavouring are right or need some adjustment. There are prissy people who think sticking fingers in food is dirty, but there's nothing disgraceful about touching food if your hands are clean, and don't let anyone tell you there is. After all, we eat lots of foods with our fingers. I can think of no more rewarding and sensuous a pleasure than plunging one's hands into a batter or dough and mixing or kneading away.

I learned to cook with my hands at a very early age, long before I ever held a spoon or a beater. I can remember making a cake – a quick, simple coffeecake – by first opening my hand like a big fork to mix and beat the batter and then cupping it like a spoon to scoop the batter from the bowl. It seemed the most natural thing in the world, and it taught me the feel of batters and doughs as nothing else could have done.

In my classes I encourage my students to get their hands into cake batters and soufflé mixtures, for once they get the feel of the texture and consistency this way, they never forget it. I find many people have difficulty learning to fold in egg whites with a spatula and tend to overfold. If you learn to fold them in by using the side of your hand to cut down and the palm to bring the mixture up and over, you soon grasp the technique of quick, light folding that doesn't deflate the egg whites. Later on in this book I'm going to tell you in detail how to mix a cake batter, fold in egg whites and separate eggs with your hands, and how to test a piece of cooked meat for doneness by pressing it with your fingertip. That's also a good way to judge whether a cake is baked. The light pressure of a finger will tell if the surface is firm and the cake underneath resilient. There are innumerable occasions in cooking when you can rely on your hands and your brain to give you these quick, accurate messages. Try mixing a salad with your fingers to learn how much dressing is needed to coat the greens – not drown them.

Next to hands, the most important tools are good knives. A knife can do practically everything in the way of cutting, slicing, mincing, chopping, even scraping and pounding. If you don't own a meat pounder, you can use the flat of a big heavy knife, such as a Chinese cleaver, to pound and flatten. Then there's a little trick I always show my students for peeling garlic – a pesky job. If you crush the garlic clove lightly with the flat of a heavy knife blade, the skin will split and come off in one piece.

Knives are the best friends a cook can have, to be treasured along with the family silver. They are just as valuable and will last equally long if properly treated – and by that I mean they should be sharpened regularly, never allowed to soak in a bath of detergent or to go in the dishwasher. Instead, merely wipe your knives clean with a damp cloth after you've used them and store them in a proper knife rack where the blades won't bang against each other or anything else.

To begin with, there are just three knives you really should have. First, and most important, comes what is variously known as a French knife or a

French chef's or cook's knife, a knife with a wide, tapering, triangular blade. Formerly all the best French chef's knives were made from carbon steel, which was soft enough to sharpen properly, but now the good-quality high-carbon stainless-steel knives are by far the best. They are expensive, but there is no economy in buying cheap knives. They just don't perform properly. A good knife will be perfectly weighted, with a blade that is wide and rather heavy at the butt near the handle, tapering to a triangle and a more pronounced thinness at the point. The reason for this shape and weight is that a chef's knife is designed to cut, slice, and chop.

To cut: *Use the thinner, pointed end of the knife to pierce the skin and to make the initial cut. Then lower the blade.*

To slice: *Hold what you are cutting firmly, bending your fingers so that the tips of the nails rest on the surface of the object and the bent fingers serve as a guide to the knife blade that will come down parallel to them, almost touching.*

After you slice, move your fingers back just the width of the next slice. Repeat. I prefer to keep a grasp on the handle of the knife with my thumb pressing the top to help guide the knife. If you are slicing something round, first cut a slice from the bottom so that the object will lie flat instead of rolling.

To 'julienne' or to cut into thin strips: *Cut first into slices, then into strips the same width. With celery you need only cut across the stalk into 3-mm. ($\frac{1}{8}$-inch) strips.*

To chop: *By guiding the thin end of the knife with your left hand, you have maximum control of even the largest blade. Thus, with a large knife you achieve a rocking motion and the heavier end of the knife is almost automatic in its ability to chop finely with a minimum of effort. There is no necessity to lift the blade from the board; the knife does the work.*

The second important knife is a slicing knife, which has a fairly thin, supple blade with a rounded or pointed end and is designed for slicing roast meats, turkey, pot roast, or corned beef brisket from paper-thin to medium-thick or very thick. This knife takes the place of the one in old-fashioned carving sets and is something no one can really get along without.

Last, but by no means least, there is the little paring knife, which may either have a triangular blade and look like a miniature chef's knife, or a small, curved scimitarlike blade and is excellent for mincing or cutting into small dice.

To mince: *To cut a single clove of garlic or a shallot, hold the bud the same way you would a larger object, with your fingers bent, and cut with the point of a well-sharpened paring knife in fine strokes, first making thin, horizontal slices almost to the end of the bud but not slicing completely through, then*

turning your knife again and cutting down in slices of the same thinness to achieve minuscule dice. Actually, the same procedure is used with a medium-sized or a large knife to chop an onion, an apple, a potato, etc., into uniform dice.

There are many other knives that can be added to these basics. You may want to have two or three sizes of chef's knife, which comes in different blade sizes from 15 cm. (6 inches) up to a giant of 35 cm. (14 inches) – the most useful are the 20-, 25- and 30-cm. (8-, 10-, and 12-inch sizes), for a large blade will, naturally, chop a greater quantity than a small one. Then you might add a boning knife, which has a thin flexible blade about 15 cm. (6 inches) long (see illustration, page 172); a smaller, triangular-bladed boning knife for chicken breasts and small birds; a bread knife with a serrated blade (also good for cutting crumbly cakes); a very long, thin, flexible ham slicer; and a Chinese cleaver. To keep your knives sharp, you should have the traditional long sharpening steel.

To sharpen a knife: *Hold it at a 20-degree angle to the sharpener and, with a quick swinging motion of your wrist and forearm, slide the blade across it. Don't lay the blade flat and scrape, just bring the edge down and across, maintaining the 20-degree angle, until the tip touches the bottom of the sharpener.* Then repeat in an upward direction with the opposite side of the blade. Do this half a dozen times whenever you use a knife and it will keep the edge keen and aligned. When the edge wears down, as it will with constant use, you can have it professionally sharpened and ground.

Look in the classified section of the telephone directory for the names of knife grinders, or ask your butcher where he has his knives ground. Knives with serrated edges do not need sharpening, of course.

The following list gives my recommendations for the equipment you should have in your kitchen. It isn't necessary to rush out and buy everything at once. Start with the equipment you really need and add to it as you go along. Get the best pots and pans you can afford. Cheap, flimsy pieces are false economy. Thin pans will not distribute heat evenly and tend to burn and scorch food. Heavy-duty pans, like good knives, are a long-term investment, and it's better to buy one decent pan than a whole set of useless ones. Sets of pans are rather pointless, anyway. There always seem to be one or two you never use. You are much better off buying pans for individual purposes, such as sauces, braising, and sautéing, plus at least one big pot of 8-litre (6½-quart) capacity that you can use for braising and pasta and soup. When it comes to materials, I happen to prefer stainless steel with an aluminium inlay between the steel layers in the bottom, or heavy-duty copper lined with stainless steel or tin, or heavy cast aluminium, with an occasional piece of enamelled iron for sauces and custards and suchlike things, but the choice is really up to you. Just be sure the pans are really heavy-duty and have tight-fitting covers. For baking, stainless-steel pans, while more expensive than tin or aluminium, are preferable because they won't warp and are easier to clean. For bread, I like the loaf pans of sheet iron, which conduct heat well and give a good brown crust. For grilling, I find the aluminium foil pans with ridged bottoms a boon because they are easy to clean and can be used over and over.

I'm all for anything that saves time and work in the kitchen and that goes for electrical appliances. There are two labour-saving devices which I think should be part of any well-equipped kitchen, because they do a better, more professional job of beating, mixing, whipping, chopping, grinding and mincing than any but the most skilled cook could accomplish – and in a fraction of the time. One is the heavy-duty Kenwood electric mixer, a formidable machine of many uses. It has a whisk for beating light things such as eggs, egg whites, batters, cream, and mayonnaise and a paddle for heavier mixtures like mashed potatoes and

pastry doughs. There's an optional dough-hook attachment for kneading bread and other yeast doughs and a positive battery of optional attachments.

The other device, a comparatively recent and quite invaluable piece of equipment, is the food processor (Magimix). Having a food processor in the kitchen is the equivalent of having an extra pair of hands. While it does many of the same jobs as the mixer, it does them in a different way, for this machine operates on the principle of centrifugal force and combines many of the attributes of the mixer and a blender. I use the food processor for all kinds of things – chopping meat; slicing, chopping, shredding and puréeing vegetables; making pastry, brioche, cake and crêpe batters as well as mayonnaise. Although I find that I use my liquidizer less now that I have a food processor, it is still an extremely useful piece of equipment for liquefying ingredients, making soups, crêpe batters, purées, bread crumbs and grated cheese, and definitely earns its kitchen space.

Throughout this book I have indicated where the mixer, food processor or liquidizer can take over in a recipe. These pieces of equipment are expensive, but they are incredibly versatile and save an enormous amount of labour which in my book means they are worth every penny. I'm constantly amazed at people who, while they think nothing of spending a hundred pounds on clothes or sports equipment for a holiday, hesitate about buying something that will save them hundreds of hours of arduous dog work – and enable them to turn out better meals with greater ease.

Kitchen Equipment Check List

KNIVES

1 20-cm. (8-inch) chef's knife
1 25-cm. (10-inch) or 30-cm. (12-inch) chef's knife
2 paring knives
1 slicing knife
1 serrated-edge bread knife
1 boning knife with 15-cm. (6-inch) blade
1 sharpening steel

Optional additions
Ham slicer
Small boning knife
Chinese cleaver

POTS AND PANS

2 1-litre (1-quart) saucepans, with covers
2 2-litre (2-quart) saucepans, with covers
1 4-litre ($3\frac{1}{2}$-quart) saucepan
1 8-litre (7-quart) braising pan, or large round or oval pot, with tight-fitting cover
1 25-cm. (10-inch) straight-sided, flat-bottomed sauté pan, with cover
1 30-cm. (12-inch) sauté pan, with cover
1 25-cm. (10-inch) frying pan of heavy metal (such as iron) with metal handle (so it can go in the oven)
1 iron crêpe pan, with 15-cm. (6-inch) bottom diameter

1 cast-aluminium omelet pan with 15-cm. (6-inch) bottom diameter, or 1 non-stick cast-aluminium omelet pan, to double for crêpes
1 fish kettle with rack, 45 or 55 cm. (18 or 22 inches) long
1 open roasting pan of heavy-gauge stainless steel, about 45 cm. × 30 cm. (18 × 12 inches) and 6 cm. (2½ inches) deep
1 stainless-steel, adjustable V-shaped rack, to fit in the roasting pan
Aluminium foil grilling pans, assorted sizes

Optional additions
Deep fryer with basket, regular or electric
10-litre (9-quart) stock pot
Double boiler, preferably heatproof glass

BAKING EQUIPMENT

3 or 4 heavy-duty baking trays
2 28-cm. × 38-cm. (11 × 15-inch) heavy-duty Swiss roll tins
3 23-cm. (9-inch) round cake tins
1 23-cm. (9-inch) square cake tin
1 20-cm. to 23-cm. (8-inch to 9-inch) tube cake tin
2 23 × 13 × 8-cm. (9 × 5 × 3-inch) loaf tins
2 20-cm. (8-inch) pie plates
2 23-cm. (9-inch) pie plates
1 23-cm. (9-inch) flan tin with removable bottom
1 23-cm. (9-inch) flan ring
1 patty-pan tin
2 or 3 wire cake racks
1 oval gratin dish, lined copper or other metal
2 ovenproof gratin or baking dishes, porcelain or pottery, medium and large
1½-litre (1¼-quart) terrine, with cover, ovenproof porcelain or earthenware, for pâtés
1-litre, 1½-litre and 2-litre (1-quart, 1¼-quart and 1¾-quart) soufflé dishes, porcelain, earthenware or ovenproof glass
1- and 2-litre (1- and 1¾-quart) lacquered tin charlotte moulds (may double for soufflés, mousses)
Deep pie dish
1 1½-litre (2½-pint) ring mould (may double for cold mousses, gelatin moulds)

1 decorative pudding mould about 1½ litres (1¼ quarts), such as a melon mould (may double for cold mousses, ice cream)

1½-litre (1-quart) pudding basin

MEASURING AND MIXING EQUIPMENT

Glass liquid measuring jugs in ¼-, ½- and 1-litre sizes (½-pint, 1-pint and 1-quart)

2 sets measuring cups

2 sets measuring spoons

Flour sifter

Kitchen scales, graduated in grams and ounces

Mixing bowls, glass and earthenware, assorted sizes

STANDARD KITCHEN EQUIPMENT

Apple corer

Potato peeler

Poultry shears

Ball scoop

Biscuit and pastry cutters

Dough scraper (can double as all-purpose scraper)

Ice-cream scoop

Small vegetable slicer with adjustable blade

Mandoline vegetable slicer (for julienne vegetables, plain and waffle-cut potatoes)

Mouli-julienne (French disc-type vegetable grater, slicer and shredder)

Cheese grater, stainless-steel, four-sided box type

Nutmeg grater

Mortar and pestle, ceramic or marble

Pepper mill

Salt mill

Food mill, for puréeing

Strainers and sieves, assorted sizes and meshes

Colander

Funnel
Tin opener
Corkscrew
Bottle opener
Screw-top jar opener
Wooden spoons and spatulas, assorted sizes
2 wooden kitchen forks
2 metal kitchen forks
2 slotted or perforated metal kitchen spoons
1 solid metal kitchen spoon
3 or 4 wire whisks, assorted sizes

2 or 3 rubber spatulas, wide and narrow blades
2 or 3 metal palette knives, wide and narrow blades
1 broad-bladed fish slice
2 skimmers, open wire and fine mesh
1 large soup ladle
1 60 ml. (2 fl. oz.) ladle, for measuring crêpe batter
Meat thermometer, the most accurate available, see page 70
Cooking thermometer
Deep-fat thermometer
Pastry board
2 pastry brushes
Rolling pin, ball-bearing or heavy French type
Plastic-lined forcing bag and sets of round, star and ribbon piping nozzles

Metal scoops for flour and sugar
Storage jars and canisters
Lemon squeezer
Large earthenware bowl or crock for marinating meats
Meat bat or pounder
Larding needle, long wood-handled type
Trussing needles and fine string
Butter muslin
Skewers, short for closing vent of poultry, long for kebabs
Metal kitchen tongs
Wood chopping block (if there is no wood countertop)

PAPER, PLASTIC AND CLEANING PRODUCTS

Aluminium foil, light and heavy-duty, short and long rolls
Cooking parchment
Greaseproof paper
Plastic wrap, short and long rolls
Plastic food bags, several sizes
Plastic freezer-storage containers
Scouring pads
Vegetable brush
Waxed paper

ELECTRIC APPLIANCES

Food processor
Hand beater
Heavy-duty mixer, optional attachments
Liquidizer
Small coffee mill (to grind coffee beans or whole spices)
Tin opener

OPTIONAL EQUIPMENT

Salad dryer
Ice-cream freezer, manual or electric
Unlined copper beating bowl and balloon whisk (for egg whites)
Brioche, tartlet and barquette tins
Stripper
Zester

Zester   Stripper

Boiling

Did you ever stop to think, when you boil an egg, poach a chicken, simmer a soup, or blanch a cauliflower, that they are all part of one basic cooking process – boiling? In one form or another it enters into many of the recipes we prepare, whether we are making a base for a soufflé or a stock for a stew. Essentially, boiling is the action of liquid, at various temperatures, on food. Meat is brought to a full boil in order to cook the surface rapidly and sear in the juices and flavours, the same thing that happens when it is seared in fat over heat, or browned under the grill. When you bring meat or poultry to a boil, the chemical reaction between the food and the liquid brings forth a frothy scum, which must be skimmed off. The scum may continue to form for as long as 5 or 10 minutes and, if you want a good finished dish, you must skim and keep on skimming to remove those undesirable elements. After this initial boiling, the heat should be turned down so the liquid merely simmers, a process that tenderizes the meat.

Vegetables, on the other hand, are boiled or blanched in order to tenderize them and to break down and expand the tissues, which brings out a well-defined, characteristic flavour. If you taste certain vegetables when they are raw, when they are partially cooked, and when they are fully cooked, you'll learn a very interesting lesson. Take a green bean, for instance. Taste it raw, taste it halfway through the cooking, and then when it is done as you like it and you'll notice the difference in flavour between the various stages.

Pasta is always immersed in rapidly boiling water and boiled very fast in order to expand the starch granules and make them tender to the bite – *al dente*, as the Italians say. There is also a school of rice cookery, to which I happen to belong, where the rice is tossed by small handfuls into a big pot of rapidly boiling water, so that the water never ceases to seethe and boil. This produces a less starchy rice than when it is cooked in only a little water, and each grain is separate rather than sticking together.

Water and other liquids boil when brought to a temperature of 100°C (212°F) at sea level and the temperature reduces one degree for every $152\frac{1}{2}$ metres (500 feet) of altitude. In high-altitude cities there is a different set of rules for boiling.

If you want to check on the various stages of boiling, it is a simple enough matter. Half fill a large saucepan or pot with water and place it on a large burner over high heat. Watch carefully as it begins to heat and tiny bubbles form on the bottom of the pan. Then the steam will start to rise and when the liquid has reached ebullition, or the boiling point, it will seethe and surge and bubble, and the bubbles will rise to the surface and break more and more rapidly. In this fast or rolling boil, the kind used to reduce stock by evaporation and intensify its flavour, or to cook pasta, the liquid moves fiercely and rapidly, rolling, rising, and vaporizing like lava in the crater of a volcano. When you are making preserves, you will notice the recipes often call for a rolling boil. Because of the density of the syrup, the boil is much more vigorous and surging and the cooking takes place in a large pot that allows plenty of room for expansion. This is also true with certain thick mixtures, such as a tomato sauce or polenta (cooked cornmeal); when they come to a boil, they puff up from the bottom of the pan rather than seething on top.

Now reverse the boiling process by turning the heat down under the pot of liquid and observe how long it takes to subside from this violent motion through the various boiling stages before the liquid reaches the faint ebullition that marks the simmering point, the gentlest form of boiling. Simmering, as used in cookbooks, is a word with a double meaning. You can refer to simmering or to poaching, which are virtually the same process. Poaching, in which something is brought to a slow simmer and kept there, is known professionally as a feeble ebullition. This is exactly what it sounds like – a boil that is hardly a boil at all, just a faint, lazy bubble that rises to the surface and slowly pops, like a carefully blown soap bubble. We talk about poaching a fish, poaching eggs, or poaching fruit in syrup. Simmering is maybe one degree less active than poaching – the feeble, steady ebullition you need when you are making a stew or a *pot-au-feu*. If you look in the pot, you will see the almost unbelievably slow bubbling, the surface of the liquid barely moving (in more poetic cookbook writing, the liquid is said to 'smile'), that helps to mingle the seasonings with the other ingredients and to relax and tenderize the flesh of the meat or poultry.

It's interesting to consider that after you have simmered a stew or a stock, sometimes for hours, either to imbue the flesh with flavour or to extract the flavour from the meat, fowl, and bones for your stock, you go to the other extreme for reducing. After straining the stock, you turn the heat very high and let it seethe, bubble, and boil away until the vaporization reduces the volume by one-half to two-thirds, intensifying the flavour and slightly thickening the liquid. The final extension of this process is the making of a *glace de viande*, or meat glaze, in which the stock is clarified and then reduced by slow steady boiling over a period of hours or days until it is no more than a thick jelly or glaze.

Blanching is another boiling technique. Again, you are using the action of boiling liquid to achieve certain results. In blanching (synonymous with parboiling, a word which has been in our cooking terminology for years), food is immersed in boiling water and allowed to steep or to cook slightly, hence, parboil. Blanching might be called a method of searing with water preparatory to further cooking.

There are all kinds of reasons for blanching. Certain vegetables are blanched to soften them slightly, or to remove their strong flavour – cabbage, for example. Peppers are blanched to cook them partially before they are stuffed and baked. Lettuce is blanched before being braised. Some vegetables are blanched, or parboiled, to shorten their cooking time, like the potatoes, carrots, or onions you want to roast in the tin with the meat.

It's not uncommon to blanch julienne strips of hard or watery vegetables, like turnips and courgettes, prior to sautéing them quickly in butter, or to blanch green beans that are then dressed in a vinaigrette sauce. In each instance, it is essential, after blanching, to plunge the vegetables immediately into ice-cold water to stop them from becoming overcooked. To prepare vegetables for freezing, you usually blanch and cool them in the same manner. Or, if you are making a pale, creamy dish like a *blanquette de veau*, you might blanch mushrooms for just a minute in water acidulated with lemon juice or vinegar to keep them white, so they look more attractive in the finished dish.

Other foods are blanched, like tomatoes, to make it easy to remove the skins. Peaches are blanched before peeling and almonds are blanched and soaked to soften the tough little skins, enabling you to rub them off easily between your thumb and finger. Salty meats, such as ham, salt pork, or bacon with a very smoky quality, may be blanched, or parboiled, to draw off the excess salt and strong odours or flavours before being added to a dish.

Yet another of the many facets of boiling is steeping – the hydrating process for making tea or extracting flavour from a dried herb or root.

Each of these related processes of boiling is extremely important to the everyday round of cooking, no matter how familiar and simple it may sound. For instance, we boil eggs. Don't let anyone tell you that an egg is 'soft cooked' or 'hard cooked'. It is *boiled*, no matter what some of the rather precious folk in the food world may say who insist on changing the terminology. 'Boiled' is a much more honest term, because we do bring eggs to the boiling point and keep them at a boil for a certain length of time. If you are making a soft-boiled egg for breakfast, you boil it for 3 minutes on the dot. Hard-boiled eggs are boiled rapidly for 2 or 3 minutes and then left to rest in the hot water, with the heat turned off, for another 8 or 9 minutes. If you are making an egg mollet, you bring it to a boil; boil $4\frac{1}{2}$ minutes, then remove it; put it in cold water at once, shell it whole, and use it as you would a poached egg.

So let's examine the whole world of boiling and learn how to apply the right technique to what we are cooking.

♨ Boiled Corned (Salted) Beef and Cabbage

This might qualify as a New England boiled dinner. It's a good, hearty, basic dish that will serve 6, with some meat left over for cold corned beef sandwiches or 4 to 6 servings of corned beef hash.

When we talk about 'boiled beef' or a 'boiled dinner' we don't really mean boiled; we mean simmered. Naturally, to create a simmer you first have to bring liquid to a boil and you do have to let the liquid boil for a little at the start of the cooking, to draw off certain elements in the beef that would cloud the broth. These form a greyish-brown scum on the surface and should be skimmed off with a skimmer or spoon.

Corned beef is beef that has been cured in a pickling solution, which used to be the way beef, pork, and sometimes lamb were preserved for the winter. It's very traditional and one of the most delicious American beef dishes. Corned beef brisket is the choicest cut because it has some fat and good marbling and makes a flavourful, tender finished product that slices well and looks good on the plate.

To cook the corned beef you will need a good big pot, an 8- to 10-litre (7- to 9-quart) size, which can be aluminium, heavy-bottomed stainless steel, anything of that sort. The size is more important than the material.

Serves 6 with leftovers

3 kg. (6 lbs.) salted or fresh beef brisket   10 large garlic cloves, peeled
1 onion, peeled and stuck with 3 cloves   1 tablespoon freshly ground black pepper

THE ACCOMPANYING VEGETABLES

6 medium onions, peeled   6 turnips, peeled
6 good-sized carrots, scraped   1 medium cabbage
6 to 10 medium potatoes

Wipe the salted beef well with a damp cloth. Put it in the pot and cover with cold water. Bring to a boil over rather high heat, and boil for 5 to 6 minutes, skimming off the grey foamy scum that rises to the surface with a wire skimmer or large spoon. This will give you a clearer, purer broth. It's very important, with any boiled meat, to skim off this scum drawn from the meat.

Add the onion stuck with cloves, the garlic cloves, and the pepper and boil another 10 minutes, skimming. Then reduce the heat to a simmer (130°C or 250°F on a burner with a thermostat), cover the pot, and let it simmer at a faint, gentle ebullition for 2 hours. At this point, test the meat for tenderness with a large fork. As this is not a very tender piece of meat, it will offer some resistance, but it should just yield to the fork. You must be careful not to overcook corned beef or the meat will become dry and stringy. It's very important to maintain some moisture in the meat. If you are not sure about the tenderness, remove the meat to a plate and cut off a tiny piece from the edge to taste. If you have a meat thermometer, check the internal temperature, which should be about 65°C (145°F to 150°F).

If the meat seems tender, turn off the heat and let it rest in the liquid. If it does not test tender, either continue cooking or, if you have started it in the morning and are ahead of serving time, leave it in the liquid and finish the cooking later.

COOKING THE VEGETABLES (1 hour before serving)

Traditionally, all the vegetables for a corned beef dinner are cooked in the pot with the meat. I have long since decided that the vegetables look and taste better if they are cooked separately in plain salted water, instead of in the briny, fatty broth. If you have sufficient pots and burners, I recommend that you follow this procedure – each vegetable will then retain its own character and flavour. However, it is perfectly acceptable to cook the potatoes with the beef, provided you scrub them and leave them in their skins so they don't absorb the fat, and to use only one extra pot, first putting in the longest-cooking vegetables, the onions and carrots, then the turnips, and finally the cabbage. Or, if you have a large pot and a steamer, put the onions and carrots in the water and steam the turnips over them. Cook the cabbage separately. Here is a timetable for the vegetables:

Onions. Put in a pot with water to cover, seasoned with 1 tablespoon salt. Bring to a boil, cover, and simmer 1 hour or until crisply tender when tested with the point of a knife.

Carrots. Follow the same procedure, seasoning the water with 2 teaspoons salt and $\frac{1}{2}$ teaspoon marjoram. Simmer 30 minutes, or until tender when tested.

Potatoes. Scrub but do not peel. Follow the same procedure, seasoning the water with 1 tablespoon salt, or simmer with the corned beef, for 30 minutes or until tender. If you are planning to make corned beef hash, cook the 4 extra potatoes, otherwise allow 1 per person.

Turnips. Leave whole if small; halve or quarter if large. Follow the same procedure, seasoning the water with 2 teaspoons salt. Simmer for 20 minutes or until tender when tested.

Cabbage. Remove coarse or discoloured outer leaves and cut in sixths. Put in a pot with water to cover, seasoned with 2 teaspoons salt. Bring to a boil and boil rapidly, covered, for 10 to 12 minutes, or until just tender but not overcooked or soggy.

I am not an advocate of using pressure cookers for vegetables. I realize that many people consider them one of the greatest kitchen aids, but I think they rob vegetables of all flavour. However, if you are a pressure-cooker addict, by all means use it for the vegetables for this dish, following your rule chart for timing, for it will certainly speed up the process.

When you are ready to serve, remove the beef from the broth (discard the broth; it cannot be saved for any other use) and let it stand on a hot platter in a warm place for 10 minutes, to firm and settle the meat. This makes it easier to carve. Surround it with the drained vegetables, the potatoes still in their jackets. Do not add butter – the vegetables are better plain. Slice only as much meat as you need, keeping the rest in one piece for future use. Serve with the vegetables, with a variety of mustards, horseradish and, if you have any, good homemade pickles.

Stock

It is a great aid and comfort always to have on hand good homemade beef, chicken and veal stock, but you have to be realistic about it. You must gauge your stock-making by the space you have to keep it. One of the greatest of all wastes is to make a big pot of stock and then have to leave most of it in the refrigerator until it has gone sour, as so often happens. Two or three days is about as long as you should keep stock in the refrigerator; if you keep it longer you should remove it and boil it up again before using. If you are keeping stock for any length of time you really have to freeze it, in which case you can safely keep it up to three months. So before you start making stock, see how much space you can spare in your freezer for long-term use and in your refrigerator for short-term cooking.

I have somewhat limited storage space, so if I want to make a small *pot-au-feu* – the French boiled dinner – for myself and have bought a piece of beef shin and a bone, I remove the meat when it's tender and make a meal of it, then keep on cooking the bone and stock until I have about 2 litres (1$\frac{3}{4}$ quarts) of good strong stock, which I cool. I then skim off the fat that rises to the top, put the stock in $\frac{1}{4}$-litre and $\frac{1}{2}$-litre or half-pint and pint containers, and keep them in the freezer, so that I can take out just enough for a sauce or a soup, rather than having to thaw the contents of a big container and refreeze what I don't need.

For chicken stock, I cook a batch of backs, necks, and gizzards until I have a good strong broth, then I eat the gizzards. I may later poach a chicken or two in the stock for *poule au pot* or a chicken salad or hash. After they have cooked, I have a much richer, double-strength stock which, when strained, degreased, and cooked down until it has reduced by one-third or one-half, gives me an elegant concentrated stock for sauces, or to clarify and use as chicken consommé. I let it stand in the refrigerator until the fat rises to the top, remove the fat, and divide the stock among small plastic containers for freezing.

If you don't have a freezer, or don't want to keep a large supply of stock on hand, you can always make a quick batch with a few gizzards, or some beef and a chicken, if you're making a *pot-au-feu*.

Buying veal for stock is expensive, even if you get the knuckles and lesser, bony cuts, but sometimes it's a necessity. Get a knuckle of veal, a piece of neck, and the less desirable parts of the shoulder and cook them, leaving the meat in only until tender, then strip the meat from the bones and make jellied veal from it; after that put the bones back in the liquid and cook them down until you have a strong veal stock. That's the economical and intelligent thing to do.

If you really can't make and store stock, tinned beef broth or tinned chicken broth are perfectly adequate, but for the most part tinned stocks are not as delicate and honest in flavour and therefore not as good for cooking, although they do serve their purpose. Don't, however, use the tinned consommé, which is too highly spiced and pronounced in flavour to make good stock.

Vegetable stocks – the water in which onions, carrots, and other aromatic vegetables have been cooked – can be saved, combined, cooked down, and used for braised dishes or those that need to be cooked with a good deal of liquid, like boiled beef. They add flavour, but unless you have an immediate use for them I think it's rather silly to fill up your freezer or refrigerator with cooked-down vegetable juices. Any space you can spare is better used for chicken, beef, or veal stock, which are real necessities.

⚜ Chicken Stock or Broth

1 kg. (2 lbs.) chicken gizzards
1 kg. (2 lbs.) chicken necks and backs
1 onion, peeled and stuck with
   3 cloves
1 leek, well washed and trimmed
   (see page 389)
1 carrot, scraped

2 garlic cloves, peeled
1 bay leaf
1 sprig of parsley
1 teaspoon dried thyme
6 peppercorns
3 l. (2½ qts) water
1 tablespoon salt

Put the chicken pieces, vegetables, garlic, herbs, peppercorns and water in a deep 8-litre (7-quart) pot or a stockpot and bring to a boil. After 5 minutes, *skim off the scum that forms on the surface with a wire skimmer or a large spoon*. Continue to boil rapidly for 15 minutes, skimming, then reduce the heat; cover the pot and simmer for 2 to 2½ hours. Season with salt to taste – about 1 tablespoon. Strain the broth through a sieve lined with several thicknesses of muslin into a large bowl and cool thoroughly in the refrigerator. Save the gizzards (they are good eating) and discard the other chicken parts and vegetables. When the stock is cold, remove the layer of fat that has formed on the surface. You will have about 2½ litres (2 quarts) of stock.

Double Chicken Broth

Put the cold, fat-free stock in an 8-litre (7-quart) pan with a whole stewing fowl or roasting chicken weighing 2 to 2½ kg. (4 to 5 pounds). Bring slowly to a boil, skim off any scum that forms on the surface; reduce the heat; cover and simmer gently until the chicken is very tender, about 1 hour for a young chicken, 2 to 2½ hours for a fowl. Remove the chicken and either serve it as poached chicken or remove the skin, take the meat from the bones, and use it for chicken dishes – salad, hash, chicken pie, or creamed chicken. Strain the broth through muslin into a bowl, cool, and skim off the fat. You now have about 2 litres (1¾ quarts) of beautifully rich, strong broth to use for cooking. Should you want to reduce it even more and clarify it, for consommé, here's how to do it.

Chicken Consommé

For chicken consommé, the broth must be absolutely fat-free and clear. Put the broth back in a pan and boil slowly until it has reduced to one-half or one-third of its original volume. To remove any lingering traces of fat, strain into a 2½-litre (2-quart) pan through a sieve lined with muslin or a linen towel. To clarify the stock, add 1 egg white, beaten to a froth, and 1 crushed eggshell. Over medium heat, *beat well with a rotary beater or a wire whisk until the stock comes to a boil and the egg white rises to the surface* (it will have gathered together any impurities in the soup that would cloud it). Stop stirring, remove pan from the heat, and let it stand for 5 minutes, to settle. Then without agitating the stock, *strain it through a*

sieve or colander lined with several thicknesses of muslin or a linen towel that you have wrung out in cold water (this traps the impurities in the egg white and any vestige of fat that might remain is chilled by the damp cloth). The liquid should just drip through into the bowl beneath; don't attempt to hurry the process or you won't get a perfectly clear consommé. When it has all dripped through, pour into plastic containers, cool, and freeze.

♛ Veal Stock or Broth

2 kg. (4 lbs.) neck of veal
　Or neck plus bony parts of the
　　shoulder
1 veal knuckle
1 calf's foot, if available
1 onion, peeled and stuck with
　2 cloves

1 teaspoon dried tarragon
1 bay leaf
3 or 4 celery leaves
1 sprig of parsley
3 l. (2½ qts) cold water
1 tablespoon or more salt

Put all ingredients except the salt in a deep 8-litre (7-quart) pot or stockpot. Bring slowly to a boil and skim off all the scum that forms on the surface. Reduce the heat, cover the pot, and simmer for 2½ hours. Add salt to taste, 1 tablespoon or more, and skim off any scum on the surface. (Test the meat. If it is tender, you can strip it from the bones to use for jellied veal, returning the bones to the stock. If not, return and continue cooking until it is.) Continue to simmer, covered, for 1 to 1½ hours more.

Remove the stock from the heat and strain through a sieve lined with several thicknesses of muslin into a bowl. Cool until the fat rises to the top and then skim it off. You will have about 2½ litres (2 quarts) of stock. Refrigerate or freeze.

Jellied Veal. Pour over the meat taken from the bones just enough fat-free stock to cover, and allow to set. The chilled veal stock should make a strong jelly, because of the gelatin content of the bones, but if it doesn't set firmly, you can stiffen it by adding up to 1 tablespoon unflavoured gelatin for each ½-litre or pint of stock. To do so, return the stock to a saucepan and heat. Soften the gelatin in 4 tablespoons cold water, then stir into the hot stock until dissolved.

Veal Aspic. If you further reduce and clarify the veal stock, as you did for the chicken consommé, you will have a delicious, sparkling clear aspic to coat a cold dish.

♛ Pot-au-Feu and Beef Stock

While there are many versions of the classic *pot-au-feu*, I have evolved one that I find very useful because it gives me the initial makings of a good flavourful beef stock which can be cooked down until very strong and concentrated, and then frozen. Reduced even further and clarified, it can be boiled down, down, down, very slowly, until it forms *glace de viande*, a highly concentrated meat glaze or essence.

In addition to the beef and chicken you will need plenty of bones – and you can throw in a few chicken necks and backs, too, which make the stock richer. This can't all be made in one pot – it would have to be fantastically large – but if you have two 8- to 10-litre (7- to 9-quart) pots, you can divide the ingredients between them. If you have only one big pot, cook the basic *pot-au-feu* one day, cool and degrease the leftover stock, and the next day boil this with bones, chicken necks and backs, vegetables, and seasonings.

Pot-au-Feu

Serves 8, plus leftover beef

FOR POT-AU-FEU

1 to 1½ kg. (2 to 3 lbs.) bones (beef, beef marrow, veal)

2½-kg. (5-lb.) piece shin of beef

1 large onion, peeled and stuck with 2 cloves

1 carrot, scraped

1 leek, well washed and trimmed

1 white turnip, peeled

2 garlic cloves, peeled

1 bay leaf

1 sprig of parsley

1 teaspoon dried thyme

1 tablespoon salt

2- to 2½-kg. (4- to 5-lb.) roasting chicken, trussed (see pages 84–5)

POT NO. 2

2½ to 3 kg. (5 to 6 lbs.) bones

1 kg. (2 lbs.) chicken necks and backs

The same vegetables and seasonings as above

ACCOMPANYING VEGETABLES FOR THE POT-AU-FEU

Medium potatoes, scrubbed, skins left on (1 or 2 per serving)

Leeks, well washed and trimmed (1 per serving)

Carrots, scraped (2 per serving)

Other accompaniments: Crisp slices of toasted French bread, coarse salt, cornichons (tiny French pickled gherkins), French mustards

Put all the *pot-au-feu* ingredients except the chicken in the first pot with water to cover. Put all the ingredients in pot number two with water to cover. Bring the water in both pots to a boil over high heat and boil for 5 minutes, skimming off the scum that rises to the surface. Reduce heat until water just simmers; cover the pots and cook for 3 hours. Check now and then to see that the water is simmering, not boiling. After 2½ hours, test the meat on the beef shin with the point of a knife. If it seems to be getting near the point of tenderness (there will be some resistance; the knife will not go in easily), add the chicken, which will take 45 minutes to 1 hour to cook. If necessary, add more water to barely cover the chicken. Continue to simmer until the chicken and beef are tender, removing the chicken if it is done before the beef, covering it with foil and keeping it warm. Let the bones in the second pot continue to cook up to 4 hours.

About 30 minutes before the end of the cooking time, put the potatoes to boil in salted water to cover, first cutting a small strip from around the centre, a little belly band, which will prevent them from bursting. Add the leeks and carrots to the *pot-au-feu*.

When the chicken and beef are tender, remove them to a large platter; scoop out the cooked vegetables and arrange them around the meats. Strain the broth from the *pot-au-feu* and bring it to a boil, carefully skimming off as much as possible of the fat that rises and forms a skin on the surface (have the pot half on, half off the heat, and boil slowly; in this way the fat will form to the side away from the heat and is more easily skimmed). Serve some of this broth in bowls, accompanied by thick slices of French bread, crisped in a 130°C (250°F, gas mark ½) oven. Carve the beef and chicken and serve with the vegetables and dishes of coarse salt, sour pickles and horseradish. Leftover beef may be used for beef salad or other cold beef dishes.

Beef Stock

Strain the broth from both pots into a large bowl through a sieve lined with several thicknesses of muslin and chill overnight. The next day, remove the layer of fat on the top; put the broth in a large pot, uncovered, and simmer very slowly for 3 to 4 hours to concentrate and reduce the stock. Strain again; refrigerate or freeze. At this point the stock may be clarified in the same way as the chicken stock, using 1 egg white, beaten until frothy, and 1 eggshell for each litre or quart of stock.

Glace de Viande. After clarifying the stock, boil it down, very, very slowly in an open pan, at the faintest ebullition, until it has reduced to a thick syrup or glaze, being careful that it does not stick or burn. This can take from 24 to 48 hours, depending on how much stock you start with. The syrup should be thick enough to coat a spoon. Strain this into a jar; cool, then cover and refrigerate or freeze.

Colouring Beef Stock. There are two ways to give beef stock a deep, rich brown colour. One way is to put the bones in a shallow tin, such as the grill pan, before boiling them, and bake in a 230°C (450°F, gas mark 8) oven for 30 to 40 minutes until nicely coloured, or to brown them under the grill about 15 cm. (6 inches) from the heat, turning once. Then cook as before, for 4 hours.

The other way, if you are making a brown sauce and want it to be glossy and richly coloured, is to make a caramel colouring and add a few drops when you make the sauce. This method is described in the chapter Thickeners and Liaisons, page 288.

Poule au Pot
(Chicken in the Pot)

I believe it was Henri IV who first advocated a chicken in every pot and *poule au pot* has passed down through the years as his memorial. It is a perfect dish for Sunday lunch. You might wish to double the recipe, for the cold edition is almost better than the hot.

Serves 4

2- to 2½-kg. (4- to 5-lb.) roasting chicken	4 carrots, scraped
1 beef marrow bone	2 medium turnips, peeled
4 to 6 leeks, well washed and trimmed	1 stick of celery
4 medium onions, peeled	1 teaspoon thyme
	2 or 3 sprigs of parsley
	1½ tablespoons salt

THE STUFFED CABBAGE LEAVES

1 good-sized head of cabbage	2 teaspoons salt
2 medium onions, peeled and finely chopped	1 teaspoon thyme
1 garlic clove, peeled and finely chopped	30 g. (1 oz.) freshly made bread crumbs
60 g. (2 oz.) butter	4 tablespoons cognac
¾ kg. (1½ lbs.) ground pork	2 eggs, lightly beaten
225 g. (½ lb.) mushrooms, finely chopped	Cabbage liquid or chicken broth for poaching
3 or 4 chicken livers, chopped	12 small new potatoes

Truss the chicken (see pages 84–5) and put it in an 8-litre (7-quart) pot with the marrow bone, vegetables, thyme, parsley, salt and enough water to cover the chicken. Bring to a boil, skim off the scum that rises to the surface; reduce the heat; cover the pan and simmer the chicken for 50 minutes to 1¼ hours, or until it is just tender (the leg will move easily). Be careful not to overcook it. Should the chicken be done before the vegetables, remove it to a hot platter and cover with foil to keep warm.

While the chicken is poaching, blanch the cabbage by boiling it in salted water to cover for 15 to 18 minutes, or until the leaves separate easily from the head. Remove and drain, reserving liquid.

To make a stuffing for the leaves, sauté the onions and garlic in the butter in a heavy frying pan over medium heat until they are barely wilted, then, with a fork, blend in the ground pork, chopped mushrooms, chicken livers, salt and thyme. Return the pan to heat and cook for 10 minutes, tossing from time to time; then add the bread crumbs, cognac, and eggs and cook the mixture over low heat until thickened. If it seems too liquid (it should be firm but moist), carefully drain off excess fat.

Gently remove the leaves from the cabbage and spread them flat on a board. *Cut out a V-shaped piece from the bottom of the coarse rib in the centre of*

folding

finished

each leaf, so it will roll easily. Put some of the stuffing on each leaf. Then roll it up carefully, tucking in the sides as you do so to make a neat package. Arrange the stuffed leaves, seam side down, side by side in a frying pan, putting them close together so they don't unroll. Pour in enough of the reserved cabbage liquid (or chicken broth, if you prefer) to cover and simmer them gently for 30 minutes.

Twenty minutes before serving, peel a band of skin from around each potato to stop it from bursting. Put the potatoes in a pan with cold water to cover and 1 tablespoon salt, bring to a boil, then boil until just pierceable with the point of a knife. Drain and return to the pan over low heat to remove any remaining moisture.

Taste the chicken broth for seasoning, and adjust if necessary. Serve the chicken on a hot platter surrounded with the stuffed cabbage leaves, the potatoes, and the vegetables from the pot. Serve each person some of the broth separately. Carve the chicken and serve. This dish is usually accompanied by small bowls of coarse salt, cornichons and grated Gruyère cheese. A Beaujolais – a Moulin-à-Vent or a Fleurie – is the best wine to serve.

Steaming

♟ Beefsteak and Kidney Pudding

Steaming in simmering water is the method used to cook steak and kidney pudding. The pastry for this is quite different from regular shortcrust – it is lubricated by finely chopped suet. I well remember, as a young man when I was first in England, eating at a small bistro near the office of some friends. Although the proprietor was a Belgian, there was always a magnificent steak and kidney pudding on Wednesdays to which he gave a rather Continental touch by using wine instead of the customary water or stock.

Serves 4

SUET PASTRY

225 g. (½ lb.) cold beef suet	1½ teaspoons salt
510 g. (18 oz.) all-purpose flour	6 to 8 tablespoons ice water

FILLING

1 kg. (2 lbs.) topside of beef or beef chuck, cut into 6-cm. (2½-inch) cubes	3 tablespoons chopped parsley
Flour	1 tablespoon salt
1 or 2 veal kidneys	1 teaspoon thyme
Or 6 to 8 lamb kidneys	1 teaspoon freshly ground black pepper
2 large onions, peeled and finely chopped	3½ dl. (12 fl. oz.) boiling water or beef stock
90 g. (3 oz.) finely sliced mushrooms	

To make the pastry, chop the suet very, very fine by hand. Combine with the flour and salt and rub together until the mixture resembles coarse meal. Add the ice water (don't add it all at once; you may not need 8 tablespoons) and pull the pastry together by rolling it into a ball and kneading it very well until it is smooth and well blended. Sprinkle it with a little flour and chill for 30 to 40 minutes.

Divide the pastry into two pieces, one twice as large as the other. Roll the larger piece into a circle about 6 mm. ($\frac{1}{4}$ inch) thick, roll it over the rolling pin, and unroll it over a $1\frac{1}{2}$-litre or $1\frac{1}{2}$-quart pudding basin, *letting it slip into the basin and easing it into the bottom of the bowl and around the sides, leaving an overlap around the top.* Roll out the smaller piece and cut from

it a strip $2\frac{1}{2}$ cm. (1 inch) wide and long enough to go around the circumference of the basin. *Dampen the edge of the pastry lining the basin and fit the strip around it.*

Toss the beef cubes lightly in flour and put in the pastry. Trim the covering membrane and fat from the veal kidneys. Cut them into $2\frac{1}{2}$-cm. (1-inch) cubes; sprinkle them lightly with flour and mix with the beef. (If you can't find veal kidneys and use lamb kidneys, they should be soaked in milk for 1 hour to take away some of their strong flavour, then dried and cut in cubes.) Add the onions, mushrooms, parsley and seasonings. Mix all the filling ingredients together well with your hands and then pour in the water or stock.

Roll the remaining piece of pastry again into a circle large enough to fit the top of the basin. Dampen the edge of the pastry strip with cold water and put on the top crust. *Pinch and crimp the two edges together to seal them well. Cover the top of the pudding with a piece of foil, tucking it over the sides of the basin and tying it with string,* then put

the basin on a clean tea towel that has been wrung out in hot water, sprinkled well with flour, and shaken to get rid of the excess.

Tie the towel securely under the rim of the basin with string; bring up the diagonally opposite corners of the towel, two at a time, and knot them over the top of the basin to provide a handle for lifting the basin out of the kettle after steaming.

Lower the basin by this handle into an 8- to 10-litre (7- to 9-quart) pot and pour boiling water into the pot until it reaches the point below the rim of the basin where the towel is tied. Bring the water to a boil over medium-high heat; reduce the heat to a simmer; cover the pot and steam the pudding for $4\frac{1}{2}$ to 5 hours. As the water boils away, replenish it.

Lift out the pudding and remove the cloth and foil. Dry the basin and wrap it in a linen napkin. Serve the pudding from the basin and accompany with boiled potatoes and a red wine.

Poached Sausages

Link sausages are usually poached in about 1 cm. ($\frac{1}{2}$ inch) of water for 4 to 10 minutes, according to size, after which they can be sautéed, grilled, or baked. The initial poaching precooks the sausages and draws off some of the fat. Large, meaty sausages such as Polish *kielbasa*, Italian *cotechino*, and French garlic sausage are best poached. Prick the sausages well on both sides with a fork before poaching to prevent the skins from bursting as they cook and allow the fat to drain out.

Sausages with Sauerkraut

Sausages and sauerkraut are a time-honoured and excellent combination. You need not use all the sausages specified – two types would be sufficient, one large (*cotechino*, or garlic sausage) and 12 small sausages (bratwurst, weisswurst, or knockwurst).

Serves 8

1 kg. (2 lbs.) fresh sauerkraut	Red wine to cover the sausage
4 strips 1-cm. ($\frac{1}{2}$-inch)-thick bacon	4 bratwurst
1 medium onion, peeled and sliced	4 weisswurst
About 6 dl. (1 pt) chicken or beef broth	4 knockwurst
1 kielbasa, cotechino, or garlic sausage	30 g. (1 oz.) butter
12 shallots or spring onions, peeled and chopped	

Wash the sauerkraut well in a colander under cold running water, lifting it up with your hands to let the water run through it. Drain well. Arrange the bacon in the bottom of a saucepan; add the sauerkraut and then the onion. Pour on enough broth barely to cover. Bring to a boil; cover; reduce the heat and simmer for 40 minutes.

Meanwhile, put the *kielbasa* or other sausage in a deep frying pan with the shallots or spring onions and add red wine barely to cover. Bring to a boil; reduce heat to a simmer and poach, turning the sausage several times, for 35 to 40 minutes.

At the same time, put the bratwurst, weisswurst and knockwurst in another frying pan, with water barely to cover, and poach for 10 minutes. Remove and drain the bratwurst; now melt the butter in that same pan and sauté the bratwurst over medium heat until lightly browned.

To serve, arrange the sauerkraut on a platter and surround it with the various sausages. Halve the smaller sausages and thickly slice the large one. Serve with boiled potatoes, a choice of mustards, and either an Alsatian Riesling or beer.

Poached Fish and Shellfish

Although fish is sometimes poached in salted water or milk, or water and white wine, the more usual way to cook it is in a court bouillon, which gives it additional flavour.

A court bouillon (the term originally meant a short sauce or small flavouring agent) is the aromatic seasoned liquid used to cook certain foods – fish, galantines (boned, stuffed, and poached poultry or meat), birds, pigs' or calves' feet, and various poached or boiled dishes. The ingredients of a court bouillon vary according to the food being cooked, but they usually include, in addition to the water, vinegar and herbs; or herbs and spices; or red or white wine (depending on the dish), seasonings, herbs and spices. A court bouillon is made by a process of boiling, reducing, simmering, and, if the liquid is to be used for a sauce after the food has been cooked, a second fast reduction by means of rapid boiling. A court bouillon may be as simple or as elaborate as you wish. Here are recipes for both types.

♛ Court Bouillon I

$\frac{1}{4}$ l. (8 fl. oz.) white wine vinegar
$1\frac{1}{2}$ tablespoons salt
1 onion, stuck with 2 cloves
1 stick of celery or a few leafy celery tops
4 or 5 slices of carrot

$\frac{1}{2}$ teaspoon thyme
6 peppercorns
1 bay leaf
2 or 3 sprigs of parsley
$1\frac{1}{2}$ l. ($2\frac{1}{2}$ pts) water

Put the ingredients in a pot large enough to hold whatever fish you are going to cook, and bring to a boil over high heat. Continue to cook at a fast boil for 5 minutes, or until the liquid is slightly reduced and the flavours concentrated. Turn the heat down so that the liquid is just simmering before lowering the fish (steaks, fillets, or whole fish) into it.

Court Bouillon II

This version includes wine and fish heads and bones, which give it a more intense flavour. If you can't get heads and bones, buy a largish, bony fish that can be discarded afterwards – a fish that is not for eating.

1 l. (1¾ pts) white wine
1½ dl. (¼ pt) white wine vinegar
1 large onion, peeled and stuck with
   2 cloves
2 carrots, scraped and thinly sliced
2 garlic cloves, peeled and crushed
1 teaspoon dried thyme
1 teaspoon dried tarragon

1 stick of celery
12 peppercorns
1 bay leaf
6 sprigs of parsley
2 tablespoons salt
1 to 1½ kg. (2 to 3 lbs.) fish heads
   and bones
2 l. (3½ pts) water

Bring all the ingredients to a full, rolling boil in a large pot and boil for 5 minutes. Reduce the heat until the liquid is simmering, cover the pan, and simmer for 1 hour. Remove and discard the fish bones and heads, or the whole fish, before adding the fish to be poached.

Fish Poached in Court Bouillon

Measure the depth of the fish at its thickest point to determine the cooking time (see page 122). Wrap the fish in muslin or place it on a double thickness of heavy aluminium foil large enough to extend above the rim of the fish cooker or cooking pot. Lower the fish into the simmering court bouillon and simmer it 10 minutes per measured 2½ cm. or 1 inch. Carefully remove it from the court bouillon by lifting the ends of the foil or muslin, and transfer it to a heated platter.

If you are making a sauce from the court bouillon, keep the fish warm. Reduce the bouillon by rapid boiling to about 6 dl. (1 pt) and strain it through a linen towel or napkin. You can make a sauce using 2 dl. (⅓ pt) of this reduced liquid, adding 4 tablespoons dry white wine, and enriching it with cream and egg (see white wine sauce for fish, page 287).

Use the white wine court bouillon II to poach large fish such as sea trout, salmon and red snapper.

Poached Fillets of Fish with White Wine Sauce

In this case, the fish is not poached in a court bouillon, but in equal parts of water and white wine, and the reduced poaching stock is used to make and flavour the sauce.

Serves 4

4 large or 8 small fish fillets
White wine and water
¼ teaspoon salt
1 sprig of parsley
1 slice of onion
45 g. (1½ oz.) butter
30 g. (1 oz.) flour

1½ dl. (¼ pt) double cream
2 tablespoons finely chopped parsley
½ teaspoon dried tarragon
Salt, freshly ground black pepper, nutmeg
2 tablespoons grated Parmesan cheese

Measure the fillets, which will be poached according to the general rule of thumb for all fish – 10 minutes per measured 2½ cm. or 1 inch of thickness (see page 122). Lay them flat in one layer in a large frying pan and barely cover with equal quantities of white wine and water. Add ¼ teaspoon salt, parsley sprig, and slice of onion. Bring the liquid to the boiling point, then reduce the heat and simmer gently for the required cooking time. Test for doneness with a fork or toothpick – if the fish just flakes, it is done. Slide a long metal palette knife under each fillet and carefully remove, without breaking, to a hot baking dish. Keep the fish warm while you make the sauce.

Strain the poaching liquid and measure. Reduce to ¼ l. (8 fl. oz.) by boiling rapidly over high heat. Melt the butter in a saucepan; blend in the flour and cook over medium heat for a minute or two, stirring with a wooden spatula, until the roux is golden and bubbling. Then mix in the reduced fish stock and stir over medium heat until the sauce is smooth and thickened. Mix in the cream, parsley, and tarragon and stir until heated through. Taste for seasoning, adding salt if necessary, a little freshly ground pepper, and a little grated nutmeg. Pour over the fish, sprinkle with grated Parmesan cheese, and put under a preheated grill until the surface of the sauce is lightly browned. Serve with tiny boiled potatoes and a purée of spinach, and drink a dry white wine – an Alsatian Riesling.

Shellfish à la Nage

One of the best ways I know to cook shellfish is *à la nage*, the French term for a style of preparation in which shellfish are both cooked and served 'swimming' in a white wine court bouillon and eaten hot, tepid, or cold. If you can get fresh-water crayfish, try this recipe with them; otherwise use large raw prawns, or small lobsters (use the timing for boiled lobsters in the following recipe).

Serves 4 to 6

COURT BOUILLON

2 or 3 carrots, scraped
2 medium onions, very thinly sliced
60 g. (2 oz.) parsley sprigs
1 teaspoon thyme
1 bay leaf

1 tablespoon salt
4 peppercorns
1 l. (1¾ pts) dry white wine
4½ dl. (¾ pt) water

THE SHELLFISH

4 dozen crayfish or large prawns
  Or 4 to 6 small lobsters

With the tines of a fork or a stripper, the little gadget that cuts thin strips from lemon rind, score the outside of the carrot and then slice it very thin – the idea is that the slices will look like flowers and be more attractive in the plate than plain old carrot rounds. Put all the court bouillon ingredients in a deep pot and bring to a rolling boil over high heat. Then drop in the crayfish and cook for 10 minutes at the boiling point – not a rolling boil. If using prawns, cook for 3 minutes. Remove at once and arrange in deep serving bowls or soup plates and ladle some of the aromatic court bouillon around them, with little bits of the carrots and onions. Sip the bouillon as you eat the shellfish. It's a good idea to have some melted butter and lemon wedges to enhance the delicate flesh of the shellfish, which are shelled at the table by the diners.

Boiled Lobsters

Most lobsters sold in markets weigh ½ to ¾ kg. (a pound to a pound and a half), but it is definitely worth buying larger lobsters if you can find them. Always look for lobsters that are active and lively, for these give the best eating. If your fish market can pick out the females, they are preferable for they have the coral, or roe. Ask to have the claws tied, if that has not been done already, so you will have no trouble with the beast. Count on one lobster per person.

You will need a large pot – an 8-litre (7-quart) size, or larger if you are cooking more than a couple of lobsters. Fill it about half full of water, season with 3 tablespoons salt, and bring to a boil. Grasp the lobsters firmly behind the head and sink them, head first, into the boiling water. This assures a sudden death. After the water returns to a boil, boil the lobsters 5 minutes for the first $\frac{1}{2}$ kg. or pound and 3 minutes more for each additional $\frac{1}{2}$ kg. or pound.

Don't cool the lobsters in the water or they will be overcooked. Remove them immediately and serve hot or, if you are serving cold lobster, let them cool.

If you are serving them hot, cut off a little piece of the shell at the head and drain the liquid from inside. Then split the lobsters in half lengthwise with a heavy chef's knife, remove the dark intestinal vein that runs down the centre of the body, and crack the claws with lobster or nut crackers. Leave the tomalley (the greenish liver) and any coral (the bright red roe) in the shell.

Serve the lobsters with melted butter, wedges of lemon, good bread, and chilled white wine. Provide lobster crackers and picks for winkling the meat from the claws.

If you are serving them cold, split and crack the lobsters and serve with mayonnaise.

Soups

Onion soup is surely one of the world's most comforting dishes. This version, slightly different from the usual, comes from Alsace, and one of the secrets of its richness is the beef stock with which it is made.

Onion Soup au Gratin

Serves 4

2 medium-large onions, peeled and
  coarsely chopped
90 g. (3 oz.) butter
1 tablespoon flour
$\frac{1}{4}$ l. (8 fl. oz.) dry white wine
$4\frac{1}{2}$ dl. ($\frac{3}{4}$ pt) beef stock

Salt, freshly ground black pepper
Pinch of nutmeg
75 g. ($2\frac{1}{2}$ oz.) grated Gruyère cheese
8 to 12 small slices of French bread
  Or small squares of bread

Sauté the onions in half the butter in a heavy saucepan over medium heat until they are limp and golden brown, shaking the pan well as they cook so they don't stick or burn. Stir in the flour, then mix in the wine and the beef stock. Season with salt and pepper to taste, and add the nutmeg. Cover and simmer over very low heat for 1 hour, then add 2 tablespoons of the cheese.

While the soup simmers, melt the remaining butter in a frying pan and sauté the bread over medium-high heat until crisply brown on both sides.

Ladle the soup into ovenproof bowls; arrange two or three of the fried bread croutons on top and sprinkle with the remaining cheese. Put in a 230°C (450°F, gas mark 8) oven or under a hot grill until the cheese melts and forms a thick browned crust.

Four-Day Vegetable Soup

I happen to think that vegetable soups made without meat stock are infinitely more intriguing. The results are often so delicate and unexpected that one is inspired to improvise constantly and find new and even more delicious combinations, for to my mind, success with vegetable soups is entirely a matter of inspiration, taste, and inventiveness.

I remember going through the refrigerator and the vegetable basket one winter day while living in France and coming up with a considerable array of bits and pieces, which I turned into a thoroughly good soup. This continued with a series of variations for four days (hence the name of the soup), resulting in three hot soups and one cold. Each time I had a totally different and distinctive product. This recipe, then, is not to be slavishly followed, but to serve as a starting point for your own ideas.

Serves 8

THE BASIC SOUP

1 large onion, peeled and finely chopped	2 small courgettes, finely diced
3 garlic cloves, peeled and finely chopped	3 or 4 leaves fresh rosemary
280 g. (10 oz.) finely chopped cabbage	Or 1 teaspoon dried rosemary, crushed
2 carrots, peeled and shredded	
1 small turnip, peeled and finely diced	1 tomato, peeled, seeded, and chopped
4 whole mushrooms, chopped	Salt, freshly ground black pepper
4 leaves and stems of Swiss chard	

Put all the vegetables and the rosemary in a deep pan with water to cover and salt and pepper to taste – about 1 tablespoon salt and 1 teaspoon pepper. Bring to a boil gradually over low heat. Cover and simmer the soup gently for $1\frac{1}{2}$ to 2 hours, or until all the flavours are well blended. Taste and correct the seasoning.

Four of us ate the soup that night, and the next day I added to the remainder another couple of peeled and chopped tomatoes, a few leaves of finely chopped spinach, another courgette, and a few leftover cooked chickpeas. I added a bit of grated lemon rind and a touch of onion about 10 minutes before serving.

For lunch on the following day I had the soup cold with a dollop of *crème fraîche* and finally, on the fourth day, I added 2 or 3 peeled and diced beetroots, another 150 g. (5 oz.) cabbage, 3 or 4 more mushrooms, and a little vegetable broth from vegetables I had cooked for lunch.

Of course, if you have some chicken or vegetable broth you can add it to your soup. The secret is to have variations of colour and texture and flavour.

Mussel Soup

Mussels make one of the most delicious of all soups. Cooking them in a tightly covered pot causes the shells to open and the shellfish to yield up their delicious liquid for the broth.

Serves 6

1½ kg. (3 lbs.) mussels
12 shallots, peeled and left whole
2 or 3 sprigs of parsley
1 teaspoon dried thyme or tarragon
Double cream to taste

90 g. (3 oz.) butter
¼ l. (8 fl. oz.) dry white wine
Garnish: Whipped cream, lightly salted; finely chopped parsley

Clean the mussels. With a scouring pad and a knife scrub and scrape off the encrustations on the shells; wash them well and pull or snip off the beards, the stringy black thread protruding from the shell. Put them in an 8-litre (7-quart) pot of heavy aluminium, enamelled iron, or stainless steel with the shallots, parsley, thyme or tarragon, butter and wine. Cover the pan tightly; bring to a boil, then reduce the heat to medium and cook the mussels for about 12 to 15 minutes. Remove the opened mussels and cook any with shells that remain shut for another 5 minutes. If they still do not open, discard them, for they are dead.

Remove the opened mussels from the shells and put them in the container of a liquidizer or food processor. Strain the broth through a triple thickness of muslin (this will trap any sand that came out of the mussel shells), then put the shallots from the mussel broth and about ¼ l. (8 fl. oz.) of the broth in the liquidizer or food processor with the mussels and blend or process until smooth. Stir this purée into the remaining strained broth, reheat, then stir in double cream to taste. Serve the soup in cups, topped with a spoonful of salted whipped cream and a sprinkling of chopped parsley.

Pasta

. . . .

Pasta is so good, and so easy to cook if you know how. The main thing to remember is that it must have a really big pot and plenty of water, which gives it room to expand and to move around, so that the pieces don't stick together. The water should be well salted, for nothing tastes worse than bland pasta. If you like, you can add a little oil to the water, which helps to prevent the strands from sticking together.

Pasta is the comprehensive Italian name for dried starch products (such as spaghetti, noodles, macaroni) that we usually call by name. The shape and size are unimportant, for the taste and method of preparation are the same.

In some towns you may find shops where pasta is freshly made. Because it is not dried until hard, like the commercial packaged products, it cooks in a very short time, a matter of 2 or 3 minutes, but it will not stay fresh too long. For best results it should be bought and cooked at once. Only the ribbony types of pasta such as fettuccine, tagliatelle and lasagne can be bought fresh. The tubular pastas are put through a machine that shapes them into cylinders and they are practically always bought dry.

When it comes to the commercial, packaged pastas, you'll find there is a tremendous difference among those of the various manufacturers. It's a good idea to try different imported and domestic pastas until you find the one that best suits your palate and bite.

How much pasta does one cook? This depends entirely on whether you are serving it as a first or a main course – and also on who is going to eat it. As the late Alice B. Toklas was wont to say, 'How do I know what appetites they will have?' How true. I know people who will cook 225 grams (a half pound) of pasta for two, and others who will stretch it to serve three or four. I feel that 450 grams or a pound is about right for 4 servings, but this is a place where you should make your own decision.

♨ To Cook Pasta

For 450 g. (1 pound) of pasta, put 4 litres (3½ quarts) of water in an 8-litre (7-quart) pot (you need a large pot because the water is kept at a rolling boil) and season it with 3 tablespoons of coarse salt. Cover the pan and bring the water to a full, rolling boil over high heat. Remove the cover; add 1 or 2 teaspoons of oil and the pasta of your choice. If you are cooking long thin strands of spaghetti or linguine, push them in the middle with a wooden spoon as the strands begin to soften so they are submerged. If the water drops below a boil, cover the pan briefly until it is back at the boil, then remove the lid.

Cook the pasta rapidly, at a seething, rolling boil. If you are cooking commercial pasta, start testing after 6 minutes. Fish out a strand with a long-handled fork or tongs and bite into it. Different pastas have different cooking times. The only way to know when it is done to your liking is to keep testing and tasting until it has reached the degree of doneness and firmness you like – but don't, please, overcook it until it is limp, soft and mushy. It should be cooked but firm to the bite – *al dente*.

The minute the pasta is cooked, drain it in a colander (with small holes) or a large sieve, then return it to the pot and toss it with your hot sauce.

While in Italy I learned a trick that I think improves pasta immensely. Instead of just adding the sauce and tossing it with the pasta, stir them together gently with two forks and then let the sauce and pasta cook over low heat for 2 to 3 minutes, so the pasta becomes imbued with the flavour of the sauce.

Pasta with Butter and Cheese
(Pasta al Burro)

Certainly the simplest and in many ways one of the most satisfying preparations of pasta is just to give it some melted butter and cheese.

Serves 4

450 g. (1 lb.) spaghettini or
  fettuccine or macaroni
125 g. (4 oz.) butter, melted or
  softened

125 to 180 g. (4 to 6 oz.) freshly
  grated cheese (Parmesan,
  Romano, or Pecorino)
Freshly ground black pepper

Cook the pasta in boiling salted water, testing after 6 minutes, until it is done to your taste. Drain well in a sieve or colander; return to the cooking pot and add the butter. Toss well with two forks, then add half the grated cheese and a few grinds of pepper and toss well again, until the pasta is coated. Serve in heated deep plates, such as soup plates, pass the rest of the cheese in a bowl and the pepper mill, for seasoning to taste.

VARIATIONS

1. Use half shredded Gruyère and half Parmesan or Romano.
2. After adding the cheese, add 1½ dl. (¼ pint) slightly warmed double cream and toss until well mixed. Freshly ground pepper is needed here as well.

Spaghetti with Garlic and Oil
(Spaghetti Aglio Olio)

Equally simple, this pungent mixture will please garlic lovers.

Serves 4

450 g. (1 lb.) spaghetti
¼ l. (8 fl. oz.) good olive oil
5 or 6 garlic cloves, peeled and
  finely chopped
Freshly ground black pepper

1 to 2 tablespoons chopped parsley,
  preferably Italian
Or 1 to 2 tablespoons chopped
  fresh basil

Cook the pasta in boiling salted water until done to your taste. While it is cooking, heat the oil until barely warm, add the garlic, and let it soak in the oil for 2 or 3 minutes. The amount of garlic depends on your tolerance – I usually gauge 1 clove per person and 1 or 2 extra. Drain the pasta and toss it with the oil and garlic, and freshly ground pepper. If you prefer, you may strain the garlic from the oil, but in doing so you lose the whole point of this dish. Cheese is superfluous with this, but chopped parsley or basil are wonderful.

VARIATIONS

1. Coarsely chop 4 or 5 garlic cloves and sauté them in 4 tablespoons olive oil until just lightly coloured. Do not allow to darken or burn or the flavour will be bitter. Combine with ½ teaspoon crushed, dried hot red pepper and 2 dl. (⅓ pt) heated olive oil. Toss the pasta with the mixture as above.
2. Add 8 to 10 anchovy fillets, coarsely chopped, to either of the oil and garlic mixtures. Toss the pasta with the sauce and garnish with chopped flat-leafed Italian parsley.

Spaghetti with Oyster Sauce

Serves 4

450 g. (1 lb.) spaghetti
4 tablespoons olive oil
3 garlic cloves, peeled and finely
  chopped

1 dozen fresh or tinned oysters,
  chopped
60 g. (2 oz.) chopped parsley, preferably
  Italian

Cook the pasta in boiling salted water until done to your taste. While it is cooking, heat 3 tablespoons of the oil in a frying pan, add the garlic, and sauté until just lightly coloured, not brown. Add the rest of the oil. Drain the oysters and add the liquid from them, and half the parsley, and heat to the boiling point. Then add the drained oysters and heat through thoroughly. Drain the spaghetti, cook it briefly with the oyster sauce, and sprinkle with the rest of the parsley.

Tomato Sauce for Pasta

If you can't get really ripe tomatoes, tinned Italian plum tomatoes make an excellent sauce.

Makes about 3 cups

3 tablespoons olive oil	1½ teaspoons salt
1 large onion, peeled and finely chopped	½ teaspoon freshly ground black pepper
3 garlic cloves, peeled and finely chopped	2 leaves fresh basil
1 kg. (2 lbs.) ripe tomatoes	Or 1 teaspoon dried basil
Or 1 l. (1¾ pts) tinned Italian plum tomatoes with their liquid	3 tablespoons tomato paste

Heat the oil in a heavy, deep saucepan, add the onion and garlic, and sauté over medium heat for a few minutes, until golden. Do not brown. If you are using fresh tomatoes, peel, seed, coarsely chop them and add. Or add the tinned tomatoes with their liquid and cook over medium-high heat for 10 minutes, or until the liquid is reduced by a third. Add the salt, pepper, basil, and tomato paste and let the sauce cook at medium-high heat for 5 minutes more.

VARIATIONS

1. Sauté 225 g. (½ lb.) thinly sliced mushrooms in 125 g. (4 oz.) hot butter for 3 minutes, tossing well. Add the tomato sauce and simmer for 2 to 3 minutes.
2. Add to the sauce 225 g. (½ lb.) Italian sausages, cut into thin slices and cooked for 4 to 5 minutes in a heavy frying pan over medium heat until the fat has drained out and they are cooked through. Drain all but about 4 tablespoons of fat, and cook 2 to 3 minutes more. Add the tomato sauce and simmer for 2 to 3 minutes.

Rice and Other Grains

There are many varieties of packaged rice on the market today, but the most popular and common are long-grain rice, and parboiled long-grain rice. Oddly enough, rice which has been parboiled, steamed and dried, takes longer to cook than the regular long-grain rice. Brown rice, much favoured by health-food fans, is a natural, unpolished rice with only the husk removed (milling and polishing make the rice white) that requires a much longer cooking time. Arborio rice from Piedmont, a very starchy Italian rice with a round, short grain, is considered by many people to be the only rice to use for a risotto, but I've made risotto for years with long-grain and parboiled rice with very good results.

Cooking rice presents a problem to many people, and there are innumerable theories about how it should be done. For long-grain rice, I have found that the old Oriental cooking method I have known all my life works the best.

☕ Old-Fashioned Boiled Rice

Makes 1 l. (1¾ pints)
Serves 4 to 6

Bring 4 litres (3½ quarts) of water and 2 tablespoons of salt to a rapid boil in a 6- to 8-litre (5- to 7-quart) pot. Throw in 350 grams (12 ounces) of rice in small handfuls, making sure that the water continues to boil throughout. Boil the rice rapidly for 15 minutes, uncovered, then drain through a sieve. Do not overcook. This will give you fluffy rice with well-separated grains, slightly firm to the bite.

If the rice seems a little moist and not fluffy, after draining return it to the pan and dry out over very low heat for 2 or 3 minutes, stirring it occasionally with a fork to fluff it up. Always stir cooked rice with a fork, or toss it with two forks. Using a spoon bruises the grains and makes them sticky.

This method also works well with the Italian short-grain rice.

Steamed Parboiled Rice

I prefer to steam parboiled rice covered. When you steam rice, remember that it will expand to three times its original volume.

Serves 4

6 dl. (1 pt) water	225 g. (8 oz.) converted rice
1 teaspoon salt	1 or 2 tablespoons soft butter or oil
1 tablespoon butter or oil (optional)	(optional)

Put the water, salt and butter or oil, if desired (this is not necessary if you are going to add butter or oil to the cooked rice), in a pan and bring it to a rapid boil. Add the rice, and when the water returns to the boil, cover the pan tightly, turn down the heat, and cook the rice over very low heat, without lifting the lid, for 20 to 25 minutes, until the water is completely absorbed. You may, for richer rice, substitute chicken stock for the water. The simplest addition is butter or oil. Add soft butter or oil to the rice. Toss with a fork until the grains are well coated.

VARIATIONS

Herbed Rice. With the oil or butter add 2 to 3 tablespoons finely chopped parsley and 1 to 2 tablespoons finely cut chives. Other herbs that might be added with the parsley and chives are chopped fresh tarragon and chervil.

Rice with Pine Nuts. After adding the butter or oil, toss the rice with 90 g. (3 oz.) pine nuts, which give a pleasant crunchiness.

Pungent Parsleyed Rice. Add to the cooked rice 6 to 8 chopped shallots that have been lightly sautéed in 2 tablespoons olive oil or butter until just limp and golden, and 2 to 3 tablespoons chopped parsley.

Saffron Rice. Crush $\frac{1}{4}$ teaspoon saffron threads in a mortar and pestle, then add to the cooking water. (Saffron is very expensive but also highly concentrated.)

Risotto

I like to use a heavy frying pan of cast aluminium, plain or enamelled cast iron, or copper and stainless steel for risotto – the Italian rice dish in which the grains, though firm, become creamy like a pudding. A pan that will distribute heat and hold it well aids the bubbling activity and gradual absorption of liquid that a risotto requires.

The next important thing is to have good stock or broth. It is best to use homemade chicken, beef, veal, or fish stock if possible. These stocks keep well in the freezer. There are so many variations of risotto that it is always a pleasure to have the wherewithal on hand to make it at the last minute. I am particularly partial to chicken and fish stock for risottos because I like to use seafood and various meats and vegetables that blend well with those flavours.

The simplest risotto is made with rice, butter or oil, onion, stock and Parmesan cheese.

Serves 4

90 g. (3 oz.) butter
1 small onion, peeled and very finely chopped
350 g. (12 oz.) rice (long- or short-grain)

$\frac{3}{4}$ to 1 l. (1$\frac{1}{4}$ to 1$\frac{3}{4}$ pts) homemade chicken or beef stock, heated
60 g. (2 oz.) freshly grated Parmesan cheese

Melt 60 g. (2 oz.) butter in a heavy frying pan; add the onion and cook over medium heat, stirring, until light golden. Add the remaining butter and, when it has melted, the rice. Stir the rice around in the butter with a fork until the grains have become coated and almost translucent.

Keep the stock hot in a pan on another burner. When making risotto, the stock is added by degrees, not all at once, so it must be kept at a simmer or the rice will not cook properly. When the rice is coated with butter, pour $\frac{1}{4}$ litre (8 fl. oz.) of the stock into a measuring cup and add to the rice. Stir vigorously for a minute with a fork, then let the rice cook over medium-high heat until the liquid is almost absorbed, stirring it now and then so it does not stick to the pan. Add another $\frac{1}{4}$ litre (8 fl. oz.) of stock and continue to cook and stir until the liquid is almost absorbed. The rice should bubble and gradually soften and become creamy – at this point, add the stock more cautiously, $1\frac{1}{2}$ dl. ($\frac{1}{4}$ pint) at a time, stirring until it is absorbed. You don't want to drown the rice with liquid, only add as much as it can absorb. You may find you need less, or possibly more, than the amount specified. As it cooks, taste a grain now and then. When the risotto is done after 25 to 30 minutes, the rice will be creamy and tender, but still *al dente* in the centre, just firm to the bite, with all the liquid absorbed. Keep stirring well in the final cooking to prevent the rice from sticking to the pan. When done, sprinkle with the Parmesan cheese and stir it in with the fork. Serve at once, on hot plates.

VARIATION

Risotto Villa d'Este (Risotto with Smoked Salmon). Cook the risotto as before, but substitute simmering fish stock for the chicken stock. When the risotto is almost done, stir in $1\frac{1}{2}$ dl. ($\frac{1}{4}$ pint) double cream and let it cook down for 1 minute. Then stir in 90 g. (3 oz.) finely shredded smoked salmon, distributing it evenly throughout the rice, 2 to 3 tablespoons finely chopped parsley, and 3 tablespoons freshly grated Parmesan cheese. Serve at once. A tablespoon or two of finely chopped fresh dill may be mixed in for an unorthodox but delicious touch.

Rice Salad

The secret of a good rice salad is to use freshly cooked rice and toss it with oil while it is hot. This coats the cooling grains and keeps them separate and fluffy.

Serves 6

1 l. (1$\frac{3}{4}$ pts) freshly cooked long-grain rice (see page 50)

3 tablespoons olive oil

90 g. (3 oz.) peeled, seeded, and
  chopped tomato
90 g. (3 oz.) finely chopped green onions
  Or red Italian onion
90 g. (3 oz.) peeled, seeded, and diced
  cucumber

90 g. (3 oz.) seeded and diced green or
  red pepper
30 g. (1 oz.) chopped parsley
2 tablespoons chopped fresh basil, if
  available
1½ to 2 dl. (¼ to ⅓ pt) vinaigrette sauce
  (see page 304)

The minute the rice is drained, put it in a bowl; add the oil and toss well with two forks until the grains are completely coated. Cool the rice at room temperature.

Mix in the chopped vegetables and herbs, add vinaigrette sauce to taste, according to how moist you like your rice salad – it should be well coated but not soggy. Toss lightly with two forks and serve in a salad bowl, which may be lined with greens, if you wish. This is a good summer accompaniment to grilled meat and poultry.

Bulghur (Cracked Wheat) Pilaf

Bulghur, or cracked wheat, a staple of Middle Eastern cooking, is light golden brown in colour, with a nutty taste and texture. It is very good with meat kebabs or grilled chicken; as an alternative to rice; and may be used, like cooked rice, for stuffings.

Serves 4

2 tablespoons butter
1 tablespoon finely chopped onion
180 g. (6 oz.) medium- or coarse-grind
  cracked wheat

½ teaspoon salt
¼ teaspoon freshly ground black pepper
4½ dl. (¾ pt) chicken stock

Melt the butter in a skillet; add the onion and sauté over medium heat for 2 or 3 minutes, stirring, until limp and golden. Add the cracked wheat and stir until the grains are well coated with butter. Add the salt, pepper and stock and bring to a boil. Lower the heat; cover the pan tightly and simmer gently for 15 minutes, or until liquid is absorbed and wheat tender.

VARIATIONS

1. Add toasted sliced almonds to the cooked pilaf.
2. Sauté 45 g. (1½ oz.) sliced mushrooms in 2 tablespoons butter and add to the cooked pilaf.

Cornmeal Mush
(Polenta)

American cornmeal mush, which is basically the same as Italian polenta, is a good and somewhat different accompaniment to meats, especially pork, game, chicken, sausages, chili and spicy Mexican dishes, or with salt cod, spinach, or just tomato sauce. Mixing the cornmeal with cold water first makes the texture less grainy.

Serves 4 to 6

225 g. (8 oz.) cornmeal
1 l. (1¾ pts) cold water
1 teaspoon salt

60 g. (2 oz.) unsalted butter
60 g. (2 oz.) grated Parmesan cheese

Put the cornmeal in the top of a double boiler and stir in ¼ litre or ½ pint of the water. Mix well. Bring the rest of the water to a boil in another pan. When the cornmeal is well mixed, stir in the boiling water and cook over very low heat, stirring constantly, until the mixture comes to a boil. Stir in the salt. Put enough water in the bottom of the double boiler to come just below the top section. Bring it to a simmer. Put on the top of the double boiler with the cornmeal mush, cover, and steam over the simmering water for 1 hour. Stir in the butter and cheese, and serve.

VARIATION

Fried Cornmeal Mush. Pour the cooked cornmeal into a loaf tin and chill thoroughly until firm and set. Remove from the pan; cut into slices and sauté in butter until crisp and brown on both sides. Or, if you prefer, brush the slices well with melted butter on one side, sprinkle with grated Parmesan cheese, and brown under a hot grill.

Dumplings and Gnocchi

Chicken with dumplings is one of those simple but good American dishes we inherited from our European ancestors. Gnocchi, the Italian name for very small dumplings, are made of different starchy mixtures – potatoes, cream-puff paste, semolina, cottage cheese stiffened with flour. After poaching, they are usually served sprinkled with butter and grated cheese and heated through in the oven, or covered with a sauce. They make a pleasant change from other starches, as an accompaniment to sautéed dishes such as chicken livers or veal, or can be eaten like pasta, as a light luncheon dish, with a cheese or tomato sauce.

One advantage of gnocchi is that they can be made in advance and either chilled and reheated in the oven, or left in the cold poaching water, with a paper towel laid on the surface of the liquid to prevent the gnocchi from drying out, then gently reheated in the water. While dumplings are usually simmered in a covered pot to expand the starch granules in the flour, gnocchi are poached uncovered. Do not let the water boil, or the vigorous action may cause the dumplings or gnocchi to disintegrate.

Old-Fashioned Chicken and Dumplings

Follow the recipe for poached chicken in double chicken broth (page 28). While the chicken is cooking, make up the dumplings, which will be added for the last 15 minutes of cooking time.

DUMPLINGS

Serves 4 to 8

225 g. (8 oz.) sifted flour
3 teaspoons baking powder
1 teaspoon salt

2 eggs
1½ dl. (¼ pint) milk

Sift the dry ingredients together. Beat the eggs and milk together lightly and blend with the flour mixture to make a fairly stiff dough. About 15 minutes before the end of the cooking time, remove the lid from the pot in which the chicken is cooking and drop rounded tablespoons of the dumpling dough over the surface of the liquid, spacing them a few inches apart as dumplings puff up. Cover the pan, keeping the liquid at a simmer, and cook the dumplings for 15 minutes, until light and cooked through. Do not remove lid while dumplings are cooking. Serve with the poached chicken.

Potato and Semolina Gnocchi

Semolina, also called farina, is a granular starch derived from the durum wheat used to make pasta.

Serves 4 to 8

¾ kg. (1½ lbs.) mealy potatoes
1 teaspoon salt
½ teaspoon freshly ground black
   pepper
Pinch of mace
3½ dl. (12 fl. oz.) milk

180 g. (6 oz.) semolina
60 g. (2 oz.) grated Gruyère cheese
2 eggs, beaten
4 tablespoons melted butter
2 to 3 tablespoons grated Parmesan
   cheese

Peel and quarter the potatoes, put in salted water to cover; bring to a boil and boil until tender when pierced with a fork or knife point. Drain; put back over low heat to dry out, shaking the pan, then mash with a fork. Season with the salt, pepper, and mace and gradually beat in the milk, using a wooden spatula or an electric mixer. Place over medium heat in a 2½-litre (2-quart) saucepan and slowly mix in the farina until the mixture is very stiff. Mix in the grated cheese, then remove from the heat and mix in the eggs. Put the mixture in a flat buttered baking tin and refrigerate for 3 hours, or until firm enough to roll.

Have ready a large pot three-quarters full of simmering salted water. Take up tablespoons of the mixture and roll into balls between the palms of your hands. Drop the gnocchi into the water, about 8 at a time, and cook them for 4 minutes at a simmer, or until they rise to the surface, which means they are cooked. Remove with a slotted spoon as they cook and arrange in a well-buttered gratin dish. When all are cooked, drizzle melted butter over the top, sprinkle with the Parmesan cheese, and heat through in a 190°C (375°F, gas mark 5) oven for 10 to 15 minutes. These will serve 4 as a light luncheon dish, or 8 as an accompaniment.

The gnocchi may also be served with a tomato sauce (see page 49).

Eggs

The egg is a perfect object lesson in the techniques of boiling and poaching. To watch a poached egg form is to see a vivid example of the firming action of the cooking process. Eggs for poaching or soft-boiling should be the freshest possible. The fresher the egg, the firmer and more shapely the white of a poached egg will be.

Poached Eggs

There are many different theories about poaching eggs, but this is the method I have found works best.

Use a frying pan or a flat-surfaced pan that is not too deep – this enables you to slip the eggs in easily. Add water to a depth of 5 to 8 cm (2 to 3 inches), ½ teaspoon salt, and ½ teaspoon vinegar, which helps the whites coagulate. Bring the water to a slow boil in which the bubbles just break the surface, not a fast, rolling boil which would whip the whites away before they could set, giving you a ragged-looking result. Have beside you paper towels or a linen cloth on which to drain the eggs, a slotted spoon or a flat, perforated skimmer for removing them from the water (I find the round, flat, well-perforated skimmer sold in Japanese stores that carry kitchen utensils ideal), and a large spoon for basting.

Break each egg into a tiny cup (such as a Japanese tea cup or an egg cup), lower the cup into the water, and very quickly tip out the egg, holding the inverted cup there for a second or two to keep the white from spreading. Don't try to do too many eggs at one time – two or three, according to the size of your pan, are about as many as can be handled easily. As soon as all the eggs are in the water, remove the pan from the heat and let the eggs poach very gently in the hot water for 3 to 4 minutes, basting the tops with spoonfuls of hot water if necessary. When the whites are firm and set, and the yolks just filmed with white, remove the eggs with the perforated skimmer and place them on the towels to absorb the excess water.

If you aren't going to use the eggs right away, lower them gently into a dish of cold water to stop the cooking, then remove, dry on towels, and put on a plate, covered with plastic wrap, until required. If the white is at all ragged, you can trim it with scissors.

Soft-Boiled Eggs

Plunge the eggs into a pan of boiling water and boil for 3 minutes after the water returns to the boil. Give very large eggs 30 seconds more. Then remove from the water and serve. If the eggs are very cold, take the precaution of pricking the end of the shell with a needle before putting them in the water, which will prevent them from cracking. There's a little egg-pricking gadget on the market now, but a needle works just as well.

Eggs Mollet

This type of boiled egg, which is used for eggs in aspic and similar dishes, both hot and cold, has a soft, runny yolk, but a white firm enough to stand up to handling – rather like an egg poached in its shell. Boil it like a soft-boiled egg, but give it about $4\frac{1}{2}$ minutes, then remove it from the hot water and immediately plunge it into very cold water to stop the cooking. As soon as the shell is cool enough to handle, shell it and either use it immediately or cover it with plastic wrap until needed.

Hard-Boiled Eggs

Put the eggs in boiling water (if they are cold, prick them first) and boil for 3 minutes, then leave them in the water, with the heat turned off, for 9 minutes. Remove and run cold water over them, or plunge them into cold water. Let them cool completely before refrigerating or shelling.

Dried Beans

The dried beans sold in supermarkets are washed and sorted before packaging and, unlike those sold loose, do not need to be picked over and washed before cooking. The recommended method of cooking is first to bring them to a boil in water to cover, boil them for 2 minutes, remove them from the heat, and let them soak, covered, in the cooking water for 1 hour. Then add extra water to cover, if necessary, and any seasonings and flavourings required in the recipe; bring to a boil, reduce the heat, and simmer, covered, until tender. Salt is added not during the initial cooking, but with the other seasonings, after the beans have softened in the water.

Breton Beans

This is the classic accompaniment to roast *gigot*, or leg of lamb, prepared in the Breton style. Half a kilo (1 pound) of dried beans equals $1\frac{1}{2}$ litres ($1\frac{1}{4}$ quarts) cooked.

Serves 6 to 8

$\frac{1}{2}$ kg. (1 lb.) haricot beans
1 onion, stuck with 2 cloves
2 garlic cloves, peeled

1 bay leaf
Salt, freshly ground black pepper
4 tablespoons tomato purée

Put the beans in a deep saucepan and add water to cover. Bring to a boil; boil 2 minutes, then remove the pan from the heat and let the beans cool, covered, in the cooking water for 1 hour. Don't let the beans sit in the liquid for longer than 1 hour or they will become too soft. Cook them soon after they have cooled.

After 1 hour, if needed, add more cold water to cover, the onion, garlic, bay leaf and 2 teaspoons salt. Bring to a boil, then reduce the heat until the liquid is simmering; cover the pan and simmer for 45 minutes. Then add the tomato purée (don't add it until the beans have had this cooking time, as the acidity of the tomato may harden them). Continue to cook until just tender, about another 20 to 30 minutes, checking for tenderness now and then. The beans should be tender when bitten, but not soft, mushy, or broken. During the cooking, check the pan to see that the liquid is simmering, not boiling, as this would break up the beans. If they seem to be getting too dry, add a little more water.

When the beans are cooked, taste them, add more salt if needed, and pepper to taste. Drain the beans and discard the onion and bay leaf. When serving the beans with roast lamb, you may, if you like, stir 1 or 2 tablespoons of the pan juices from the roast into them, just before serving, and garnish them with a sprinkling of chopped parsley.

VARIATION

White Bean Salad. Follow the directions for cooking the beans, but do not add the tomato purée. Drain and cool. Put the beans in a bowl with 125 g. (4 oz.) finely chopped spring onion and 4 tablespoons chopped parsley. Add 3 dl. ($\frac{1}{2}$ pint) vinaigrette sauce (see page 304) and toss well. Allow to stand 1 to 2 hours before serving to mellow the flavours. If desired, the salad may be garnished with rings of thinly sliced red onion and 1 tablespoon chopped parsley.

Vegetables

Many people believe in cooking vegetables by plunging them into quantities of boiling water and then boiling them rapidly until they are tender. It does no harm, especially if you are cooking root vegetables or green beans. However, I have experimented considerably with vegetable cookery and I find that I get extremely good results simply by putting vegetables in a pan, barely covering them with cold salted water (about 1 teaspoon salt per $\frac{1}{4}$ litre or $\frac{1}{2}$ pint of water), putting on the lid, and bringing them to a boil over low heat and then simmering them very gently until they are tender. I have had splendid results with new potatoes, young carrots, green peas and other tender things. Somehow gentle cooking in a minimum of water for the minimum time seems to give them a fresher taste.

When I cook corn on the cob, I put it in cold water and just bring it to a boil, without cooking further. It is done perfectly, without that starchy 'cooked' taste I dislike in most corn on the cob.

There are other vegetables, notably asparagus and green beans, that I like to cook rapidly in water to cover in an open pan. Asparagus I lay flat in a frying pan, cover with cold salted water, bring to a boil, and then cook very fast until it is barely tender, removing the stalks to a paper-towel-lined dish as they are ready. Depending on the thickness of the stalks, and there is always some variation, asparagus will take from 7 to 12 minutes to cook. You can't leave it – you must watch and test carefully until it is done to your personal taste and bite. You can tell when the spears are done by picking one out with tongs and gently shaking it – if the stalk bends slightly and the tip droops over and bobs back and forth, it is done: it should be crisply tender and a brilliant green. I cook green beans in the same way, picking one out and biting into it after 5 or 6 minutes' fast boiling, at which point it is easy to determine how near it is to being done.

If you try this minimum-water method, you'll find that it works pretty well for most vegetables. There are, of course, exceptions. Spinach should be put in the pan with only the water that clings to the leaves after washing, covered, and wilted down very rapidly over high heat. Other fast-cooking leafy greens, such as chard leaves, need very little water, just enough to keep them from sticking to the pan, and only a light sprinkling of salt. I cook artichokes in plenty of rapidly boiling salted water, with a lemon slice and clove of garlic, in a covered pot large enough to allow the water to circulate around them.

When it comes to cooking, it is impossible to give hard-and-fast cooking times. The only way to know if a vegetable is done is to test it with a fork or the point of a small sharp knife or to take one piece out and bite into it. The timing depends on so many things – the age, the size, the natural degree of tenderness (mangetout, for instance, need hardly any cooking, nor do very young green peas), and whether the vegetable in question is whole or cut up. Most green vegetables will cook in 15 minutes or less – be sure not to overcook them; root vegetables will take longer.

🍳 Basic Vegetable Purée

Many vegetables, after being boiled, can be turned into the soft, smooth mixture we call a purée by being put through a sieve or food mill and whipped with butter and seasonings. A liquidizer or food processor does a speedy and smooth job of puréeing and mixing.

Firm vegetables are best suited to purées. Some good candidates are potatoes, parsnips, carrots, celeriac, swedes, white turnips, salsify, Jerusalem artichokes, cauliflower, broccoli, French beans, green peas, spinach, cooked dried beans, lentils and chickpeas (or tinned chickpeas). Certain purées go well together in combination, such as potato with celeriac, or carrot, or swede.

For 1 kg. (2 pounds) sieved vegetable, use from 60 to 90 g. (2 to 3 oz.) butter, depending on the consistency of the vegetable. If the mixture is on the dry side, beat in a few tablespoons of double cream or soured cream. Potatoes, which need plenty of moisture, are usually beaten with boiling milk as well as butter. Here are some simple variations on the purée:

Puréed Potatoes

Mashed or whipped potatoes, more elegantly known as *purée de pommes de terre*, ideally should be light, fluffy and creamy and they must be made at the last minute so they won't sit and become soggy. Opinions differ as to whether the potatoes should be cooked in their jackets or not. I believe that if they are floury and mealy they should be peeled.

Serves 6

Peel 1 kg. (2 pounds) potatoes and cook them in salted water to cover until they are tender. Drain them, return them to the pan, and let them dry over medium heat for a few minutes. Mash the potatoes with a wooden or wire masher or put them through a food mill or potato ricer into a bowl. Add 1½ to 2 dl. (¼ to ⅓ pt) boiling milk and about 75 g. (2½ oz.) softened butter and whip the potatoes with a whisk or wooden spatula or in the bowl of an electric mixer, using the whisk attachment. The potatoes must be smooth, very hot and rather loose in texture. Do not let them get too thick and pasty or they will lose their delicacy. Season them with freshly ground pepper to taste and transfer them to a heated serving dish. Add a dot of butter and serve them very hot. To keep the potatoes hot, put them in a well-buttered pan set over hot water and cover them with buttered waxed paper.

Purée of Celeriac

Serves 6

Simmer 1 to 1¼ kg. (2 to 2½ pounds) celeriac in salted water to cover until it is just tender. Peel it, cut off the little root ends, and cut the bulbs in quarters. Put the bulbs through a food mill. Whip the purée with 90 g. (3 oz.) butter, 1 teaspoon freshly ground pepper and additional salt, if needed. Spoon it into a heated vegetable dish, sink a large piece of butter in the centre, and serve it at once.

Or you may combine the celeriac purée with an equal quantity of puréed potatoes and whip them together with 125 g. (4 oz.) butter and 3 to 4 table-spoons double cream. Spoon the purée into a heated vegetable dish and top it with a square of butter and some chopped parsley.

Carrot Purée

Serves 6

Scrape 1 kg. (2 pounds) carrots and cut them into two or three pieces. Simmer them in salted water to cover until they are tender, drain them well, and put them through a food mill. Finish the purée in any of the following ways:

1. Blend the carrots with 90 g. (3 oz.) butter, $\frac{1}{8}$ teaspoon nutmeg, and additional salt, if needed. Spoon the purée into a heated serving dish and top it with bits of butter and some chopped parsley.

2. Mix the carrots with 60 g. (2 oz.) butter and 4 tablespoons double cream. Blend the purée well with a spatula, spoon it into a serving dish, and top it with chopped parsley.

3. Combine the carrots with an equal quantity of puréed potatoes. Add 90 g. (3 oz.) butter and 6 tablespoons double cream, and whip the purée with a wooden spatula or a heavy whisk until it is smooth and creamy.

Puréed Parsnips with Madeira

Serves 6

Wash and trim $2\frac{1}{2}$ to 3 kg. (5 to 6 pounds) parsnips and put them in a 6- to 8-litre (5- to 7-quart) pan with salted water to cover. Simmer the parsnips until they can be pierced, drain them, and let them cool until they can be handled. Peel them and cut them into pieces 7 to 10 cm. (3 to 4 inches) long. Put the pieces through a food mill and combine the purée with $1\frac{1}{2}$ dl. ($\frac{1}{4}$ pt) melted butter, $1\frac{1}{2}$ dl. ($\frac{1}{4}$ pt) madeira, 4 tablespoons double cream, $\frac{1}{4}$ teaspoon nutmeg and salt to taste. Beat the purée well, adding more butter or cream if it seems too dry. Spoon it into a $1\frac{1}{2}$ l. ($1\frac{1}{2}$ qt) baking dish, sprinkle it with finely chopped walnuts, and top it with pieces of butter. Heat the purée in a 190°C (375°F, gas mark 5) oven for about 20 minutes, or until it is heated through. Serve it very hot with game or roast fowl or pork.

Vegetables à la Grecque

Although this style of poaching tender young vegetables in a flavourful court bouillon, known as *à la Grecque*, did originate in Greece, it has now become completely identified with the French cuisine. As the vegetables are eaten cold, rather than hot, they can be made in quantity and kept in the refrigerator in containers, to be brought out when you want a simple first course or cold vegetables for a summer buffet. Serve the different vegetables in the small serving dishes called *raviers*, or in flat pottery or glass dishes. A sprinkling of chopped fresh parsley or, if you like the flavour, chopped fresh coriander, makes a pleasant garnish.

POACHING LIQUID

$1\frac{1}{2}$ dl. ($\frac{1}{4}$ pt) oil (olive, groundnut, or corn)

4 tablespoons white wine vinegar

4 *tablespoons dry white wine or vermouth*

1 *teaspoon salt*

½ teaspoon freshly ground black pepper
1 bay leaf
1 or 2 garlic cloves, peeled
Dash of Tabasco

1 teaspoon dried thyme, tarragon,
   oregano, or basil
   Or, even better,
   1 tablespoon chopped
   fresh herbs

SELECT FROM THE FOLLOWING VEGETABLES

Young tender French beans
Whole spring onions or tiny white
   onions
Small, firm mushroom caps
Leeks, whole or halved
Fennel bulbs, halved or quartered
Fingers or cubes of aubergine
Small, firm courgettes, halved or thickly
   sliced

Celery hearts (tight white cores),
   halved
Flower buds of broccoli or cauliflower
Tiny young carrots
Tiny pattypan squash
Artichoke bottoms or quartered
   artichokes, trimmed and choke
   removed

Do not simmer vegetables together, as they will have different cooking times. Cook your selection separately.

Put the court bouillon ingredients in a large shallow pan or deep frying pan, then add the cleaned, trimmed vegetable and just enough water barely to cover. The court bouillon is sufficient for ½ kg. (1 pound) of French beans or carrots, or 1 large aubergine, cubed, or 8 artichoke bottoms, or a dozen mushroom caps.

Bring the liquid to a boil very slowly over medium heat, then reduce the heat and poach until the vegetable is just crisply tender when pierced with a fork or the point of a small sharp knife. Do not overcook. Remove from the heat, taste the liquid for seasoning, and add salt, if needed; then let the vegetable cool in the liquid. When cool, transfer to a refrigerator container or serving dish. Strain the poaching liquid and use again for other vegetables. If necessary, add more water.

Fruit

Poaching in a simple syrup of sugar and water or wine is a classic method of preparing fruit for dessert. As the syrup is merely the cooking agent, it should not be overly sweet. Firm-fleshed large fruits, such as peaches, pears, apricots, or pineapples, are best for this process. You can also poach cherries and softer fruits, such as plums, gooseberries and rhubarb, but they won't be as firm or as attractive as the larger fruits.

♛ Poached Peaches

Serves 4

225 g. (8 oz.) sugar
¼ l. (8 fl. oz.) water
2½-cm. (1-inch) piece of vanilla bean
   Or ½ teaspoon vanilla extract

4 ripe but firm, unblemished peaches

Combine the sugar, water, and vanilla bean in a heavy saucepan large enough to hold the peaches. Bring to a boil, and boil slowly for 8 minutes to make a simple syrup.

Meanwhile, put the peaches in a deep pan, pour over them enough boiling water to cover, bring it to a boil again, reduce the heat, and simmer the peaches for 3 minutes. This parboiling helps the skins to slip off easily and slightly softens the fruit. Remove the peaches from the water and peel them. Drop them into the syrup, reduce the heat, and poach them at a feeble simmer until just tender when pierced with a fork, from 4 to 12 minutes. Do not overcook. The time depends on the ripeness of the peaches. Remove the peaches to a serving dish, bring the syrup to a rolling boil, and reduce by boiling fast for 4 to 5 minutes, watching carefully to see that it does not turn dark and caramelize. Let it cool slightly, then pour over the peaches and chill before serving.

Pears Poached in Red Wine

Serves 6

6 dl. (1 pt) red wine
280 g. (10 oz.) sugar
1 lemon slice

2 cloves
6 firm and slightly underripe pears

Combine the wine, sugar, lemon and cloves in a large flat-bottomed pan, such as a sauté pan. Bring to a boil over high heat, stirring until the sugar dissolves. Peel, core, and halve the pears, dropping each peeled half into a bowl of water acidulated with 1 tablespoon lemon juice to prevent discolouring. Reduce the heat so the syrup is simmering, drain and add the pears, and poach until tender, turning them once, for 10 minutes, or until just tender when pierced with a fork, but not overdone (the time depends on the size and firmness of the pears). They should still hold their shape and not be mushy. Serve hot, with a little of the syrup, or cool in the syrup and serve cold, again with a spoonful or two of syrup.

Apple Sauce

Serves 4

When making apple sauce, you need just enough water to create the steam necessary to soften the apples, as they themselves contain a lot of liquid. Apples also vary so much in tartness that it is folly to sweeten them before cooking.

Peel $1\frac{1}{2}$ kg. (3 pounds) of cooking apples, cut them into sixths, and cut out the cores with a small sharp knife. As you peel them, drop them into a bowl of cold water acidulated with 1 tablespoon lemon juice, to prevent them from turning brown. Place apples in a heavy saucepan and add $1\frac{1}{2}$ dl. ($\frac{1}{4}$ pint) water. Cover and cook over medium heat at a gentle simmer until they are almost soft. Taste and add sugar, a little at a time, then taste again. When the apples are sweetened to your taste, continue simmering uncovered for 2 or 3 minutes to melt the sugar and cook down the sauce. If you like your apple sauce spiced, add $\frac{1}{4}$ teaspoon of your favourite spice (such as ground cinnamon, nutmeg, mace, or cloves) when adding the sugar. For a smoother apple sauce, put the cooked apples through a food mill to make a purée.

Roasting

Whenever I think of roasting, my mind returns to our big family kitchen, which was equipped with a very large wood-burning stove. When we had guests for dinner, my mother or Let, who was our sometime-chef after my mother gave up her hotel business, prepared a glorious standing rib roast. First, she would go to her butcher, who obeyed her every wish and command, pick out the roast at least $2\frac{1}{2}$ weeks ahead of time, and ask that it be hung an additional time, until the day she wished to roast it. She felt, and rightly, that well-aged beef had better flavour and better texture, as well as greater tenderness. Sometimes it would arrive covered with green mould, which was trimmed off before cooking, and I learned that this made the roast taste better.

My mother would buy quite a lot of extra suet and render it in the huge professional roasting tin that had been used in the hotel kitchen. It was a big, oblong black tin with rather shallow sides and in it was a rack with very short legs, just enough to elevate the meat from the tin bottom. On the day of the party, the suet was rendered in this tin until it was bubbling hot, wafting a lovely beef-scented air through the house. The roast, rubbed with flour, salt and pepper, was put with this bubbling fat into a very hot oven and that first enticing sizzle as the meat hit the rack gave a wonderful preview of what was to come. The meat was basted regularly with the fat, then taken from the oven when it had just about reached its peak of perfection and placed on a hot platter on the back of the stove. The rack was removed and a good deal of the fat poured off – a ticklish business – and the tin returned to the oven to bake the Yorkshire pudding while the roast rested. The pudding batter, poured into the hot fat and popped into a 230°C (450°F, gas mark 8) oven, rose to the most glorious golden-brown crispness and puffiness and took on a marvellous beef flavour. There was never any Yorkshire pudding left over. With the roast beef and Yorkshire pudding we had gravy and sometimes potatoes roasted in the fat to a crisp, well-done brownness, a most glorious combination. That was my introduction to roasting, and it created in me a passionate love for properly roasted meat that has lasted all my life.

Roasting is one of the oldest and most spectacular forms of cooking. Originally, roasting was done on a spit in front of the fire. What we call roasting, meat cooked by dry heat in the oven, was known until the end of the nineteenth century as baking. Spit-roasting was the popular way of cooking a piece of meat, while baking had a rather plebeian implication, as if you couldn't afford a spit for your fireplace.

Years ago, in the great houses, the spits were operated by dogs or by the scullery maids. I remember seeing in a house in France, between Cognac and Angoulême, traces of the sixteenth- and seventeenth-century kitchen which the owners had left for their own and their friends' enjoyment, while creating a modern kitchen in another part of the house. In the old fireplace was a treadmill spit that had been worked by dog power – or by manpower, which must have been a most exhausting job. A more civilized and later form of spit was operated by counterweights, and there was also a rather primitive form of tin oven that stood in front of the fire, with a curved reflector back to intensify the heat and a tin underneath to catch the drippings.

Anyone who has a spit on his outdoor grill or in his fireplace can testify to the delicacy and deliciousness of meat roasted in this way. A side of beef, a baron or leg of lamb, even a tiny rack of lamb will all come forth with great flavour and perfect texture. Some years ago, when I visited André Surmain in Majorca, he cooked a suckling pig on an electrically driven spit in front of a fire, and it was one of the most delicious pigs I have ever eaten.

Unfortunately, few of us these days can have a large fireplace with a revolving spit, and flat-dwellers can't even have a charcoal barbecue with a rotisserie, so our roasting is done in the oven. Modern ovens are ideal for roasting – efficient, foolproof and accurate because they are well calibrated, which means they are tested for calibration, or the accuracy of the thermostatic control. Occasionally, if you have an oven tested, you may find it will be 10 to 20 degrees centigrade (25 to 50 degrees Fahrenheit) off one way or the other, something that can easily be adjusted then and there.

There is a great deal of controversy about temperatures for oven roasting. Some contend that low-temperature roasting, at 170°C (325°F, gas mark 3), results in juicier meat and less shrinkage. Another school believes that the most effective method is to sear the meat at 230°C (450°F) or even 250°C (500°F) for 45 minutes to an hour; searing means sealing the surface by exposing it to high heat. Then reduce the heat to 180°C or 170°C (350°F or 325°F) for the remainder of the cooking period. There's a lot to be said for this method. It seems to me that, in most cases, high-temperature roasting gives a crustier exterior and juicier interior. However, there is always the chance – and this is the result of a great deal of testing on my part – that roasting too long at a high temperature gives you a well-done streak around the meat, while the inner part is pink or rare, as the case may be. In some ways you get a more even flavour and perhaps a more delicate texture from roasting throughout at a low temperature. I'm not going to take sides on this, because I roast both ways, and there are even some things, a fillet of beef or a chicken, indeed most birds, that I roast completely at a high temperature. I find that if chicken is roasted at 220°C (425°F) or even 230°C (450°F) for the entire cooking time, the result is crisper and better than if it is seared and cooked at a lower temperature, or cooked the whole time at 170°C (325°F).

Roasting is a dry-heat process in which the meat or bird is cooked on all sides by even heat circulation. (For this reason, microwave ovens are not satisfactory for roasting, as the interior of the meat cooks first.) The roast should always be placed on a rack in a shallow roasting tin – either one of the adjustable V-shaped racks or a flat rack – or on the grill rack and pan. Look at the display of roasting tins on page 67 and you'll realize how easily you can improvise. The important thing is never to put the meat directly in the tin as contact with the fat and juices will give the underside of the roast a soggy, stewed quality, no matter how carefully you roast it. With a rack and shallow tin the heat penetrates all sides evenly and the bottom will have the same crusty finish as the top.

I believe, as my mother did, that basting is an important part of roasting. A well-basted roast of beef has a character all its own. I don't think rack or leg of lamb needs basting, but a shoulder can benefit. Certainly veal is improved by regular basting – in fact, I prefer to braise veal so that it gets more moisture and flavour – and even pork can take some basting. Turkey and most game birds are all the better for basting. If you want my honest opinion, a big spoon is better to use for basting than those bulb basters, which I don't think do an efficient job. A big basting spoon holds plenty of the juices and should be used frequently during roasting.

Probably one of the greatest aids to roasting ever invented is the meat thermometer, and by this I do not mean the old-fashioned meat thermometer with a dial listing recommended temperatures for different meats, from rare to well done. I remember when meat thermometers like this first came on the market, recommending internal temperatures that were quite ridiculous: 60°C (140°F) for rare beef, 77°C (170°F) for pink lamb, and 85°C (185°F) for turkey. Well, that may have been to the taste of the people who made up the meat charts these thermometers were based on but not to those of us who like our meat rare and our birds succulent. At 60°C you get beef that is medium- or medium-to-well-done, lamb roasted to 77°C is grey and tasteless, and at 85°C the breast of the turkey is dried out.

Neither did these recommendations take into account the all-important factor that the internal temperature of meat or poultry continues to increase for 10 to 15 minutes after it comes out of the oven. It cooks, so to speak, by its own stored-up heat, so the temperature goes up another 10 to 15 degrees. If you roast beef to 52°C (125°F) or 55°C (130°F) and let it rest for 15 or 20 minutes, it will be the perfect temperature and the juices will have had time to settle and the connective tissues to become firm, so that the meat carves more easily and is tender to the knife and to the bite. If you cook lamb to 55°C or 58°C (130°F or 135°F), no more, and then let it rest, you'll have delicious French-style pink, rarish lamb, rather than a stringy, grey-brown horror.

For years we were warned that pork had to be roasted to 82°C to 85°C (180°F to 185°F) to kill any possible trichinosis parasites. Well, now that they have found the bacteria are killed at 65°C to 68°C (150°F to 155°F), we cook pork to no more than 74°C (165°F), which gives a much better, juicier result. The same goes for veal. If veal, a rather dry meat, is cooked to 71°C to 74°C (160°F or 165°F), preferably with some liquid (the process is actually nearer braising than roasting), it comes out juicy and perfectly done. Always remember that meat absolutely must have that 15-minute rest period (the exception would be a tiny rack of lamb, which shouldn't rest quite as long, as it would cool off too much).

If you are buying a meat thermometer, the most accurate available are based on the type used in laboratories and test temperature in just about a minute. Unlike most you'll still find on the market, these delicate thermometers must never be left in the meat while it is roasting; the high oven heat would ruin them. Instead, they should be inserted in the thickest part of the meat during the latter part of the estimated roasting time. Don't let the thermometer touch the bones as bones conduct heat, and that could throw your reading off. (You'll probably notice that roasts with the bone in cook somewhat faster than boneless ones – for that very reason.) Leave the thermometer in only until the needle settles.

Because these sensitive thermometers register from 0°F, you can also use them to test the temperature of the meat before it goes into the oven. It's useful to make a note of this, because you can learn by experience how long it takes for a roast to reach the required internal temperature, depending on whether it has been frozen and thawed, left in the refrigerator, or allowed to warm up to room temperature.

I believe, incidentally, that meat should be left at room temperature before roasting, not taken straight from the refrigerator. There is a lot of controversy about this. The late Michael Field and I had a constant battle about it, because he insisted that it made absolutely no difference and I insisted that it did. I have always felt that meat left for 1 or 2 hours at room temperature cooks faster. If my roast is really big, I may leave it out for 3 to 4 hours. If you test the meat with your thermometer after taking it from the refrigerator and after letting it warm up, you'll see the difference it makes.

Testing with a meat thermometer is a much more accurate way of roasting meat than following the old so-many-minutes-per-pound method that the meat charts in many books give you, which never allows for the fact that two roasts of exactly the same weight may be of different shapes and thicknesses, a factor that will definitely affect the cooking time. To prove my point, recently I cooked two legs of lamb of almost identical weight but different thicknesses. One was rather flat, the other fully cushioned, compact, and rounded. The flatter leg, tested with the meat thermometer, took 40 minutes less cooking time than the plump, cushiony one. These are the little differences that one has to take into account when roasting in the oven. The variation in time can be just as great if you are roasting on a spit outdoors, even more so, for here the wind and the temperature of the air can noticeably affect the cooking time.

Roasting is a tricky and fascinating process. Even a meat thermometer is not always an infallible guide. I find it is chiefly my fingers that, through experience, can tell me by the way the meat feels whether or not it is done. The surface should feel firm to the touch, neither soft and yielding nor hard and resistant, with a springy resilience underneath. As you become a more experienced roast cook, you will learn to trust your hands, your sense of timing, and your accumulated knowledge. If you roast a great deal, on the spit and in the oven, you will find it an enormous benefit to make your own meat chart, with a schedule of the temperatures and times you have found to be perfect for your own taste. Yours may well differ from mine, or from those given in other cookbooks, but only you know what your preferences are.

I'm often asked whether I find any difference between fresh and frozen meat after it has been cooked. I have done many blindfold tests, with students and with friends, and I can honestly say that I don't. Provided the meat is of top quality and has been commercially flash-frozen, the flavour and texture are just as good, sometimes even better. I'm not talking, of course, about the special you bring home from the butcher and throw into the freezer, because that will never be very satisfactory. Unless meat is professionally frozen, ice crystals will form inside.

Frozen roasts should be thawed, or they take too long to cook, although I find that small cuts such as steaks and chops are better cooked from the frozen stage and the regular cooking time doubled. If it's an emergency and you haven't time to thaw the roast, put the meat in the oven at 170°C (325°F) and roast it slowly.

While roasting may be one of the more demanding of the kitchen arts, requiring care, thought, and accuracy, it is also one of the most worthwhile. A fine joint, or a roast bird, is a magnificent sight when it is finished, arranged on a platter or carving board with some appropriate garnish, and brought to the table or the buffet for the carving ceremony.

Carving used to be one of the necessary skills of any host. Well I'm afraid that most people today would not qualify as good carvers. I do know a few who are, including some women, but the art of carving in public, which used to be considered one of the delightful happenings at dinner with good friends, seems to have gone by the board. If you are proud of the meat you have roasted, you should be even prouder of it after you have carved it, so I suggest you study the carving drawings on pages 405–9 and practise a bit. Then, don't hide your talents in the kitchen, but let your guests have the pleasure of watching you carve a standing rib roast, a rack of lamb, or a turkey at table.

Lamb

♨ Roast Leg of Lamb

At one time, lamb was very unpopular in America – all because it was usually overcooked. I don't blame anyone turning against lamb that has been roasted until it is grey-brown, stringy and unpalatable. Fortunately, I grew up in a home where lamb was treated properly.

Lamb is perfect when it is from rare to pink. The French like it very rare. Most Americans prefer it pink. I'm on the side of the very rare, but I will settle for pink. I suggest you try it pink first and see how juicy and delicious it can be when it is not overcooked, and then gradually you may find you want it rare. I can assure you that once you have had properly cooked lamb, you'll never again roast it to death.

A leg of lamb is covered with a tight, papery tissue called the fell, which should be removed before cooking. If the butcher has not already removed it, take a very sharp, pointed paring knife and loosen the fell from the fat and flesh, then cut or tear it off in chunks. It usually comes off easily. At the same time, remove a good deal of the fat from the lamb – this will improve the flavour considerably. Now you are ready to prepare the lamb for roasting.

Serves 8 to 10

$2\frac{1}{2}$- to 3-kg. (5- to 6-lb.) leg of lamb,
   fell and most fat removed
6 to 8 garlic cloves

2 to 3 tablespoons cooking oil
1 teaspoon dried rosemary
Salt, freshly ground black pepper

Make 10 to 12 small incisions all over the top of the lamb with a small sharp paring knife, pushing the point in about $2\frac{1}{2}$ cm. (1 inch) deep. Lightly crush the garlic cloves with the side of a heavy knife or cleaver, or with a meat pounder, to break the skins so they peel easily. Peel the garlic and cut the cloves into thin slivers. With your finger, push the slivers of garlic into the incisions in the lamb. Then rub the roast all over with a little of the oil, massaging it in with your hands.

Crush the rosemary in the palm of one hand, pressing it down with your other thumb to break up the spiky little leaves. (Rosemary is an easy herb to grow in the garden or in a pot, and you'll save money by drying your own.) Rub the crushed rosemary on to the lamb and then sprinkle it with freshly ground black pepper. Preheat the oven to 180°C (350°F, gas mark 4).

I find a grill pan is perfect for roasting a leg of lamb. It allows the heat to circulate all around the meat so that it cooks more evenly and doesn't need basting. Oil the rack of the pan lightly and put the joint on it. Just before you put the joint in the oven, sprinkle it with salt. Many people will tell you that this will draw out the juices, but it is my feeling that when meat is salted just before roasting, the seasoning penetrates better and aids the flavour, while the oven heat helps to seal the surface.

Put the lamb in the oven and forget it for 1 hour. After an hour, test the internal temperature with a meat thermometer to see how it is progressing. Insert the thermometer into the meatiest part of the leg, being careful not to let it touch the bone. The desirable finished temperature for the lamb, rare, is 58°C (135°F). At the end of the first hour, the temperature should be between 32°C and 38°C (90°F and 100°F), depending on the thickness of the meat. At this point, if you wish to serve the lamb with Bordelaise (see page 289) or mint sauce (see over), prepare the sauce and set aside.

When the thermometer registers around 32°C, you know that you have perhaps 25 to 30 minutes to go. If it is only 29°C, you may need 35 to 40 minutes more. Return the joint to the oven, let it cook 15 to 20 minutes, then retest. When it has reached 58°C (135°F) remove the lamb to a carving board or a hot platter and let it rest for 10 to 15 minutes in a warm place before carving. Lamb fat congeals at a low temperature, so be sure always to serve the lamb on hot plates and a hot platter. For carving technique, see the drawing on page 408.

Roast leg of lamb is delicious served with just the pan juices. Sautéed potatoes are very good with it, and so is ratatouille, a Provençal vegetable stew with great affinity for lamb, or white beans mixed with a little cooked tomato, Breton style (see page 58). Many people like mint sauce with lamb. To make it: wash, dry, and finely chop enough fresh mint leaves to make 4 tablespoons. Dissolve 2 teaspoons sugar in 2 tablespoons boiling water and add to the mint leaves with a good pinch of salt and 3 tablespoons wine vinegar. Taste, and add more sugar or vinegar as needed. The sauce should be thick. Let stand 30 minutes before serving for the flavours to mellow. Makes about $1\frac{1}{2}$ dl ($\frac{1}{4}$ pt).

Alternative Method for Roasting

Preheat the oven to 230°C (450°F, gas mark 8). Roast the lamb at that temperature for 25 to 30 minutes to sear, then reduce the heat to 170°C (325°F, gas mark 3) and continue roasting as before. You may want to try both this and the preceding method to find out which you prefer. Both have virtues. Roasting part of the time at a high temperature gives you a crustier surface, but I find that it makes the outside of the meat slightly overdone. Roasting at one temperature for the entire time causes less shrinkage and more evenly coloured slices when the lamb is carved. Take your pick.

Roast Leg of Lamb, Baker's Style

This differs from the basic roast leg of lamb only in the garnishing.

Prepare the lamb as directed in the master recipe, putting it on a rack in a shallow roasting tin in a 180°C (350°F, gas mark 4) oven.

Peel 1 kg. (2 pounds) of small new potatoes, put them in salted water to cover, bring to a boil, and boil, covered, for 10 minutes. Drain the parboiled potatoes. After the lamb has roasted for 30 minutes, arrange the potatoes in the roasting tin. Melt 90 g. (3 oz.) unsalted butter in a small pan and, as the lamb and potatoes roast, baste potatoes well every 10 to 15 minutes with the juices and butter. When the lamb has about 15 minutes' roasting time left, sprinkle both lamb and potatoes with salt and freshly ground black pepper. When the meat thermometer registers 58°C (135°F), transfer the lamb from the roasting rack to a carving board and let it rest for 10 to 15 minutes in a warm place, keeping the potatoes warm in the turned-off oven. Carve, arrange the slices on a hot platter, and pour the juices from the tin over them. Arrange the roast potatoes around the meat and garnish them with a sprinkling of chopped parsley. A purée of green beans is a good accompaniment. Drink a good red Bordeaux or a light red Burgundy.

Beef

You'll hear a lot of different advice about the proper roasting temperature for beef. Some people believe in searing the meat first at a high temperature, then reducing the temperature for the rest of the cooking time. Others prefer to roast the beef throughout at one temperature – high, medium, or low. I'm going to give you two methods for a rib roast of beef. In one the beef is seared first at a high temperature and then cooked until done at a low temperature. In the other method, it is cooked throughout at very low heat. Choose the method you prefer according to the way you like your beef. The seared joint will be crisp on the outside with a well-done streak near the surface and a rare eye of the rib. The slow-roasted beef will be perfectly cooked throughout and an even pink from the fat to the bone. Both are excellent eating and both are excellent methods of roasting beef. Carve both joints thin for the best flavour, appearance, and eating. Thick slices lack the delicacy fine beef should have. Do not trim off all the fat when carving. I am among those who feel that the true flavour of the meat lurks in the fine crisp fat – and anyone who really doesn't care for the fat can always cut it off at the table.

☺ Pre-Searing Method for Rib Roast of Beef

Choose preferably a 4- or 5-rib roast cut from the wing or prime ribs, to serve 6 people, with some leftovers; if you are having a large dinner party you may need a 7- or 8-rib roast. Have the joint 'cut short' – with the short ribs removed. The chine bone should be removed by the butcher, the ribs left intact, and the joint well trimmed of any connective tissue and gristle and the excess fat. A properly prepared rib roast should be well balanced – even in size and compact. Rub the meat well with ½ teaspoon freshly ground black pepper and ½ teaspoon of thyme if you wish. For added zest, you can also rub the fat and bone with a crushed garlic clove, but this is a matter of taste. Preheat the oven to 250°C (500°F, or gas mark 9).

Place the joint on a rack in a shallow roasting tin and roast bone side down at 250°C (500°F, gas mark 9) for 35 to 40 minutes, basting twice with 2 to 3 tablespoons melted butter or beef fat. Reduce the heat to 170°C (325°F, gas mark 3) and continue to roast the beef for 30 minutes longer. Test the internal temperature by thrusting the meat thermometer into the thickest part of the eye of the rib, being careful not to touch the bone at any point. Remove the thermometer and continue roasting, basting every 20 minutes with the pan juices or melted beef fat. You may salt the joint after any of the bastings. Test again for temperature after 30 minutes and make a final test within 20 minutes after that. Estimate about 12 to 14 minutes of cooking time per $\frac{1}{2}$ kg. (pound). When the joint reaches 50°C to 52°C (120°F to 125°F), depending on how you like your meat, remove it to a hot platter or carving board and let it rest in a warm place for 15 to 20 minutes. Turn up the oven to 230°C (450°F, gas mark 8). Bake the Yorkshire pudding (see below) while the beef is resting and being carved. To carve, turn the joint on the side that gives it the best balance for carving and hold it in place with the back of a heavy fork while carving with a good sharp knife (for carving, see page 405). Serve it with the juices and Yorkshire pudding, or with a Bordelaise or Béarnaise sauce. If you like roast potatoes with your roast beef, place peeled, parboiled pieces of potato in the roasting tin after the searing period and cook them with the meat, turning once during the cooking time and basting along with the beef. Salt and pepper them and arrange them around the carved joint, or serve them in a separate dish with a sprinkling of chopped parsley.

YORKSHIRE PUDDING

Serves 8

2 eggs
$\frac{1}{4}$ l. (8 fl. oz.) milk
125 g. (4 oz.) sifted flour
$\frac{1}{2}$ teaspoon salt

$\frac{1}{2}$ teaspoon freshly ground black pepper
4 tablespoons beef drippings (melted beef fat), heated

Beat the eggs with a whisk or electric hand beater until quite light, then gradually beat in the milk and flour. Or you can put those ingredients in a liquidizer or mixer and blend or beat just until the batter is smooth. Season with the salt and pepper. Preheat the oven to 230°C (450°F, gas mark 8). Put a baking tin measuring 28 × 35 × 6 cm. (11 × 14 × 2$\frac{1}{2}$ inches) in the oven and let it get very hot. Remove and pour in the hot drippings and then the batter. Put on the centre shelf of the oven and bake for 10 minutes, then reduce the heat to 190°C (375°F, gas mark 5), and continue to bake for 15 to 20 minutes, or until the pudding has risen and is puffed and brown. Do not open the oven door during the first 20 minutes of baking. Cut in squares and serve immediately with roast beef.

☺ Low-Temperature Method for Rib Roast of Beef

Use the same cut as for the preceding technique. Leave the meat at room temperature for several hours, then rub it well with $\frac{1}{2}$ teaspoon freshly ground black pepper and $\frac{1}{2}$ teaspoon rosemary. Place it on a rack in a shallow roasting tin and take the internal temperature of the meat. Preheat the oven to 130°C (250°F, gas mark $\frac{1}{2}$). Roast at 130°C (250°F, gas mark $\frac{1}{2}$), without basting for approximately 20 minutes per $\frac{1}{2}$ kg. (pound). After 2 hours, take the internal temperature, salt the roast well, and add another grind or two of black pepper. Continue to roast the meat for 1 hour more. Again take the temperature and calculate the approximate time it will take for the joint to reach 50°C to 52°C (120°F to 125°F). If you want to accompany the roast with Yorkshire pudding, see preceding recipe for preparation. When the meat is done, remove it to a hot platter or carving board and let it rest for 15 to 20 minutes before carving. For a change serve the joint with a Bordelaise sauce, parsnip purée flavoured with Madeira (see page 62), and watercress.

COLD ROAST BEEF

Served cold or allowed to cool out of the refrigerator until it is almost at room temperature, roast beef makes a delicious, tempting offering for a buffet. For a cold buffet serve it sliced paper thin with a selection of mustards and breads. For a cocktail buffet cut it into strips, place it on fingers of bread cut to the same size, and spread with mustard or horseradish butter.

☺ Roast Fillet of Beef

To my thinking, a beef fillet, an expensive but meltingly tender boneless piece of meat which should always be served very rare, is best roasted quickly at a high temperature with several bastings. Now that so many cookers are equipped with self-cleaning ovens, high-temperature roasting, an inevitably messy business, presents few problems and seems to be increasingly popular.

When you buy the fillet, have the filet mignon (the thin tapering piece at one end of the fillet) removed, as it is too thin for roasting. Use it for another recipe – beef scallops or brochette of beef. Ask the butcher to bard the fillet, that is, to wrap it with thin sheets of pork fat or flattened beef suet and tie it well (see illustration following).

Serves 8 to 10

2- to 2½-kg. (4- to 5-lb.) fillet of beef,
   well trimmed, with all fat and
   tendon removed, then barded
   with fat

90 g. (3 oz.) butter, melted
   Or 3 tablespoons butter and
     3 tablespoons olive oil
   Or 6 tablespoons rendered beef suet
     (see note following)

Preheat the oven to 250°C (500°F, or gas mark 9). Place the barded fillet on a rack in a shallow roasting tin and roast at 250°C for 25 minutes, basting it well every 8 minutes with melted butter, butter and oil, or rendered suet. Suet gives it a lovely flavour. Remove the barding fat after the fillet has roasted for 20 minutes to allow the surface to brown. After 25 minutes, test the internal temperature of the beef by inserting a meat thermometer – for rare fillet, it should register 50°C (120°F). When the meat reaches that temperature, remove it to a hot platter or a carving board and let it rest for 5 minutes before carving. Unlike other beef joints, a delicate rare fillet is always carved into slices 1 cm. (½ inch) thick. Serve it with a Béarnaise sauce (see page 294). Potatoes Anna and a purée of broccoli go well with this. Drink a fine red Burgundy.

Note. To render any suet, cut into small pieces and cook in a heavy frying pan over medium-low heat until the fat is liquefied. Strain before using.

Pork

Pork is probably the most delicious – and the most misunderstood – of all meats. Served hot in winter it is a hearty, warming dish, and in summer served cold, it attains the utmost in delicacy and flavour. If I had to narrow my choice of meats down to one for the rest of my life, I am quite certain that meat would be pork.

In recent years there has been a tendency in pig breeders to cut down the fat content of pork – like almost everyone else, the pig has been placed on a reducing diet. As a result, there is a trend to meat that is not quite so lavishly fat-streaked and marbled as formerly, and this sometimes has the effect of toughening the fibre.

☗ Roast Pork Loin

Probably the most commonly used cut of pork is the loin, the stretch from the shoulder to the leg (see page 382) that takes in the ribs and the loin and chump chops with the tenderloin or fillet. It is usually sold divided into the fore loin and the hind loin. Or you can buy the entire loin. The roast may be bought boned and tied, or left with the bones intact. In this case, the chine bone that runs the length of the loin should be removed or cut through to facilitate carving, and the roast should be trimmed of excess fat and securely tied.

Serves 6

2½-kg. (5-lb.) pork loin, trimmed of skin and excess fat and tied

2 to 3 garlic cloves, peeled and cut into thin slivers

1 teaspoon dried thyme or summer savory

Coarse salt, freshly ground black pepper

12 small new potatoes, scraped or peeled

6 small carrots, scraped and whole Or 3 large carrots, scraped and quartered

12 small white onions, peeled*

Watercress for garnish

*If onions are dropped into boiling water for 20 seconds, their skins will slip off easily.

About 1 hour before roasting the pork, pierce the fat all over with the point of a small sharp knife and insert slivers of garlic into the holes. Rub the loin lightly with thyme or summer savory and then with coarse salt. Preheat the oven to 170°C (325°F, gas mark 3).

Put the loin, fat side up, on a rack in a shallow roasting tin and roast at 170°C (325°F) for 25 to 30 minutes per ½ kg. (pound), about 2¼ to 2½ hours.

Parboil the potatoes, carrots, and onions for 5 minutes in salted water to cover (this softens them slightly, so they cook faster) and arrange them around the meat in the roasting tin for the last hour of roasting time. When you add the vegetables, baste them with the juices and sprinkle the loin with a little salt and pepper. Continue to roast the meat until the internal temperature reaches 75°C (165°F). Check 30 to 40 minutes after adding the vegetables to find how near the meat is to that mark, inserting the thermometer at the thickest part, but not touching the bone.

When the meat is done, transfer it to a hot platter and let it rest in a warm place for 10 to 15 minutes before carving. Arrange the roasted vegetables around it and garnish with watercress.

Carve the joint downwards, cutting between the bones. If the meat has been boned, cut in slices about 1 cm. (⅜ inch) thick. Skim the fat from the meat juices and serve them with the pork. A dish of sautéed, glazed apple rings (see page 201) is a perfect accompaniment. Wine for such a dish might be a chilled Alsatian Riesling.

Marbelized Fresh Ham

The fresh ham or leg of pork is a most satisfactory joint for a large number of people, and equally good hot or cold. I find that my Italian pork store in New York always handles fresh hams, and is well acquainted with boning and stuffing them with herbed and other mixtures that make them particularly succulent. I like to leave the scored skin on and roast it to crisp, chewy perfection, but most people prefer to have the skin removed.

This rather elaborate dish is best served cold. Roast it early in the morning and let it cool until evening, without refrigerating, if possible. If you must refrigerate, leave it out of the refrigerator for at least several hours before serving. This is a good choice for a buffet party.

Serves 16 to 20

100 g. (3½ oz.) white raisins	1 teaspoon crushed dried sage
1½ dl. (¼ pt) dry sherry	Coarse salt, freshly ground black
8 garlic cloves	pepper
60 g. (2 oz.) chopped Italian	90 g. (3 oz.) unsalted butter
(flat-leaf) parsley, packed	75 g. (2½ oz.) apple jelly
125 g. (4 oz.) shelled pistachio nuts	1 teaspoon crushed aniseed
5½- to 7-kg. (12- to 15-lb.) fresh	(optional)
ham, boned, rolled, and well tied	

Soak the raisins in sherry to cover until puffed, then drain. Reserve sherry.

Chop 5 garlic cloves and the parsley rather coarsely, and chop ¾ of the pistachio nuts very coarsely. Make deep incisions in the ham with a long, heavy, wooden-handled larding needle, turning the needle before removing it so that it makes small cavities in the meat – these need not be done in any pattern. Combine raisins, chopped garlic, parsley, and chopped pistachios and stuff the mixture into the cavities with your fingers, packing it in as tightly as possible – a wooden chopstick is a good aid. Push in the remaining whole pistachios here and there.

Mince the remaining garlic and blend with the crushed sage. Rub the outside fat with the mixture, then sprinkle with salt and pepper. Put the ham on a rack in a roasting tin and roast in a 170°C (325°F, gas mark 3) oven for 25 to 30 minutes per ½ kg. (pound). Combine the sherry drained from the raisins, the butter, and the apple jelly in a small saucepan and heat gently until butter and jelly are melted. If you like the flavour of anise, add the crushed aniseed to the mixture – this will result in a more highly perfumed ham. Baste the ham every half hour with the mixture as it roasts. Keep the basting mixture warm while using it.

When the ham reaches an internal temperature of 74°C or 165°F (insert meat thermometer in the thickest part) remove it from the oven and let it cool. If you are going to chill the ham, brush it well with the juices from the tin, wrap in plastic wrap, and refrigerate until ready to serve.

Carve the ham into thin slices. They will be beautifully marbled with the mixture of raisins, nuts, and herbs. Serve the ham with a Cumberland (see page 82) or a rémoulade sauce and white beans vinaigrette (see page 59) sprinkled with chopped fresh basil and parsley and garnished with tomato sections. Crisp Italian bread goes well with this meal, as does a fine French champagne of a pleasant vintage. The famous mustard fruits of Cremona (available in speciality groceries) are admirable with this ham.

Note. If the ham is much larger, increase the stuffing ingredients proportionately.

Glazed Ham

Although I use a ready-cooked, boiled ham for this, I find that many of the hams sold in supermarkets and stores these days need a certain amount of cooking and flavouring to be really palatable. They are much tastier if basted with sherry, Madeira, cider, wine or ginger-ale during baking. A cooked ham need only be baked until it reaches an internal temperature of 55°C (130°F), just sufficient to heat it through, but an uncooked ham should be boiled or baked to an internal temperature of 71°C to 74°C (160°F to 165°F). Country hams, which are prepared by small smokehouses in the different counties and often sold by mail, are vastly superior to the average, rather bland supermarket ham. Generally, they are well and slowly cured and heavily smoked, which gives them a more pronounced flavour and better texture. When you buy these hams, follow the directions that come with the ham for the length of cooking time. Occasionally the ham may be very salty and need some soaking in cold water to remove the excess salt. To check, cut off a bit of the ham, sauté it in a little fat until thoroughly cooked and then taste it.

A whole ham can weigh from $4\frac{1}{2}$ to 9 kg. (10 to 20 pounds), but if that is just too much meat for you, you can buy half of a ham, either the meatier butt end or the less expensive but equally tasty shank end. Allow about 225 g. ($\frac{1}{2}$ pound) of ham per person, or 350 to 450 g. ($\frac{3}{4}$ to 1 pound) for a shank end with a lot of bone. If you want an even smaller joint, buy the smoked butt, a cut from the foreleg, which is fattier but less expensive than ham from the hind leg.

A whole ham makes 16 to 20 servings,
a half ham makes 8 to 10

1 cooked ham, weighing about $4\frac{1}{2}$ to 5 kg. (10 to 12 lbs.), or half of a ham, weighing about 3 to $3\frac{1}{2}$ kg. (6 to 8 lbs.)

$4\frac{1}{2}$ dl. ($\frac{3}{4}$ pt) dry sherry, Madeira or white wine

60 to 90 g. (2 to 3 oz.) dry bread crumbs

1 tablespoon dry mustard

125 g. (4 oz.) brown sugar

2 tablespoons Dijon mustard

Preheat the oven to 180°C (350°F, gas mark 4). Put the ham, skin and fat side down, in a large, deep roasting tin with the wine and bake approximately 10 to 15 minutes a $\frac{1}{2}$ kg. (a pound) for a whole ham, 15 to 18 minutes for a half ham, basting from time to time with the liquid. When tested with a meat thermometer, inserted in the thickest part but not touching the bone, the internal temperature should be 55°C (130°F).

Remove the joint from the oven and trim off the skin or rind and all but about 6 mm. ($\frac{1}{4}$ inch) of the fat. Mix together the bread crumbs and dry mustard and rub the mixture into the fat with your hand. Press brown sugar into the crumbs and dot all over with Dijon mustard. To glaze the ham (that is, to melt the sugar and give the fat a glossy brown finish), put the ham under the grill, if it is deep enough, about 25 cm. (10 inches) from the heat, and watch carefully to see that the mixture does not scorch – the sugar should melt into the crumbs and leave a nice glaze. Otherwise turn up the oven heat to 230°C (450°F, gas mark 8), and bake 15 to 20 minutes more, or until nicely glazed.

With hot ham, serve potato and semolina gnocchi (see page 55), a purée of spinach and a mustard hollandaise or Cumberland sauce.

With cold ham, serve a salad of white beans and tiny bits of chopped tomato, cucumber and green pepper, tossed with a well-flavoured vinaigrette sauce and garnished with thinly sliced red Italian onions. A hot corn or spinach soufflé is also a nice accompaniment to a cold ham, with a selection of French and German mustards. Champagne or a very fruity Alsatian white wine or a rosé wine goes well with either hot or cold ham.

CUMBERLAND SAUCE

Remove the zest (the orange part of the rind) from 1 orange with a potato peeler and chop it very fine. Put in a small pan with 3 dl. ($\frac{1}{2}$ pint) of Port wine or Madeira and cook over medium-high heat until the liquid is reduced to one third. Add the juice of the orange, 1 tablespoon lemon juice, 125 g. (4 oz.) currant jelly, and a pinch of cayenne pepper or ground ginger. Stir until the jelly is melted, then serve the sauce. Makes about 3 dl. ($\frac{1}{2}$ pint).

Roasted Spareribs

An excellent cut of pork to consider for roasting – the spareribs – are cut from the rib part of the belly. Succulent and versatile as they are, in the last few years good spareribs have been ruined by too many sweet and sour sauces intended to make them taste glamorous or Oriental or some such thing. To be quite frank, I think there is nothing as good as simple roasted spareribs seasoned merely with salt and pepper.

Serves 4

2 sides spareribs, about 2 kg. (4 lbs.), heavy bone or gristle section removed	Coarse salt, freshly ground black pepper

Put the ribs on a rack in a shallow roasting tin and roast them in a 180°C (350°F, gas mark 4) oven for 30 minutes, then season the ribs well with salt and pepper, turn, season the other side, and continue roasting them for another 30 minutes. At the end of an hour they should be nicely browned and fairly crisp on the outside. Roast them another 10 to 15 minutes if you like them very well done.

Remove the ribs to a carving board and cut between the ribs into smallish sections. Heap them on a hot platter and serve with sauerkraut cooked in chicken broth with a few juniper berries. Add perfectly boiled potatoes in their jackets and you will have a delightful feast. Drink the beer of your choice.

Chicken

Perhaps my predilection for good chicken is something I was born with because both my parents were ardent chickenphiles. More likely it is due to the fact that nothing is better than a well-cooked, well-presented roast chicken. Game, turkey, and goose all have their charms and their advantages, but it is incontrovertible that a perfect roast chicken is one of the world's superb dishes.

Not that chickens don't vary. Seldom can we get the fine chickens that are raised by interested poultry farmers on organic food and with plenty of room to scratch around. These chickens, which used to be common in the markets, have all but disappeared. Instead, the majority of the chickens we buy are raised behind wire and very quickly, which results in a beautiful clean carcass with plenty of meat, but little of the flavour of the old-time birds. I wish that some public-spirited person would start a chain of farms around the larger towns from which we could order the old-fashioned, well-fed, hand-plucked chickens of perfect size. Such a product could command a premium price from restaurants and all of us who pine for a really flavourful bird.

There is another stumbling block to achieving a perfectly roasted chicken. That is the matter of how long the bird should be cooked. If it is roasted until the white meat attains the exact point of juiciness, there is bound to be a touch of pink in the joints of the dark meat. This repulses many people who shun the thought of underdone chicken (which happens to be very good). If the chicken is cooked until the juices at the thigh joint run clear, the white meat will be dry and, to my taste, totally uninteresting. Perhaps the answer is always to roast two chickens, one perfectly cooked, the other overcooked. One can, of course, carve the chicken in the kitchen and put the pink-juiced dark meat under the grill for a minute or two to satisfy those who cannot reconcile themselves to that pinkness, but it is my feeling that if they once tried the white meat at its proper stage, they would overcome their prejudice.

A roasting chicken of 2 to 2½ kg. (4 to 5 pounds) is the right size for 4 people. Because of modern methods of preparing and plucking chickens, there is no need to pluck the bird. I find, though, that with these new methods the chickens are plucked too well, for the process also removes most of the tiny oil sacs that used to help give colour to the skin during cooking. It is well-nigh impossible to get a brilliantly brown skin on a roast chicken now without cheating a bit. That is one of the prices paid for a labour-saving device.

♨ Perfect Roast Chicken

Serves 4

2- to 2½-kg. (4- to 5-lb.) roasting chicken
½ lemon
225 g. (8 oz.) unsalted butter, softened
Salt, freshly ground black pepper
3 tablespoons flour
3 dl. (½ pt) chicken or veal stock, heated

1 tablespoon chopped fresh tarragon
Or 1 teaspoon dried tarragon,
crushed
2 dl. (⅓ pt) double cream
1 tablespoon chopped parsley
Watercress

Preheat the oven to 220°C (425°F, gas mark 7). Wipe the chicken with a damp cloth. Rub the inside with the cut lemon, squeezing the juice on to the bone structure as you rub. Cream together half the butter, 1 teaspoon salt, and ½ teaspoon pepper and put the mixture into the cavity. Truss the bird as follows. Thread a long trussing needle with twine and push the legs and thighs back with your hands. *Run the needle through the thigh joints and across the bird and pull through.* Then cross the pieces of twine, bring them up to the legs, and *wrap them around the legs, tying them close together. Bring the twine down and under the tail end then bring it up to the legs again and tie it securely.* Turn the bird over. *Take the two ends of the twine and bring them down, running the twine back and around the wings. Tie the ends securely.* This method will truss the bird tightly and well.

Rub one side with butter. Put the chicken on its side, buttered side up, on a rack in a shallow roasting tin. Roast the chicken in a 220°C oven for 20 minutes. Protecting your hands with a wad of paper towels, turn the chicken on its other side, and brush the upper side lavishly with melted butter. Roast it for 20 minutes longer; turn it on its back and baste it well with the pan juices. Sprinkle the bird with about $1\frac{1}{2}$ teaspoons salt and $\frac{1}{2}$ teaspoon pepper. Roast it breast side up for 20 minutes, then baste with the juices.

After the bird has cooked almost an hour, siphon off about 3 tablespoons of the fat from the roasting tin and transfer it to a heavy saucepan. Blend in 3 tablespoons flour to make a smooth roux (see directions on page 286). Simmer the roux over low heat for several minutes, increase the heat, and gradually stir in the hot chicken or veal stock. Stir the sauce with a whisk until it is thickened and simmer it over low heat for 4 to 5 minutes. Season the sauce with the tarragon and salt to taste. Remove the pan from the heat and stir in the double cream. Cook the sauce over low heat, stirring, until it is thick and smooth. Correct seasoning if necessary, then stir in parsley. Keep hot until ready to serve. Or, if you prefer, just remove the excess fat from juices, mix in a little hot stock and serve with the bird.

Test the bird for doneness: if the leg and thigh move easily, it is done – sometimes overdone for my taste. Puncture the skin at the thigh joint. If the juices that run out are still a bit pink, it is very close to being done. If they run clear it is definitely done – or overdone. Another way to test for doneness is to insert a meat thermometer into the fleshiest part of the thigh (do not touch the bone). It should register 75°C (165°F) for a perfectly cooked chicken. A 2-kg. (4-pound) chicken should not take more than 1 hour and 15 minutes to roast, but you cannot be exact about timing because the bone structure and the amount of flesh and fat on the bones all affect the cooking time.

When the bird is done, remove it to a hot platter and garnish it with watercress. Surround the chicken with sautéed potatoes. For the best serving and eating, carve the chicken into quarters (poultry shears are a great help here). I find that the sliced breast of a roast chicken makes a pretty dull-looking plate, but a juicy, delicious quarter is something else entirely. Serve the sauce in a sauceboat.

Traditionally, potatoes, a salad, and a pleasing red wine are the perfect companions for roast chicken. You might try a Moulin-à-Vent, or even a Côte Rotie with it.

If you wish to serve the chicken cold, do not refrigerate it, or let it get completely cold. When you remove the bird from the oven, let it cool at room temperature and serve it when there is just a suspicion of warmth left – the flavour is much better and the bird juicier.

Old-Fashioned Sunday Roast Chicken with Stuffing

Stuffed roast chicken has traditionally figured – and still does – on many families' Sunday dinner menus. Usually the bird is overcooked, and the stuffing is often the best part. However, if you use a stuffing that is light, not dense and pasty, and roast the bird for the correct length of time, it can be a delicious dish.

Serves 6

125 g. (4 oz.) unsalted butter	1 teaspoon grated lemon zest
1 large or 2 medium onions, finely	(see page 376)
chopped	1 teaspoon rosemary, crushed in a
1 garlic clove, finely chopped	mortar
20 soft black Italian or Greek	90 g. (3 oz.) finely diced ham
olives, pitted and coarsely	150 g. (5 oz.) fine fresh bread crumbs*
chopped	60 g. (2 oz.) plus 1 tablespoon parsley

*Use bread crumbs made from non-sweetened white bread.

Salt, freshly ground black pepper
2½-kg. (5-lb.) roasting chicken, giblets
  reserved

8 to 10 thick rashers of good smoked
  bacon
1 sprig of parsley
4 tablespoons cognac

First make the stuffing: melt 90 g. (3 oz.) butter in a heavy frying pan with a cover. Add the onions and sauté for 2 to 3 minutes. Cover the pan and steam the onions over very low heat until they are soft and pale gold, about 7 to 8 minutes. Add the garlic, olives, lemon zest, rosemary and ham. Toss the mixture lightly with the bread crumbs and 60 g. (2 oz.) chopped parsley until well blended. Season to taste with salt and pepper. Preheat the oven to 200°C (400°F, gas mark 6).

Wipe the chicken inside and out with a damp cloth, stuff with the stuffing, and close the vent with tiny clamps or with tiny skewers laced with twine. Truss the chicken (see preceding recipe) and rub it lightly with butter. Put it on its side on a rack in a shallow roasting tin. Cover with 4 or 5 bacon rashers. Roast for 35 minutes, then turn it on to its other side. Cover the upper side with bacon, baste with the juices, and roast 35 minutes longer. Turn the chicken breast side up and remove the bacon. Sprinkle it with salt and pepper, brush with 2 tablespoons melted butter, and roast it for 30 minutes more, basting once or twice with the juices. Test for doneness as described in the recipe for perfect roast chicken.

While the chicken is cooking, simmer the giblets, including the liver, in 3 dl. (½ pt) water with ½ teaspoon salt, 2 or 3 grinds of black pepper, and a parsley sprig for 15 to 20 minutes. Strain the broth and reserve it. Chop the giblets and reserve them. When the chicken is done, transfer it to a hot platter and remove all but 3 tablespoons of the fat from the pan. Add the reserved broth and giblets to the pan, bring the mixture to a boil, and simmer for several minutes, stirring to scrape up the brown bits from the bottom of the pan. Add the remaining chopped parsley and the cognac and reduce the sauce a little by boiling over high heat for 1 to 2 minutes. Pour into a sauceboat and serve with the chicken and stuffing. Braised celery or endive and a bowl of fresh watercress go exceedingly well with the chicken. Drink a Moulin-à-Vent.

Poussins

Poussins or baby chickens of about ½ kg. (1 pound) make a delicious entrée for a dinner party or, when allowed to cool, a wonderful cold food for picnics or a late supper. They are often difficult to find, but you can usually get them from your market if you order ahead of time. Allow 1 per person.

Stuffed Poussins

Serves 6

90 g. (3 oz.) finely chopped shallots
125 g. (4 oz.) or more unsalted butter
Giblets and livers from the poussins
1 tablespoon chopped fresh tarragon
*   Or 1½ teaspoons dried tarragon,*
*   crushed*
½ l. (¾ pt) cooked rice

Salt, freshly ground black pepper
3 tablespoons chopped parsley
30 g. (1 oz.) chopped pistachio nuts
6 poussins
1 lemon, halved
Watercress for garnish

Prepare the stuffing: sauté the shallots in 90 g. (3 oz.) butter until they are just limp. Chop the giblets (including the liver) rather fine, and toss them in the butter with the shallots. Add the tarragon, rice, 1 teaspoon salt, ½ teaspoon pepper, parsley and pistachios. Toss lightly to blend well. If the mixture seems dry, melt 45 to 60 g. (1½ to 2 oz.) of butter and blend in lightly to moisten.

Wipe the poussins inside and out with a damp cloth. Rub the cavities with the cut lemon. Stuff the birds lightly, skewer the vents and truss the birds. Arrange them on their sides on a rack in a very shallow roasting tin and rub the top sides well with butter. Roast in a 200°C (400°F, gas mark 6) oven for 20 to 25 minutes, then turn them onto the other side. Rub the top side well with butter and roast 20 minutes more. Turn breast side up, baste with the juices, sprinkle with salt and pepper, and roast for 10 to 12 minutes. Be careful not to overcook them. Test the legs for doneness by wiggling the legs and puncturing the joints, as described in the recipe for perfect roast chicken.

Transfer the birds to a hot platter, remove and discard the strings, and garnish with watercress. Serve the poussins with tiny green peas, the pan juices and a good salad. Drink a Fleurie.

If you wish to serve the birds cold, do not stuff them unless you like cold stuffing – it is actually quite good. Baste the birds well and be sure to undercook them slightly, as they will continue cooking for a few minutes as they cool.

Turkey

It is very hard nowadays to buy a hand-plucked, fresh-killed turkey, but if you can find a market that sells them, they are definitely worth buying.

There are really no hard-and-fast rules for roasting and cooking times. It all depends on the shape of the bird, the amount of fat, the way the flesh is distributed, and the internal temperature when it goes into the oven. I am always horrified when newspapers at Christmas time give supposedly infallible timetables for roasting. Nothing could be more designed to produce badly cooked birds – perhaps one reason that turkey is so unpopular with a great many people. Certainly there are few things worse than an overcooked turkey, except perhaps an undercooked one. It must be at the point of perfection to be right. Cooking a turkey perfectly depends on one's attention to the work at hand and sense of the moment when it is done. A perfectly cooked turkey is one of the major achievements of a cook.

♕ Roast Turkey with Two Stuffings

Stuffings for turkey vary a great deal, but a simple bread stuffing is my favourite, perhaps with a separate meat stuffing, of well-seasoned sausage meat and ground veal, for the neck cavity. After many years, it is my considered opinion that stuffing tastes much better when cooked in a baking dish than inside the bird – it gets nice and crispy, not soggy, and is altogether much more satisfactory and easier to serve. Baste it, as it bakes, with juices from the roasting tin and it will be delicious. So, if you are a traditionalist, roast your turkey with the stuffing inside, but bake some of the bread stuffing separately and you will see what I mean. Leftover stuffing is no problem. Just sauté it in butter.

Serves 16

BREAD STUFFING FOR THE BODY CAVITY

*180 g. (6 oz.) very thinly sliced
green onions*
*225 to 325 g. (8 to 12 oz. unsalted
butter*
*2 tablespoons finely chopped fresh
tarragon*
*Or 1 tablespoon dried tarragon,
crushed*

1 tablespoon salt
*1½ teaspoons freshly ground black
pepper*
125 g. (4 oz.) finely chopped parsley
*About 570 g. (1¼ lbs.) freshly made
soft bread crumbs**
90 g. (3 oz.) pine nuts

* Use crumbs made from unsweetened white bread.

STUFFING FOR THE NECK CAVITY

*1 kg. (2 lbs.) good sausage meat
(made without filler to extend
the meat)
Or 1 kg. (2 lbs.) ground pork with
about 30 per cent fat
1½ teaspoons salt
1 teaspoon dried thyme*

*1 teaspoon Tabasco
1 teaspoon ground coriander
1 teaspoon freshly ground black
pepper
½ kg. (1 lb.) ground veal or ham
125 g. (4 oz.) pine nuts
60 g. (2 oz.) finely chopped parsley*

THE TURKEY AND SAUCE

*9-kg. (20-lb.) turkey, preferably one
that is fresh-killed, hand-plucked
and unfrozen; neck, gizzard,
heart, and liver reserved
Juice of 1 to 2 lemons
About 225 g. (8 oz.) unsalted butter
Salt, freshly ground black pepper
Whole piece of bacon or pork rind, big
enough to fit on the roasting rack*

*Or large sheet of well-greased
heavy-duty aluminium foil
1 onion, stuck with 2 cloves
1 garlic clove
1 teaspoon dried tarragon
1 sprig of parsley
3 dl. (½ pt) brown sauce (see page 288)
4 tablespoons Madeira or cognac*

Prepare the stuffing for the body cavity: sauté the scallions in 225 g. (8 oz.) butter over medium heat until they are just limp. Add the tarragon, salt, pepper, parsley and bread crumbs. Toss to blend. Mix in pine nuts and moisten with as much additional melted butter as needed to make a light, not soggy, mixture. Taste and correct seasoning.

Then prepare the stuffing for the neck cavity: combine the sausage meat or ground pork with the salt, thyme, Tabasco sauce, ground coriander, pepper, ground veal or ham, pine nuts and parsley. Mix the stuffing well. Sauté 1 or 2 teaspoons in a small frying pan in 15 g. (½ oz.) butter until brown and cooked through (never taste uncooked pork) and taste to check seasoning; correct if necessary.

Wash the turkey well inside and out, or wipe with a damp cloth, and rub the cavity with lemon juice. Stand the bird on its tail and stuff the neck cavity with the meat mixture, taking care not to stuff it too tight. Pull the flap of the neck skin over the stuffing and attach it to the skin on the back of the bird, either by securing it with small skewers or clamps or sewing it with a large needle and fine twine.

Turn the bird breast side up and stuff the cavity lightly with the bread mixture. Do not force stuffing into the cavity or you will not only have soggy, messy stuffing, but run the risk of the bird's splitting during roasting as the steam from the stuffing inflates it slightly. Stuff a piece of crumpled foil into the opening of the vent to prevent the stuffing from oozing out during roasting and close the vent with clamps or skewers or sew it together with fine twine. Truss (following the directions for chicken on page 84) and rub the turkey well with butter and a small amount of salt and pepper. Put an adjustable rack in a large shallow roasting tin and put the bacon or pork rind or well-greased aluminium foil on the rack where the turkey breast will be. Put the turkey on the rind or foil, breast side down, and cover the top loosely with a piece of foil. Roast in a 170°C (325°F, gas mark 3) oven for 1 hour. Remove the bird from the oven; baste it well and turn it on to one side. Roast it for 45 minutes; baste and turn it on to the other side. Roast for 45 minutes, then turn it breast side up. Baste it, rub it with soft butter, and roast for 1 hour more. At this point start the broth: put the reserved neck, gizzard, heart and liver in a saucepan with the onion, garlic, tarragon, 1½ teaspoons salt and 6 dl. (1 pt) water. Bring the mixture to a boil, skim off any scum that rises to the surface, and add the sprig of parsley. Reduce the heat and simmer the mixture for 35 to 40 minutes. Strain and reserve broth. Chop the giblets and liver very fine and set aside.

Test the turkey for doneness by inserting a meat thermometer into the thickest part of the thigh, but not touching the bone. It should register 77°C to 80°C (170°F to 175°F). Or test the leg to see if it moves easily and puncture the thigh joint; the juices should be pinkish-red. Be sure not to over- or undercook it.

When the turkey is done, remove it to a hot platter or carving board and let it rest in a warm place for 15 to 20 minutes before carving.

Remove all but 3 tablespoons fat from the tin and pour in the broth. Stir to scrape up all the brown bits from the bottom. Pour the liquid into a saucepan and reduce it by half over rather high heat. Add brown sauce, chopped giblets, and Madeira or cognac. Bring the sauce to a boil; reduce heat and simmer for several minutes. Taste sauce and correct seasoning. Serve it in a sauceboat.

Puréed potatoes (see page 61) with plenty of butter and cream and sautéed Brussels sprouts or turnips sautéed with mushrooms are fine accompaniments. Drink a fine red Burgundy.

Roast Turkey without Stuffing

For cold turkey and various dishes made with cold or cooked turkey, the bird is best roasted unstuffed.

Serves 8 to 10

5½- to 6½-kg. (12- to 14-lb.) turkey*   125 g. (4 oz.) or more unsalted butter
Juice of 1 to 2 lemons   Salt, freshly ground black pepper

* Your turkey should preferably be hand-plucked, fresh-killed, and unfrozen.

Wash the interior of the turkey or wipe it out with a damp cloth. Rub cavity well with lemon juice. Blend 60 g. (2 oz.) butter with 1 teaspoon salt and $\frac{1}{2}$ teaspoon pepper and put it in the cavity. Close the vent and truss the turkey carefully (the same as for chicken; see page 84). Rub one side well with butter and put the bird, buttered side up, on a rack in a shallow roasting tin. Roast it in a 170°C (325°F, gas mark 3) oven for 1 hour. Turn it onto the other side, protecting your hands with a wad of paper towels, rub it with butter, and season with 2 teaspoons salt and 1 teaspoon pepper. Roast the turkey for 1 hour more, turn it breast side up, and baste well with the juices. Roast it for another 25 minutes and baste it again. If the bird is browning too much, put a piece of foil loosely across the top. Roast it for 30 minutes more, then test for doneness by wiggling the legs to see if they move easily or by piercing the thigh joint with a carving fork. If the juices run pale pink, remove the turkey from the oven. It will continue to cook as it cools. You can also test for doneness by inserting a meat thermometer into the thickest part of the thigh, not touching the bone. It should register between 77°C to 80°C (170°F and 175°F).

Turkey roasted without stuffing may be eaten hot with a sauce suprême (see page 287), or with a simple bread sauce, but it is at its best cooled, sliced, and served with a tart homemade mayonnaise flavoured with lemon juice, a rice salad (see page 52), crisp vegetables, and perhaps hot corn bread and butter with good preserves. Drink a full-bodied white Burgundy with it.

Goose

Goose is one of the most flavourful and juicy birds we have, with rich, dark, succulent flesh. Although it is often difficult to get freshly killed geese, there are excellent frozen geese on the market, available in sizes from 3 to $5\frac{1}{2}$ kg. (6 to 12 pounds) which make very tasty and tender eating. Frozen geese should be thawed before roasting, from $1\frac{1}{2}$ to 2 days in the refrigerator or 6 to 10 hours at room temperature (for the medium size) or 4 to 5 hours in cool water. Leave the goose in its wrapping to thaw and when thoroughly thawed, refrigerate until you are ready to stuff and cook the bird. Goose needs to be roasted with a fruity stuffing to flavour the bird.

☺ Roast Goose
with Prune and Apple Stuffing

Serves 8

A 3½- to 4½-kg. (8- to 10-lb.) goose, fresh or frozen and thawed

STUFFING

90 g. (3 oz.) butter

60 g. (2 oz.) finely chopped onion

225 to 280 g. (8 to 10 oz.) fresh
   bread crumbs

2 teaspoons salt

225 g. (8 oz.) cooked peeled chestnuts
   or canned chestnuts

350 g. (12 oz.) peeled and chopped
   apples

225 g. (8 oz.) pitted prunes, soaked for
   2 days in Madeira to cover

1 teaspoon thyme

½ teaspoon nutmeg

GRAVY

Giblets and neck from goose, liver
   reserved

4 tablespoons white wine

1 teaspoon salt

3 or 4 peppercorns

1 sprig of parsley

1 small onion, stuck with 1 clove

1 small carrot, scraped and halved

The goose liver

1 small onion, peeled and chopped

2 tablespoons goose fat (from the
   roasting tin)

Beurre manié (see page 283)

Remove the giblets and neck from the cavity and reserve for the stock.
Remove excess fat from the body cavity. You can render this fat slowly in a
heavy frying pan and keep it for cooking – goose fat is pure, full of flavour,
and marvellous for sautéing potatoes, meats, and poultry.

To make the stuffing, melt the butter in a large frying pan; add the onion
and sauté over medium heat until limp and golden. Remove from the heat and
mix in the bread crumbs, moistening them well with the butter. Then add the
remaining stuffing ingredients and mix them well together with your hands
or a wooden spatula. Stuff the goose about two-thirds or three-quarters full
(the fruit and crumbs will expand during the roasting). There will be some
leftover stuffing, which can be put in a baking dish and baked in the 180°C
(350°F, gas mark 4) oven alongside the goose the second half of its roasting
time. It never matters if you overestimate on stuffing; in fact it is better to do
so as everyone always wants more than the cavity will accommodate. You
usually calculate 2 to 3 dl. (⅓ to ½ pint) of stuffing per ½ kg. (pound) of bird,
though a bird with a small cavity may take no more than 1½ dl. (¼ pt) per
½ kg. (pound).

After stuffing the goose, truss it, and sew up or skewer the vent (see sketches on page 84). Rub the skin with salt, which helps to crisp it. Place the goose breast side up on a rack in a roasting tin – a goose has so much natural fat there is no need to baste it or to protect the breast from overcooking. Preheat the oven to 200°C (400°F, gas mark 6).

Roast for 1 hour at 200°C to start rendering fat from the bird. Then prick the skin all over with a fork, to let the fat escape; reduce the temperature to 180°C (350°F) and roast for another hour. As the fat renders from the goose, remove it to a large jar, using a large spoon or bulb baster, and keep it for cooking. Leave some fat in the tin each time.

While the goose is roasting, put the neck and giblets (but not the liver) in a pan with 4½ dl. (¾ pt) water, the wine, seasonings, parsley, clove-stuck onion, and carrot. Bring to a boil; boil 1 minute, skimming off the scum, then reduce the heat; cover and simmer slowly for 1 hour, adding a little more water if the stock reduces too much; it should cover the giblets. Strain the stock, chop the giblets fine and reserve for the sauce. Quickly sauté the goose liver and the chopped onion in 2 tablespoons of the fat rendered from the goose. As soon as liver is firm, remove and chop fine.

A 3½- to 4½-kg. (8- to 10-lb.) goose will take 2 to 2¾ hours to cook. After the second hour, test to see how near done it is by pressing the leg meat with your fingers (protected with paper towels). When done, the meat should feel soft and the juices from the thickest part of the thigh, when it is pricked with a fork, should run yellowish, with a little pink but not red tinge. If the goose needs more cooking, reduce the oven heat to 170°C (325°F, gas mark 3), for the rest of the roasting time.

Bake the excess stuffing in the oven during the last 1¼ hours of cooking, basting it two or three times with a tablespoon or two of the goose fat to keep it moist. If it gets too brown on top, cover the dish lightly with aluminium foil.

When the goose is done, remove it to a hot platter and allow it to rest for 15 minutes while you make the sauce. Skim the fat from the tin juices; add the giblet stock to the tin and bring to a boil by setting the tin on a burner over medium-high heat, scraping with a wooden spatula to lift the brown glaze from the bottom. Pour the juices into a pan and thicken to taste by stirring in *beurre manié* and simmering until the sauce thickens. Stir in the chopped giblets and liver.

Good accompaniments for this rich, fruit-stuffed bird would be a purée of potatoes (see page 61) or a purée of parsnips (see page 62) and a green vegetable such as broccoli or spinach. Serve extra stuffing and sauce separately.

For carving directions, see page 409.

Duck

Duck has a thick layer of fat under the skin that acts as insulation for the meat, so rather than cooking ducks at a high temperature, they are best roasted in a moderate 180°C (350°F, gas mark 4) oven to allow time for the fat to render from the duck, otherwise the meat would be overcooked before the fat was drawn off. To get a lovely crispy brown skin on duck, raise the heat to 250°C (500°F, or gas mark 9), for the last 15 minutes of roasting time. One school of thought holds that if you leave all the accumulated fat in the tin and keep basting the duck with it, the skin will be crisper. You might try that method sometime and see how you like it. However, if you're going to raise the temperature at the end, there shouldn't be more than 3 dl. ($\frac{1}{2}$ pint) of fat in the tin, or you'll have a very smoky, grease-splashed oven.

Ducks sold for roasting usually weigh from 2 to 2$\frac{1}{2}$ kg. (4 to 5 pounds), but because of the fat, you don't get many servings from them. One duck will serve 2 amply, 4 at a pinch, depending on the rest of the menu. Ducks are sold both fresh and frozen. They can be left wrapped and thawed in the refrigerator for 1 to 1$\frac{1}{2}$ days, at room temperature for 4 to 5 hours, or in cool water for 2 to 3 hours. After thawing, roast at once, or refrigerate.

☺ Roast Duck with Peaches

Serves 4 to 8

2 2- to 2$\frac{1}{2}$-kg. (4- to 5-lb.) ducks, fresh
   or frozen and thawed
$\frac{1}{2}$ lemon
Coarse salt
4 tablespoons port or madeira
3 dl. ($\frac{1}{2}$ pt) brown sauce (see page 288)

4 tablespoons brown sugar
8 peach halves (fresh, peeled peaches
   or firm canned peaches)
30 g. (1 oz.) unsalted butter
4 tablespoons bourbon or rum

Wipe the ducks, remove the giblets and neck (they can be saved for making stock) and the loose fat from the cavity and around the neck. Rub the ducks well, inside and out, with the lemon. Rub salt inside the ducks and all over the skin, which helps to crisp it. Truss the ducks and arrange them on a rack in a shallow roasting tin. Preheat the oven to 180°C (350°F, gas mark 4).

Roast the ducks at 180°C for 1 or 1$\frac{1}{2}$ to 2 hours, according to how well-done you like your ducks. At 1 hour, duck will be rare (I happen to like it that way); at 1$\frac{1}{2}$ hours, medium rare.

When the ducks have been in the oven for 30 minutes, prick the skin all over with a fork. This lets the fat drain out as it melts and keeps the skin crisp. During the roasting, prick once or twice more. As the fat accumulates in the tin, remove any excess with a spoon or bulb baster and put in a jar for future use. Leave about 3 dl. ($\frac{1}{2}$ pt) of the fat in the tin each time to prevent the juices from burning and scorching. If you like a really crispy brown skin, about 20 minutes before the ducks are done, increase the heat to 250°C (500°F, or gas mark 9), and roast for 15 minutes longer. (Reduce the cooking time by 5 minutes to allow for the higher temperature.)

To test duck for doneness, press the flesh of the thigh with protected fingers and wiggle the leg. The flesh should feel soft and the leg move easily. Prick the thigh with a fork. For medium-rare duck, the juices should be slightly rosy, not bloody, but not yellow and clear, a sign that the duck is well done. Well-done duck will have overcooked, dry and tasteless meat.

When the ducks are done, remove them to a hot heatproof platter and let stand for 10 minutes to allow the juices to settle before carving. Meanwhile, make the sauce and grill the peaches. Skim off the fat from the roasting tin; add the wine and bring the wine and juices to a boil over medium-high heat, scraping up the brown glaze from the tin with a wooden spatula. Add this liquid to the brown sauce, bring it to a boil in a saucepan, reduce the heat, and simmer for 2 to 3 minutes to reduce it slightly.

Spread the sugar on the cut sides of the peaches; cut up the butter and dot it over the sugar; put the peaches in a baking dish or on a baking tray and grill until the sugar and butter are melted and bubbly and the peaches heated through. Arrange the peaches around the ducks; heat the bourbon or rum in a small pan; ignite it; pour the flaming spirit over the peaches and serve. The flaming may be done at the table if you like.

Duck does not slice well, as the breast has little meat. The best way to carve duck is to cut it into halves or quarters with poultry shears (see page 114) and serve each person a half or a quarter. To go with the duck, you might have fried cornmeal squares or a purée of potatoes and celeriac (see page 61) and either a braised vegetable or a salad of chicory and julienne strips of beetroot. Drink a red wine – a Bordeaux or a Côtes du Rhône.

Game Birds

Most roast game is delicious in itself and gains nothing from being smothered with other flavours. The most agreeable complements to game birds are juniper berries, tarragon, onion, leeks, cabbage and sauerkraut. These do not all go with all birds, but they are fairly interchangeable.

The currant-jelly school of thought, like the cranberry school, is to my mind to be avoided. If one has regard for fine wine, which goes so magnificently with game, there is certainly no reason to attempt to mask the flavour of the bird with sharp sweets.

One of the most pleasing foundations or accompaniments for game is a very American food – corn – in the form of cornmeal mush cut into squares or oblongs and sautéed in butter until brown and crisp. The texture and taste blend well with the wild, gamy flavour and give a definite quality to certain dishes. I much prefer corn to wild rice, which most people feel is the answer to what to serve with all game.

Another delicious accompaniment I like is the giblets of the game birds chopped and sautéed in plenty of butter with salt, freshly ground pepper, and perhaps a touch of cognac or wine, and spread on toast fried in butter or on the sautéed cornmeal mush previously mentioned.

Roast Pheasant

Pheasants raised in captivity are sometimes a better bet than wild birds, as they are usually sold when they are the right age for the oven. They generally weigh about 1 to 1½ kg. (2½ to 3 pounds), and one pheasant will serve 2 or 3.

Serves 2 to 3

1 1¼- to 1½-kg. (2½- to 3-lb.) pheasant	4 sprigs of fresh tarragon
125 g. (4 oz.) or more unsalted butter	Or 2 teaspoons dried tarragon
4 sprigs of parsley	Sheet of fresh pork barding fat*

*Pound it thin, to fit over the breast of the bird.

Because pheasant is rather dry, wipe the pheasant inside and out with a damp cloth. Put about 30 g. (1 oz.) butter in the cavity with the parsley and tarragon. Butter the skin of the bird well and bard the breast with the sheet of fat, tying it on securely (see illustration). Put the pheasant
on its side on a rack in a shallow roasting tin and roast it in a 190°C (375°F, gas mark 5) oven for 15 minutes, basting every few minutes with the juices and melted butter. Turn it on its other side and roast it for another 15 minutes, basting again. Turn the bird breast side up; cut the string that secures the barding fat so that the fat just lies loosely on the breast and roast it for 10 to 15 minutes, basting frequently. Test the pheasant for doneness by piercing

the meat near the thigh and leg joint. If the juices run pale pink, the bird is juicily done. If the juices run clear, the bird is thoroughly done and the breast meat will be fairly dry. If the pheasant needs additional cooking, remove the barding pork; baste the bird well and continue to cook for about 15 minutes or until it is done to taste. The average time for roasting pheasant is about 45 minutes, although many people prefer it roasted a full hour or even more.

Serve the pheasant with crisply sautéed cornmeal mush squares, bread crumbs sautéed in butter and, if you wish, a velouté sauce made with chicken broth and cream and seasoned with chopped tarragon. To my taste, a good red Burgundy of a recent vintage or a fine full-bodied white Burgundy go equally well with roast pheasant.

Roast Wild Duck

The cooking of duck is a highly individual matter. There are those who cannot stand the sight of blood running in a roasted bird. Then there are others to whom a well-done duck is absolutely unthinkable. Something can be said for both attitudes. I adore rather underdone duck, but I have a friend who roasts hers, stuffed, for over an hour, and when I eat them I am convinced that they are far and away the finest ducks I have ever tasted.

Some cooks feel that wild duck should be marinated in wine or brandy, or a combination of the two, with herbs and seasonings. It is my belief that something as precious as a good duck needs very little to improve its superb flavour save the good butter, wine, brandy and simple seasonings used during its roasting. Duck does not need a marinade unless it is a pretty fishy-tasting and -smelling bird – and then it won't be improved much whatever is done to it. However, if you do have to cope with this kind of bird, an onion stuck with a few cloves and some red wine will help to make it more palatable. Rub the interior well with a cut lemon or lime before popping the onion into the cavity and let the bird marinate in wine for some time before roasting.

I have also found that wild duck benefits from being rubbed with butter or olive oil and then basted with butter during the cooking period. Sometimes I vary the process and baste during roasting with a blend of red wine and melted butter. Wild ducks are also enhanced if they are flambéed after they issue from the oven. A good cognac, Armagnac, or gin are the most acceptable spirits. The gin, heavy with juniper, is a very satisfactory flavour for finishing off the duck.

The length of time you roast wild duck depends on your taste and that of your guests. One duck, unless it is large, will serve only 1 person, so if you wish to go to the trouble you may time each bird separately.

FOR EACH SERVING

1 wild duck

3 or 4 juniper berries

  Or ½ teaspoon dried thyme

60 g. (2 oz.) unsalted butter

2 tablespoons red wine, port, or
  madeira

Salt, freshly ground black pepper

2 tablespoons cognac (optional)

Be sure the birds are well cleaned; wipe outside and cavity with a damp cloth. Put juniper berries or thyme and 15 g. (½ oz.) butter in the cavity of each bird. Rub the skin with 15 g. (½ oz.) butter (or use olive oil) and put the duck on a rack in a shallow roasting tin. Melt the remaining butter and combine with an equal amount of red wine, port, or madeira. Roast ducks in a 230°C (450°F, gas mark 8) oven for 17 to 18 minutes, basting them once or twice with the wine mixture. Season the cooked ducks with salt and pepper and flambé them with cognac if you wish (see page 96). For convenience, split the ducks in half with shears before serving. Serve some of the roasting juices with the ducks.

If you like your ducks better done, roast them in a 230°C oven for 20 minutes, then reduce heat to 180°C (350°F, gas mark 4), and continue to roast 25 to 30 minutes longer, or to your preferred degree of doneness, basting frequently. Remember, though, that wild duck should not be roasted for more than 45 minutes in all, unless it has a stuffing.

To vary the flavour for the duck cavity, try a stalk of celery, a quarter of an onion, 1 or 2 crushed garlic cloves or a sprig of thyme or parsley or a combination of these. You may also put a sheet of barding pork fat over the breast of the bird, although this is not necessary if it is to be cooked quickly.

With the duck, serve a barley casserole (especially good when cooked with the duck, giblets) or wild rice, and cabbage, kale, Brussels sprouts or glazed turnips – there are many contrasting vegetables that go well with duck. An orange and onion salad with watercress, endive, or cos lettuce with a rosemary vinaigrette is also a pleasing contrast. However, eschew the salad if you are going to give the duck the great wine it deserves. Duck can take a fine aged Burgundy – a Clos de Vougeot, an Echézeaux, or a Clos de Bèze – or one of your best Bordeaux. Other than that, a good Rhône, such as a red Hermitage, is excellent.

Venison

Of all the furred game, venison is the most generally available, both to the hunter and to the non-hunter. Good venison can be found in shops in the larger cities where fine meats and poultry are sold, either fresh or frozen. If the animal is old and the meat less than tender, it is best to relegate it to a ragout or have it minced for hamburgers. The most desirable cuts for joints are, of course, the saddle, the rack, and the haunch or leg. According to your preference, you should decide if you want the meat hung for a long time until it develops a really 'gamy' flavour or if you would rather have it hung only for several days and eaten fresh or after marination. This is a question you have to answer for yourself, although my feeling is that a fine young deer is delicious roasted without having been marinated.

Marinade for Venison

1 carrot, peeled and cut into julienne
  strips
1 onion, peeled and thinly sliced
1 stick of celery, cut into small pieces
1 garlic clove, peeled
Several sprigs of parsley
1½ teaspoons dried thyme

1 bay leaf
1 teaspoon dried summer savory
1 teaspoon freshly ground black
  pepper
1½ dl. (¼ pt) olive or groundnut oil
1½ dl. (¼ pt) red wine vinegar
1 l. (1¾ pts) dry red wine

Combine all ingredients. Marinate any cut of venison for roasting in the mixture for 2 to 5 days, turning it once or twice a day.

Roast Rack of Venison

A rack of venison, which is not very large and will serve only 2, may be roasted on the spit or in the oven and it is best when roasted quickly and basted well. Marinate the meat first for 3 to 5 days.

Serves 2

1 rack of young, tender venison
2 tablespoons olive or groundnut oil
1 teaspoon dried thyme or rosemary
½ teaspoon freshly ground black
  pepper

60 g. (2 oz.) unsalted butter, melted
4 tablespoons dry white wine
30 g. (1 oz.) freshly made bread crumbs
30 g. (1 oz.) butter
30 g. (1 oz.) chopped parsley

Prepare the rack by trimming the ribs well and scraping the ends of the rib bones to remove meat and fat, the way a butcher prepares a rack of lamb (this, in butcher's terms, is known as 'Frenched'). Wrap exposed bones with pieces of foil to prevent them charring. Preheat the oven to 230°C (450°F, gas mark 8). Rub the meat and bone well with the oil, thyme or rosemary, and pepper. Put the meat on a rack in a shallow roasting tin and roast at 230°C for 15 minutes. Combine the melted butter and white wine and baste the meat well with it. Continue to roast for 5 minutes, then reduce the temperature to 200°C (400°F, gas mark 6), and roast 5 minutes longer. Test the internal temperature with a meat thermometer by inserting it lengthwise into the thickest part of the meat, but not touching the bone. It should register 55°C (130°F). Remove the rack from the oven; turn off the oven and preheat the grill. Sauté the bread crumbs in 30 g. (1 oz.) butter until lightly browned, then combine with the parsley, mixing well, and press them into the meaty part of the venison with your hand until they adhere well. Put the rack under the hot grill, about 10 cm. (4 inches) from the heat, and leave it just long enough for the surface of the crumbs to brown. Transfer the rack to a hot platter and let it rest for 5 minutes before carving it into chops. Serve with crisp sautéed potatoes and a green vegetable such as broccoli. Drink a Juliénas from Beaujolais.

Roast Haunch of Venison

The haunch is the leg and part of the loin. If it is from a fine young animal have the meat hung for 10 days to 2 weeks.

Serves 8

1 large or 2 small garlic cloves, peeled and chopped	Salt
Freshly ground black pepper	4½ dl. (¾ pt) dry red wine
1 teaspoon dried thyme	3 dl. (½ pt) strong veal or chicken broth
1 venison haunch, weighing 3½ to 5½ kg. (8 to 12 lbs.)	2 teaspoons tomato paste
125 g. (4 oz.) unsalted butter, softened	Beurre manié (see page 283)
	3 tablespoons Madeira
	Watercress or parsley

Combine the garlic, 1 teaspoon pepper and the thyme. Blend the mixture well with your hands and rub it vigorously into the meat. Let it stand for 1 hour.

Preheat the oven to 230°C (450°F, gas mark 8). Spread the roast with 30 to 45 g. (1 to 1½ oz.) softened butter and put it on a rack in a shallow roasting tin. Roast at 230°C, basting it once with the rest of the butter, for 30 minutes. Reduce heat to 180°C (350°F, gas mark 4) and continue to roast for 1 to 1½ hours for a 3½-kg. (8-pound) haunch or proportionately longer for a larger one, allowing 12 to 15 minutes per ½ kg. (pound). After roasting for 1 hour, test with a meat thermometer, inserting it in the thickest part of the meat but not touching the bone. When the venison is done, the internal temperature will be 55°C (130°F). If it is anywhere near that, continue to test at 10-minute intervals. About 15 minutes before you estimate the meat will be done, sprinkle it with salt.

While the meat is roasting, put the red wine in a pan. Bring to a boil, then reduce the heat and simmer until the wine is reduced to 3 dl. ($\frac{1}{2}$ pt).

Remove the cooked venison to a hot platter and let it rest for 10 to 15 minutes before carving. Skim the fat from the juices in the tin and combine the juices with the stock and red wine, scraping well to incorporate the brown glaze in the tin. Pour the liquids into a saucepan and mix in the tomato paste, 1 teaspoon pepper, and salt to taste. Bring the liquid to a boil; reduce the heat and drop in small balls of *beurre manié*, stirring the sauce and simmering it until thickened to your taste. Add the Madeira and simmer the sauce a little longer to eliminate the alcohol – about 5 minutes.

Garnish the roast with watercress or parsley and serve polenta (cooked cornmeal) with it. Serve the sauce separately and drink a good red Bordeaux.

If you prefer to marinate the haunch before roasting, put it in a large nonmetallic bowl, pour the marinade over it, and leave for 5 days, turning the meat over at least once a day. When ready to roast, remove it; dry well on paper towels and roast as above, using $1\frac{1}{2}$ dl. ($\frac{1}{4}$ pt) of the strained marinade in place of $1\frac{1}{2}$ dl. ($\frac{1}{4}$ pt) of the wine.

Vegetables

Certain root vegetables, notably onions, potatoes, carrots and parsnips, are delicious when roasted, either in the tin with the roasting meat or separately in a tin of rendered beef fat or suet, which gives them the same lovely flavour they get from the meat drippings.

You'll have noticed that a couple of the meat recipes had roasted vegetables as an accompaniment. I've found by experience that they cook better, especially if the meat is being roasted at a medium temperature, if they are first parboiled for 5 minutes, to soften them slightly. Small new potatoes may be roasted whole, either peeled or in their thin skins, with a little belly band of skin cut from around the centre to prevent them from bursting. Larger potatoes should be peeled and halved or quartered, according to size. Small carrots or parsnips may be left whole, larger ones halved or quartered. The small white onions are better for roasting than the large yellow ones. Prepare the vegetables; parboil them, bringing them to a boil in water to cover with 1 teaspoon salt; drain and then arrange them in the tin, around the roast, for the last hour of cooking time. Or put them in a roasting tin containing about 1 cm. ($\frac{1}{2}$ inch) of hot rendered beef fat or suet and roast in a 220°C (425°F, gas mark 7) oven for 40 minutes, or until just tender when pierced with a fork or the point of a small sharp knife.

Grilling

Grilling, the application of intense direct heat to meat and other foodstuffs, is probably the oldest, most basic, and most functional of all the cooking processes. It can be done over an outdoor fire, a charcoal, gas, or electric barbecue grill, or under the oven grill. I remember, as a child, our grills at the beach over fires of the driftwood we gathered. Our fuel was mainly the bark from fir and spruce trees, which was very plentiful along the beach because of the Oregon lumber industry. Believe me, nothing was better for grilling than that wonderful aromatic bark when it had burned down to glowing, white-encrusted coals. Our primitive little grill stuck over the fire did noble work with hamburgers, frankfurters, marshmallows speared on sticks, and all those other things that children love to eat outdoors. Sometimes we would nail a split salmon to a plank and grill it alongside the fire, as the Indians used to do.

The words 'grilling' and 'broiling' are practically synonymous, although in America broiling refers to cooking food under the broiler, or grill, of an oven, while grilling is the term applied to cooking over charcoal. One grills or broils on a grill, originally known as a gridiron. According to my infallible authority, the Oxford English Dictionary, grilling was 'the process of broiling on a gridiron or similar apparatus over or before a fire', and a grill was a piece of meat or fish broiled on a gridiron. Hence the adoption of the term 'grill room' for restaurants or hotel dining rooms where grilled foods are prepared and served. In French, the verb to broil is *griller* and broiled fish is a *grillade*.

The first gridirons, of which you see drawings in old English and American cookbooks, were little four-footed iron grills that were placed over coals in the fireplace. This could be a very messy way of cooking. The fat dripped on to the coals, sending forth smoke and odours, although fortunately, to a great extent these dissipated up the chimney. When I was a child, the only way we could grill in the kitchen was to remove the lid from the wood stove and put a grill over the open flame. Although this chancy process managed somehow to bring forth some delicious morsels, our grilling had to be performed with the windows open to let out the smoke, and the fat that dripped into the fire caused quite a mess. Thank goodness, the advent of gas and electric cookers changed all that.

Today, most of our grilling is done with gas or electricity. It is my personal feeling that electric grills do a more efficient job than gas ones. As it takes time to become accustomed to the performance of any grilling unit, whether it is the newest type or an older one, it is always a good idea to try it out with various pieces of meat and poultry to establish the correct timings and distances from the heat for your particular unit. You also have to learn how to adjust the flame for best results if you are using one of the older gas grills.

It's fun to play around with grilling, to experiment with the basic rules of distance and timing and then set up your own chart. The timing will vary according to the unit and to how you like your meat cooked. Grilling is not just a matter of throwing a piece of meat under the grill or over a charcoal fire, it is a pretty scientific process you should master, for in these days of quick meals and diets, grilling has become one of the most popular forms of cooking. Not only is it functional and fast, but the direct heat cooks out a great deal of the fat in meat or poultry and chars the surface, giving great flavour. The main difference between grilling over charcoal and under a gas or electric grill is the distance from the heat, as the heat of charcoal is much more intense.

There are, of course, some drawbacks to grilling. It will not tenderize meat, so you should only grill the more tender cuts and those that are best suited to the process, like beef and lamb. I refrain most of the time from grilling pork, including pork chops, because the intense heat tends to dry out and harden the flesh. I find braising or sautéing gives the meat more succulence. The same is true of most cuts of veal, except perhaps for a *paillard* of veal, a very thin slice from the leg which is pounded until it is even thinner, then brushed with oil or butter and grilled for less than a minute very close to the heat. Veal chops or veal steaks, on the other hand, need the moist heat of braising and sautéing.

Fish lends itself well to grilling, provided you baste it well and don't overcook it. Prawns and scallops are delicious, but I don't recommend it for larger shellfish, such as lobster. To me, a grilled lobster is a dried-out, tasteless disaster. Among the organ meats, liver and kidneys respond well to fast grilling, and so do little chicken hearts and livers cooked on skewers. This method of stringing pieces of meat, fish, and vegetables on sticks or skewers, known in France as *en brochette* and in other parts of the world as kebabs or kabobs, is as old as time. It may well have been one of the first ways anyone ever grilled over an open fire.

When you come to think about it, there are comparatively few foods that don't lend themselves to grilling. You could cook a whole breakfast under the grill, if you wanted to – grilling your grapefruit, your bacon, and your toast. Although it may not have occurred to you, toasting is really grilling bread. In France, as a matter of fact, toast is *pain grillé*, grilled bread. Maybe you are old enough to remember how bread used to be toasted before we had electric toasters – on a long-handled wire toasting fork in front of the fire, first on one side, then on the other.

There's another aspect of grilling that dates back to the old days when a piece of solid metal called a salamander was heated in the fire until it was red hot and then passed over the surface of a finished dish to give it a lovely brown glaze. One of the most famous of all the traditional English and American desserts, *crème brûlée* – a baked custard sprinkled with a thin layer of sugar which is then exposed to intense heat until it caramelizes and forms a thin, brittle crust – used to be finished this way. Now we caramelize the sugar under the grill. Then there are all the dishes which we serve gratinéed – spread with crumbs, dotted with butter or sprinkled with cheese, and put under a hot grill for a few minutes until the top is delicately browned and takes on a deliciously toasty quality. Or the grill may be used to glaze a dish covered with a mornay or hollandaise sauce – perhaps poached fish fillets, or vegetables, or sauced oysters.

Grilling is a fascinating cooking technique and probably the one requiring the most active participation on the part of the cook.

GENERAL RULES AND RECOMMENDATIONS FOR GRILLING

Generally speaking, your meat will cook better and faster if you remove it from the refrigerator and let it warm up at room temperature for $1\frac{1}{2}$ to 2 hours. Refrigeration cools meat considerably and it takes time for the heat to overcome this interior chill. While frozen meats may be grilled without defrosting, you will have to allow twice as long a grilling time as for a fresh cut. Sear them about 5 cm. (2 inches) from the heat on both sides, to seal the surface, then lower and grill 10 cm. (4 inches) from the heat, rather than the usual $7\frac{1}{2}$ cm. (3 inches), for the rest of the cooking time. Fish can also be grilled from the frozen state, at the normal distance but for double the cooking time. Chicken, duck, and other poultry or game birds should be thawed before grilling.

Whatever type of grill you have, it should always be preheated at the highest setting until good and hot.

Do not preheat the grill pan and rack, unless you are cooking an extremely thin piece of meat, such as a *paillard* of veal, that grills very fast and is not turned, and therefore needs heat on both sides. Just lubricate the rack well by rubbing it with oil or butter or beef fat so the meat doesn't stick to it and, if you wish, line the grill pan with foil, which will help to reflect heat upwards and make cleaning simpler. Thin fish fillets are best grilled on oiled foil, which you can put over the rack or in the pan itself. As to distances from the heat, you will have to figure out for yourself, according to the type of unit you have, how to increase and decrease the distance. If your grill has a grid positioner, so much the better. Mainly, you will just have to figure out how to move the oven racks and pans around or, if you have one of the older gas units, how to regulate the heat by increasing or decreasing the flame. As a general rule, a distance of about $7\frac{1}{2}$ cm. (3 inches) from the heat to the surface of the meat is the best level for cuts of normal thickness (about $3\frac{1}{2}$ cm. or $1\frac{1}{2}$ inches) and for thin fish fillets. Chicken, poultry and foods that easily get overcooked, like scallops, prawns and whole fish, are better at a distance of 10 cm. (4 inches). Steaks or lamb chops can be brought closer to the heat towards the end of the cooking time, if you wish, for that last touch of charring. Very thin cuts, say a flank steak, on the other hand, should be no more than $3\frac{1}{2}$ to 5 cm. ($1\frac{1}{2}$ to 2 inches) from the heat, as they must cook very rapidly indeed.

Always trim excess fat from meat before grilling, to prevent flare-ups. As to seasoning, there are great differences of opinion about whether you should salt and pepper meat before, during, or after grilling. Personally, I like to season meat before I grill it, but I really don't think it makes one bit of difference. If you feel like experimenting, as I have done in the past, take three pieces of the same meat cut and season one before, one during, and one after and you'll find there is practically no difference in texture and flavour. You don't have to worry about the salt drawing out the meat juices, because the intense heat will seal the surface almost immediately.

While tender cuts need no marinating and seldom, if ever, any basting, fish, shellfish, chicken, game birds and offal like kidneys and liver that have no natural fat do need to be basted or brushed with butter or oil to keep them from drying out.

I am of the opinion that marinating does little or nothing to render tough cuts of meat grillable. They are better braised. However, there are times when you might want to marinate a flank steak, meat kebabs, poultry and game, or fish and shellfish to give added and enhancing flavour. A teriyaki marinade of soy sauce, oil, sherry and flavourings can be used for many different foods such as grilled chicken, wild duck, flank steak, prawns, or strips of meat or chicken wound on skewers and grilled in the Japanese style. You can make a very simple marinade for game, poultry, or meat with equal parts of dry vermouth and olive oil flavoured with dried or chopped fresh herbs – tarragon or rosemary for chicken, thyme for beef or lamb, thyme and rosemary for most game. Wine and oil marinades, like the one given for beef shashlik (page 119), are also good for game birds, kebabs, and thick cuts of lamb. No marinade should ever be without oil. Unless there is some lubrication, the meat may dry out. What is the difference between a marinade and a basting liquid? Technically, a marinade is a thin sauce in which food is soaked before it cooks and a basting liquid is a thin sauce that is brushed on or spooned over the food as it cooks, but as you also baste with a marinade, sometimes they are one and the same.

Beef

♟ Grilled Steak

Steaks are bought by thickness, not by weight. Because of the variance in size and shape between the different cuts, it is very difficult to gauge how much a steak is going to weigh. It's my feeling that a $2\frac{1}{2}$- to $3\frac{1}{2}$-cm. (1- to $1\frac{1}{2}$-inch) steak is the minimum thickness for grilling; anything thinner is better sautéed.

When you buy a steak, you must consider the grade. The better the grade, the tenderer the cut. When picking out steak, look for meat that is deep red in colour and well marbled with creamy-coloured fat. If you can, have the steak specially cut for you rather than picking up a ready-packaged steak in the supermarket. The butcher will weigh the steak after cutting it to the thickness you want.

Allow roughly 180 to 225 g. (6 to 8 ounces) of boneless meat per serving. If you are not buying a boneless cut like the rump or entrecôte but rather a larger bone-in steak such as a sirloin or porterhouse, estimate 350 to 450 g.

($\frac{3}{4}$ to 1 pound) meat per serving to compensate for the weight and waste of the bone. You'll find a description of steaks for grilling on page 378. If you have some left over, don't worry. Cold steak makes great sandwiches.

GRILLING METHOD FOR ANY $3\frac{1}{2}$-CM. ($1\frac{1}{2}$-INCH) STEAK

Preheat the grill. Trim excess fat from the steak, leaving a rim about 1 cm. ($\frac{1}{2}$ inch) thick. Slash the rim to keep it from curling.

Brush the grill rack with oil or rub it with some of the fat trimmed from the steak. Salt and pepper one side of the meat and arrange it, seasoned side up, on the rack of the grill pan. Before putting the steak under the grill, press it with your finger. It will feel very soft. Remember this later when you test the cooked steak.

Put the pan under the grill with the surface of the steak $7\frac{1}{2}$ cm. (3 inches) from the heat, or as close to $7\frac{1}{2}$ cm. (3 inches) as possible.

For a very rare steak, grill for 8 to 12 minutes, 4 to 6 minutes a side. For a rare steak, grill for 10 to 14 minutes, 5 to 7 minutes a side. When I'm grilling a steak, I sometimes give it an extra half-minute on the first side, because it doesn't really begin to sear until it has been under the grill for a half-minute. Halfway through the cooking time turn the steak with metal tongs, not with a fork, which would pierce the flesh and let the juices escape, and season the second side before grilling it.

There are two schools of thought about how often to turn a steak during cooking. Some people like to sear one side, turn and sear the second side, turn it back again and cook on each side for the rest of the cooking time. Frankly, I don't think it does anything for a steak to keep on turning it back and forth. Once is enough.

About 2 minutes before the end of the cooking time, test the steak to see if it is done to your liking. There are three ways you can determine this. One is to remove the pan from the grill and insert your meat thermometer horizontally through the side (not in the top) of the steak to the centre, but not touching the bone, if there is one. The internal temperature for a very rare steak is about 50°C (120°F to 125°F) and for a rare steak about 55°C (130°F to 135°F). Medium, if you must, would be 60°C to 63°C (140°F to 145°F). The second way is to make a little cut in the meat near the bone or the rim of fat with a small sharp knife and check the inside of the meat. If it is done the way you like it, that's fine. If not, return the pan to the grill and continue to cook the steak for a minute or so longer. The third test, which is the one professionals use and you will gradually learn to rely on, is to press the centre of the steak lightly with your finger (it won't burn you), remembering how it felt when raw. A rare steak will feel firm on the surface but soft within. Were it to be medium, the steak would feel slightly resistant and a well-done one, perish the thought, would be quite firm. Practise touching steak grilled to the stage you prefer and you'll soon become accustomed to testing this way.

When your steaks are grilled, put them on hot plates or a hot platter. Or, if you are going to carve a large steak at table, on a carving board. I like to put a pat of butter on a steak the minute it comes out of the grill, either plain unsalted butter or butter mixed with a herb such as crushed rosemary or thyme. Use a ratio of about $\frac{1}{2}$ teaspoon dried herb to 30 g. (1 ounce) butter. The butter melts and runs over the meat, mingling with the juices when you cut into or carve the meat and making a little sauce.

A good steak needs little or no embellishment. You can sit down and eat it just as it is, or you can have grilled tomatoes or grilled mushrooms with it, or a green salad, or you can shoot the works and have potatoes or chips, a green vegetable and a salad. That's up to you. If you wish to be really elegant, you might have a Béarnaise sauce, sautéed potatoes and a vegetable or salad.

TIMINGS FOR STEAKS OF OTHER THICKNESSES

For a steak $2\frac{1}{2}$ cm. (1 inch) thick, grill 5 cm. (2 inches) from the flame: 3 minutes a side for very rare, 4 to 5 minutes a side for rare.

For a steak 5 cm. (2 inches) thick, allow the longer grilling time given for a $3\frac{1}{2}$-cm. ($1\frac{1}{2}$-inch) steak, grilling at $7\frac{1}{2}$ cm. (3 inches) from the heat.

Charcoal-Grilled Steak

The main difference between oven grilling and charcoal grilling is the distance from the heat, as the heat of charcoal is more intense. Otherwise the timing is much the same.

Start grilling when the coals have burned down until they have a white feathery covering of ash. The heat at grill level, which should be from 12 to 18 cm. (5 to 7 inches) above the coals, will be between 170°C and 190°C (325°F and 375°F), ample for grilling almost any steak or poultry, chops, or fish. If you are grilling a steak, start at a temperature of about 180°C (350°F) at grill level, which you can easily check with a special flat grill thermometer. To sear the steak first, raise the firebox or move the grill closer to the coals, and sear quickly on both sides, close to the coals, then move the steak farther from the heat to finish the cooking. Or if you would rather char the meat at the end of the cooking time instead, follow the same procedure of raising the firebox or lowering the grill. Steaks should be seared, charred and cooked for equal time on each side.

London Grill
(Grilled Flank Steak)

Serves 4

Although this thin fibrous steak, the triangular piece on the underside, below the loin, is not a tender cut, it is delicious if grilled very fast and sliced very thin. Get the choicest, most expensive flank steak, which will be a tenderer, better quality.

Remove the tough membrane on the outside of the meat with a sharp knife. Rub the steak well on both sides with coarse salt, freshly ground black pepper and a little Tabasco.

Preheat the grill. Rub the grill rack with oil; arrange the flank steak on the rack and put the grill pan and rack on the top oven shelf, so that the surface of the steak is 3½ to 5 cm. (1½ to 2 inches) from the heat. Grill for 3 to 4 minutes on each side for rare meat – which this has to be.

Carve into very thin slices on the diagonal, slicing across the fibres, which will give you tender, edible pieces of meat. Serve with sauce diable (see page 290) and sliced French bread. Flank steak also makes great sandwiches.

VARIATION

Teriyaki Flank Steak. Trim but do not season the meat. Put the steak in a dish or deep platter in which it can lie flat and pour teriyaki marinade (see page 111) over it. Marinate for 2 to 3 hours, turning the steak occasionally. Grill as before, 3½ to 5 cm. (1½ to 2 inches) from the heat, for 3 to 4 minutes a side. When you turn the meat, brush the upturned side with the marinade.

Grilled Hamburgers

It is difficult to grill hamburgers well, as they are likely to dry out, though a chip of ice in the centre of each patty helps. I prefer to sauté hamburgers (see page 169), but if you wish to grill your hamburgers, they should always be cooked to the rare stage.

Allow 225 g. (8 ounces) hamburger for a main-dish serving. Form the meat into 2½-cm. (1-inch)-thick patties, putting a chip of ice in the centre of each, and season the outside with salt and freshly ground black pepper. Preheat the grill and grease the grill rack. Arrange the patties on the rack and brush the tops with melted butter or beef fat, or a mixture of oil and butter. Grill 10 cm. (4 inches) from the heat for 3 minutes, then turn with a broad-bladed fish slice and brush the second side with butter. Grill 3 minutes on the second side. This will give you a rare hamburger. Serve with chips and sliced tomato or sliced onion.

Poultry
....

♨ Grilled Chicken

Birds of 1¼ kg. (2½ pounds) are best for grilling as there is more meat on them than on the small ones. Half a chicken per serving is usual. If you feel this is too much chicken for one person, you can carve the chickens into quarters after they are grilled. (If your grill is rather shallow, carve the chicken into quarters before grilling.) Have the chickens split lengthwise and the necks and backbones removed.

Serves 4

2 1¼-kg. (2½-lb.) chickens, split,   1½ dl. (¼ pt) melted butter or oil
    backbone and neck removed.   Salt, freshly ground black pepper

Preheat the grill. Rub the rack of the grill pan with melted butter or oil. Rub salt and freshly ground pepper into both the skin and bone sides of the chickens and then rub them well with butter or oil. Arrange the chickens, bone side up, on the grill rack. Grill 10 cm. (4 inches) from the heat for 12 to 14 minutes, basting once or twice with the butter, then turn with tongs; brush the skin side with butter and continue to grill, skin side up, brushing once or twice more with butter, for 12 to 14 minutes. If necessary, move the chicken closer to the heat for the last 2 or 3 minutes to brown and crisp the skin, but be careful it doesn't burn.

Test for doneness by piercing the joint between thigh and body with the point of a knife. If the juices are slightly tinged with pink, but not red, the chickens are cooked. If red, cook a minute or two longer. Serve with a green vegetable or a green salad.

Teriyaki Grilled Chicken

Serves 2

A 1¼-kg. (2½-lb.) chicken, split

TERIYAKI MARINADE

1½ dl. (¼ pt) soy sauce (preferably   2 tablespoons grated fresh ginger root
    Japanese or Chinese)   Or finely chopped candied ginger
1½ dl. (¼ pt) olive oil   with the sugar washed off
4 tablespoons dry sherry   1 tablespoon grated tangerine or
2 garlic cloves, peeled and finely   orange rind
    chopped or crushed

Arrange the chicken in a shallow dish or pan. Combine the marinade ingredients and pour over the chicken. Marinate from 1 to 3 hours, turning the chicken frequently to make sure it is well soaked with the marinade. You can leave it in the marinade, refrigerated, for up to 24 hours if you wish. Otherwise marinate for 1 hour at room temperature or 3 hours in the refrigerator.

Preheat the grill. Grease the grill rack with oil and arrange the chicken on it, bone side up. To prevent the soy marinade from caramelizing and burning, place the chicken under the grill about 12 cm. (5 inches) from the heat, farther away than it would normally be. Grill bone side up for 12 to 14 minutes, depending on thickness, brushing once or twice with the marinade from the dish. Turn the chicken over with tongs, brush the skin side with the marinade, and continue grilling for another 12 to 14 minutes, brushing or basting twice with the marinade. If the skin of the chicken seems to be blistered or burning, lower the grill pan another 2½ cm. (inch). To test for doneness, pierce the joint between the body and the thigh with a small sharp knife. The juice that trickles out should be faintly tinged with pink. If it is red-tinged, grill a minute or two longer, but do not overcook or the chicken will be dry. Serve on hot plates, with rice and sautéed mangetouts or a green salad.

Grilled Poussins

These baby chickens weigh only ½ kg. (1 pound). Have them split, and grill and baste them as for grilled chicken, but give them only 8 to 10 minutes a side. Serve 1 chicken per person.

Grilled Chicken with Flavoured Butter

One of the easiest and best ways to prepare grilled chicken is to make a flavourful mixture of butter creamed with herbs or garlic or shallots, rub some of it on the bone side, and stuff some under the skin so that the flavour penetrates and the butter lubricates the flesh. Tarragon-flavoured butter is especially good.

Serves 4

FLAVOURED BUTTER FOR 2 1¼-KG.
(2½-POUND) CHICKENS, SPLIT

90 g. (3 oz.) unsalted butter   *½ teaspoon freshly ground black pepper*
1 teaspoon salt

CHOOSE ANY OF THE FOLLOWING

4 large garlic cloves, very finely
   chopped

60 g. (2 oz.) finely chopped shallots

45 g. (1½ oz.) finely chopped
   parsley
   Or half parsley and half chopped
      chives

2 tablespoons choppped fresh tarragon
   Or 1½ teaspoons crushed dried
      tarragon

2 teaspoons finely chopped fresh
   rosemary
   Or 1 teaspoon well-crushed dried
      rosemary

Mix the butter, salt, pepper and chosen flavouring in a bowl, mashing them well together with a wooden spoon or working them with your hands, until thoroughly mixed (or prepare the butter by mixing the ingredients in a liquidizer or food processor).

Lift up the skin of the chicken at the top of the breast and slip your hand under it. Push your hand down between the skin and breast – the membrane connecting skin to flesh will rupture easily as you do so – and then between the skin and flesh of the leg and thigh. Take some of the flavoured butter in your hand and rub it over the leg and thigh meat under the skin and then pat a thin layer over the breast meat.

Turn the chickens over and rub the bone side with a little of the butter. Melt the remaining butter in a small pan and reserve for brushing the chickens. Grill the chickens as for grilled chicken, brush melted butter once on the bone side; turn, brush twice on the breast side.

Serve the chickens with sautéed potatoes and a green salad.

Grilled Duckling

Duckling is more interesting grilled than roasted. *The duckling should be cut in half lengthwise with poultry shears, from the vent at the tail, along the side of the breastbone, and then down the centre of the back.* Allow half a 2- to 2½-kg. (4- to 5-pound) duckling per serving, as there is little meat on the carcass. You may, if you prefer, cut each half in two after grilling and serve it to 4 people.

2- to 2½-kg. (4- to 5-lb.) duckling, split

½ lemon
Salt, freshly ground black pepper

Remove as much fat as possible from the carcass of the duck, then rub the bone side with the cut lemon. Rub both bone and skin side with salt and pepper.

Preheat the grill. Put the duck halves, bone side up, on the grill rack and pan (as the duck is so fatty, there is no need to grease the rack). Arrange the pan so the duck is 10 to 12 cm. (4 to 5 inches) from the heat and grill on the bone side for 20 minutes. Remove the pan from the grill and pour off the fat; turn the duck pieces with tongs and prick the skin all over with a fork to release the fat. Return to the grill and continue grilling for a further 20 to 30 minutes on the skin side, or until the skin is crisp and well browned. If at any time the duck seems to be browning too fast or the skin is in danger of burning, move the pan farther away from the heat.

Test the duck for doneness by piercing the joint between thigh and body, as for grilled chicken. If the juices are faintly tinged with pink, the duck is done. If red, grill a minute or two longer. Remove the duck to a heated platter or a carving board, if you wish to cut it into quarters. Serve with glazed turnips or tiny green peas. A salad of sliced oranges and onions is also good with grilled duck.

VARIATION

Grilled Peppered Duckling. Omit the pepper when seasoning. After the duck has grilled on the second, skin side for 10 minutes, remove it from the grill. Prick the skin again. Holding each half with several thicknesses of paper towels, press the skin into 2 tablespoons coarsely crushed black peppercorns on a plate until well coated. Lower the grill pan and rack so the skin of the duckling will be 15 cm. (6 inches) from the heat (to prevent the peppercorns from burning) and grill for 10 to 20 minutes. For the last 2 or 3 minutes raise the pan until the duck is about 5 cm. (2 inches) from the heat so the pepper forms a brown, crunchy coating.

Lamb

♟ Grilled Lamb Chops

Thick loin or best-end-of-neck chops are the best for grilling. As they have a good deal of fat and most people like their lamb chops grilled rare or pink (medium rare), you should move the chops nearer to the heat, about 5 cm. (2 inches) away, 2 minutes before the end of the grilling time in order to char the fat. Thin chops $2\frac{1}{2}$ cm. (1 inch) thick are best grilled fast and close to the heat or the meat will be overcooked before the fat is brown.

Grilling time depends not only on the thickness of the chops but also on the intensity of heat put out by your grill. The following chart gives approximate times and distances for chops of different thicknesses. The time given is total grilling time. Allow half the time per side.

THICKNESS	DISTANCE FROM HEAT	GRILLING TIME
$2\frac{1}{2}$ cm. (1 inch)	5 cm. (2 inches)	5 to 6 minutes for rare
		6 to 8 minutes for medium rare
$3\frac{1}{2}$ cm. ($1\frac{1}{2}$ inches)	10 cm. (4 inches)	6 to 8 minutes for rare
		8 to 10 minutes for medium rare

GRILLING METHOD

Preheat the grill. Rub the grill rack with oil.

Season the chops on one side with salt and pepper and arrange on the rack or in the foil pan. Grill according to the chart, turning the chops with tongs midway through the grilling time and seasoning the second side with salt and pepper when turned.

If necessary, raise the chops to within 5 cm. (2 inches) of the heat for the last 2 minutes to brown the fat.

To check for doneness, make a tiny slit in the meat, near the bone. Or, if the chops are very thick, insert a meat thermometer horizontally into the thickest part of the meat, not touching the bone. The internal temperature should be 58°C or 135°F for rare, 60°C or 140°F for medium rare.

Serve the lamb chops on very hot plates, as the fat congeals quickly. Crisp fried potatoes or grilled tomatoes and watercress are good accompaniments.

Other Meats

Grilled Liver Steaks

Allow 150 to 225 g. (⅓ to ½ pound) liver per serving.

Preheat the grill and brush the grill rack with oil or melted butter. Arrange the liver steaks on the rack and brush them well with melted butter. Brush the liver well with butter as it cooks, turning once. The liver should be lightly browned on the outside and pink on the inside. Do not overcook. Remove from the grill to a hot platter and sprinkle with salt and pepper. Serve with Béarnaise sauce and sautéed or boiled potatoes.

Grilled Ham Steaks

Steaks cut from a boiled ham require minimum grilling otherwise they dry out. Buy ham steaks 2½ to 3½ cm. (1 to 1½ inches) thick. Slash the fat around the edge to prevent it from curling.

Preheat the grill and grease the rack. Arrange the steaks on the rack and grill 5 to 7½ cm. (2 to 3 inches) from the heat for 2½ minutes a side, until just lightly browned. Do not overcook. If you wish to glaze the ham slice, brush it with equal quantities of honey and Dijon mustard.

Grilled Sausages

You can grill either pork sausages or the Italian or Greek sweet or hot sausages. Prick them well with a fork and cook them in boiling water for 3 to 4 minutes to blanch and precook them and to draw out some of the fat. Drain, dry, and arrange on a greased grill rack or aluminium foil pan. Grill 7½ cm. (3 inches) from the heat, turning once, for about 9 to 10 minutes, or until nicely browned on all sides.

Grilled Veal Kidneys

Allow 1 kidney per serving. Remove the skin and any fat from the kidneys, *split them in half lengthwise, and cut out the hard core of tubes and fat with scissors or a small sharp knife.*

Preheat the grill and brush the grill rack with melted butter or oil. Arrange the kidneys, cut side up, on the rack and brush them well with melted butter or oil. Grill 7½ cm. (3 inches) from the heat for 5 minutes, turn halfway through the cooking time. Brush the kidneys well during the cooking with butter or oil. When properly grilled, kidneys should be delicately browned on the outside and juicily rare inside. Transfer to hot plates, sprinkle with salt and pepper, and spoon a little melted butter over each serving. Sprinkle each kidney with 1 teaspoon chopped parsley, if you wish. Serve with chips, watercress, and hot mustard.

VARIATION

Devilled Kidneys. Grill the kidneys for 4 minutes, then dip them in a mixture of melted butter, lemon juice and Tabasco (1 tablespoon lemon juice and ½ teaspoon Tabasco to 5 tablespoons melted butter). Roll them in fresh bread crumbs, return to the grill, and grill quickly on both sides just until the crumbs are browned. Serve with mustard sauce (see page 287).

Kebabs

This oldest method of grilling (antedating the gridiron) which consists of simply stringing pieces of meat on a twig or sharpened stick and holding them over the fire is now known as kebab cookery. With the advent of metal, the stick was discarded in favour of the sturdier, reusable skewer or brochette, an implement that has survived virtually unchanged for centuries.

While almost anything in the meat, poultry, game and fish line can be strung on skewers and grilled, grilled lamb and beef, in the form of shish kebab and shashlik, are undoubtedly the most popular. They are virtually the same. Shish kebab is the Turkish name and shashlik the Russian for this style of meat cookery.

Lean, tender cuts of meat are best for kebabs: lamb shoulder or leg; pork loin or leg; the sirloin and rib cuts of beef. Veal tenderloin or shoulder, while also excellent, needs plenty of lubrication. For each serving, allow 225 to 350 g. ($\frac{1}{2}$ to $\frac{3}{4}$ pound) meat. For shish kebab and shashlik, the meat is usually marinated, to add flavour.

Shish Kebab

Serves 4 to 6

$1\frac{1}{2}$ kg. (*3 lbs.*) lean lamb, either leg or
   shoulder, with most of the fat
   removed, cut in $3\frac{1}{2}$- to 5-cm.
   (*$1\frac{1}{2}$- to 2-inch*) cubes

MARINADE

3 dl. (*$\frac{1}{2}$ pt*) olive oil
5 tablespoons lemon juice
2 garlic cloves, peeled and crushed

1 teaspoon salt
1 teaspoon freshly ground black pepper

OPTIONAL VEGETABLES

Small tomatoes
Green pepper, cut in $3\frac{1}{2}$-cm. (*$1\frac{1}{2}$-inch*)
   cubes
Mushroom caps
Aubergine, unpeeled, cut in $3\frac{1}{2}$-cm.
   (*$1\frac{1}{2}$-inch*) cubes

Small white onions, parboiled for 5 to
   10 minutes, according to size
4 tablespoons olive oil
   Or melted butter

There should be practically no fat on the meat. Trim off as much as possible.

Combine the marinade ingredients in a glass, stainless-steel, or pottery bowl, add the meat, and marinate for from 2 to 48 hours, turning frequently.

Remove the meat cubes from the marinade (there is no need to dry them) and string them on steel or iron skewers, about 35 cm. (14 inches) long, leaving about 5 cm. (2 inches) of space at the handle and tip of the skewers. Push the pieces close together. This gives a juicier, rarer result than spacing out the meat, as it protects the inner surfaces from the heat. If you like to cook vegetables on the same skewer as the meat, alternate the meat cubes with any or all of the optional vegetables. Or you may string the vegetables on separate skewers and cook them alone.

Preheat the grill. Remove the rack from the grill pan. Arrange the skewers across the pan, handles resting on one side, tips on the other (you should be able to get about six skewers on the pan). Brush with oil. Grill with the surface of the meat approximately $7\frac{1}{2}$ cm. (3 inches) from the heat, turning the skewers often and brushing with the marinade, for about 9 minutes for rare, 12 minutes for medium rare. Test by making a small cut in one of the cubes to see if it is done to your taste. Do not overcook. Serve with rice or bulghur pilaf (see page 53).

If you are grilling the vegetables separately, after putting them on skewers brush them liberally with olive oil or melted butter and sprinkle lightly with salt and pepper. Keep brushing them with oil or butter as you turn the skewers – mushrooms are especially likely to dry out if not well lubricated.

Beef Shashlik

Serves 4 to 6

$1\frac{1}{2}$ *kg. (3 lbs.) lean beef sirloin, cut in*
  5-cm. (2-inch) cubes

RED WINE MARINADE

$1\frac{1}{2}$ *dl. ($\frac{1}{4}$ pt) dry red wine*   1 *teaspoon freshly ground black*
$1\frac{1}{2}$ *dl. ($\frac{1}{4}$ pt) olive oil*   *pepper*
2 *tablespoons lemon juice*   1 *tablespoon chopped fresh dill*
3 *garlic cloves, finely chopped*   *Or 1 teaspoon dried dill weed*
1 *teaspoon salt*

OPTIONAL VEGETABLES

Small tomatoes   *Squares of green pepper*
Mushroom caps   2 *tablespoons oil*

Combine the marinade ingredients in a glass or pottery bowl; add the beef cubes and marinate from 4 to 48 hours, turning frequently.

When ready to cook, thread the beef on skewers, as for shish kebab, alternating the cubes, if you wish, with the optional vegetables. Arrange the skewers on the grill pan and brush with oil, lubricating the vegetables well.

Preheat the grill. Grill the shashlik $7\frac{1}{2}$ cm. (3 inches) from the heat, turning and brushing with the marinade, until the meat is crusty on the outside and rare within, about 8 to 9 minutes for rare and 9 to 10 minutes for medium rare. Test by making a small cut with a knife in one of the cubes. Serve the shashlik with rice, bulghur pilaf (see page 53), or potatoes Anna.

Fish and Shellfish

♨ Grilled Fish Fillets

Fresh or frozen fillets are the most universally available form of fish. You can buy fillets of cod, haddock, sole, dabs, salmon (usually the thinner part, from the tail), hake, whiting, brill, plaice and turbot. Or you can buy something anonymous, just called 'fillets', which can mean any variety of fish.

Grilling fish fillets is tricky. They must be watched carefully and, as they are usually very tender when grilled and break easily, great care should be taken when removing them from the grill pan. A firm, long-bladed metal palette knife or long-bladed fish slice which can be slid under the entire length of the fish is best for this purpose. You can also use a hinged grill with two mesh sides and a handle, the kind in which prawns and small fish are grilled over charcoal. There are different types available. The smaller the mesh, the easier it is to handle delicate fish. Another good way to cook fillets, especially the very thin ones that are best grilled on one side only and not turned, is to place a long piece of foil on the grill rack, leaving two overlapping ends to serve as handles. Lightly oil the foil and arrange the fillets on it. Then all you have to do to remove them is to grasp the foil handles firmly and carefully slide the fillets onto a hot platter. If you are grilling fillets on one side only and not turning them, it is also a good idea to preheat the grill pan first in the oven, so the heat will help to cook the underside of the fish.

Frozen fillets are best grilled without thawing and may be turned easily up to the point at which they have thoroughly thawed. Grill them as you would fresh fillets, but double the cooking time.

Serves 4

1 kg. (2 lbs.) fish fillets

BASIC BASTING MIXTURE

$1\frac{1}{2}$ dl. ($\frac{1}{4}$ pt) melted unsalted butter or vegetable oil	*1 teaspoon salt*
	$\frac{1}{4}$ teaspoon freshly ground black pepper
Or a mixture of butter and oil	*2 tablespoons lemon juice*

Combine the basting ingredients in a small pan. Measure the fish at the thickest point. According to the thickness of the fillets, either line the grill pan with foil or arrange a piece of foil over the grill rack (place very thin fillets on the rack to bring them nearer the heat, thicker ones in the pan). In either case, leave an overhang of foil to help in removal. If the fillets are thin, heat the pan and rack while preheating the grill.

When ready to cook, remove the grill pan and rack. Brush the foil well with oil or melted butter, which will prevent the fish from sticking to the foil. Arrange the fillets on the foil in a single layer and brush them well with the basting mixture. Grill with the surface of the fish $7\frac{1}{2}$ cm. (3 inches) from the preheated unit, estimating 10 minutes per $2\frac{1}{2}$ cm. (inch) of maximum thickness (very thin fillets may take only about 3 minutes). If the fillets are thinner at the ends than in the centre, it is best to underestimate a little or the ends will be overcooked. If the fillets are thick enough to turn, 2 to $2\frac{1}{2}$ cm. ($\frac{3}{4}$ to 1 inch), grill for half the estimated time on one side, then turn, using a fish slice; brush well with basting mixture and grill for the remainder of the time on the second side. If too thin to turn, baste during the cooking. The fish is done if the flesh flakes easily when tested with a toothpick or fork.

Transfer the cooked fillets to hot plates or a heated platter and pour over them any of the basting mixture left on the foil.

Sprinkle the fish fillets with chopped parsley. Serve with wedges of lemon and, if you wish, with boiled potatoes dressed with melted butter and chopped parsley and a green vegetable or a green salad. Herbed butter, lemon butter, or mustard sauce (see page 287) are also good with grilled fillets.

Grilled Fish Steaks

Fish steaks can be grilled and basted in the same manner as fish fillets, but the surface of the fish should be 10 cm. (4 inches) from the heat, 13 to 15 cm. (5 to 6 inches) if the steaks are frozen. Estimate 10 minutes of cooking time per measured $2\frac{1}{2}$ cm. (inch) of maximum thickness and twice as long for frozen fish. Thin fish steaks will need no turning, but if they are $2\frac{1}{2}$ cm. (1 inch) or more thick, they should be turned with a broad-bladed fish slice after half the cooking time. When done, slide a fish slice under the steaks and transfer to hot plates or a heated platter. Serve with wedges of lemon and garnish with parsley or watercress sprigs. Allow 1 small steak or half a large steak (about 225 g. or 8 oz. of fish) per serving.

Grilled Marinated Halibut Steaks

Thick steaks of firm-fleshed fish such as halibut can be marinated before cooking, which gives them flavour and prevents them from drying out.

Serves 2 to 4

2 halibut steaks, 2½ cm. (1 inch) thick

MARINADE

6 tablespoons olive oil

2 small garlic cloves, finely chopped

1 teaspoon dried basil

1½ teaspoons salt

1 teaspoon freshly ground black pepper

1 tablespoon lemon juice

Combine the marinade ingredients in a glass or pottery dish large enough to hold the halibut steaks in one layer. Add the steaks and marinate for 2 hours, turning them two or three times in the marinade.

Line a grill pan or rack with foil; oil or butter the foil; put the steaks on the foil and grill 10 cm. (4 inches) from the heat for 5 minutes a side, brushing with the marinade. Serve on hot plates with fried courgettes (see page 206) and boiled potatoes. Garnish with chopped parsley.

♨ Whole Grilled Fish

Whole fish, either small ones or those of fairly good size, are delicious grilled. Have the fish scaled and gutted and the head and tail left on (unless this would make it too large for your grilling facilities).

Rub the skin with oil on both sides and then with coarse salt and freshly ground black pepper. Slash the skin in two or three places with a sharp knife, to prevent its splitting when grilled. You can also salt and pepper the inside of the fish and put a slice or two of lemon inside, or, if you wish, stuff a few sprigs of fresh herbs or a sprinkling of dried herbs inside. Crushed or chopped herbs may be rubbed on the skin with the seasonings. Thyme, rosemary and summer savory are good herbs for fish.

Measure the fish at the thickest point to estimate the cooking time – the rule for any type of fish cookery is to allow 10 minutes per 2½ cm. (inch) of measured thickness. *Place a strip of foil on the grill rack or in the grill pan;*

brush it with oil and arrange the fish on
it to allow for easy turning.

Grill the fish approximately 10 cm.
(4 inches) from the preheated grill,
according to size: large fish 10 to
15 cm. (4 to 6 inches) from the heat;

smaller fish 5 to 10 cm. (2 to 4 inches) away, allowing 10 minutes per measured $2\frac{1}{2}$ cm. (inch) of thickness for total cooking time. Halfway through the cooking turn the fish with a large fish slice, using the foil to help. Be careful not to overcook or let the skin char too much. If the heat seems too intense, lower the pan $2\frac{1}{2}$ to 5 cm. (an inch, or two). Test the flesh with a toothpick or a fork 3 or 4 minutes before the end of the estimated time. If it flakes, it is done.

When done, transfer to a heated platter and serve at once with an appropriate sauce, such as mustard, hollandaise, Béarnaise, or caper sauce.

You may also split the whole fish and grill it, removing the head but leaving the backbone in (which seems to keep the juiciness and flavour). Lay the split fish skin side down on the oiled foil, brush the flesh well with melted butter, and grill $7\frac{1}{2}$ cm. (3 inches) from the heat, allowing 10 minutes per measured $2\frac{1}{2}$ cm. (inch). Do not turn the fish but baste it several times during the cooking with melted butter. Season with salt and pepper.

Estimate about 350 g. ($\frac{3}{4}$ pound) whole or split fish per serving, to allow for the inedible parts.

Grilled Scallops

Serves 4

680 g. ($1\frac{1}{2}$ lbs.) scallops
$1\frac{1}{2}$ dl. ($\frac{1}{4}$ pt) milk or beer
60 to 90 g. (2 to 3 oz.) freshly made
bread crumbs, from unsweetened
white bread

Salt, freshly ground black pepper
125 g. (4 oz.) unsalted butter,
melted
1 tablespoon finely chopped parsley

Rinse the scallops under cold running water. Drain and dry thoroughly on paper towels. Dip the scallops in the milk or beer and then roll them lightly in the crumbs. Arrange in a shallow foil pan and put the pan on top of the grill pan and rack. Sprinkle with salt and freshly ground pepper to taste and spoon 4 tablespoons of the melted butter over them. Grill 10 cm. (4 inches) from the heat just until the crumbs are lightly browned. Do not overcook, or the scallops will be tough. Transfer to a serving dish and sprinkle with the rest of the melted butter and the chopped parsley.

Grilled Prawns

Serves 4 to 6

1 kg. (2 lbs.) large raw prawns
in the shells

MARINADE

3 dl. ($\frac{1}{2}$ pt) olive oil
2 garlic cloves, very finely chopped
3 dl. ($\frac{1}{2}$ pt) dry white wine

1 teaspoon salt
1 teaspoon freshly ground black pepper
4 tablespoons finely chopped parsley

With kitchen scissors, slit the shell of each prawn down the back and remove the black intestinal vein. Break off the shell, leaving the tail shell on. Combine the remaining ingredients in a bowl. Add the prawns to this marinade and let them soak, turning frequently, for 2 to 3 hours.

Preheat the grill. Arrange the prawns in a large aluminium foil pan or on the grill rack and pan, and grill about 10 cm. (4 inches) from the heat for 5 to 7 minutes, according to the thickness of the prawns, turning them halfway through the cooking time and brushing with the marinade as you turn them. If you have a hinged grill (the type used for grilling prawns or small fish over charcoal), you can arrange the prawns in this before putting them on the grill rack; they will be easier to turn.

Vegetables

The vegetables best for grilling are those with plenty of natural moisture, such as mushrooms, tomatoes and aubergine, which is better grilled than sautéed, for in sautéing it tends to soak up too much oil.

Grilled Mushrooms

Use large flat caps for grilling. Break off the stems and reserve them for some other use. Brush the caps well with melted butter or oil and arrange them on a well-oiled grill rack, cap side up. Grill 10 cm. (4 inches) from the grilling unit for 2 to $2\frac{1}{2}$ minutes, then remove the pan from the grill. Turn the mushrooms over and in each cap put either $\frac{1}{4}$ teaspoon butter, a tiny piece of partially cooked bacon, or 1 or 2 drops of olive oil. Sprinkle each one with salt, a grind of pepper, and a tiny dash of Tabasco. Return to the grill and cook another $2\frac{1}{2}$ minutes. Transfer carefully to a serving plate or to slices of toast, so as not to lose the liquid in the caps. These are good with grilled steak, chicken, or liver.

Grilled Tomatoes

Serves 6

6 large, ripe tomatoes
Salt, freshly ground black pepper
2 slices day-old bread

1 garlic clove, peeled
2 tablespoons olive oil
2 tablespoons chopped parsley

Slice about 6 mm. ($\frac{1}{4}$ inch) off the top, stem end of the tomatoes, then give each one a slight squeeze to loosen some of the seeds; sprinkle the top with salt and turn the tomatoes upside down on paper towels to drain. Preheat the grill.

Rub both sides of the bread well with the garlic clove, to impart some garlic flavour to it, then break the bread into small pieces and reduce to fine crumbs in the liquidizer or food processor. Blend the crumbs with the olive oil. When excess liquid has drained from the tomatoes, after about 10 minutes, turn them over and spread the crumb mixture on the tops, then sprinkle the crumbs with a little salt and a grind or two of black pepper.

Arrange the tomatoes on the rack or in a baking dish and grill them about 10 to $12\frac{1}{2}$ cm. (4 to 5 inches) from the heat. Grill until the tomatoes are heated through and the crumbs nicely browned, about 10 minutes. Do not let the crumbs burn. Remove from the grill; sprinkle the tops with chopped parsley and serve with grilled meats.

Grilled Aubergine Slices

Soak 2 or 3 finely chopped or crushed garlic cloves in 1½ dl. (¼ pt) olive oil for 1 hour.

Wash 1 large or 2 small aubergines; trim off the stem end and about 5 mm. (¼ inch) of the rounded end and cut them into 1-cm. (½-inch)-thick slices, leaving the peel on. Allow 1 or 2 slices per serving, according to size.

Preheat the grill. Oil or butter a baking tray large enough to hold the aubergine slices in one layer (or do them in batches, according to how many slices you are grilling). Brush the slices lavishly on one side with the garlic-flavoured oil and sprinkle them with a little salt and freshly ground pepper. Arrange them on the baking tray and put them under the grill with the surfaces about 12½ cm. (5 inches) from the heat. Grill until lightly browned, about 5 minutes, brushing with a little more oil if they seem to be getting dry. When browned, turn them over with a fish slice; oil, salt, and pepper the second side and grill again until browned, about another 5 minutes. They should be just cooked through. Remove them; sprinkle with a little chopped fresh parsley, if desired, and serve with grilled steak or hamburgers. Or sprinkle with chopped fresh mint and serve with grilled lamb. You can also serve hamburgers or thin slices of grilled steak or of roast leg of lamb on top of the aubergine slices, omitting the herb. Serve this combination with spicy tomato sauce, if you like.

VARIATION

About 2 minutes before the aubergine slices are cooked on the second side, sprinkle them lightly with grated Parmesan cheese and replace under the grill until the cheese melts and browns.

Grilled Peppers

Unless you are eating green or red peppers raw in a salad, grilling is the best way to deal with them. Grilling chars the thin, papery skin so that you can easily scrape it off with the back of a knife and slightly cooks the flesh to a flavourful juiciness. You can also char the skin of peppers by impaling them on a fork and turning them over a gas flame, but the grilling method is really easier. Allow 1 to 2 peppers per serving, according to size.

Wash and dry the peppers, leaving them whole, and place them on the rack of the grill pan. Grill under a preheated grill, about 3½ to 5 cm. (1½ to 2 inches) from the heat, until the skin scorches and blackens, turning them from side to side until the entire surface is blistered and charred. This may take as long as 25 minutes. Remove from the grill and when just cool enough to handle, scrape the charred skin from the flesh with the back of a silver or stainless-steel knife – don't tear the flesh. Then remove the stems and seeds. Halve, quarter, or cut into slices. Heat a little finely chopped garlic in olive oil (1 garlic clove to 4 tablespoons oil), and toss – or dress – the hot peppers with the garlic-flavoured oil, salt, freshly ground black pepper to taste and a few drops of lemon juice. Serve with grilled meats and chicken. Or let the peppers cool after skinning and seeding them; cut into strips; marinate in vinaigrette dressing and serve as for vegetables vinaigrette (see page 307), as a first course or part of an hors d'oeuvre selection.

Fruit

Certain fruits can be sprinkled with sugar, dotted with butter and grilled, to make a fast, light and delicious dessert.

Grilled Grapefruit

For each serving, allow half a grapefruit. Remove the seeds with the point of a knife or spoon. Cut round the membranes and between the outer peel and the pulp with a grapefruit knife to loosen the sections. Arrange the halves on a baking tray and sprinkle them lightly with about 2 teaspoons brown sugar. Add about $\frac{1}{2}$ teaspoon Grand Marnier to each one. Dot with 1 teaspoon butter cut into small pieces. Preheat the grill. Grill the grapefruit until the topping is brown and bubbly – about 5 minutes. If you serve these for breakfast, omit the Grand Marnier.

Grilled Peaches

Allow 1 peach per serving. They should be ripe but firm. Put the peaches in a bowl, pour boiling water over them to loosen the skins, and leave for 1 to 2 minutes. Peel off the skins, halve the peaches, and remove the stones. Arrange them on a buttered or oiled baking tray, cut surface up. Sprinkle the cut surfaces lightly with brown sugar and dot with 1 teaspoon butter cut into small pieces. Preheat the grill. Grill the peaches 10 to $12\frac{1}{2}$ cm. (4 to 5 inches) from the heat until the sugar and butter are brown and bubbling – about 5 minutes – and the peaches soft but not mushy.

Grilled Pineapple

Cut the leafy top and the bottom from a whole, ripe pineapple. Slice, skin and all, 1 cm. ($\frac{1}{2}$ inch) thick crosswise. Cut the rind and the eyes from the pineapple slices. Arrange the slices on a buttered baking tray. Sprinkle each slice with 1 teaspoon brown sugar and dot with 1 teaspoon butter cut into smaller pieces.

Preheat the grill. Grill the slices 10 to $12\frac{1}{2}$ cm. (4 to 5 inches) from the heat until the sugar and butter are brown and bubbling – about 5 minutes. Serve 2 or 3 slices per person, according to size.

VARIATION

Flamed Pineapple. Arrange the grilled slices on a heatproof serving dish. Heat 6 tablespoons light or dark rum in a small pan; ignite with a match and pour flaming over the hot pineapple.

Grilled Bananas

Butter a baking tray and arrange whole, peeled ripe bananas on it. Allow 1 per person. Spread each banana with 2 teaspoons soft butter; sprinkle it with 1 teaspoon brown sugar and squeeze 2 or 3 drops of lemon or lime juice over it.

Preheat the grill. Grill the bananas 10 to $12\frac{1}{2}$ cm. (4 to 5 inches) from the heat, about 5 minutes, until the fruit is soft and the butter and sugar browned and bubbly.

Gratinéed Dishes

Oysters Casino

About the only time oysters are grilled is when they are served on the half shell as a hot appetizer, with a topping of herbed butter or buttered bread crumbs. Usually they are grilled and served on beds of rock salt, which prevents the shells from tipping over and keeps them hot.

Serves 4

6 rashers bacon
24 oysters on the half shell
Rock salt
225 g. (8 oz.) unsalted butter, at room temperature
60 g. (2 oz.) finely chopped shallots or spring onions
60 g. (2 oz.) finely chopped parsley
90 g. (3 oz.) finely chopped green pepper
2 tablespoons lemon juice
1 teaspoon salt
½ teaspoon freshly ground black pepper

Arrange the bacon rashers on the grill rack and grill about 5 cm. (2 inches) from the heat until half cooked. Remove; drain on paper towels and cut each piece of bacon into 4 pieces.

Arrange the oysters on beds of rock salt in 4 aluminium foil pie plates. Blend the butter, shallots, parsley, green pepper, lemon juice, salt and pepper well by beating them together with a wooden spatula or blending them in a liquidizer or food processor. Put the herbed butter on top of the oysters and cover with a piece of bacon. Put the pie plates on baking trays and slide them under the hot grill with the oysters about 5 cm. (2 inches) from the heat. Grill just long enough to brown the bacon and heat the oysters through. Put the pie plates on serving plates and serve as a first course.

Lobster au Gratin

Serves 4

90 g. (3 oz.) unsalted butter
350 g. (12 oz.) bite-sized chunks of cooked lobster meat
4 tablespoons cognac
4 tablespoons dry white wine
1½ dl. (¼ pt) double cream
3 dl. (½ pt) hollandaise sauce (see page 292)

Melt the butter in a frying pan; add the lobster and sauté briefly over medium heat, tossing and turning it with a wooden spatula, until just heated through.

Add the cognac to the pan; light with a match and shake the pan until the flames die. Stir in the white wine and the cream and cook for 5 minutes. Do not boil. Pour the lobster mixture into a 2-litre (2-quart) baking dish or casserole and cover it with the hollandaise sauce. Put under a hot grill, 10 to 12½ cm. (4 to 5 inches) from the heat, just long enough for the sauce to brown and glaze. Do not overcook or the hollandaise will separate. Serve immediately, with rice.

Crème Brûlée

Contrary to popular belief and despite the name, this is not a French dish, but an English one. It first appeared in a seventeenth-century English cookbook of Dorset recipes as 'burnt cream'. Then it became one of the great specialities of Trinity College at Cambridge, where, I think, it probably acquired the more elegant name. There are many recipes for this dessert and many ways of preparing it. The baked custard part is easy to make, but the topping of caramelized sugar (that is, sugar melted until it is brown and bubbly) which gives the dessert its name is a tricky process – you must have a good hot grill and watch the sugar carefully to make sure it doesn't burn, moving the dish farther from the heat if it seems about to. If you don't get a completely caramelized topping the first time you make this, don't worry. It takes time and practice.

Serves 8

9 egg yolks	6¼ dl. (22 fl. oz.) double cream
6 tablespoons sugar	2½ cm. (1 in.) piece of vanilla bean
Pinch of salt	100 g. (3½ oz.) sugar

Beat the egg yolks in a bowl with a rotary beater, whisk, or electric hand mixer until thick, then add the sugar and salt and continue beating until thick, creamy and light yellow. Meanwhile, heat the cream with the vanilla bean in a heavy saucepan over medium heat, stirring occasionally to prevent the cream from sticking to the pan and scorching, until it comes to the boiling point (tiny bubbles will appear around the edges and the surface will start to move). Remove from the heat and drizzle the cream slowly into the egg mixture, stirring vigorously with a whisk or a wooden spatula, until thoroughly mixed. Remove and discard the vanilla bean. Put the mixture in a heavy enamelled-iron or stainless-steel pan and cook over medium heat, stirring constantly, for 3 minutes. Do not let the custard get near the simmering point or it will curdle. Strain the custard into a 1-litre (1-quart) heatproof baking dish of enamelled metal, heatproof glass, or porcelain. Preheat the oven to 170°C (325°F, gas mark 3).

Place the baking dish in a roasting tin and set it in the centre of the middle rack of the oven. Pour hot water into the roasting tin to reach to two-thirds the depth of the dish (baking the custard in this hot-water bath prevents it from overcooking or curdling). Bake the custard for 45 to 50 minutes, or until it is set but not overcooked. Cooking time depends on the thickening power of the yolks. Insert a skewer or thin-bladed knife into the custard. It should come out clean. Watch carefully while the custard cooks to see that the water does not boil; if it is getting too hot, add some cold water to the pan.

When the custard is baked, carefully remove the tin from the oven and the dish from the tin. Let the custard cool thoroughly, then cover the top of the dish with plastic wrap and refrigerate until firm and cold (the recipe can be prepared to this point in advance, as much as a day ahead).

A few hours before serving, preheat the grill to its hottest temperature. Set the chilled custard on a large piece of waxed paper and, using a fine sieve, carefully sift 100 g. (3½ oz.) sugar evenly over the surface of the custard, making a layer about 6 mm. (¼ inch) thick. The waxed paper will catch any sugar that spills over and this can be resifted.

Place the dish on the grill rack, so that the sugar is about 2½ cm. (1 inch) from the heat, and grill until the sugar melts, caramelizes, and forms a crust. Watch carefully to see that the sugar does not burn, moving it farther from the heat if it starts to scorch, and turning the dish around, if necessary, so the sugar melts evenly. When the sugar has caramelized, immediately remove it from the oven and chill in the refrigerator for about 2 hours. The caramelized top should be hard and brittle, and sound hollow when tapped with a finger. Crack the crust as you serve the dessert and give each person a bit of crust along with the custard.

Braising

'Braising' is a term that is far too seldom used in our gastronomic vocabulary. You'll hear people say, 'I'm making a pot roast', or 'I'm going to make a stew of this meat', or 'I think I'll simmer this in wine', and what it all comes down to, whether they know it or not, is braising, or cooking with moist heat, probably one of the earliest and certainly one of the most effective ways to tenderize tough cuts of meat, game, or mature birds, wild or domestic.

Incidentally, that phrase 'pot roast' didn't come into the American kitchen lexicon until quite late. Many of the early cookbooks, including those of New England and Michigan, referred to the dish we know as Yankee pot roast as 'beef à la mode', and it's quite likely this was one of the dishes that came across the border into New England, Pennsylvania, and Michigan with the

French Canadians and even travelled as far as the South. And beef à la mode is just another form of braised beef.

Braising has always been extremely popular in Europe, for good reasons: first, because there used to be fewer tender cuts; second, because using less tender cuts was a thrifty way to eat; and third, because Europeans, in the last seventy-five or eighty years, anyway, have eaten more game, per capita, than we in the United States, so they have devised ways of braising game birds and furred game that make them more toothsome, tender and flavourful.

Braising differs from boiling and poaching in one important respect: it is standard practice, in most cases, to brown the meat well before adding the liquid that forms the essential vapours. These aromatic vapours provide the long, moist, tenderizing treatment that produces a well-flavoured and delicious piece of meat. Aiding the liquid are the additions – herbs, vegetables, sometimes calves' or pigs' feet or a piece of pork rind – that give the dish a distinctive taste. Sometimes these are part of a marinade in which the meat is bathed for several hours or days before being cooked until it is thoroughly imbued with the various flavours. Certain braised meats, notably the *daubes* of the south of France, are marinated and then cooked in the marinade without browning, but this is not the general rule.

The choice of liquids for braising is wide, and the results are surprisingly and delightfully diverse. Water, naturally, is one, but it needs excellent seasoning and some enriching and thickening ingredient such as a veal knuckle or calves' or pigs' feet, which add natural gelatin. Stock or broth provides its own flavour, enhancing both taste and texture. Wine or beer may be combined with stock or used alone. Cider, other juices, and tomato purée are occasionally combined with the flavourings to give a different character to the dish.

Braising can range from a simple matter of browning a piece of meat, adding liquid and flavourings, and simmering it in a covered pot, to a more complex and interesting process based on what is known as a *mirepoix*, a mixture of finely cut flavouring vegetables that form a bed on which meat, birds, or occasionally whole fish are braised. The *mirepoix* usually consists of three or more vegetables cut in very fine matchstick strips, or julienne, cooked together in a little fat until just wilted and then arranged on the bottom of the pan in which the braised meat or bird will cook. These vegetables usually include the two great flavouring root vegetables, carrot and onion; in addition, leek, turnip, celery, fennel, or even parsnip might also be tossed in, and they are all wilted down into a lovely soft bed which exudes a delicious aroma and juice that gives great flavour to the meat. Sometimes a little stock, white wine, sherry, or a touch of wine vinegar is added before the meat or bird is braised.

After braising, the *mirepoix* may be puréed to make a sauce for the dish (if it is cooked a long time, it almost becomes a purée automatically) or it may be served around the meat or bird as an accompaniment.

The *mirepoix* is not only used with less tender cuts. Sweetbreads, as tender a morsel as you are likely to find, are often cooked on a *mirepoix* in order to transfer the lovely mixed vegetable flavours to them and to form the basis for a sauce.

Traditionally, the first step in braising is to brown the meat in fat over fairly high heat on top of the stove. It may be dipped in flour, and sometimes in seasonings, before browning, or sprinkled with flour after the initial browning. The flour, which browns too, thickens the liquid and gives a rich deep colour. However, I'm a firm believer in browning meat under the grill. It's just as efficient, really easier, and I happen to prefer the result. Not only does it draw out fat, rather than adding it, but it gives the crusty exterior and flavour conveyed by a word sometimes used in the past for braised dishes – *carbonnade* or *carbonadoes*. Say it, and you get the feeling of meat browned almost to the point of being charred or carbonized. I'm pretty sure that in the old days when meats were spitted and roasted in front of a fire, they were browned this way before being put into a pot and simmered over the coals.

Braising can be applied just as well to small pieces of meat as to large cuts. A beef stew, a navarin of lamb, veal Marengo, all of the many and varied stews and *daubes* and goulashes and ragouts, including *carbonnade Flamande*, that succulent dish of beef and onions simmered in beer, are braised dishes. Even a simple little Irish stew, although the meat isn't browned first but merely cooked with liquid and vegetables, qualifies as braised lamb. Think about it, and you'll see how they all fit the pattern.

I am also of the opinion that any braised dish is best when allowed to cool completely after cooking (which makes it easier to remove the excess fat) and reheated before serving. This somehow seems to mellow the flavours and give the dish a better finish.

The French, the English and, to a certain extent, the Italians have come up with some extraordinarily fine braised game dishes. The French, with their supreme regard for the beauty of a finished product, make a dish of game birds and vegetables called a *chartreuse* (the name, like that of the liqueur, comes from La Grande Chartreuse monastery near Grenoble, where the dish was invented centuries ago by the Carthusian monks, originally as a moulded composition of vegetables alone). The vegetables are precisely cut and arranged in a pattern around the container so that when the dish is unmoulded it is revealed as an exquisite *pièce montée*, a delicate shell of rows of carrots, turnips, French beans, green peas, sometimes truffles, enclosing the game filling. A *chartreuse* is a magnificent example of the chef's art, as beautiful to look upon as to eat.

In a homelier vein, one finds such delicious combinations as the great Alsatian dish of pheasant with sauerkraut, an ideal way to use mature birds, as the sharpness of the sauerkraut, the flavour of the wine and seasonings, and the pungency of the sausage merge into a bouquet of mouthwatering tastes that do something sensational to that tough old bird. In that respect we might define braising as the art of making the tough not only tender but infinitely more desirable and tasty.

It's a delight to discover the miracle of braising. When you wander through the supermarket and go through the meats, especially those less tender cuts that look so good but may taste worse than they look, a picture of the *mirepoix* will come into your mind and you'll know how to transform them into thoroughly delicious and lip-smacking dishes. I'm a great believer in having an idea in my head when I go shopping and then embroidering on that idea as I go through the market and see what looks good that day. This is intelligent shopping. Instead of making up your mind before you shop what you are going to have for dinner, you wait until you get to the market and have the fun of making out your menu there, based on that idea lurking at the back of your mind.

Of course, as I mentioned before, it's not only tough cuts that benefit from braising, so don't limit yourself to the meat counter. Chicken can be braised. So can delicate foods like sweetbreads, fish, even vegetables. However, one must be extremely careful when braising fish not to overcook it, but just to give it that benediction of the *mirepoix* and the wine or other liquid that supplies the necessary moisture, for here the cooking is done more by flavoured steam than by simmering liquid.

If you have never tasted a braised vegetable, you'll find it is a revelation, completely· different from one that is eaten raw, plainly cooked, boiled, sautéed, or fried. Root vegetables like fennel and onions are superb when braised. So are leafy greens like lettuce and endive, or red cabbage. Once you have learned how to braise one vegetable, you can move on to a ragout of different kinds of vegetables, first giving the longer-cooking vegetables time to become tender, then adding to the aromatic, steaming mélange those that are quicker-cooking. You might start with artichoke bottoms, small white onions, and carrots and then add blanched French beans, asparagus, fresh peas. One has to have a good sense of texture and timing but the resulting combination, in which the taste and texture of one vegetable favours another in a most exciting and unusual way, is well worth the care you put into it. This is just one example of how, having learned the basic principles of braising, you can come up with new ideas and combinations of tastes in your own fashion.

♨ Swiss Steak

Swiss steak is a dependable, economical, easily prepared braised beef dish that has been an American favourite for a long time. How, I wonder, did it ever get that name? It's not Swiss, and it's not really steak, in our accepted usage of that word. Be that as it may, it's delicious, simple, and enables you to make a good meal from an inexpensive and less tender cut of meat that needs long, slow cooking to make it tender. The best cuts for this are a piece of chuck steak from the shoulder or a silverside of beef. If you are shopping in the supermarket, where meats are precut and packaged, look at the chuck steak carefully. If it has part of the blade bone in it and a lot of fat, don't buy it. You are better off paying a little more and buying a piece of silverside, which is all meat, rather than a piece of chuck with a lot of waste. The meat should be cut like a steak, from 5 to 6 cm. (2 to 2½ inches) thick, weighing about 1 to 1¼ kg. (2 to 2½ pounds), which will serve 4 persons of good appetite. If you find a chuck steak without too much fat and just a tiny bit of bone, buy it. You can cut around the bone. Meat that has the least bone is the best buy, even though you may pay more for it.

To cook the Swiss steak you'll need a very heavy frying or sauté pan with a tight-fitting cover, about 6 to 7½ cm. (2½ to 3 inches) deep, made of iron, cast aluminium, stainless steel, enamelled cast iron, or pottery. You'll also need kitchen tongs and an old dinner plate or a cleaver or meat pounder, to pound the flour into the steak.

Serves 4

1 to 1¼ kg. (2 to 2½ lbs.) chuck steak or silverside, cut 5 to 6 cm. (2 to 2½ inches) thick

70 g. (2½ oz.) or more of flour

1 teaspoon freshly ground black pepper

2 onions, peeled and sliced

2 garlic cloves, peeled and chopped

3 to 4 tablespoons butter, butter and oil, bacon fat, or beef dripping

1½ teaspoons salt

2½ to 3½ dl. (8 to 12 fl. oz.) red wine

1½ dl. (¼ pt) water, beef stock, tinned beef broth, or beef bouillon

Put the meat on a cutting board and sprinkle the top quite heavily with flour – at least 2 or 3 tablespoons. Then grind ½ teaspoon pepper over it. Using the edge of the dinner plate like the edge of your hand, the back of a cleaver, or a meat pounder, pound the flour into the meat until a good deal of the flour is absorbed, working first along the width of the meat and then the length. Keep pounding so that the plate makes pressure marks in the meat and the flour holds in there. When you have done one side, dust off the excess flour and repeat the flour-and-pepper process on the other side. The steak should absorb 4 to 5 tablespoons of flour, which will give body to the sauce as it cooks and thicken it – this is the technique that makes it Swiss steak.

After the flour is pounded in, let the meat rest for 10 minutes. Slice the onions and chop the garlic during this time.

Melt the fat in the pan over medium-high heat (190°C or 375°F, if you have a burner with a thermostat) until it is bubbling and sizzling, but not smoking. Dip the meat in the remaining flour and place it in the hot fat. Let it bubble and sizzle over medium-high heat for 4 to 5 minutes, until deliciously brown on the underside, being careful not to let the flour burn. Just as you are about to turn the steak, add the onions and garlic to the pan. Turn the steak, brown it on the other side, and let the onions and garlic take on colour. Sprinkle with the salt, remove the pan from the heat, and add the red wine and water, stock, or bouillon – or use half water and half stock. The wine will give the sauce a good colour and richness, and when blended with the broth and water the flavour is not too intense. You should add just enough liquid to come halfway up the steak – you don't want to inundate it, as you will get some liquid from the onions as they cook down.

Return pan to the heat, reduce to a simmer, cover tightly, and simmer for $1\frac{1}{2}$ hours. Test for doneness with a fork or the point of a sharp knife and turn the steak. If it is tender enough (the fork or knife should penetrate the meat easily), taste the sauce to see if it needs more salt and pepper or more chopped garlic. If it still needs cooking, cover again and continue simmering until tender. You don't want the meat to be so tender that it loses all its texture, but it should be tender enough to cut easily.

When done, transfer the steak to a hot platter and, using a slotted spoon to drain off the liquid, spoon the onions over it. Then see if there is a lot of fat on the top of the sauce – there shouldn't be, unless your beef was too fat. To remove excess fat, let the sauce boil up for a minute, then remove it from the heat and skim off the fat on the surface.

Pour the sauce over the steak, putting any surplus in a small bowl or gravy boat to be served separately, and sprinkle with some chopped parsley. Plain boiled potatoes or boiled buttered noodles go well with this, and a salad. Drink the same kind of red wine you used in cooking and follow with cheese and fruit.

Veal

Veal, a rather dry meat, benefits immeasurably from the slow, moist braising process and the flavourings that enhance and accentuate its delicate taste and texture. If you must depend on veal that is less than perfect, braising is probably the best way to deal with it.

☺ Braised Shoulder (or Leg) of Veal

This is a classic and more complex form of braising than that used for Swiss steak. First you make a *mirepoix*, which acts as a bed for the meat and adds flavour, and a veal stock for the sauce (if you have veal stock in the freezer, you can use that), so there are several steps in the preparation.

For our meat we have chosen a boned, rolled, and tied shoulder of veal. You may use either the boned shoulder or the more expensive boned leg, and have it rolled and tied for you by the butcher who does the boning.

The first step is to make the veal stock. This can be done the morning of the day you cook the veal, or the day before and refrigerated, or weeks before and stored in the freezer. Veal stock is always good to have on hand, so even though this is not the more elaborate stock you would make for soup, just a liquid for the sauce, it pays to make a larger quantity than you need and freeze what is left.

The actual braising may be done, for the most part, in the morning and finished later in the day, which enables you to cool the broth and skim off all the fat before finishing the dish. It's a time-consuming process, but worth it because the results are satisfactory in every way.

For cooking, you will need a deep 6-litre (5-quart) pot to make the stock and a large, heavy 6- or 8-litre (5- or 7-quart) braising pan for cooking the *mirepoix* and the veal. Any suitably heavy material such as cast aluminium, enamelled cast iron, stainless steel, or lined copper will do. It should have a tight-fitting cover and be large enough to hold the meat comfortably.

Serves 6 to 8

THE VEAL BROTH

1 to 1¼ kg. (2 to 2½ lbs.) bones from the veal, plus 1 veal knuckle	1 stick of celery
	1 sprig of parsley
2 l. (1¾ qts) water	Salt
1 onion, stuck with 2 cloves	

Put the veal bones, knuckle, and water in the pot and add the onion, celery and parsley. Bring to a boil. Skim off any scum that rises to the surface. Reduce the heat to low, cover, and cook at a faint boil for 1½ hours. Taste the stock and add as much salt as you feel it needs. Cook for a further 45 to 60 minutes, then strain the stock through a wire sieve into a large bowl and allow to cool. When cool, remove the fat from the top. If done ahead, store the stock in a screw-top jar or a covered bowl and refrigerate or freeze, depending on when you are going to use it. You will have about 1½ litres (2½ pints) of which you will need 3½ dl. (12 fl. oz.) for the sauce.

THE MIREPOIX

2 large onions, peeled

2 large carrots, peeled

1 small white turnip, peeled

2 or 3 sticks of celery

Several sprigs of parsley

3 large or 6 small garlic cloves, peeled

4 tablespoons groundnut oil

    Or 2 tablespoons groundnut oil and

    30 g. (1 oz.) butter

2 tablespoons wine vinegar

1 tablespoon salt

Slice the onions and cut the slices in half or thirds. The other vegetables should be cut into thin julienne, or pieces of about matchstick size. Slice the carrots and cut into small strips, then cut the strips in half. Slice the turnip and cut into small strips. Cut the celery into small strips and then into shorter pieces. Leave the parsley sprigs and garlic whole.

Heat the oil, or oil and butter, in the braising pan, add the vegetables, and let them wilt down in the fat. Add the wine vinegar – this gives a slight acidity that offsets the sweetness of the onions, carrots and turnip. Add the salt. Cover the pan and simmer for about 30 minutes. The vegetables will throw off a good deal of highly flavourful liquid, which will add to the richness of the sauce and the finished dish.

THE MEAT AND SAUCE

2 kg. (4 lbs.) of boned, rolled, and tied
    shoulder of veal

Salt, freshly ground black pepper

1½ teaspoons thyme

1 bay leaf

45 to 90 g. (1½ to 3 oz.) butter

3 tablespoons flour

3½ dl. (12 fl. oz.) veal stock

1 tablespoon glace de viande
    (optional; see page 32)

There are two ways to brown meat for braising. One is to brown it carefully on all sides in a pan in a mixture of butter and oil. The other, and to me the more satisfactory, way is to brown it under a preheated grill, turning it from one side to another as it browns so that it colours evenly. This is a less fatty way of browning meat, especially good if you are watching calories.

Arrange the meat on the grill rack and place it about 10 cm. (4 inches) from the heat. Watch very carefully, turning it as it colours, until it achieves a nice rich brownness. Salt the meat lightly as it browns, using 2 teaspoons of salt – I find that if you add salt at this point it cooks into the meat and seasons it better.

When the meat is browned, you may continue the braising process, or if you wish, you can leave it until the next day. In this case, let the meat cool before wrapping it in foil and refrigerating it.

To continue the braising, preheat the oven to 230°C (450°F, gas mark 8). Draw the chopped cooked vegetables (the *mirepoix*) together into the centre of the braising pan to form a bed for the veal. You want a little liquid so the veal will cook with moist heat, but not too much. If the *mirepoix* has given off so much liquid that it covers the vegetables, remove some with a spoon and reserve it to use in the sauce.

Sprinkle the vegetables with 1 teaspoon of thyme and add the bay leaf. Put the veal on the bed of vegetables and sprinkle the meat with the remaining thyme.

The veal may be braised in a covered pan on top of the range at a low simmer, or in the oven. I prefer to braise in the oven, where the meat is surrounded by the aromatic steam from the pan. Lay a piece of buttered foil lightly across the top of the braising pan; place the pan in the 230°C oven and cook for 30 to 35 minutes. Then reduce the heat to 180°C (350°F, gas mark 4), and continue to cook, allowing approximately 20 minutes per $\frac{1}{2}$ kg. or pound from the time the meat goes into the oven. The internal temperature of the meat, when tested with a meat thermometer, should be 71°C to 74°C (160°F to 165°F) depending on how pink you like your veal. I feel that if it is slightly pink in the centre, it is juicier and more pleasing to the palate than if it is cooked completely all through, but this is a matter of personal taste.

When the veal is cooked, remove it to a warm platter and keep it warm while you make the sauce. Drain the liquid from the braising pan through a sieve into a bowl and skim off any fat. Reserve the *mirepoix* vegetables and keep them warm.

Melt 45 g. (1$\frac{1}{2}$ oz.) of the butter in a heavy saucepan, add the flour, stirring in well, and cook over medium heat, stirring until the mixture is golden and bubbling. Add the liquid from the braising pan and the 3$\frac{1}{2}$ dl. (12 fl. oz.) of veal stock and stir constantly until the sauce comes to a boil and thickens. Reduce the heat, season to taste with salt and pepper and, if you have *glace de viande* (see page 32), add 1 tablespoon to the sauce to give it a beautiful richness and glaze. Otherwise, as the sauce simmers, stir in the remaining butter, one third at a time.

Cut the strings and remove them from the veal. Arrange the veal on a hot serving platter and surround with some of the *mirepoix* vegetables. You may garnish the platter with watercress or parsley, putting it at one end so it does not interfere with the carving. Serve the sauce separately in a bowl.

Buttered noodles, or new potatoes sprinkled with parsley and chives or chopped fresh mint and butter are excellent with the veal, and you may have cooked French beans, tossed in butter, or a salad.

Stuffed Breast of Veal

Hot or cold, a stuffed breast of veal is both spectacular and as simple as any dish can be. This is the least expensive cut of veal and the braising process makes it very tender and flavourful. A good butcher who has been trained to bone meat properly will be able to bone the breast and cut a pocket in it for the stuffing, so that when stuffed it may be formed into a good shape that will slice easily. If this is not possible, buy the breast unboned and merely have the pocket cut in it – you can remove the little rib bones after the meat is cooked by breaking them away from the joints and pulling them free from the flesh. In either case, you will need some bones for the braising – either those removed from the breast or a veal knuckle or some veal neck bones.

Serves 6

1 3-kg. (6-lb.) breast of veal (unboned
  weight), boned and with a pocket
  cut in it*

THE STUFFING

45 g. (1½ oz.) butter
1½ dl. (¼ pt) olive oil
3 large onions, peeled and finely chopped
350 g. (¾ lb.) fairly lean sausage meat
  (if unavailable substitute ground pork
  with 25 per cent fat)
225 g. (½ lb.) ham, finely chopped

1 tinned truffle, finely chopped (optional)
60 g. (2 oz.) freshly made bread crumbs
1 teaspoon dried thyme
Salt, freshly ground black pepper
⅛ teaspoon ground cloves
¼ teaspoon ground or grated nutmeg
2 eggs, slightly beaten

THE BRAISING MIXTURE AND SAUCE

Mirepoix of 1 onion, 1 carrot, 2 garlic
  cloves, 4 sprigs of parsley, all
  finely cut
1 bay leaf
Bones from veal breast or 1 veal knuckle
3½ dl. (12 fl. oz.) veal stock, chicken
  stock, or white wine
450 g. (1 lb.) tomatoes, peeled, seeded,
  and finely chopped

125 g. (4 oz.) pitted, soft black olives
90 g. (3 oz.) pine nuts
4 tablespoons chopped parsley

* If the breast of veal you buy has not been boned, *cut away the flesh around each rib with a sharp knife*, then snap the rib off, leaving the main neck intact. Remove the bone to which the ribs were attached. *Cut a deep pocket, almost to the edge of the meat, for the stuffing.*

Prepare the stuffing for the breast. Heat the butter and 3 tablespoons of oil in a frying pan, add the onions, and sauté over medium heat until just limp. Add the sausage meat or ground pork, ham, truffle and 1 tablespoon of the liquid from the tin, bread crumbs, thyme, 1½ teaspoons salt, 1 teaspoon pepper, cloves and nutmeg. Blend the stuffing well, remove from the heat, and mix in the eggs. *Stuff the pocket in the breast,* moulding with your hands so that it is fairly even in shape.

Secure the stuffing by sewing up the pocket with a trussing needle and fine string or by closing the opening with skewers or clamps.

Heat the remaining oil in a heavy frying pan and brown the stuffed breast on both sides over medium-high heat. Butter the bottom of a braising pan large enough to take the breast and arrange in it the *mirepoix* of cut vegetables, the bay leaf and the veal bones. Lay the breast on this bed and add the stock or wine and the tomatoes. Cover the pan and braise the meat in a 170°C (325°F, gas mark 3) oven for 2 to 3 hours, or until a meat thermometer inserted into the veal registers 77°C (170°F). If the liquid reduces too much (it should be just sufficient to cover the vegetables), add more stock or wine.

Remove the cooked meat to a hot platter. Purée the pan juices and vegetables by putting them through a food mill or by pushing them through a sieve with a wooden spoon, pressing the vegetables well. Reheat the purée in a saucepan with the olives, pine nuts, and parsley, bringing the sauce to a boil and then simmering it for 5 minutes. Serve the breast of veal, sliced about 2 cm. (¾ inch) thick, with the sauce and with tiny new potatoes browned in butter and a purée of French beans. Drink a Beaujolais.

To serve the stuffed breast cold, slice and serve with a spinach salad dressed with olive oil, lemon juice and a touch of soy sauce, with finely chopped onion, a little chopped garlic, and a handful of pine nuts added just before it is tossed. Or you might vary this and have the cold meat with a dish of hot macaroni and the reheated sauce from the veal, plus a salad of lettuce and raw mushrooms.

Veal Chops Niçoise

Veal chops are extraordinarily good when braised with the proper seasonings.
Thickly cut loin chops of the choicest veal are the best to buy.

Serves 6
THE TOMATO SAUCE

6 dl. (1 pt) tinned Italian plum
  tomatoes
3 garlic cloves, peeled
1 small onion, finely chopped
1 teaspoon salt
½ teaspoon freshly ground black pepper

45 g. (1½ oz.) butter
1 or 2 leaves fresh basil
  Or ½ teaspoon dried basil
2 tablespoons tomato paste

THE BRAISED CHOPS

6 veal loin chops, cut 5 cm. (2 inches)
  thick
4 tablespoons flour
6 tablespoons olive oil
Salt, freshly ground black pepper
3 garlic cloves, peeled and finely
  chopped

36 stoned whole, soft black olives
  (preferably French)
2 tablespoons fresh basil leaves, cut
  into strips
  Or 1 teaspoon dried basil, ground
1 tablespoon freshly chopped parsley
  (optional)

First make the sauce. Put the tomatoes, garlic, onion, salt, pepper, butter and
basil in a saucepan and cook down over medium heat until the mixture is
reduced by one-third. Add the tomato paste and cook for 5 minutes, or until
the sauce is reduced to about 3 dl. (½ pt). Taste, and correct the seasoning.

Sprinkle both sides of the chops lightly with flour, shaking off excess. Heat
the oil in a frying or sauté pan and sear the chops quickly on both sides over
medium-high heat, salting and peppering them as they cook, until delicately
browned. Add the tomato sauce and garlic, cover, and simmer for about
20 to 40 minutes (depending on the age of the veal) or until tender but not
overcooked; the point of a knife should penetrate easily. Add the stoned olives
and basil and heat through. Taste, and correct seasoning.

Arrange the chops and sauce on a mound of saffron rice and garnish, if
desired, with finely chopped parsley. Drink a brisk white wine from Provence,
well chilled.

Veal Birds Western Style

Veal birds are another very good way of braising veal. For this you need slices
of veal cut from the leg and pounded very thin. If the meat you buy is not thin
enough, *put it between two pieces of waxed paper and flatten with a meat pounder.*

meat pounder

Serves 4 to 8

8 slices of veal cut from the leg, about
 12½ cm. (5 inches) square, pounded
 1 cm. (⅜ inch) thick
150 g. (5 oz.) butter
150 g. (5 oz.) finely chopped onion
45 g. (1½ oz.) finely chopped
 mushrooms
2 garlic cloves, peeled and finely chopped
Salt, freshly ground black pepper
90 g. (3 oz.) fresh bread crumbs
1½ tablespoons fresh dill, finely cut
 Or 1½ teaspoons dried dill weed

1½ dl. (¼ pt) white wine
16 thin strips of dill pickle
Melted butter (about 3 tablespoons)
2 tablespoons oil
4½ dl. (¾ pt) chicken or veal broth
Beurre manié *for thickening (see
 page 283)*
2 dl. (⅓ pt) soured cream
Chopped fresh dill or dried dill weed,
 chopped parsley

For the stuffing, melt half the butter in a frying pan, add the onion, and sauté until just limp. Blend in the mushrooms, garlic, 1 teaspoon salt, ½ teaspoon pepper, bread crumbs, fresh or dried dill and about 1½ dl. (¼ pt) white wine, or just enough to moisten the mixture. Spread some of the filling on each slice of veal and put 2 strips of dill pickle in the centre. Sprinkle a little melted butter on the filling and roll the veal slices up. Tie them securely at each end and in the centre with fine string.

Heat the remaining butter and the oil in a deep, heavy frying or sauté pan. Lightly brown the veal birds on all sides over medium-high heat, salting and peppering them as you turn them. Add the broth and simmer the birds, covered, for about 1 hour, or until just tender but not overcooked or stringy. Transfer the birds to a hot platter and keep warm while making the sauce.

Thicken the pan juices with small balls of *beurre manié*, following the method given on page 283, simmering the sauce for 3 or 4 minutes. Keeping the heat medium low, mix in the soured cream, adding it in the centre and stirring with a wire whisk or wooden spoon to incorporate it into the sauce. Let it just heat through, being careful not to let it boil or the soured cream will separate. Add a little more dill (about 1 tablespoon chopped fresh or 1 teaspoon dried dill weed) and about 2 teaspoons chopped parsley.

To serve, arrange the birds on a platter around a mound of freshly cooked fluffy rice, spoon some of the sauce over them, and serve the rest separately in a bowl. Braised leeks go well with the birds. Drink a brisk white wine such as Pouilly-Fumé.

Beef

The beef cuts generally chosen for braising are the topside, top sirloin, rump, silverside, brisket and chuck. Thin slices from the round, cut into squares, are often stuffed, rolled, and braised. Thick or thin round and chuck steaks also benefit from the liquids and additions employed in the braising process. The Swiss steak on page 137 is a perfect example. As all beef cuts vary in texture and degree of tenderness, the cooking times tend to differ. Testing, by inserting the point of a small sharp knife into the meat after it has cooked for a certain amount of time to see how much resistance it encounters, is really the only way to determine when the meat is done.

Brisket is a popular cut for braising. It has a rich, full flavour and, with its even layers of fat and lean, slices well and looks appetizing whether served hot or cold. The famous French dish *boeuf à la mode* can be made with brisket, which in the following recipe is first marinated to give it additional flavour and to tenderize the meat.

♔ Boeuf à la Mode
(French-Style Pot Roast)

Serves 6

3-kg. (6-lb.) brisket of beef	1 teaspoon dried thyme
2 pigs' feet (preferably long cut; see page 383), split lengthwise	4 tablespoons cognac
	Red wine to cover
Salt, ground nutmeg, freshly ground black pepper	4 tablespoons rendered beef fat (see page 78)
1 large onion, peeled and studded with 3 cloves	60 g. (2 oz.) butter
	3 to 4 tablespoons tomato paste
1 onion, peeled and sliced	1 stick of celery
1 large carrot, peeled and sliced	1 leek, trimmed and well washed
3 garlic cloves, peeled	2 sprigs of parsley

ACCOMPANIMENTS

12 to 18 small white onions, peeled,
* with a cross cut in stem end*
30 g. (1 oz.) butter
6 leeks, trimmed and well washed

6 whole carrots, scraped
12 small potatoes
1 tablespoon chopped parsley

When you buy the beef, have a good deal of the fat cut away, and ask the butcher to split the pigs' feet for you.

Arrange the brisket and pigs' feet in a large earthenware, enamelled, or glass bowl (don't use metal containers for a marinade containing wine). Salt the brisket well and sprinkle it lightly with nutmeg and freshly ground black pepper. Add the clove-studded onion and sprinkle the sliced onion and carrot over the meat. Add 2 garlic cloves, the thyme, a heaped teaspoon of freshly ground black pepper, the cognac, and enough red wine to barely cover the meat. Let the meat stand in the marinade for 6 to 12 hours.

When you are ready to cook the meat, heat the beef fat and butter in a heavy braising pan. Remove the brisket from the marinade and dry well with paper towels. Brown the meat on all sides in the hot fat over medium-high heat until it is evenly coloured. Remove the sliced carrot and onion from the marinade with a slotted spoon and cook them briefly with the beef. Add the pigs' feet, cover the pan, reduce the heat, and simmer for at least 30 minutes. Strain the marinade and add to the beef with the remaining garlic clove, the tomato paste, celery, leek and parsley. Bring to a boil, then cover and cook in a preheated 150°C (300°F, gas mark 2) oven for 2 hours.

Remove the meat from the pan and add the small onions, which have been briskly cooked and tossed in the butter until lightly browned, the leeks and the carrots. Return the beef to the pan, cover, and continue to cook in the oven until it is just tender – not grainy and overdone. Transfer the meat to a hot platter and keep warm. If the vegetables are not quite done, continue to cook them in the oven until they are. Meanwhile, boil the potatoes in salted water to cover, either peeled or in their jackets, until done.

Pour off the sauce from the pan, strain it, and skim off the fat. Arrange the vegetables on the platter around the meat. Sprinkle the meat with the chopped parsley. Serve the skimmed sauce separately, in a sauceboat. Serve the dish at once.

Leftover cold beef makes a perfectly splendid salad with the addition of diced onion, celery, boiled potatoes, hard-boiled eggs, strips of green pepper and a vinaigrette sauce (see page 304).

Estouffat de Noël
(Braised Beef with Wine and Brandy)

One of the most famous dishes of Gascony, in France, is the *estouffat*, or *estouffade*, a dish of braised beef cooked in a covered earthenware casserole, always with Armagnac, the brandy of the region. This *estouffat de Noël* is a traditional Christmas Eve dish, to which the Armagnac and the gelatin content of the pork rind give a special rich, luscious body and taste. If you can't get pork rind, substitute a pig's foot, split.

Serves 8 to 10

½-kg. (1-lb.) piece of pork rind or	Grated nutmeg
1 pig's foot, split lengthwise	3-kg. (6-lb.) piece topside of beef, neatly
8 shallots, peeled and quartered	tied to keep its shape
3 or 4 onions, peeled and quartered	Salt, freshly ground black pepper
1 carrot, peeled and cut into long strips	3½ dl. (12 fl. oz.) Armagnac
1 garlic clove	4½ dl. (¾ pt) good full-bodied red wine,
1 teaspoon dried thyme	such as a Rhône

Preheat the oven to 180°C (350°F, gas mark 4).

Put the pork rind or pig's foot on the bottom of an 8-litre (6½-quart) casserole or pot. On this, make a bed of the vegetables, add the garlic, thyme and a sprinkling of grated nutmeg. Salt the beef lightly. Make an indentation in the centre of the vegetables and in it lay the beef. Add the Armagnac and red wine. Cover the pot with a piece of aluminium foil and then the lid.

Put in the oven and cook for 35 minutes, then reduce the heat to 150°C (300°F, gas mark 2) and cook for 1 hour. Then reduce the heat to 130°C (250°F, gas mark ½) and cook for at least 2, preferably 3, hours or more (long, slow cooking is essential to the success of this dish). Or you may simmer the *estouffat* on top of the stove for 1½ hours, then finish the cooking in a 130°C oven.

Remove the casserole or pot from the oven about an hour before serving to let the fat settle on top. Skim off the fat and reheat the beef in the sauce. Or you can make the *estouffat* the day before and let it cool overnight, then remove the fat and reheat the meat before serving – to my mind the dish tastes better when made ahead and allowed to cool completely. Before serving, taste the sauce and correct the seasoning. Serve the *estouffat* with either boiled potatoes or macaroni to soak up the lovely sauce. Cut up the pork rind or the meat from the pig's foot and serve it with the beef. Drink the same kind of red wine you used for cooking.

Viennese Goulash

The principal flavouring for a Hungarian goulash is paprika, which should also be Hungarian and of the best quality. Hungarian paprika has much more flavour than the standard supermarket type and is well worth buying for any dish requiring paprika. You'll find it in speciality shops that sell spices and herbs. The difference in this recipe, which is a Viennese variation, is the paste of caraway seeds, garlic and lemon zest stirred in for the final cooking time, which gives a fresh and spicy flavour.

Serves 6

60 g. (2 oz.) butter	Salt, freshly ground black pepper
2 tablespoons salad oil	1 teaspoon thyme
6 medium onions, peeled and thinly sliced	1½ dl. (¼ pt) tomato purée
30 g. (1 oz.) Hungarian paprika	4 tablespoons flour
4 tablespoons white wine or wine vinegar	4½ dl. (¾ pt) beef broth
1½ kg. (3 lbs.) beef rump or chuck, cut into 5-cm. (2-inch) cubes	1 tablespoon caraway seeds
	Zest of 1 lemon, finely chopped
	2 garlic cloves, peeled

Heat the butter and oil in a large sauté pan or a 6-litre (5-quart) braising pan. Add the onions and sauté until golden over medium heat, stirring them so they do not stick to the pan or brown. Mix in the paprika and wine or vinegar. Cook 4 minutes. (Spices such as paprika and curry powder should always be cooked a little in fat, to bring out the flavour and prevent the raw taste that occurs when they are not cooked first.) Push the onions to the side of the pan, add the beef cubes, a few at a time, and sear them on all sides. Don't overcrowd the cubes or they will reduce the heat too much and not brown properly. Remove them to a plate as browned.

When all the beef is browned, replace it in the pan, season to taste with salt and pepper, add the thyme and tomato purée, and simmer over medium-low heat until the liquid is reduced to a glaze. Sprinkle the beef with the flour, and toss with a spatula until the flour is well coloured. Add the beef broth (there should be just enough to cover the meat) and simmer, covered, until the beef is tender when pierced with the point of a knife – about 2 hours.

Meanwhile, grind the caraway seeds, the finely chopped lemon zest (the yellow part of the rind, without any pith) and the garlic to a paste with a mortar and pestle. When the beef is cooked, stir this paste into the goulash and cook a further 10 minutes to blend the flavours. Serve with noodles.

Jeanne Owen's Chili con Carne

American south-western chili con carne certainly qualifies as a braised beef dish, for it is, by definition, a stew. This recipe, while not for purists, is rather different and utterly delicious. It improves with ageing, so make it the day before you wish to serve it, and reheat.

Serves 6

5 tablespoons olive oil
1½ kg. (3 lbs.) lean round steak, cut into 2½-cm. (1-inch) cubes
2 onions, peeled and finely chopped
3 garlic cloves, peeled and finely chopped
Salt
1 l. (1¾ pts) boiling water

1 teaspoon caraway seeds
2 teaspoons sesame seeds
½ teaspoon oregano
2 to 4 tablespoons chili powder, or to taste
125 g. (4 oz.) pitted green olives
2 450-g. (1-lb.) tins kidney beans, drained and well rinsed

Heat the oil in a large sauté pan or 6-litre (5-quart) braising pan, add the beef, a few cubes at a time so the pan is not too crowded, and sauté over brisk heat, turning to brown on all sides. Add the chopped onions and sauté over medium heat for 2 or 3 minutes, then add the garlic. Season with salt to taste, add the boiling water, the caraway and sesame seeds, and the oregano. Reduce heat, cover, and simmer for 1 hour.

Gradually stir in the chili powder, testing frequently until you achieve the degree of flavour and hotness that suits your palate. Then add the olives, cover, and simmer for another hour. Taste, and correct the seasoning, then mix in the kidney beans and heat through. Toasted French bread, tortillas, or corn bread go well with this, and a crisp green salad. Beer is the only drink that can stand up to the spiciness of the chili.

Oxtail Ragout

Oxtail is a part of the animal that many people ignore because they don't know how to cook it. Braised oxtails make a delicious and eminently simple meal. This is another dish that tastes better if made a day or two in advance, chilled, the fat completely removed, and then reheated, after the flavours have had a chance to blend and mellow. I also like to brown the oxtails under the grill, which draws out their excess fat and makes them beautifully brown and crispy.

Serves 6

2½ or 3 kg. (5 or 6 lbs.) of oxtails,
  cut into joints for serving
Salt, freshly ground black pepper
3 tablespoons oil
45 g. (1½ oz.) unsalted butter or
  beef drippings
3 large onions, peeled and thinly sliced
4 carrots, scraped and halved

2 white turnips, peeled and sliced
4 whole garlic cloves, peeled
Bouquet garni (see page 373)
1¼ l. (1 qt) beef broth
1½ dl. (¼ pt) madeira
Beurre manié (see page 283;
  optional)
2 tablespoons chopped parsley

Put the pieces of oxtail on the grill rack and pan and grill until nicely coloured and crispy around the edges, about 15 minutes, salting and peppering them as they brown, and turning them once.

In a frying pan, heat the oil and butter or beef drippings left in the grill pan, add the onions, and sauté over medium heat until golden and limp. With a slotted spoon, transfer the onions to an 8-litre (7-quart) braising pan, add the carrots to the frying pan, and sauté them lightly for 3 minutes. Add these, the turnips, and the garlic cloves to the braising pan, lay the oxtails on top, and add the bouquet garni. Add the beef broth (there should be just enough to barely cover the oxtails), bring to a boil over high heat, skim off the scum that rises to the surface, and continue to boil and skim for 5 minutes. Reduce the heat, cover, and simmer for 3 to 3½ hours, adding more liquid if it reduces too much (it should just cover the oxtails). Test the meat for tenderness with the point of a small sharp knife – it should penetrate the meat easily. Add the madeira and cook, covered, for 10 minutes. Taste the broth for seasoning, adding salt, pepper and a touch of thyme if it needs more herb flavour. Let the ragout cool and skim off the fat, then reheat before serving. Or chill it in the refrigerator for a day or two before serving.

Reheat the ragout, and when heated through remove the oxtails and vegetables to a hot platter. Discard the bouquet garni and let the broth cook down over high heat for 2 or 3 minutes.

I prefer the broth the way it is, but you can thicken it, if you wish, with small balls of *beurre manié* (see page 283), dropping them into the broth a few at a time and simmering until the sauce is thickened as you wish. Pour broth or sauce over the meat and sprinkle with the parsley. Serve with boiled potatoes, rice, or buttered noodles. A good green salad is the best accompaniment to this hearty dish, which can take a robust red wine, a Bordeaux or Rhône.

Lamb
....

The flavour of good lamb comes through the braising process admirably. Just about every part of the animal – leg, shoulder, breast, shanks and chops – takes well to the various styles of slow cooking that meld meat and seasonings into a savoury succulent dish.

Probably the most basic braised lamb dish, which manages to be both simple and elegant, is Irish stew. Recipes for Irish stew can be found in Escoffier, Montagné, and practically every lexicon of good cooking – and they differ a great deal. Good Irish stew is not a thin soup with meat and vegetables floating in it, but a hearty dish of meat, potatoes and onions cooked slowly until rather thick in texture. In the purest version, it contains neither carrots nor turnips.

♟ Irish Stew

Serves 6

$1\frac{1}{2}$ kg. (3 lbs.) lamb cutlets, best end
   of neck or middle neck
Butter (to grease the casserole)
5 or 6 medium potatoes, peeled and sliced
3 teaspoons chopped parsley, mixed
   with $1\frac{1}{2}$ teaspoons dried thyme

3 large onions, peeled and sliced
Salt, freshly ground black pepper
$4\frac{1}{2}$ dl. ($\frac{3}{4}$ pt) water
2 to 3 tablespoons chopped parsley

Trim the fat from the cutlets, leaving the meat on the bones. Butter a 2- to $2\frac{1}{2}$-litre ($1\frac{1}{2}$- to 2-quart) casserole. Preheat the oven to 150°C (300°F, gas mark 2).

Arrange a layer of one-third of the potatoes in the bottom of the casserole and cover with a layer of cutlets topped with a third of the parsley-thyme mixture. Add a layer of half the onions, then a third more potatoes, the remaining cutlets, herbs, remaining onions, and finally, the remaining potatoes and herbs. Season well with salt and pepper and add the water. Cover and cook the stew in the preheated oven for 2 to $2\frac{1}{2}$ hours, or until the meat is tender and the potatoes and onions soft. Serve in soup plates with a sprinkling of parsley on top, and drink beer with it.

Irish stew always benefits from being cooked the day before and allowed to cool thoroughly. Skim off any fat and reheat the stew.

Braised Shoulder of Lamb
with Ratatouille

Serves 6

2- to 2-½ kg. (4- to 5-lb.) shoulder of
  lamb, boned and tied
6 garlic cloves, peeled and cut into
  slivers
2 or 3 anchovy fillets, cut into small
  pieces
Salt, freshly ground black pepper
Olive oil
1 teaspoon dried basil
  Or 2 tablespoons chopped fresh basil
6 dl. (1 pt) tinned Italian plum
  tomatoes

2 medium onions, thinly sliced
4 small courgettes, trimmed and cut
  into 1-cm. (½-inch) slices
1 green pepper, halved, seeded, and
  cut into thin strips
1 medium aubergine, peeled and
  diced
90 g. (3 oz.) pitted, soft black olives
6 tablespoons chopped parsley

Make small incisions in the meat with the point of a small sharp knife and
insert half the slivered garlic (reserve the rest for later) and the anchovy
pieces in the incisions. Rub the meat well with salt, pepper, and olive oil and
put it on a rack in a roasting tin. Roast for 30 minutes in a 200°C (400°F, gas
mark 6) oven.

Meanwhile, make the ratatouille. In an 8-litre (7-quart) braising pan heat
5 tablespoons olive oil; add the onions and sauté over medium heat until just
wilted and pale gold. Add the reserved garlic, the courgettes and the green
pepper. Sauté over rather brisk heat for 5 minutes, then add the aubergine.
Mix the vegetables well with a wooden spatula; season them with 2 teaspoons
salt, 1 teaspoon pepper, and the basil.

Remove the lamb from the oven and place it in the middle of the vegetable
mixture in the braising pan. Add the tomatoes and bring the mixture to a boil
on top of the stove. Reduce the oven heat to 170°C (325°F, gas mark 3) and
braise the lamb in the oven, covered, for 1½ to 1¾ hours, or until the lamb is
tender and the ratatouille cooked down and well blended. Add the olives and
4 tablespoons chopped parsley and cook 10 minutes longer.

Transfer the lamb to a hot platter and remove the strings. If the ratatouille
is too liquid (it should be thick, without visible liquid), reduce it over rather
high heat for a few minutes, stirring it well so it doesn't stick. Taste and
correct the seasoning. Slice the meat and serve with the ratatouille spooned
over and around it. Sprinkle the dish with the remaining parsley and serve
with crisp hot French bread. Drink a light red wine, such as a Mâcon.

Pork

Braised Pork Hocks, Italian Style

Pork hocks are a good and economical buy so I have adapted the classic Italian recipe for *ossi buchi*, or braised veal shanks, to pork hocks.

Serves 4

45 g. (1½ oz.) butter
3 tablespoons oil
4 meaty pork hocks
1 teaspoon salt
½ teaspoon freshly ground black pepper

3 dl. (½ pt) dry white wine
1½ dl. (¼ pt) chicken or beef broth
3½ dl. (12 fl. oz.) tinned Italian
  plum tomatoes

GREMOLATA GARNISH

1 large garlic clove, peeled and coarsely
  chopped

Zest of 1 medium lemon, removed with
  a zester or grater
75 g. (2½ oz.) chopped parsley

Heat the butter and oil in a deep heavy frying or sauté pan that has a cover. Add the pork hocks and brown well on all sides over medium-high heat, salting and peppering them as they cook. Add the wine, broth, and tomatoes, cover the pan, and simmer for 2 hours, or until the meat is tender and coming away from the bone.

Meanwhile, prepare the *gremolata*, a garnish that gives a very fresh spicy flavour. Combine the garlic, lemon zest, and parsley. When the pork hocks are cooked, transfer them to a hot platter, spoon the sauce over them, and sprinkle with the *gremolata*.

Serve with rice.

Braised Pork Chops with Sauerkraut

Braising is a good way to cook pork chops, which become dry and tough if grilled.

Serves 4

4 rashers of thickly cut bacon
1½ kg. (3 lbs.) fresh sauerkraut
1 large onion, sliced
Salt, freshly ground black pepper
30 g. (1 oz.) rendered pork fat or butter

4 pork chops, cut from the loin and
  2½ cm. (1 inch) thick
1 garlic clove, finely chopped
Beer, about ¾ l. (1¼ pts)

Arrange the bacon rashers in the bottom of a heavy braising pan. Rinse the sauerkraut well under cold running water in a colander, then squeeze out as much water as possible with your hands (this gets rid of most of the salt in which it was pickled). Cover the bacon with half the sauerkraut and the sliced onion, then sprinkle it with 1 teaspoon pepper.

Melt the pork fat or butter in a frying pan and brown the chops quickly on both sides over medium-high heat. When the meat is browned, arrange it on top of the sauerkraut in the pan, season to taste with salt and pepper, sprinkle with garlic, and pour the pan juices over it. Add the rest of the sauerkraut, sprinkle with a little more pepper, and add enough beer to cover. Bring it to a boil, reduce the heat, cover, and simmer for 1 hour.

Serve with sautéed apple rings (see page 201), boiled or mashed potatoes, and beer.

Poultry and Game

♨ Coq au Vin
(Chicken in Red Wine)

Probably the most famous and classic example of braised chicken is the French *coq au vin*. This dish is very much akin to beef *bourguignon*, hardly surprising as they both come from Burgundy and share the regional combination of glazed onions, mushrooms, and salt pork.

Serves 6

125 g. (4 oz.) butter	18 small white onions, peeled*
4 tablespoons oil	2 teaspoons sugar
2 medium onions, thinly sliced	Salt, freshly ground black pepper
100 g. (3½ oz.) flour	1 bay leaf
2 1½-kg. (3-lb.) chickens, cut into serving pieces	4 sprigs of fresh thyme Or ½ teaspoon dried thyme
125 g. (4 oz.) salt pork, diced small	2 tablespoons chopped parsley
18 firm white mushroom caps	Red wine – preferably Burgundy

* If the onions are dropped into boiling water for 20 seconds, their skins will slip off easily.

Heat 90 g. (3 oz.) of the butter and 3 tablespoons of the oil in a heavy frying pan and add the sliced onions. Sauté over medium heat until lightly browned. Lightly flour the chicken pieces. Push the onions to one side of the pan and brown the chicken pieces over medium-high heat, a few at a time, removing them to a large casserole as they are browned.

In another frying pan, render the salt pork by cooking until the fat has melted and the pieces of pork are brown and crisp, then add the mushroom caps and toss in the fat until lightly browned. Heat the remaining butter and oil in another frying pan and sauté the onions until lightly browned, then sprinkle with the sugar and cook, tossing, until caramelized. Transfer all the cooked ingredients to the casserole with the chicken, season to taste with salt and pepper, and add the bay leaf, thyme, and parsley.

Rinse the pan in which the chicken was browned with 1½ dl. (¼ pt) red wine, scraping up the brown glaze from the pan. Pour this into the casserole and add enough additional wine to just cover the chicken and vegetables. Cover the casserole and cook in a 180°C (350°F, gas mark 4) oven for 40 minutes, or until the chicken is tender. Serve with small boiled potatoes.

Chicken Calandria

This rather unusual, spicy chicken, named for its originator, is like many braised dishes best made a day in advance and reheated.

Serves 4

180 g. (6 oz.) white cornmeal or polenta	½ teaspoon caraway seeds
2-kg. (4½-lb.) roasting chicken, cut into serving pieces	Pinch (⅛ teaspoon) each: mace and marjoram
1½ dl. (¼ pt) olive oil	¾ l. (1¼ pts) boiling water
3 medium onions, peeled and finely chopped	Salt
3 garlic cloves, peeled and finely chopped	150 g. (5 oz.) whole, blanched almonds
3 dl. (½ pt) dry red wine	125 g. (4 oz.) pitted green olives, preferably the small Spanish olives
1 teaspoon sesame seeds	4 tablespoons chili powder

Put the cornmeal on waxed paper or a pie plate. Add the chicken pieces, and coat them lightly on all sides. Shake off any excess and reserve the cornmeal. Heat the oil in a 6-litre (5-quart) braising pan. Add the chicken pieces and sauté them lightly on all sides over medium-high heat. Lower the heat to medium, add the onions and garlic and let them just wilt down. Mix well with the chicken. Add the wine, sesame and caraway seeds, mace, marjoram and boiling water. Season with salt to taste, cover, reduce the heat, and simmer for 10 minutes, until flavours are blended. Then mix in the almonds, olives and chili powder, cover, and simmer until tender, another 20 to 30 minutes. It can be refrigerated at this point. Before serving, reheat. Mix 3 tablespoons of the leftover cornmeal with $1\frac{1}{2}$ dl. ($\frac{1}{4}$ pt) water and stir it into the pot to thicken the liquid. Stir until the cornmeal expands and thickens, 2 or 3 minutes. Serve at once, with French bread and a green salad. With this spicy chili-flavoured dish, beer is the best thing to drink.

Duck with Beans

Serves 4

370 g. (13 oz.) dried beans
1 onion, stuck with 1 clove
1 teaspoon oregano
1 tablespoon salt
3 slices salt pork, diced
$2\frac{1}{2}$- to 3-kg. (5- to 6-lb.) duck, cut into
   serving pieces, like a chicken

75 g. ($2\frac{1}{2}$ oz.) flour, seasoned with
   1 teaspoon salt
1 medium onion, chopped
1 teaspoon dried basil
Freshly ground black pepper

Soak the beans overnight in water to cover. Next day, drain, put in a saucepan with the clove-stuck onion, oregano and boiling water to cover. Bring to a boil, reduce the heat, cover, and simmer very, very gently until tender, which can take up to $1\frac{1}{2}$ to 2 hours. Do not let the beans boil; it is the gentle simmering that keeps them whole. Add more liquid if it cooks away. When the beans are almost cooked, season them with 1 tablespoon salt – always salt dried beans after they have cooked for a while, not before, or they will toughen. Drain the cooked beans and reserve the liquid.

Cook the diced salt pork in a frying pan over medium heat until the fat is rendered and the salt pork crisp. Remove and reserve the crisp pieces. Coat the duck with the seasoned flour, shaking off the excess, and brown it on all sides in the hot fat over medium-high heat.

Mix the beans with the crisp pieces of salt pork, the chopped onion, and the basil. Season to taste with black pepper. Put half the beans in the bottom of a large casserole, arrange the duck pieces on top, and cover with the rest of the beans. Add the reserved bean liquid and enough boiling water to cover the beans. Cover and cook in a 180°C (350°F, gas mark 4) oven for $1\frac{1}{2}$ hours, or until beans and duck are cooked. Add more liquid if necessary – the dish should not have too much liquid, but should be just moist.

Serve with crisp French bread, an orange and onion salad, and drink a red Rhône wine.

Braised Pheasant

Wild pheasants are frequently tough, and best when braised with some contrasting flavour. If a good-sized mature bird comes your way (you can tell whether it is mature or not by the size of the spurs on the feet and the feel of the breast bone, which in an older bird is not supple but rigid and hard), this is a good way to cook it.

Serves 4

1 mature pheasant	3 or 4 cooking apples (see page 357)
½ lemon	3 teaspoons sugar
About 180 g. (6 oz.) butter	1 tablespoon lemon juice
Salt, freshly ground black pepper, grated nutmeg	5 tablespoons calvados
4 tablespoons oil	2 dl. (⅓ pt) double cream

Clean the pheasant well and rub the interior with the cut lemon. Butter the cavity and sprinkle it with nutmeg. Butter the exterior of the bird and rub with salt, pepper, and nutmeg.

Heat the oil and 60 g. (2 oz.) butter in a large frying pan until bubbling and brown the bird on all sides over medium-high heat until evenly coloured. Liberally butter the inside of a braising pan or earthenware casserole of 6-litre (5-quart) capacity. Core, peel, and slice the apples thick, then spread them over the bottom of the casserole. Sprinkle them with the sugar, ½ teaspoon salt, ¼ teaspoon nutmeg and dot with butter – about 45 to 60 g. (1½ to 2 oz.), cut into small pieces. Add the lemon juice. Place the pheasant on the apples and cover the pan or casserole tightly – if the lid does not fit tightly, first cover the top with a piece of aluminium foil, tucking it over the sides; this will seal in the steam and juices. Cook in a 180°C (350°F, gas mark 4) oven for 1 hour, remove, and test for tenderness by inserting the point of a knife in the thigh; juices should run clear.

If tender, remove to a hot flameproof platter; heat and ignite the calvados and pour it flaming over the bird. Remove the apple mixture to a small pan; mix in the cream and bring to a boil. Simmer for 4 minutes and serve as a sauce with the pheasant.

To serve, carve the pheasant into quarters, arrange on a platter, and top with the sauce. Garnish the platter with mounds of buttered rice tossed with chopped pistachio nuts and chopped parsley.

Vegetables

Braised Fennel

Certain root vegetables braise very successfully. One is fennel, which takes on a completely different character, losing the strong anise taste of its raw state.

Serves 4

2 heads of fennel	Salt, freshly ground black pepper
75 g. (2½ oz.) unsalted butter	1 tablespoon chopped chives
3 dl. (½ pt) chicken or beef broth	

Fennel has feathery green tops on long white stalks that look rather like dill. These should be trimmed off at the point where the bulbous part of the fennel begins. Also remove any discoloured or very tough and stringy outer leaves. Cut the heads into quarters.

Melt the butter in a frying pan; add the fennel quarters and brown them lightly over medium heat on all sides. Add the broth, bring the liquid to a boil, then reduce to a simmer, cover the pan, and let the fennel cook gently (it should not boil) until just tender when pierced with the point of a knife, about 30 to 40 minutes, according to size. Season with salt and pepper to taste, remove the fennel to a hot vegetable dish, turn up the heat, and let the liquid reduce by about half, until it is rather thick. Pour over the fennel and sprinkle with chopped chives.

Braised Celery

This is an eternally popular dish, which is best made with celery hearts. Trim off the large, coarse outer stalks, leaving only the tight bunch of tender white stalks and leaves in the centre.

Serves 4

60 g. (2 oz.) unsalted butter	4 tablespoons strong chicken or beef stock
4 celery hearts, split lengthwise	½ teaspoon freshly ground black pepper
1 teaspoon salt	1 tablespoon chopped parsley

Melt the butter in a heavy frying pan or saucepan, add the celery hearts, sprinkle with salt, add the stock, and cook, covered, over medium heat, turning the hearts carefully with two spoons once during the cooking time.

until just tender and pierceable, about 30 minutes. Remove the celery to a vegetable dish. Boil pan juices down to 5 tablespoons and pour over the celery. Season with pepper, sprinkle with parsley, and serve.

Braised Lettuce

This leafy vegetable is extraordinarily good braised and served with lamb, beef, game and roast or braised chicken. I have found that the old recipes for braised lettuce give too long a cooking time, so I have formulated my own somewhat revolutionary way of preparing it, which to my palate, produces a pleasanter result.

Serves 6

6 heads of lettuce	225 g. (8 oz.) bacon
2 leeks	Chicken, beef, or veal stock
Or 2 medium onions	60 g. (2 oz.) unsalted butter
2 carrots	Salt, freshly ground black pepper

Remove the outer leaves from the lettuce, then wash the heads under cold running water, pulling the leaves apart to loosen them and wash away all sand between them. Wrap the heads in paper towels to dry. Trim the root end and all but $2\frac{1}{2}$ cm. (1 inch) of the green top from the leeks and wash them well under cold running water, separating the leaves to rinse out lurking sand. Dry and cut into fine julienne (matchstick-sized) strips. If leeks are not available, use onions, peeled and thinly sliced. Peel the carrots and also cut into julienne strips.

Arrange the carrots and leeks or onions in a layer in a heavy sauté pan and top them with 2 rashers of the bacon, cut into small pieces. Arrange the dried lettuce heads on the bed of vegetables and cover with the remaining bacon rashers. Add enough stock to barely cover the lettuce. Bring the liquid to a boil over high heat, then reduce the heat to low, cover the pan, and simmer, covered, for 20 minutes, or until just tender and pierceable. Carefully remove the lettuce heads with wooden spoons or tongs and drain on paper towels. Strain the stock. It may be saved and used for soups or stews.

Melt the butter in large frying pan, add the drained lettuce, and reheat in the butter. Season with salt and pepper to taste. Transfer the braised lettuce to a heated serving dish and spoon some of the butter over it.

Red Cabbage with Chestnuts

Red cabbage goes well with game and red meats. The following recipe, which comes from the central part of France, works as a complete vegetable course – the chestnuts supplying the starch.

Serves 6 to 8

2 kg. (4 lbs.) red cabbage
75 g. (2½ oz.) unsalted butter
1 kg. (2 lbs.) peeled chestnuts

1½ teaspoons salt
1 teaspoon freshly ground black pepper
Chicken broth

Wash the cabbage, quarter it and cut out the core, then cut it into very thin shreds with a large chef's knife.

Melt the butter in a heavy sauté pan over medium heat. Add the cabbage, chestnuts, salt and pepper, and just enough chicken broth to cover. Bring the liquid to a boil, then reduce the heat to low, cover, and simmer for 40 to 45 minutes.

Sauerkraut

Sauerkraut is often overlooked as an accompaniment to meat and poultry, yet its tart, fermented flavour is a perfect balance for any form of pork – from roasts and barbecued spareribs to pigs' knuckles and sausages – or to boiled beef, rich and fatty goose and duck, turkey and many game birds.

The best buy is the fresh sauerkraut packaged in plastic bags, but tinned sauerkraut is also acceptable. Fresh sauerkraut is very salty and should always be rinsed well before using.

Serves 4 to 6

2 450-g. (1-lb.) packages of fresh
    sauerkraut
4 to 5 slices salt pork or bacon, cut
    3 mm. (⅛ inch) thick
Freshly ground black pepper
Bouquet garni (see page 373)

2 peeled garlic cloves
10 crushed juniper berries
    Or 2 tablespoons gin
Chicken stock, white wine, or
    beer to cover, 1 l. (1¾ pts)

Rinse the sauerkraut well in a colander under cold running water, tossing it with your hands. Drain well. Line the bottom of a large heavy pot with the salt pork or bacon (if you use salt pork, soak it in cold water for 30 minutes to remove the excess salt). Put layers of sauerkraut into the pot, grinding black pepper on each layer. Tuck in among the layers the bouquet garni and garlic, then add the juniper berries or gin. Pour on enough liquid (I prefer chicken stock, which gives a more delicate flavour) to cover, bring to a boil, then reduce the heat to a simmer and simmer slowly for 2 to 4 hours. The longer it cooks, the better it tastes.

Braised Peas with Lettuce

By cooking tender young green peas this French way, they retain all their flavour and texture because the damp lettuce leaves add moisture to the heat, while the touch of sugar brings out their sweetness.

Serves 4

125 g. (4 oz.) unsalted butter	*1 teaspoon salt*
1 head lettuce	*1 teaspoon sugar*
1½ kg. (3 lbs.) green peas, shelled	

Wash but do not dry the lettuce. Melt the butter in a heavy 2½-litre (2-quart) saucepan and cover the bottom of the pan with damp lettuce leaves. Put the peas on top, sprinkle them with the salt and sugar, and cover with more damp lettuce leaves. Cover tightly and cook over low heat for 20 to 25 minutes, or until the peas are just tender. Serve the peas with or without the lettuce.

Braised Onion Slices

Braising is an excellent way to cook onions because it gives them a great deal of flavour. The whisky, though not traditional, makes them extra special.

Serves 6

2 tablespoons olive oil	*1 teaspoon salt*
30 g. (1 oz.) butter	*½ teaspoon freshly ground black pepper*
4 large yellow onions, peeled and cut into 2½-cm. (1-inch)-thick slices	*4 tablespoons chicken or beef broth*
	4 tablespoons Scotch whisky

Melt the oil and butter in a heavy frying or sauté pan. Add the onions and sauté them over high heat for 2 minutes to brown them slightly. Add the salt, pepper and broth. Reduce the heat to low, cover, and simmer for 10 minutes, or until just tender when pierced with the point of a sharp paring knife. Add the whisky and cook for a further 5 minutes, until the alcohol has evaporated and the sauce is slightly reduced. These are delicious with roast or grilled beef, roast lamb, or roast chicken.

Sautéing

There is a great deal of confusion about what is sautéing and what is frying. In America, the fact that something is cooked in a frying pan or flat pan in fat does not mean that it is fried; there frying is like baptism in certain religious sects – there must be total immersion. Occasionally you'll encounter the term 'pan-fried', which is just an American way of saying 'sautéed'.

What, then, is sautéing? Sautéing is cooking food on top of the stove in a relatively small amount of fat in, preferably, a heavy-duty sauté pan or frying pan, and it's a fast, deft procedure. A sauté pan, known in France as a *sautoir* or *sauteuse*, is specially constructed and designed for sautéing. It is a straight-sided, heavy bottomed pan about $6\frac{1}{2}$ to $7\frac{1}{2}$ cm. ($2\frac{1}{2}$ to 3 inches) deep that comes in different diameters, usually 25, 30 and 35 cm. (10, 12 and 14 inches). The handle is longer than that of most frying pans because in sautéing you have to shake the pan and sometimes toss the food in it. It should also have a tight-fitting cover for sautés, such as chicken, that are cooked covered after the initial browning in fat.

You can use other pans for sautéing – a frying pan, especially one of heavy iron or of cast aluminium, with or without a non-stick lining, or any fairly shallow, flat, long-handled pan large enough to accommodate in one layer the food you are going to sauté, plus that tight-fitting cover. (See illustration for an assortment of equipment.) Provided it is not made out of a flimsy material or is difficult to handle, almost any pan of this sort is acceptable. Heavy lined copper, stainless steel with aluminium plate on the bottom, and cast aluminium are good materials for sauté pans and frying pans. However, if a sauté includes wine or egg yolks, it is inadvisable to cook it in an unlined aluminium or iron pan, for chemical reaction between the metal and the wine (or other acid foods, such as vinegar or tomatoes) or the egg yolk can discolour your sauce. It doesn't harm the food, it's just a matter of aesthetics.

The simplest and most basic form of sauté, which does not need covering, is the one you'll find on menus all around the world – a sauté meunière, or sauté in the style of the miller's wife (presumably because it implies a light dusting of flour on the food). This is usually applied to fish – sole meunière, trout meunière – the delicate flesh of which needs quick cooking and a little protection from the heat, hence the flour. The fish are first sprinkled with flour and then sautéed quickly in butter, or butter and oil, turned to give a lovely golden colour on both sides while the inside stays tender and not dried out or overcooked. This, with a blessing of salt and pepper, a squeeze of lemon and a sprinkle of parsley, is the sauté meunière, one of the most famous of all ways of preparing fish. Nothing could be simpler or better. It's a triumphant example of a sauté.

A similar sauté, perhaps the best known next to the meunière, applies to thin, thin slices of meat, usually veal escalopes or scaloppine, slices cut from the leg and pounded flat. These are sometimes floured, sometimes not, and sautéed very quickly in butter, oil, or a combination of the two. The seasoning may be merely salt and pepper and a little lemon juice, or there may be herbs, or white wine, or Marsala wine, the classic Italian version, to make a little sauce for the meat. This is a quick dish, in and out of the pan before you know it, and seldom, if ever, covered. The other famous meat dish is beef Stroganoff, made with thin slices of tenderloin sautéed very fast in butter and oil, just to sear them so they remain deliciously rare inside. The slices are removed and soured cream and seasonings mixed into the pan juices, then briefly combined with the beef and served in what is really a minute sauté, although too often it is bastardized into a stew, which it was never meant to be. Then, of course, we have offal, the kidneys, liver, sweetbreads, brains, all those delicious little bits that need the fast cooking of a sauté to keep them juicy and tender.

Chops can be sautéed very successfully, though here the thickness of the meat requires that they be cooked further, covered. Pork chops, for instance, are often quickly sautéed, covered, and simmered very slowly with flavourings and a touch of liquid until tender, then served with a sauce made from the pan juices, after the chops are removed. You can also sauté them and then put the pan, covered, in the oven so the chops braise slowly under a moist blanket of vegetables and liquid – or the whole process can be carried out on top of the stove. I once did a year of demonstrations around the country and one of the dishes people loved most was a very interesting sauté of lovely thick pork chops, browned quickly along with 1 or 2 rashers of thick bacon, then covered with sauerkraut, a little finely chopped garlic, freshly ground pepper, and beer, and simmered, covered, until the chops were tender and beautifully flavoured with the smoky bacon and pungent sauerkraut. It's basically the same recipe as the one on page 154.

Chicken sautés, which are legion in the dictionary of cooking, fall into two categories – the ones that are browned, and the ones that are not. Those that are sautéed a golden brown, perhaps with the aid of a light dusting of flour, are known as a *sauté brun*, a brown sauté. For the other, the white or *sauté blond*, the chicken is merely seared on the surface, but not allowed to colour. It's a very minor difference. For a brown sauté the pieces are browned on both sides, for a blond sauté they are cooked just until the outside is firm and the colour creamy. The pieces are then seasoned with salt and pepper, covered, and cooked gently for 5 to 8 minutes. The next step in a chicken sauté is to add liquid – a small amount of white or red wine, sherry, port or madeira, stock or tomato juice, or tomato purée – and the flavouring additions, which can be herbs, certain spices, chopped garlic, shallot, or onion, tiny bits of ham, tomato, green pepper, mushrooms, or many different ingredients, all of which are put in at a point about midway in the cooking, usually after the sauté has simmered, covered, for about 10 minutes. These additions help to tenderize and flavour the flesh of the chicken and create the infinite variations possible with a basic chicken sauté. Some of them will be added with the liquid before covering and simmering the sauté; others will be added after it has simmered for a while.

Once the chicken has simmered to tenderness, remove it to a hot dish and keep it warm while you cook down the pan juices for a sauce, perhaps adding more wine or more herbs to finish it off. Sometimes a recipe will call for a touch of *glace de viande*, beef stock reduced to a jelly, which gives the finished dish a nice glaze, or a little butter, which also enriches the sauce and gives a pleasant body and glaze. Or if the recipe were for a creamy sauté, you'd add cream, or egg yolks mixed with cream, or the sauce might be thickened with cornflour, arrowroot, or *beurre manié*. The sauce would be poured over the chicken or served with it, according to the recipe.

Sautéing is a process with many facets. A surprisingly large number of everyday cooking procedures fall within the realm of sautéing. I can remember one day, years ago, when I was demonstrating omelet-making. As

I melted the butter in the pan, added the eggs, shook the pan, and swirled the omelet around I suddenly realized something that I had never considered before – an omelet is a sauté of egg! Scrambled eggs are also a sauté, if you define the process, because again one melts the butter, adds the eggs, and moves them around gently until they have cooked to perfect, creamy delicacy.

Vegetables, another tender and delicate food, sauté very nicely. Depending on their texture they can be sautéed raw, like onions, or after parboiling. Tiny French beans, for instance, are blanched or parboiled in water, drained very well, and then sautéed in plenty of butter with a vigorous shaking of the pan so that the beans don't overcook but just acquire the flavour that comes from that quick, hot kiss of butter. Asparagus can be blanched, drained, and cooked in butter in the same way (but one has to handle them very gently lest the tips break), with a finishing touch of some grated cheese. Onions for a vegetable course, cut in very thin rings, are either sautéed gently in butter to a delicate deep ivory colour or more intensely until they turn quite brown and crisp on the edges, then seasoned with salt and pepper. Thicker slices that take longer to cook may be finished off by adding cheese and covering the pan so the onions steam and the cheese melts, or by adding wine such as Madeira or sherry, covering the pan, and letting the onions steam and cook down in the wine.

Apple rings are very often sautéed as an accompaniment to meat, especially pork, or to certain chicken dishes. The apples are cored, cut into slices, and sautéed in butter and oil with a light sprinkling of sugar until they are delicately browned and caramelized. After caramelizing they may be flambéed with a little calvados or cognac. And pears, pineapples, or bananas can be sautéed quickly in butter for an easy dessert.

It's a far cry, in every way, from frying to sautéing. We talk about fried ham. Well, there's no such thing. It is sautéed in butter, maybe after being parboiled in the sauté pan with water to draw out some of the salt and make it tender. The pan is dried, the butter added, and the ham gently sautéed to a delicate brown tenderness, after which the ham is removed and those of us in America who like the famous red-eye gravy add some water to the pan to dissolve the glaze.

People who say they can't prepare a meal for company without spending hours over a hot stove are just foolish. In slightly over an hour, they can make a simple *salade composée*, a light soup or seafood starter, and a chicken, veal, or pork sauté with a vegetable, and with cheese and fruit have an excellent meal for 4. Sautéing is an almost foolproof form not only of quick cookery but of good cookery. I love sautés. One of the persons who taught me most about cooking over a period of years, Jeanne Owen, made at least thirty different chicken sautés, all absolutely delicious. She'd do one with white wine, salt and pepper and then add perhaps a dash of tarragon or a little thyme, or a red wine sauté with shallots and onion and garlic, or a sauté with garlic, tomato, and rosemary, each one taking no more than 25 to 30 minutes and producing a magnificent meal for 2 or 4 with practically no effort. So you see, once you master the sauté you are well on your way to becoming a good cook and a good host or hostess.

Beef

♔ Steak au Poivre

One of the simplest of all sautés is a steak *au poivre*, which is now popular throughout the world, although I can remember the time when you found it only in France. Gradually, people became so enamoured of this delicious combination of pepper-flavoured beef and cognac, sometimes a little cream, that you find it served just about everywhere.

The best cut for individual steaks *au poivre* is the entrecôte, the boneless, tender eye from the sirloin. The steak should be 4 cm. (1½ inches) thick.

To cook the steaks you will need a heavy-duty frying pan or sauté pan large enough to accommodate the two steaks, side by side, with some room left over. They must not be squeezed together.

Serves 2

2 entrecôte steaks, about 4 cm. (1½ inches) thick	45 g. (1½ oz.) unsalted butter
1½ tablespoons black peppercorns	3 tablespoons salad oil
1 teaspoon or more salt	5 tablespoons cognac

About 2 hours before you plan to cook the steaks, remove them from the refrigerator and leave at room temperature. Before cooking, trim any excess fat from the side of the steak with a small, sharp paring knife, leaving just a thin strip for lubrication – a good piece of sirloin will be well marbled with fat and that will also lubricate the meat as it cooks. Fat is the flavour-giver for meat, and if you cut off all the fat you will take away some of the flavour of the meat, the part that settled in the fat.

Now crush or grind the peppercorns very, very coarse. If your pepper mill doesn't grind coarsely enough, it is advisable to crush them in a mortar and pestle, or to wrap them in a towel and beat them with a mallet, or you may use a liquidizer or food processor, which does the job fast and isn't so arduous.

Sprinkle the top of each steak with $1\frac{1}{2}$ teaspoons of the ground peppercorns, and with the heel of your hand (which has the most strength in it), press the pepper into the meat. Turn the steaks and repeat on the other side. Let the steaks rest for 15 minutes before sautéing. Just about 2 minutes before you put the steaks on to cook, sprinkle one side with salt, using about $\frac{1}{2}$ teaspoon for each steak. Many people tell you that this will draw out the juices, but I maintain that when meat sears as fast as this does, the salt is absorbed and the surface immediately sealed.

Heat the butter and oil in the frying or sauté pan over medium-high heat – 220°C (425°F) if you have a plate with a thermostat. As oil can be heated to a higher temperature than butter without burning, the oil prevents the butter from burning at the rather high heat one uses to sauté steak. For this reason, you should also use unsalted rather than salted butter, which is more inclined to burn. If you prefer, you may omit the butter and use all oil, or you can substitute beef drippings, if you have any, or chop up the fat you trimmed from the steak, throw that into the pan, and let it melt and render into fat.

When the fat is sizzling but not smoking (if it smokes, it is too hot, and you will have to throw it out and start again), place the steaks, salted side down, in the hot fat. The steak will sizzle as it hits the fat and you don't want it to stick, so shake the pan very gently to move the steaks around. Cook for about 3 minutes on that side, shaking the pan back and forth very gently, then salt the uncooked side, turn the steaks with tongs, and cook 3 minutes on that side. Now reduce the heat to medium – 180°C (350°F) on a thermostat – or below medium, turn the steaks again, and cook a further 3 minutes on each side – that's 3 minutes a side for searing plus 3 minutes a side for cooking at the lower temperature.

To make sure the steak is done to your taste, remove the pan from the heat, and with a very sharp paring knife and a fork make a small incision in the thickest part of the steak and push the meat apart to see if it is cooked as you like it. If not, you may give the steaks a minute or two more. Six minutes a side should give you a really rare steak. Eight minutes a side will give you medium-rare steak.

Remove the steaks to a hot platter and keep warm. Shake the pan well, remove it from the heat, and pour the cognac into the pan. Strike a long kitchen match and very carefully place it at the side of the pan – the fumes of alcohol from the heated cognac will immediately ignite and burn with a great flame, so keep your head and hands well out of range as you do this. Hold the pan by the handle and shake it gently until the flames die down – they will have burned off all the excess fat and lifted the brown glaze from the bottom of the pan, making a little sauce for the steak. Should a tiny bit of flame linger, fan it out quickly with your hand. Pour the sauce over the steak and serve at once.

Contrary to what some people think, the pepper should on no account be scraped off the steak before you eat it, but eaten and enjoyed. It's really like a condiment, and it is that lovely charred peppery taste and crunchy crustiness on the outside that makes steak *au poivre* the great dish it is. You may serve the steaks as they come, or cut them into thin diagonal slices. Sautéed potatoes, a green salad, and a good red wine are all you'll need with this delicious steak.

♟ Sautéed Hamburgers

A good hamburger is one of the most basic meat dishes you can make, but even here there are one or two tricks you should know. In my opinion, hamburgers are best sautéed in a heavy frying pan in oil, a combination of butter and oil, or clarified butter (see page 361), all of which can be heated to a higher temperature without burning than plain butter. I think this gives a juicier, crustier hamburger than grilling, and it is easier to control the degree of doneness. You will need a heavy iron frying pan, or whatever you normally use for sautéing (with a non-stick frying pan, you won't need much fat, just about 1 tablespoon for flavour), and a large spatula for turning the hamburgers.

Serves 4

1 kg. (2 lbs.) minced beef, preferably	*2 tablespoons groundnut oil*
topside or chuck, with 20 to	*Or equal quantities of oil and butter*
25 per cent fat	*Or clarified butter*
Coarse salt, freshly ground black pepper	

Divide the meat into 4 equal portions, seasoning it to taste with salt and pepper, and form it gently and lightly into patties with your hands, almost tossing it back and forth. Be careful not to press or overhandle the meat. Too much handling makes for heavy, solid patties, and that is not what you want at all. The meat should just hold together. You can make your patties round or oval, thick or fairly flat, according to how you like them. For rare hamburgers, make them thick. For medium, make them thinner. They won't be perfectly shaped. They'll be sort of free-form but that's all right. Taste is more important than appearance.

Heat the oil, or whatever you are using, in a heavy frying pan. There should be just a film of fat on the surface. When it is hot, but not smoking, put the patties in the pan and cook briskly on one side for 4 minutes over fairly high heat until good and brown. Turn them carefully with a large spatula and cook 4 minutes on the other side. Press the browned surface gently with your finger. See how much firmer it is than the uncooked meat. Then press the sides. These will be less firm because the centre meat has not cooked as much.

At this point you can almost gauge how near to done the hamburgers are. Reduce the heat slightly and, if you like them rare, give them 2 more minutes on each side. Press them again and you'll find they are slightly resistant to the touch. Transfer them to hot plates and serve at once. When you cut into the hamburger and find it done to your liking, remember the way the patty felt when pressed. This is a very simple test, but it will give you confidence in the message your fingers can send to your brain. A grilled steak can be tested in the same way.

Beef Liver Bourguignon

Beef liver, which is not as delicate in flavour as calves' liver, benefits from a flavourful red wine sauce. As with all offal, beef liver should be sautéed quickly and not overcooked or it will be tough and unpleasant. Speed is essential for this dish, so you should make the croutons first.

Serves 4

2 slices white bread
180 g. (6 oz.) unsalted butter
3 garlic cloves, finely chopped
6 rashers bacon or salt pork, diced
60 g. (2 oz.) flour
Salt, freshly ground black pepper

4 good-sized slices of young beef liver,
　1 cm. (⅜ inch) thick
4 medium onions, peeled and sliced
1½ to 2 dl. (¼ to ⅓ pt) red wine
1 tablespoon chopped parsley and chives

Trim the crusts from the bread, cut each slice in two diagonally and then in two diagonally again, making 8 triangles. Heat half the butter in a heavy frying pan and when the butter is hot and sizzling, add the garlic and the bread pieces and sauté them quickly, turning frequently, over medium-high heat, until brown and crisp. Be careful not to let the butter, garlic, or bread burn. Remove to paper towels to drain, and keep warm in a 95°C (200°F, gas mark ¼) oven.

Wipe out the pan with paper towels, removing all butter and residue, then add and melt the remaining butter, add the bacon dice, and sauté over medium heat until the fat is rendered and the pieces are brown and crisp. Remove to paper towels and drain. Season the flour with 1 teaspoon salt and ¼ teaspoon pepper and coat the beef liver lightly with the flour, shaking off any excess.

Heat the butter and fat in the pan until hot and sizzling, add the liver slices, and sauté quickly over medium-high heat until browned on each side, about 3 to 4 minutes on one side and 1 minute on the other – the liver should still be rare, pink, and juicy in the centre. Remove to a hot platter, cover with foil, and keep warm. Add the onions to the fat in the pan and sauté until limp and golden, then replace the bacon dice, add just enough red wine to cover, reduce heat, and simmer gently for 5 minutes.

Add the liver slices to the sauce and let them just heat through, then arrange the liver slices on a hot platter, pour the sauce over them, top with the fried bread triangles, and sprinkle with parsley and chives. Serve at once. Serve with potatoes Anna and pass the rest of the sauce in a bowl. A red Burgundy or similar full-bodied red wine is best with this.

Zrazys Nelson

This Polish recipe involves three different sautés – potatoes, cucumbers with mushrooms, and thin slices of tender fillet of beef.

Serves 6

8 to 10 medium-small potatoes, boiled in their jackets until done but slightly undercooked and firm, so they slice easily

225 g. (8 oz.) or more unsalted butter

Salt, freshly ground black pepper

4 cucumbers, peeled and thinly sliced

18 firm white button mushrooms, thinly sliced

60 g. (2 oz.) flour

4½ dl. (¾ pt) double cream

1 tablespoon tomato purée

12 slices of beef fillet, about 1 cm. (½ inch) thick

Peel the potatoes and slice about 5 mm. (¼ inch) thick. Heat 60 g. (2 oz.) butter in a heavy frying pan and sauté the potatoes in batches over medium-high heat until nicely browned and crisp at the edges. Add more butter as needed. As they are cooked, sprinkle lightly with salt and pepper and transfer them to a large serving platter, making a bed for the beef. Keep warm in a 130°C (250°F, gas mark ½) oven.

Rub out the pan with paper towels, add and heat 60 g. (2 oz.) butter and, when bubbling, add the cucumbers and mushrooms and sauté over fairly high heat, tossing and turning, until cucumbers are soft and mushrooms lightly browned. Mix in the flour. Gradually add the cream and cook over medium heat, stirring constantly, until thickened. Mix in the tomato purée and season to taste with salt and pepper. Keep warm while sautéing the beef.

Melt 60 g. (2 oz.) butter in another heavy frying pan or sauté pan and, when hot and bubbling, sauté the beef slices on both sides very quickly over high heat, a few at a time, for about 2 to 3 minutes a side, or until nicely browned on the outside but still rare inside. Do not overcook. As they are cooked, sprinkle them lightly with salt and arrange on the bed of potatoes. Cover with the cucumber–mushroom sauce and serve.

Poultry and Game

♟ Chicken Sauté with White Wine and Tarragon

For sautéing, chicken is cut into serving pieces – either quartered into 2 breast halves with wings attached and 2 legs and thighs, or disjointed into smaller pieces, with the wings separated from the breast, and the legs from the thighs. Although you can buy chicken cut in pieces in the supermarket, it has usually been pretty sloppily done. Often the chicken has merely been sawed or hacked into pieces, leaving splintery bits of bone. It is preferable, and also more economical, to buy a whole chicken and cut it up yourself, which not only gives you neat, perfect serving pieces, but also the gizzards, neck, and back to make into stock. The wing tips, which are not very meaty, can be cut off and added to the stock pot.

Take a sharp knife and, using your fingers to locate the joint, cut through the connecting skin and flesh. *Bend the leg back, away from the body, until the hip joint appears. Cut through at the connecting joint.* Cut skin between leg and thigh, locate joint, and cut through. Next, *remove the wings from the breast,* (unless you are doing a dish that calls for the wing bone to be attached, such as the recipe that follows or chicken Kiev).

*Now grasp the chicken by the back
and hold it so that you can cut through
the entire length of the bird with a large
sharp knife; this means cutting through
the ribs and straight down to the wing
joint.* Bend the back and then with a
heavy knife cut through the bones at
the shoulder to sever the breast from
the carcass. The back may be cut in
two crosswise and simply used for
stock. Cut the breast in half up the
centre with your knife, slicing
through the wishbone at the top.
You will now have eight serving
pieces as illustrated.

You can vary this sauté endlessly, by using different herbs, vegetables,
stock, sherry, or red wine in place of the white wine, or by blazing the cooked
chicken with brandy. The tarragon in this recipe can be replaced with
parsley, if you prefer.

Serves 4

90 g. (3 oz.) unsalted butter
*2 spring chickens, each weighing
  about 1 kg. (2 to 2½ lbs.)*
Salt, freshly ground black pepper

1½ dl. (¼ pt) dry white wine
2 tablespoons chopped fresh tarragon
Or 2 teaspoons dried tarragon

Melt the butter in a large, heavy frying or sauté pan that has a tight-fitting cover. When it is hot (the slight foaming of the melted butter should subside, but do not let it turn brown), brown the chicken pieces over medium-high heat, turning them as they brown so that all sides are evenly coloured. Lower the heat, sprinkle the chicken with salt and pepper to taste, cover the pan, and simmer gently for 5 to 8 minutes. Remove the cover and check the pieces, rearranging them so they cook evenly. Add half the wine, cover the pan again, and cook for another 10 minutes. If you are using dried tarragon, put it to soak in the remaining wine.

Uncover the pan and move the breast and wing sections to the top, arranging them over the leg and thigh pieces. The dark meat takes longer to cook and during the final cooking should be at the bottom of the pan, closest to the heat. Sprinkle the chicken with the tarragon (if dried, remove it from the wine by straining it through a little sieve – reserve the wine), cover again, and cook the chicken until tender, but still moist and juicy. This will take 5 to 10 minutes, so check after 5 minutes.

Remove the cooked chicken to a hot serving platter. Add the rest of the wine to the pan, turn the heat to high, and stir the juices with a wooden spoon or spatula until they boil and blend, scraping up the brown bits from the bottom of the pan. Boil until reduced by half, then pour the juices over the chicken and serve immediately. With this you might have boiled rice or bulghur pilaf and a green vegetable, such as green peas, braised French style (see page 162), or just French bread and a green salad. Drink the same kind of wine you used for cooking.

Chicken Sauté with Armagnac

Only the white meat is used for this delicate and suave sauté.

Serves 4

125 g. (4 oz.) unsalted butter	6 shallots, peeled and very finely chopped
4 half chicken breasts, with wings attached	2 egg yolks
	2 dl. (⅓ pt) double cream
Salt, freshly ground black pepper	5 tablespoons Armagnac

Melt the butter in a large, heavy frying pan and when the foaming stops add the chicken and sauté over medium-high heat on both sides until golden. Season with salt and pepper to taste, reduce the heat, cover, and cook gently for 15 to 20 minutes, or until the breasts are just cooked through. Remove the chicken to a hot flameproof serving platter, or put in the top part of a chafing dish, and pour a little (about 2 tablespoons) of the melted butter over it.

Add the shallots to the pan and cook them in the remaining butter until just limp and golden, stirring them so they do not brown. Beat the eggs and cream together lightly in a measuring jug or small bowl and stir into them a couple of tablespoons of the hot pan liquid, which tempers the yolks and prevents them from curdling when added to the pan. Pour the mixture into the pan and stir constantly over low heat until the sauce is well blended and slightly thickened. Do not allow it to get too hot or to boil or the eggs will curdle. Remove from heat and keep warm.

Heat the Armagnac in a small pan, ignite with a match, and pour blazing over the chicken. When the flames die down, spoon the sauce over the chicken and serve immediately. Serve with a potato purée and French beans tossed in butter. Drink a Pinot Chardonnay or Pouilly-Fumé.

Chicken Panné

Chicken breasts pounded until very thin, like veal scaloppine, sauté very fast and stay beautifully tender and succulent. It is extremely important not to overcook the breasts, or they will dry out – the chicken is done as soon as the coating is browned. Panné means that the chicken is coated with flour, beaten egg and crumbs.

You can ask the butcher to bone chicken breasts but it is much more economical to do it yourself. If you are working with a whole chicken, follow the procedure for cutting up on page 172, eliminating the last step; in other words, leave the breasts whole – don't split them until you have boned them.

First, break the breastbone by pressing firmly on it with the flat of your hand. Pull the skin from the breast with your fingers.

Turn the chicken breast over and slip your fingers between the flesh and the rib cage. Pull the rib cage away from the flesh.

Then take your small sharp chicken-boning knife and scrape the flesh away from the wishbone and larger bone at the top of the breast, pulling the bone out with your fingers as it is loosened. Should you wish to remove the long stringy white tendon that runs the length of the breast, hold the protruding end of the tendon firmly with your fingers, scrape with the knife to loosen it from the flesh, then give it a firm tug and it will come out easily.

Serves 6

3 whole chicken breasts	3 tablespoons or more groundnut oil
125 g. (4 oz.) flour	Salt, freshly ground black pepper
3 eggs, beaten	4 tablespoons cognac
125 to 150 g. (4 to 5 oz.) freshly made fine bread crumbs	2 egg yolks
90 g. (3 oz.) unsalted butter or more	3 dl. (½ pt) double cream

Cut the breasts in half up the centre. Put each half breast between two sheets of waxed paper, lay it on a wood counter or chopping block, and pound with a meat pounder until about 1 cm. (⅜ inch) thick, as you would for veal scaloppine (see page 144). As you pound, push the pounder outwards to flatten and spread the flesh. As each piece is flattened (it will almost double in size), put it between sheets of waxed paper. Put the flour on a large piece of waxed paper, the beaten eggs in a shallow baking dish or pie plate, and the bread crumbs on another large sheet of waxed paper, lining them up in that order. Dip the chicken pieces, one at a time, first in the flour, coating both sides lightly (as you lift the breast out, pat and shake it gently to get rid of excess flour), then lay it in the egg, turning to coat both sides, then lay the breast in the crumbs. Toss the crumbs over the breast, making sure both sides are well coated, then transfer to a baking tray lined with waxed paper. Put waxed paper between the breasts so they do not stick together, then refrigerate until ready to cook, to firm and set the coating. This can be done several hours ahead of time.

When you are ready to cook them, remove the breasts from the refrigerator. Heat the butter and oil in a large, heavy frying pan (preferably plain iron or non-stick) over high heat until it is hot and bubbling, but not browned or smoking. Put the chicken breasts in the pan in a single layer, no more than 2 at a time. They should not be crowded together or they will steam rather than sauté. As you put the pieces in the pan, turn the heat to medium-high. Brown quickly on both sides, sprinkling the breasts with salt and pepper as they cook. This will take no more than a minute or two a side, just until the coating is lightly browned. Adjust the heat so the crumbs do not burn. Add more butter and oil between batches, if necessary, and each time heat until bubbling.

When the pieces are cooked, transfer them to a hot platter. When they are all cooked, turn off the heat, replace the breasts in the pan, and pour the cognac over them. Ignite the cognac with a match and shake the pan until the flames die down. Remove the chicken pieces to a platter and keep warm in a 130°C (250°F, gas mark ½) oven while making the sauce.

Beat the egg yolks in a small bowl and mix with the cream. Heat the juices in the pan and add a little of the hot pan juices to the egg-cream mixture, to warm the eggs through so they will not curdle when put into the pan. Pour the mixture into the pan and cook over medium heat, stirring, until smooth and lightly thickened. Do not let the sauce get near the simmering point or it will curdle. Taste the sauce and adjust the seasoning. You may need salt and pepper. Serve the chicken pieces on hot plates and spoon sauce over each piece. Puréed broccoli goes well with this, and tiny new potatoes, or rice.

Sauté of Chicken Livers

Chicken livers make a very easy, fast sauté. Prepare the toast or noodles before starting the livers.

Serves 4

60 g. (2 oz.) unsalted butter

4 shallots, finely chopped

½ kg. (1 lb.) chicken livers, trimmed of connecting threads and any bitter green or blackish discolourations

Salt, freshly ground black pepper to taste

2 tablespoons chopped parsley

Melt the butter in a heavy frying pan and when hot, add the shallots and sauté over medium heat, stirring, for 3 or 4 minutes until limp and golden. Add the chicken livers, raise the heat to high, and sauté, tossing and turning them, until well browned on all sides and just cooked through, about 5 minutes. Do not overcook or they will toughen; they should still be pink inside. Season with salt and pepper to taste, sprinkle with the parsley, and serve immediately on crisp toast or on a bed of noodles cooked with a garlic clove, drained well, and tossed with butter, salt and pepper, and a little grated nutmeg. The sautéed livers may also be folded into individual omelets, just before they are rolled and turned out.

Rabbit Sautéed with Tarragon

If you buy a whole, cleaned and skinned rabbit, weighing about 1½ kg. (3 to 3½ pounds), it should be cut into serving pieces. The two back legs may be left whole or cut into thighs and drumsticks, the smaller front legs should be left whole, and the saddle, the choicest part, cut in two. The giblets may be cooked in the pan with the rabbit to add flavour. Sauté the liver separately in a tablespoon of butter, as it should not be cooked long.

Serves 4

60 g. (2 oz.) flour
1 teaspoon salt
½ teaspoon freshly ground black pepper
2½ teaspoons dried tarragon
1 young, tender rabbit, weighing about
   1½ kg. (3 to 3½ lbs.)

60 g. (2 oz.) unsalted butter
4 tablespoons oil
3 dl. (½ pt) dry white wine
30 g. (1 oz.) chopped parsley

Place flour, salt, pepper, 1½ teaspoons tarragon and rabbit in a plastic bag and shake well, to coat the rabbit. Remove and shake off excess flour.

Heat the butter and oil in a large frying or sauté pan with a tight-fitting cover. When hot but not brown, add the rabbit and brown the pieces over medium-high heat, turning them carefully with tongs. When they are browned, add half the wine, reduce the heat, cover, and simmer for 15 minutes. Remove the cover, turn the pieces, and rearrange so they cook evenly, then cover and simmer until tender – from 20 to 30 minutes, according to the age and tenderness of the rabbit. There should be no resistance when the flesh is pierced with the point of a small, sharp knife. When tender, remove the pieces of rabbit to a heated platter, add the remaining wine, and turn up the heat. Add the remaining tarragon and the parsley; bring the liquid to a boil and boil rapidly until reduced by half, then pour the pan juices over the rabbit and serve. Crisply sautéed potatoes and a celery salad with a mustard vinaigrette dressing go well with this. Serve with the same kind of white wine used for cooking.

Sautéed Pheasant with Cabbage

When I was young, we often indulged in sautéed pheasant. Somehow the delicate game flavour was more pronounced than when the pheasant was roasted. For sautéing, the pheasant must be young and tender, and I also feel it should be done in two frying pans, one for the dark meat, which takes longer to cook, and one for the white meat. One pheasant will serve 2 to 4, depending on the size of the birds and the size of the appetites.

Serves 4 to 8

2 young pheasants, disjointed into serving pieces like chickens	¼ teaspoon paprika
	6 to 8 rashers of good bacon
60 g. (2 oz.) flour	90 g. (3 oz.) unsalted butter
Salt, freshly ground black pepper	1 medium head of cabbage
¼ teaspoon dried thyme	3 dl. (½ pt) double cream

Put the pheasant pieces in a plastic bag with the flour, 1 teaspoon salt, ½ teaspoon pepper, the thyme and the paprika and shake until the pieces are lightly coated with the seasoned flour. Remove and shake off excess.

Divide the bacon between two heavy 25-cm. (10-inch) frying pans (one should have a tight-fitting cover). Cook the bacon over medium heat until the fat is rendered and the bacon is just beginning to crisp. Remove it, drain on paper towels, and keep warm in a 130°C (250°F, gas mark ½) oven.

Add half the butter to one pan and, when it has melted into the bacon fat and is hot and sizzling, add the dark meat pieces, skin side down, and sauté over medium-high heat until brown on one side, then turn and brown the other side. Five minutes after starting the dark meat, put the remaining butter in the other pan and, when hot and sizzling, add the white meat pieces, skin side down, and brown over medium-high heat. Then turn and brown the second side.

While the pieces are browning, shred the cabbage and parboil it in salted water for 10 minutes. Drain well.

Reduce the heat under both pans and continue to cook the pheasant until just tender, about 15 to 20 minutes, adding the cabbage to the dark meat, and covering the pan so the meat will be tenderized by the steam. Five minutes before the end of the cooking time, uncover, season both white and dark meat with salt and pepper to taste, add the cream to the pheasant and cabbage, and simmer until tender. If the white meat is cooked first, remove it to a hot platter, cover with foil, and keep warm. Combine the pheasant and cabbage on the platter and garnish with the crisp bacon. Serve with small boiled potatoes.

VARIATION

If you like a juniper flavour, tuck a few juniper berries in with the cabbage.

Sautéed Quail

Tiny quail, with their delicate flesh, are delicious sautéed. Do not overcook these little birds, and serve 1 or 2 per person, depending on size.

Serves 3 to 6

60 g. (2 oz.) unsalted butter	2 dl. (⅓ pt) white wine
4 tablespoons groundnut oil	1½ dl. (¼ pt) cognac
6 quail	225 g. (8 oz.) seedless or seeded white
1 teaspoon or more salt	grapes
Freshly grated nutmeg	6 rounds of buttered toast

Heat the butter and oil in a large frying pan with a cover until very hot, but not brown. Add the quail and sauté them on all sides until delicately browned, turning frequently. Season with salt to taste and grate a little nutmeg over them. Add the white wine, reduce the heat, and simmer the quail, covered, for about 10 minutes. Turn off the heat, remove the cover, add the cognac to the hot pan, ignite it, and flame the birds, shaking the pan gently until the flames die down. Add the grapes. Cover and simmer for about 8 minutes, or until quail are tender. Serve them on the toast croustades and garnish with the grapes. A purée of parsnips with butter and Madeira and a salad of chicory with a well-flavoured vinaigrette sauce goes well with this.

VARIATION

Remove the breasts from the quail (use legs and carcasses for stock), and sauté in 45 g. (1½ oz.) butter and 3 tablespoons oil until delicately browned, season with salt and nutmeg, add 4 tablespoons white wine, and simmer, covered, until just tender, about 10 minutes. Do not flame or add grapes. Serve on toast croustades.

Veal

As I've said, the meat that takes best of all to sautéing is veal, the thin slices cut from the leg and pounded until they are paper-thin and flat that are known as scallops, escalopes, or scaloppine. The pounding tenderizes the meat, enabling it to be cooked very quickly, in about 5 to 8 minutes depending on thickness and tenderness. Although pale pink, top-quality veal is expensive, it is a better buy than the darker, pinkish-red veal that comes from an older animal (really, young beef) and therefore is not so tender. Two to three thin scallops, according to size, are enough for a serving, and 750 g. (1½ pounds) of very thin scallops should be enough for 4 to 6 people. The important point is to cook them fast, and not to overcrowd the pan, which reduces the heat and makes them steam rather than sauté. The following is a very simple, basic recipe for sautéed veal scallops.

♙ Veal Scallops Fines Herbes

Serves 4

8 large or 12 medium veal scallops (about 680 g. or 1½ lbs.), pounded until thin

60 g. (2 oz.) flour

90 g. (3 oz.) unsalted butter

3 tablespoons olive oil

2 tablespoons finely chopped chives

2 tablespoons finely chopped parsley

1 tablespoon finely chopped tarragon

Or 1 teaspoon dried tarragon

1½ dl. (¼ pt) dry white wine

Salt, freshly ground black pepper

Coat the scallops lightly with flour, brushing off excess. Heat the butter and oil in a heavy frying pan and when hot but not brown (butter should just stop foaming) add the scallops, a few at a time, and sauté them quickly over high heat, about 3 or 4 minutes a side, until delicately browned. Remove and keep warm while you do the rest of the scallops. Add the chopped herbs and wine and cook for 2 minutes at high heat. Season to taste with salt and pepper and serve immediately, with the pan juices poured over the scallops. Serve with sautéed potatoes and julienne strips of blanched, sautéed carrot and courgette (see page 200).

Veal Kidneys Flambé

Serves 4

4 veal kidneys
60 g. (2 oz.) unsalted butter
3 tablespoons oil
1½ dl. (¼ pt) cognac or Armagnac
Salt, freshly ground black pepper
1½ teaspoons Dijon mustard

1 tablespoon Worcestershire sauce
¼ teaspoon Tabasco
3 dl. (½ pt) double cream
Beurre manié (see page 283)
1 tablespoon chopped parsley

Clean the kidneys, removing the outer membrane and the core of fat and white tubes in the top (see page 117). Cut in medium-thin slices. Combine the butter and oil in a large frying pan and heat until hot and bubbling, add the kidneys, and sauté very quickly (about 4 minutes) over high heat, shaking the pan and tossing and turning the kidneys several times until browned. Turn off the heat, add the cognac or Armagnac, and ignite with a long kitchen match, standing well back. Flame the kidneys, shaking the pan until the flames die. Season with salt and pepper to taste, the mustard, Worcestershire sauce and Tabasco, and stir in the cream. Add small balls of *beurre manié* and cook over medium heat, stirring, until the sauce is just lightly thickened. Do not overcook or the kidneys will toughen. Taste and correct the seasoning. Sprinkle with chopped parsley and serve with rice and a green salad.

♟ Sautéed Sweetbreads with Ham

When sweetbreads are sautéed they should be soaked in ice water, blanched, and weighted to firm the texture before they are trimmed and cooked.

Serves 6

3 pairs sweetbreads
225 g. (8 oz.) or more unsalted butter
12 slices bread, trimmed of crusts
12 thin slices cooked country ham
12 large mushroom caps
100 g. (3½ oz.) plus 2 tablespoons flour
Salt, freshly ground black pepper
1 tablespoon lemon juice

¼ teaspoon nutmeg
3 eggs, lightly beaten
90 to 125 g. (3 to 4 oz.) fresh bread crumbs
1½ dl. (¼ pt) brandy or calvados
3 to 4½ dl. (½ to ¾ pt) double cream
¼ teaspoon Tabasco
2 tablespoons chopped parsley

Soak the sweetbreads in ice water for 30 minutes. Put in a deep saucepan with water to cover, 1 teaspoon salt, and 1 tablespoon lemon juice (which helps to keep them white), bring to a boil, reduce the heat, and simmer for 10 minutes. Remove and plunge into ice water to stop their cooking any further. When cool enough to handle, remove the covering membrane, connecting tubes, and particles of fat. Put the sweetbreads on a baking tray, cover with greaseproof paper, put another baking tray or chopping board on top, and weigh down with several tins of food. Leave for 2 hours. This makes the sweetbreads firm and compact enough to slice.

When ready to cook, remove the sweetbreads and halve them lengthwise into 12 even 'cutlets'.

Heat 90 g. (3 oz.) butter in a very heavy frying pan and when it is hot and has stopped frothing, add the bread squares, a few at a time, in a single layer and fry just until golden on both sides. Do not allow the butter to get too dark or burn, or the bread to get too dark. Add more butter if necessary. Remove, drain on paper towels, and keep hot in a 130°C (250°F, gas mark ½) oven. Heat the ham slices in 30 g. (1 oz.) butter, drain, and put on the toast. In another frying pan, sauté the mushroom caps over medium-high heat in 45 g. (1½ oz.) butter, tossing them so they cook on all sides, until lightly browned – about 3 to 4 minutes. Remove and keep warm.

Season 100 g. (3½ oz.) flour with 1 teaspoon salt, ¼ teaspoon pepper, and the nutmeg. Dip the sweetbread 'cutlets' into the seasoned flour, then into the beaten eggs, and then into the bread crumbs. Heat 90 g. (3 oz.) butter in a large frying pan and when it stops frothing, add the sweetbreads and sauté, a few at a time, over medium-high heat, until delicately browned on all sides. When all are cooked, return to the pan, turn off the heat, pour in the brandy or calvados, ignite it, and flame the sweetbreads, shaking the pan until the flames die. Remove to a platter, cover with aluminium foil, and keep warm while making the sauce.

Blend 2 tablespoons flour with the butter and juices in the pan, adding a little more butter if the mixture seems too floury, and cook over medium heat, stirring, until it starts to bubble. Gradually stir in the cream and the Tabasco and cook over low heat, stirring, until thickened. Taste and correct the seasoning.

To serve, top each ham slice with one piece of sweetbread. Spoon the sauce over the sweetbreads and top with a mushroom cap. Sprinkle with parsley. Serve two per person.

Traditionally, this elegant dish was finished and served *sous cloche* – under a glass bell. The toast, ham and sweetbreads were put on individual gratin dishes, covered with a heatproof glass bell, and gently reheated in the oven, then covered with the sauce and served under the bell, or *cloche*.

Pork and Lamb

Pork Chops Niçoise

Sautéed pork chops are succulent and delicious. For sautéing, they should be cut $2\frac{1}{2}$ to $3\frac{1}{2}$ cm. (1 to $1\frac{1}{2}$ inches) thick, and those from the loin or rib section are preferable. You can trim some of the fat from the chops, render it, and use it for the sautéing.

Serves 6

3 to 4 tablespoons rendered pork fat or olive oil

6 pork loin chops, cut $2\frac{1}{2}$ to $3\frac{1}{2}$ cm. (1 to $1\frac{1}{2}$ inches) thick

4 ripe tomatoes, peeled, seeded, and finely chopped
Or 3 dl. ($\frac{1}{2}$ pt) canned Italian plum tomatoes

3 garlic cloves, peeled and finely chopped

1 medium green pepper, seeds and ribs removed, finely chopped

1 tablespoon fresh, chopped basil
Or 1 teaspoon dried basil

350 g. (12 oz.) black olives (preferably the Niçoise olives)

Heat the pork fat or oil in a heavy frying pan and brown the chops lightly on each side over fairly high heat, allowing about 3 minutes a side. Do only as many chops at one time as will fit into the pan without crowding. Add extra fat or oil if required. Replace the chops in the pan and add the tomatoes, garlic, green pepper and basil. Cover the pan and simmer for 25 minutes, turning the chops once during the cooking. Add the olives and continue cooking for another 10 minutes over low heat, or until the chops are tender when tested near the bone with the point of a small sharp knife. Serve with rice mixed with chopped parsley.

Devilled Breast of Lamb

One of the most delicious of all ways to cook economical breast of lamb is first to poach it in a *court bouillon* and then cut it into pieces, crumb, sauté, and serve with a sauce diable.

Serves 6 to 8

2 or 3 1½-kg. (3-lb.) breasts of lamb, trimmed of most of their fat

2 large onions, peeled and each stuck with 2 cloves

12 to 14 garlic cloves, peeled

1 leek, well washed and trimmed

1 carrot, peeled

1 bay leaf

2 teaspoons salt

1 teaspoon rosemary

Water or stock to cover

2 eggs, lightly beaten

150 g. (5 oz.) flour

125 g. (4 oz.) dry bread crumbs

6 tablespoons clarified unsalted butter (see page 361)

Or 3 tablespoons unsalted butter and 3 tablespoons oil

Put the lamb breasts in a deep pan with the onions, garlic, leek, carrot, bay leaf, salt, rosemary and enough water or stock to just cover the lamb. Bring to a boil, skim off any scum that forms on the surface, reduce the heat, and simmer the lamb for 1 hour, or until it is quite tender when tested with the point of a small, sharp knife. Remove and drain the breasts, put them in a shallow dish or tin (such as a roasting tin), cover them with aluminium foil, and weigh them down with a board or baking tray with tinned goods on top. Let the meat cool and then chill it.

When ready to prepare, pull the rib bones from the breasts and cut the meat into serving pieces, about 2½ to 3½ cm. (1 to 1½ inches) wide. Put the eggs, flour, and bread crumbs in separate pie plates. Dip the lamb pieces in the flour, then into the egg, then roll them in the crumbs.

Heat the butter or butter and oil in a large, heavy frying pan. Sauté the lamb in the hot fat, a few pieces at a time (do not crowd too many in the pan), over medium-high heat until delicately brown and crisp on both sides. Serve on a very hot platter with a sauce diable (see page 290). Crisp shoestring potatoes and a large bowl of plain watercress are excellent with this. Drink a Beaujolais, such as a Fleurie.

Fish
....

While sautéing, like frying and grilling, ranks among the more common ways of cooking fish, all these processes require care and attention if the delicate flesh is to be perfectly cooked and not overdone.

For a simple sauté, or sauté meunière, the fish is cooked in a small amount of unsalted butter or, better yet, butter and oil (remember, the oil, which can be heated to a higher temperature, keeps the butter from burning), turned once during the cooking process, seasoned with salt and pepper, and sprinkled with chopped parsley.

Sometimes the fish is lightly floured before cooking, and a bit of additional butter may be added at the last minute with a few drops of lemon juice. Clarified butter is excellent for sautéing, as it does not burn as readily as plain butter. If you use clarified butter (see page 361), no oil is necessary.

Sautéing is best done at the very last minute – otherwise the fish will become stale and uninteresting if it stands too long. Small whole fish, split fish, fish fillets, or thin fish steaks may all be sautéed. Frozen fish can be sautéed without thawing, but the cooking time will be almost double, and care must be taken that the skin does not become overcooked. Among fish suitable for sautéing whole are small trout, plaice, flounder, sole, whiting, dabs, sardines and smelts.

☙ Sautéed Trout

Select 4 whole trout of the same size and measure the fish from belly to backbone at the thickest point (see page 122) to estimate the cooking time – the rule for any type of fish cookery is to allow 10 minutes per $2\frac{1}{2}$ cm. (inch) of measured thickness.

Serves 4

4 whole trout
30 g. (1 oz.) flour
100 g. ($3\frac{1}{2}$ oz.) unsalted butter
4 tablespoons vegetable oil, preferably
  groundnut

Salt, freshly ground black pepper
1 tablespoon chopped parsley

Put the flour on a sheet of waxed paper, add fish and coat lightly with flour on both sides, shaking off excess. Heat 60 g. (2 oz.) butter and the oil in a large, heavy frying pan and when hot but not smoking, add the fish and cook them for half the estimated cooking time over medium-high heat, then turn and cook for the remainder of the time on the other side. Salt and pepper to taste as they cook. Test the fish for doneness with a fork or toothpick – if they flake easily, they are done – and remove to a hot platter. Add the rest of the butter to the pan, swirl it around until it melts, add the chopped parsley, and pour the sauce over the fish. Serve at once with lemon wedges and plain boiled potatoes. A white wine such as a Muscadet from the Loire or a Pinot Chardonnay from Burgundy is good with sautéed trout.

VARIATIONS

Vary the flavouring by adding chopped dill, chives, or tarragon to the pan.

Sautéed Trout Amandine. Sauté 100 g. (3½ oz.) thinly sliced almonds in 60 g. (2 oz.) butter in the pan in which the fish were cooked until delicately golden, shaking the pan several times and lightly salting the nuts as they cook. Spoon over the trout and serve immediately.

Sautéed Fish Steaks

Turbot, salmon, and halibut steaks are excellent candidates for sautéing. Have the steaks cut about 2½ to 3½ cm. (1 to 1½ inches) thick from the best, centre part of the fish (if the fish is very large, divide the steaks in half before or after cooking) and allow one steak or half a steak, according to size, for each serving. Measure the fish at the thickest point and allow 10 minutes cooking time per 2½ cm. (inch).

For 2 large or 4 medium salmon or halibut steaks, heat 60 g. (2 oz.) unsalted butter and 4 tablespoons oil in a large, heavy frying pan until fat is hot but not smoking. Add the steaks and cook over medium-high heat for the allotted time, turning them once halfway during the cooking, until lightly browned on the outside. As for trout, serve with additional melted butter and chopped parsley, lemon wedges and boiled or sautéed potatoes. If you prefer a sauce with the steaks, skip the melted butter and have a hollandaise or Béarnaise sauce (see pages 292 and 294).

Fish Steaks Sauté Provençale

This unusual *sauté provençale*, a variation on the simple sauté, is a good way to prepare almost any fish that can be cut into steaks – cod, haddock and snapper, as well as halibut and salmon.

Serves 4

3 tomatoes, peeled, seeded, and chopped
30 g. (1 oz.) unsalted butter
2 large or 4 medium halibut or
    salmon steaks
30 g. (1 oz.) flour

6 tablespoons olive oil
2 large garlic cloves, finely chopped
4 tablespoons chopped parsley
Salt, freshly ground black pepper
4 tablespoons white wine

Cook the tomatoes slowly in the butter until they are almost a paste, but with enough of the pieces left to give them texture – about 20 minutes.

Measure the fish steaks at the thickest point to estimate the cooking time (see page 122). Spread flour on greaseproof paper, add fish, and coat lightly on both sides, shaking off excess. Heat the oil in a large, heavy frying pan until hot but not smoking, add the fish, and cook for half the estimated time. Turn the fish and add the garlic, shaking the pan gently. Then add 3 tablespoons chopped parsley, shaking the pan once more, and season the steaks with salt and pepper to taste. Cook for the rest of the time, then transfer the fish to a hot platter. Pour the wine into the pan and swirl it around. Pour the pan juices over the fish and garnish with the cooked tomatoes. Sprinkle with the remaining tablespoon of parsley and serve with lemon wedges. Drink a white wine – a Blanc de Blancs is a good choice.

Sautéed Fish Fillets

Sautéed fillets need very careful handling, constant attention, and a minimum of cooking. Some are so thin that they take barely more than 3 minutes. Cooking by measured thickness is vitally important here, for an overcooked fillet resembles nothing so much as well-seasoned cardboard.

If you are cooking frozen fillets from the frozen state, double the cooking time.

Fillets vary so much in size that it is hard to say whether to allot 1 or 2 per person. To be on the safe side, estimate approximately 150 to 225 g. ($\frac{1}{3}$ to $\frac{1}{2}$ pound) of fish per serving. Flour the fillets lightly. In a heavy frying pan heat 60 g. (2 oz.) unsalted butter and 4 tablespoons oil until the fat is hot but not smoking. Add the fillets and cook them until they are done, turning them once and taking great care to prevent them from breaking. Serve them with additional melted butter, chopped parsley and lemon juice.

Crab

♨ Sautéed Crabmeat

Crabmeat, which is bought ready-cooked and needs only heating through, is one of those foods that can be sautéed at the table in a chafing dish or any similar portable cooking unit as easily as in the kitchen, which makes it a good choice for a small party or a tête-à-tête dinner.

Serves 4 as a starter, 2 as a main course

4 tablespoons clarified butter (see page 361)
4 very thin slices of French bread
4 very thin slices of lemon
350 g. (¾ lb.) lump or leg crabmeat
2 tablespoons lemon juice
2 tablespoons cognac
5 tablespoons fish stock
5 tablespoons white wine
2 tablespoons each: chopped parsley and chopped chives
1 teaspoon salt
Freshly ground black pepper
2 tablespoons shredded raw carrot
Additional chopped parsley (about 1 tablespoon)

Heat the clarified butter in a sauté pan, frying pan, or blazer pan of a chafing dish, add the slices of French bread, and sauté on both sides until golden and crisp. Transfer them to heated plates.

Put the lemon slices in the pan and heat through in the butter (add more butter if the bread has absorbed it all), then transfer them to the plates with the fried bread croutons.

Add the crabmeat to the pan and toss lightly in the butter, sprinkle with the lemon juice; heat the cognac in a small pan to release the fumes of alcohol, then touch a match to it and pour flaming over the crab. Shake until the flames die, then pour in the stock and wine and let the mixture simmer gently until the crabmeat is just heated through – do not overcook it. Add the chopped parsley and chives, salt, several grinds of pepper and a few shreds of carrot. Spoon the mixture on to the croutons and garnish with additional shredded carrot and chopped parsley. Serve with hot French bread and butter, and drink a white Burgundy.

Eggs and Omelets

As I mentioned before, scrambled eggs are really sautéed eggs and as with other delicate sautés, you must take great care not to overcook them – the important thing is knowing the point at which to stop, for the eggs will go on cooking with their own internal heat after they are removed from the stove. People have different ways of making scrambled eggs, but I have got the best results by using a small, 23-cm. (9-inch), non-stick omelet pan for from 2 to 4 eggs and a 25-cm. (10-inch) frying pan for larger quantities. I recommend that you start with the smaller quantity as it is easier to control.

⌂ Perfect Scrambled Eggs

Serves 1

2 eggs
Salt, freshly ground black
   pepper
1 or 2 dashes of Tabasco

1 teaspoon water (for lighter
   scrambled eggs)
30 g. (1 oz.) butter (plus extra
   softened butter for richer eggs)

Break the eggs into a bowl, add salt, pepper, and Tabasco, and beat lightly with a fork. For lighter scrambled eggs, also beat in the water. If you like your scrambled eggs thick and eggy, don't use any water.

Melt the butter, 15 g. ($\frac{1}{2}$ oz.) for each egg, in a non-stick frying pan over medium-high heat and when hot but not sizzling, pour in the eggs. As soon as the eggs begin to coagulate, start making pushing strokes with a rubber or wooden spatula so you get curds. Lift the pan off the heat from side to side with a circular motion while you push. As the heat in the eggs increases, the curds will form faster and you will have to keep lifting the pan from the heat and pushing faster. When the curds are soft but not too runny, quickly transfer the eggs to a plate. You have to know exactly when to stop applying heat or the eggs will be overcooked, hard little lumps.

If you want very rich eggs, sometimes called 'buttered eggs', as you push the curds in the pan add small pieces of softened butter, which will melt in and make the eggs taste even more luscious.

If you are adding chopped herbs, sliced sautéed mushrooms, chopped sautéed scallions, or grated cheese, lace them in as you scramble the eggs. For finely cut ham or smoked salmon, heat gently in the butter before adding and scrambling the eggs.

🍳 A Perfect Omelet

Making an omelet requires deftness, speed, plenty of practice, and a pan 23 cm. (9 inches) in diameter, with rounded sides and a heavy bottom that will hold the heat. If you use a cast-aluminium or cast-iron pan, it must be used only for omelets and never washed on the inside, merely wiped out with a damp cloth, or the omelet will stick. Should it stick, rub the pan with a sprinkling of coarse salt and a paper towel to remove the residue, then rub with a drop or two of oil and a clean paper towel.

However, after many years of omelet-making I have come to the conclusion that the best pan to use is one with a non-stick lining, to which the egg will never cling, no matter how often you wash the pan or use it for other things.

My favourite non-stick omelet pan is made of cast aluminium, 23 cm. (9 inches) in diameter, sloping to a heavy bottom 15 cm. (6 inches) across. Only the bottom is heavy; the pan itself is light enough to lift and shake with one hand. In this pan it is possible to make an omelet without using any kind of tool – all you need to do is shake the pan vigorously and the eggs will move around and start to set of their own accord.

Don't worry if you can't make a perfect omelet at first. This is a technique you acquire by constant practice and by learning to judge the point when the omelet has set just enough and can be rolled and tipped out. The whole process takes only about 30 seconds, so you can make as many omelets as you need in practically no time. Always make your omelets individually. It's much more difficult, and not very satisfactory, to make a huge one in a big pan and then divide it up.

Serves 1

2 very large or 3 small eggs	1 tablespoon water
Scant ½ teaspoon salt	15 g. (½ oz.) butter
Pinch of pepper	
Or dash of Tabasco	

Break the eggs into a bowl, add the seasonings and water, and beat lightly with a fork – don't overbeat, only enough to blend yolks and whites.

Heat your omelet pan over high heat until a drop of water bounces when flicked onto the surface. Add the butter and swirl it around until it melts and foams, which will happen almost immediately if the pan is the right heat. If it browns or burns, the pan is too hot. Remove it from the heat, wipe out the butter with paper towels, swing the pan in the air a little to cool it, and start again.

When the butter stops foaming, quickly pour in the eggs and, shaking the pan with one hand so it moves over the heat, *stir the eggs lightly with a fork as if you were making scrambled eggs.* (If you use a non-stick pan, use a wooden spatula, not any sort of metal tool, or *just shake the pan which will move the eggs around enough.*)

When the eggs have set to the degree you like (I like mine French style, still creamy in the centre, but you may prefer yours a little more set), *start rolling the omelet with the fork or spatula, at the end of the pan near the handle.*

If you are adding a filling, do this before starting to roll. Tip the pan forward so the omelet rolls on to itself.

Now reverse your grip on the handle, holding it from underneath, hold a plate close to the pan with your other hand, and start to invert the pan, which will tip the omelet onto the plate in a neat roll, with the edges underneath and a lovely smooth surface on top. Serve immediately. Omelets can't wait.

If you are making more than one omelet, wipe the pan with paper towels after each one, reheat, and add fresh butter to the pan.

OMELET FILLINGS

Four or five tablespoons of any of the following, freshly cooked or reheated, may be added to the omelet just before it is rolled, and any excess spooned over the top before serving:

Sliced mushrooms, sautéed or creamed
Creamed chicken or chicken hash
Buttered green vegetables, such as pieces of asparagus, broccoli, spinach
Creamed fish
Crumbled crisp bacon
Thin strips of ham, frizzled in butter
Ripe tomatoes, peeled, seeded, chopped and sautéed
Sautéed lamb kidneys, cut into small pieces
Croutons of bread, fried in olive oil, with or without garlic
Sautéed sliced onions

Or use any other mixture of your choice, provided it is hot. Grated cheese (2 to 3 tablespoons) should be added just before the eggs are set, so it can melt. Herbs, such as finely chopped chives, parsley, and chervil for an omelet fines herbes, or finely chopped watercress should be mixed into the eggs before they are cooked. Use 1 tablespoon fresh herbs.

Vegetables

If you have never tasted a sautéed vegetable, you're missing something. Like the Chinese stir-frying technique (which it closely resembles), sautéing keeps the crispness and flavour of vegetables intact. Certain vegetables, such as mushrooms, thinly sliced carrots, courgettes, onions, green peppers and corn kernels, which lend themselves to this fast technique, need no prior cooking. Firmer vegetables, such as turnips, potatoes, cauliflower, Brussels sprouts, French beans and broccoli, need to be parboiled or blanched first until tender but still crisp.

Buttered Brussels Sprouts

Brussels sprouts, members of the cabbage family, are underrated because they are usually very badly cooked to a mushy tastelessness with little or no character. Sautéing keeps them crisp and interesting.

Serves 4

1 kg. (2 lbs.) Brussels sprouts of
   roughly equal size
90 g. (3 oz.) butter

½ teaspoon freshly ground black pepper
Several drops of lemon juice

Trim the sprouts, being careful not to cut away too much of the stem end. Remove discoloured outer leaves. Put them in a 2-litre (2-quart) saucepan with enough boiling, salted water to come one-third of the way up the pan, bring to a boil, and blanch, covered, for 5 minutes, until barely cooked through. Drain well.

   Melt the butter in another pan, add the sprouts, and cook, covered, shaking the pan well, for 3 to 4 minutes. Season with the pepper and lemon juice. These are good with grilled or roast meats.

VARIATIONS

1. Sauté 60 g. (2 oz.) thinly sliced almonds in 30 g. (1 oz.) butter and add to the sprouts.
2. Combine sprouts with an equal quantity of whole, cooked, peeled chestnuts, heated in butter and seasoned to taste, and a few pieces of crumbled crisp bacon.

Carrots Vichy

I'm sure the reason most of us shun carrots is that they are prepared so indifferently in restaurants – boiled to death and combined with tinned peas or dressed with a mere sliver of butter. As a result they have no trace of flavour. This classic way of cooking them is certainly a change for the better.

Serves 4

1 kg. (2 lbs.) fairly small carrots
1 teaspoon salt
60 g. (2 oz.) butter
4 tablespoons water
½ teaspoon sugar

¼ teaspoon marjoram
1 tablespoon chopped parsley
4 tablespoons double cream
   (optional)

Scrape the carrots and cut them into very thin rounds. Put them in a saucepan with the salt, butter and water and cook, covered, over medium heat, shaking the pan from time to time and making sure the carrots do not brown or cook too fast, until they are just tender when pierced with the point of a small, sharp knife. Add the sugar and marjoram and toss well, then sprinkle the carrots with parsley and serve. If you like, add the cream to the carrots just before sprinkling them with parsley.

Sautéed Cauliflower

Cauliflower is another vegetable that tends to be rather dull and uninspiring. Sautéed to buttery crispness, cauliflower has a flavour that is so different you'll find it hard to know what you're eating.

Serves 6

1 very large cauliflower	*Salt, freshly ground black pepper*
Or 2 medium cauliflowers	*1 teaspoon lemon juice*
180 g. (6 oz.) butter	

Parboil the cauliflower in boiling, salted water to cover for 4 to 6 minutes. Drain well and slice very thin or chop rather coarse – the centre may not even be warmed through, but don't worry about that. Melt the butter in a large heavy frying pan and when foaming, add the cauliflower and toss it well over very, very low heat for a few minutes until it has absorbed almost all the butter. Season to taste with salt, pepper, and lemon juice.

Celery in Butter

When celery is boiled and dressed with butter it loses all its lovely flavour and becomes something best forgotten. Perhaps this is the reason that most people eat only raw celery and never know how delightful it can be when quickly sautéed.

Serves 4

1 large head of celery, cleaned and
   trimmed
90 g. (3 oz.) butter

1 teaspoon salt
½ teaspoon freshly ground black pepper

Cut the celery head into thin slices. Heat the butter in a heavy saucepan, add the celery, season with the salt and pepper, and cook, covered, tossing from time to time with a fork, until just tender, about 5 to 6 minutes. Taste, add more salt and pepper if needed, and serve with roast pork or lamb.

Sautéed Mushrooms with Turnips

Serves 6

225 g. (8 oz.) mushrooms
6 medium turnips
125 g. (4 oz.) butter

Salt, freshly ground black pepper
1 tablespoon chopped parsley

Wipe the mushrooms with a damp cloth and slice them lengthwise, through cap and stem, 6 mm. (¼ inch) thick. Peel the turnips and slice 6 mm. (¼ inch) thick. Parboil the sliced turnips in boiling salted water to cover for 8 to 12 minutes, watching them carefully to see they do not overcook – they should be tender but still crisp. Drain them well, add 45 g. (1½ oz.) butter and ¼ teaspoon freshly ground pepper, and keep warm over low heat.

Melt the remaining butter in a frying pan, add the mushrooms, and sauté them quickly over fairly high heat, tossing them in the pan and seasoning them as they cook with ½ teaspoon salt and ¼ teaspoon pepper. Combine the turnips with the mushrooms and cook them together, shaking the pan gently to mix them, for 2 minutes. Transfer to a heated serving dish and sprinkle with parsley. Serve with roasted, grilled or braised meats, or with duck or game.

♨ Sautéed Potatoes

This version of sautéed potatoes is made with potatoes boiled in their skins, which hold them together.

Serves 4 to 6

1 kg. (2 lbs.) potatoes
90 g. (3 oz.) butter
1 teaspoon salt

Freshly ground black pepper
1 tablespoon chopped parsley

Boil the potatoes in their skins in salted water to cover until they are just tender when pierced with a knife, about 20 minutes. Drain, and when cool enough to handle, slice them into rounds about 6 mm. ($\frac{1}{4}$ inch) thick.

Heat the butter in a heavy frying pan until foaming. Add the potatoes and sauté them over medium-high heat until they begin to brown. Turn them carefully with a spatula and cook until browned on the other side. Season them with salt and a few grinds of pepper, carefully transfer to a heated serving dish, and sprinkle with chopped parsley.

VARIATION

Lyonnaise Potatoes. Melt 60 g. (2 oz.) butter in a frying pan, add 4 medium onions, sliced, and sauté over medium heat, turning them frequently, for 10 minutes. Add 1 teaspoon sugar and salt to taste, cover, and cook for 4 or 5 minutes more, until soft. Add the onions to the sautéed and seasoned potatoes and toss the two vegetables together lightly until well blended. Transfer to a heated serving dish and sprinkle with parsley.

Sautéed Spinach

Serves 4

1 kg. (2 lbs.) fresh spinach, well washed	$\frac{1}{2}$ teaspoon freshly ground black
4 tablespoons olive or groundnut oil	pepper
1 garlic clove, finely chopped	$\frac{1}{4}$ teaspoon nutmeg
2 tablespoons soy sauce	

Remove the heavy stems from the spinach, put it in a heavy pan with just the water clinging to the leaves, cover, and boil over high heat until it is wilted down but not cooked, about 2 minutes. Pour off any liquid.

In a frying pan heat the oil with the garlic, add the drained spinach, soy sauce, pepper and nutmeg, and toss them well for 2 or 3 minutes. Taste and add salt if necessary – it probably won't be, as the soy sauce is salty.

Sautéed Chicory with Brown Butter

Chicory, with its tight white head, is another salad green that is traditionally braised and served as a vegetable with roast meats, poultry, or game. In this recipe, browned butter is used as a sauce.

Serves 6

6 heads of chicory
200 g. (7 oz.) unsalted butter

Juice of $\frac{1}{2}$ lemon
Salt, freshly ground black pepper to taste

Because chicory is specially blanched and packed, it does not require washing. Just trim off a little of the root end, remove any discoloured or broken outer leaves, and wipe with a damp cloth.

Melt 90 g. (3 oz.) of the butter in a frying pan or saucepan, add the chicory in a single layer, and sauté on all sides over medium-high heat until lightly coloured. Reduce the heat, cover the pan, and cook for about 10 minutes, then turn them over and cook, covered, until just tender and pierceable, about 30 to 40 minutes.

To prepare the brown butter, warm the remaining butter over medium heat in a small, heavy frying pan, shaking the pan from time to time, until the butter turns a deep brown-tinged gold. Do not let it burn and get dark.

Arrange the cooked chicory on a hot platter or serving dish and sprinkle with the lemon juice and salt and pepper to taste. Spoon the brown butter over them and serve at once.

Glazed Turnips

These are a classic accompaniment to roast duck. Often they are basted at the last minute with some of the pan juices from the duck.

Serves 4

6 to 8 small white turnips
125 g. (4 oz.) butter

1 teaspoon salt
1 teaspoon or more sugar

Peel the turnips and with a very sharp knife shape each into two ovals about the size of a walnut but slightly longer – you should get two or more ovals from each turnip.

Heat the butter in a heavy frying pan, until foaming, add the turnips, sprinkle them with salt, and cook very slowly over medium-low heat, shaking the pan and turning them often, for about 10 minutes. Sprinkle with 1 teaspoon sugar, shake the pan, and keep cooking and turning the turnips until they are lightly glazed and tender but still crisp. For a heavier glaze, add a little more sugar. Serve with roast duck, goose, or venison.

🍲 Shredded, Sautéed Courgettes

Courgettes carry a lot of water, and if you are going to sauté them you have to get rid of some of that water first. A very popular way to cook courgette now is to shred it, squeeze out the water, and then sauté it quickly in butter.

Serves 4

6 medium courgettes, about 1½ kg. (3 lbs.)
60 g. (2 oz.) butter
  Or 30 g. (1 oz.) butter and 2 tablespoons olive oil
Salt, freshly ground black pepper

2 garlic cloves, peeled and chopped
  Or 2 finely chopped shallots
¼ teaspoon dried basil
  Or 2 teaspoons chopped fresh basil (optional)

Wash the courgettes and slice off the stem end and the brown part of the blossom end. Dry. Shred the courgettes, using the coarse side of a grater, a Mouli-julienne with shredding disc, or a food processor with the larger shredding attachment. Put them in a heavy tea towel and twist the towel to squeeze the excess water from the courgettes.

Melt the butter, or oil and butter, add the courgettes and garlic or shallots, and sauté over moderately high heat, turning with a spatula and shaking and tossing in the pan, until tender but not soft and mushy. Do not allow to brown. While sautéing, season with salt and pepper to taste and, if desired, basil.

Sautéed Courgettes with Walnuts

Serves 6

6 medium-small courgettes
45 g. (1½ oz.) butter
3 tablespoons olive oil
1 garlic clove, unpeeled

Salt, freshly ground black pepper
125 g. (4 oz.) coarsely chopped walnuts
1 tablespoon chopped parsley

Clean and trim the courgettes as in previous recipe. Cut into 6-mm. (¼-inch) slices. Put them in a colander, sprinkle with salt to draw out the water, and leave for an hour to drain. Rinse the slices and dry them.

Heat 30 g. (1 oz.) butter and the oil in a heavy frying pan or sauté pan and when foaming, add the courgettes and garlic clove and sauté, shaking the pan constantly, until the slices are tender but still crisp. (The unpeeled garlic clove gives a little touch of flavour; discard it after cooking.) While cooking, taste a slice to see if it needs additional salt. If so, salt while tossing and give the slices a few grinds of pepper.

Add $\frac{3}{4}$ of the walnuts to the courgettes, shake the pan to blend them together, and heat the nuts through. Transfer to a heated vegetable dish, add the remaining butter and walnuts, and garnish with parsley. This is excellent with roast lamb or with poultry.

Three-Vegetable Sauté

Recently I have been experimenting with vegetable dishes and I've come up with some interesting combinations and techniques. One is a mixture of thin strips of swede (the large yellow turnip), white turnips, and peeled broccoli stalks, a part of the vegetable that has a delicious flavour all its own and is all too often thrown away. The vegetables are blanched and then very quickly sautéed.

Serves 4

1 swede	90 g. (3 oz.) butter
3 small white turnips	Salt, freshly ground black pepper
Heavy stems from a bunch of broccoli	

Peel and slice the swede and white turnips and cut them into julienne strips of matchstick thickness about 8 or 10 cm. (3 or 4 inches) long (yellow turnips are rather hard to slice, so use a heavy chef's knife or a Chinese cleaver). Carefully peel the broccoli stalks, using a vegetable peeler or a small, sharp paring knife, and cut them into julienne strips of the same size and thickness as the turnips. Combine the three vegetables and drop them into a pan of boiling, salted water. When the water comes back to the boil, let them blanch for 1 minute only. Then immediately drain them and plunge them into cold water to stop their cooking (you can do this blanching an hour or two ahead of the time you are going to cook the sauté). Drain and dry well.

When you are almost ready to serve, melt the butter in a heavy frying pan or sauté pan that has a cover. Just toss the vegetables in the hot butter until heated through, the way you would toss a salad, then cover them and cook for a minute or two – no longer. They should not be cooked until soft and limp; they must retain their colour and be just crisply tender. Season with salt and pepper to taste and, if you feel they need it, melt a little more butter in the pan and pour it over them.

VARIATION

Instead of using turnips and broccoli stems, cut carrots and courgettes into strips of the same size and thickness, blanch them in the same way, and then toss in the butter and cook until just crisp and tender.

Fruit

Sautéing is an easy and delicious way to prepare firm fruits, such as apples, pears and pineapples.

Fried Apple Rings. Wash and core but do not peel apples and cut crosswise in 1-cm (½-inch) slices. Sauté in hot unsalted butter, allowing about 15 g. (½ oz.) for every 2 slices, until brown on both sides, but not mushy. Serve with pork dishes, or with ham and sausage for breakfast.

Glazed Apple Rings. Cook as above but sprinkle the rings as they cook with a little sugar and let it blend with the butter to glaze the apples slightly.

Sautéed Pears. Peel, core, and quarter ripe but firm pears. Sauté them in hot butter, about 15 g. (½ oz.) per pear, sprinkling them with a little sugar as they cook so they glaze slightly. Cook only until lightly glazed, not until they get mushy or break up. Serve with a little pear brandy (*eau-de-vie de poire*) poured over them.

Sautéed Pineapple. Sauté slices or fingers of fresh pineapple in hot butter, 15 g. (½ oz.) per slice, or per two fingers. After turning the slices or fingers, sprinkle them with brown sugar so they glaze slightly. Serve plain or flavoured with a little dark rum.

Bananas à l'Archestrate. Slice bananas very thin and sauté them in hot butter, 15 g. (½ oz.) per banana, over a high flame, tossing them well and sprinkling them with 1 tablespoon sugar per banana, until they brown, caramelize, and get crispy. Flame with 1 tablespoon warmed cognac per banana and serve spooned over vanilla ice cream – the hot bananas and the frigid ice cream make a sensational dessert.

Frying

In America, the word frying is, strictly speaking, used to mean deep-frying. Food which is cooked in a frying pan in a minimum of fat is said to be sautéed, or pan-fried.

To fry means to immerse completely in deep fat raised to a high temperature so that the entire surface of the food is quickly seared and becomes brown and crisp. Foods are fried in different ways, for different reasons. Some, like potatoes, are fried in their natural raw state, others are dipped in flour or batter, or first coated with flour, then dipped in egg, and finally in bread or biscuit crumbs.

In these calorie-conscious days, deep-frying has got a bad name. People are prone to think of fried foods as being greasy and fattening, but if they are fried correctly, there will be minimum absorption of fat. The most important thing to remember is that the heat must be kept at the right frying temperature and allowed to reheat to that temperature between batches, so that the surface of the food is immediately sealed by the hot fat. Once fried, the food should be removed to paper towels to drain off any excess fat on the outside and then put in a low-temperature oven to keep warm until the rest of the food is fried and ready to serve. If you remember these simple rules, you'll have perfectly cooked food every time, not a soggy, grease-soaked disaster.

When we think of deep-frying, the first thing that comes to mind is the chip or French fried potato, which you'll find on the menus of luncheonettes, fast-food chains, cafés and small restaurants all over the United States and Britain. While good French fries can be very good indeed, unfortunately they have become so universal and universally bad that they are one of the curses of the American diet. Pity the poor potato, cut into thick chunks, soaked in cold water, dried, then rudely thrust into a cauldron of hot fat without any care as to the accuracy of temperature or timing, so it emerges limp and soggy on the outside and hard in the centre. That needn't be so. If you follow my recipe for perfect French fries on page 216, you'll know how good this crisp little morsel can be.

While French fries have no coating of any kind, other vegetables, French fried courgettes for example, may be lightly dusted with flour to give them a nice brown coating. Or, like French fried onion rings, they may be dipped in batter. Batter forms a light, crisp, puffy envelope for delicate things such as fruits, fish, vegetables, and tender little chunks of sweetbreads or brains and a protective insulation that prevents them from overcooking and becoming hard and inedible. Breading, where the food is first lightly coated with flour, then dipped in beaten egg and finally in crumbs, is another kind of insulation. As the coating meets the hot fat it creates a quick, crunchy, golden-brown crust, keeping the food inside tender or creamy.

Properly fried food can be sublime. Just think of *beignets soufflés*, those little fritters of cream puff dough that puff up and expand in the hot fat to an ethereal lightness, delicate batter-coated tempura, the Japanese version of French-frying, and the very similar Italian *fritto misto* (or mixed fry) where pieces of fish or meat or vegetable are dipped into batter and deep-fried to a delicious crunchiness. I first encountered *fritto misto* at an Italian trattoria in London that I used to frequent when I lived there as a young man. The chef understood what frying should be. His *fritto misto* of early vegetables – tiny French beans, artichoke bottoms, small pieces of carrot, potato and onion – dipped in batter and quickly and expertly cooked, was an inspiring example of this much maligned and misused technique.

The American colonists were great exponents of cooking in deep fat. One of the staples of their diet was fried cakes of all kinds – doughnuts, and so on. Later, as they began to make bread from yeast, setting the dough to rise overnight in rooms that were much cooler than ours are today, chunks of the risen dough would be broken off in the morning, dropped into hot fat to puff and brown, then consumed for breakfast with maple syrup. There used to be a small inn on Nantucket that for many years kept this tradition going, serving 'dough gobs', as they were called, two or three days a week. How homely, simple, and delectable they were! Then there are cake doughnuts, doughnut holes, and those luscious jelly doughnuts made from bread dough that one bites into and encounters the hidden sweetness of jam or jelly – innocent, unpretentious food, but wonderfully exciting to the palate.

At a later period in America's food history came croquettes, the elegant type of fried food considered proper for ladies' luncheons. These were made from ground poultry, meat or fish bound together with a very heavy white sauce, seasoned, shaped into balls or ovals, coated with flour, egg and crumbs, and cooked in hot fat until golden brown. Croquettes were usually served with a sauce, green peas, and sometimes (showing an unfortunate lack of judgement) another fried food – game chips, or Saratoga chips as they were called because they were said to have originated in Saratoga, the unwitting invention of a chef who sliced his fried potatoes too thin and ended up with crispy chips.

All kinds of fats can be used for frying. Many recipes used to call for lard, which, like rendered beef fat, gives very good flavour. Nowadays oil, mainly groundnut oil, corn oil and sunflower oil, is the preferred fat for frying because it is colourless, odourless, and can be heated to quite high temperatures without burning or darkening. Personally, my preference is for groundnut oil, which I use almost exclusively because it satisfies my frying requirements better than any other.

Oil can be used over and over, provided you strain it after every use and now and then clarify and purify it by frying in it a few pieces of raw potato, which collect those little burned bits that get left behind. Discard it when it gets very dark or starts to smell rancid. Never be skimpy with the oil you use for frying and never overcrowd the pan. There should be enough oil comfortably to cover whatever is being fried and space for the food to move around.

The first requisite is a deep fryer. You can take your choice of an electric deep fryer with a thermostatic control; the traditional wide, deep pan designed for deep-frying that has a basket that fits into the pan and hooks on to the side handles to drain; any deep, heavy 4- or 5-litre (4-quart) pot or an electric frying pan. With a non-electric pan you'll also need a cooking thermometer and, if you are using an electric frying pan or a pan without a frying basket, something to fish the fried food out with, such as a slotted spoon, a wire skimmer, or one of the flat, mesh skimmer-lifters the Japanese use for tempura – anything, in fact, that will simultaneously lift and drain the food. For batter-fried foods, you'll also need tongs for dipping the foods in the batter and lowering them into the fat.

While there's no denying that deep-frying is a messy job that smells up the kitchen and one that needs care and attention if you are to get worthwhile results, it does have advantages. It is the fastest of all cooking techniques, and once you have acquired the skill and a sense of timing, you'll be able to turn out a meal in no time flat and serve the food immediately, crisp, hot and deliciously tasty.

☺ Fried Courgettes

This is one of the simplest and very best fried dishes I know – quick, easy and delicious.

You need a good deep fryer (see introduction and illustrations, page 203). Be sure to check the oil temperature, remembering to let the fat heat between batches as the addition of cold food will cool it off. If you're using a frying basket, heat it in the fat first; otherwise it, too, will cool the fat. You should also keep at your side a baking tray lined with paper towels on which the fried courgettes can drain and keep warm in the oven. Preheat the oven to 130°C (250°F, gas mark $\frac{1}{2}$) before you begin frying.

Serves 6

6 to 8 small, firm courgettes	Groundnut oil for deep-frying
Salt, freshly ground black pepper	30 g. (1 oz.) flour

Wash and dry the courgettes and cut off the ends. Cut in half lengthwise and then into long strips of matchstick thickness. Place these sticks in a colander over a bowl, sprinkle with about 1 tablespoon salt, cover with a piece of greaseproof or waxed paper or foil, and allow to stand for 1 hour or more. This salting draws some of the liquid from the courgettes and results in quicker cooking and a better texture.

When you are ready to fry, put the oil in the deep fryer. Fill it no more than half full – fat foams up when food is added. If the fryer is electric, set the thermostat for 190°C (375°F). If you are using a pot on a surface burner, have a cooking thermometer handy to test the temperature. Heat the frying basket in the oil. (If you don't have a frying basket, you can drop the courgette pieces directly into the fat and remove them with a wire skimmer or slotted spoon, but with a basket you can remove all the fried courgettes at once and there is no risk of any getting overcooked.)

While the oil is heating, drain the courgette sticks, first tasting one. If it is very salty, rinse the sticks briefly with cold water to remove the salt. Toss the courgettes, salted or rinsed, on paper or linen towels to dry them thoroughly. Then remove to paper towels and dust with the flour, sifting it over them and shaking them around until lightly coated.

When the oil reaches 190°C transfer a handful of the courgette sticks to the frying basket and immerse in the hot fat. There will be a sizzling and the fat will bubble up, so stand back or you may get splashed with hot oil. The courgettes will cook very, very quickly. In about 2 to 3 minutes they will brown lightly and become crisp. Immediately remove to the baking tray lined with paper towels and taste one to see if they are cooked through. Keep them hot on the baking tray in the warm oven. Before adding more courgettes to the oil, let the temperature return to 190°C. When all the courgettes are fried, serve immediately, fresh and hot – they will not hold or freeze. Salt and pepper them just as they are served. If they are salted ahead of time they can turn soggy.

Batter-Dipped Foods

♟ Fried Prawns

Deep-fried prawns can be sheer delight – crisp, tender, greaseless and flavourful – or they can be a soggy mess. The secret of these fried prawns is the lightness and crispness of the beer batter which encases them – the yeast in the beer has a leavening effect on the batter. Make the batter ahead of the time you plan to fry the prawns and let it rest, anywhere from 1 to 2 hours to overnight. This allows the ingredients to expand and amalgamate after the vigorous beating and the batter will be crisper for it.

Serves 4

*680 g. (1½ lbs.) of raw prawns in the
  shell (these should be fairly good-sized)*

BEER BATTER

100 g. (3½ oz.) flour   *2 dl. (⅓ pt) beer, at room temperature*
2 eggs, separated   *Freshly ground black pepper*
1½ teaspoons salt   *Oil for deep-frying*
2 tablespoons salad oil

Wash the prawns very carefully and dry on paper towels. Take a pair of sharp kitchen scissors and cut along the curved back of the shell towards the tail, then break off the body shell with your finger, leaving the tail shell on. Cover the cleaned and shelled prawns with plastic wrap until ready to fry.

To make the batter, put the flour in a bowl and add the 2 egg yolks (the whites will be used later), the salt, the oil, the beer and a grind or two of pepper. Starting in the centre, stir clockwise with a wire whisk until well mixed and free of lumps. Cover the bowl with plastic wrap and allow to rest for at least 1 to 2 hours or overnight. Then stir the batter. In a separate bowl beat the 2 egg whites with a wire whisk until stiff but not dry and very gently fold them into the batter.

Preheat the oven to 130°C (250°F, gas mark ½). Line a baking tray with paper towels and put it near the stove. Half fill the deep fryer with oil and heat it to 190°C (375°F).

Put the prawns, one at a time, on a small ladle or large spoon and dip them into the batter so that they become completely coated, then lower them into the hot fat. Cook about 4 or 5, not more than 6, at a time – the batter expands in the fat and besides you don't want to lower the temperature too much. It will take about 3 to 4 minutes for the prawns to brown and cook through.

As the prawns are fried, lift them out in the basket or with a flat mesh skimmer (which can also be used to skim any stray pieces of batter from the fat) and let them drain and keep warm on the baking tray in the oven.

Serve at once with either a tartare sauce (see page 297) or a Béarnaise sauce (see page 294), or merely with mayonnaise and wedges of lemon. These may be served as a starter, as a cocktail tidbit, or as a main course. For a main course, you could have coleslaw with them, which you will find on page 311.

Fritto Misto

Although it is not traditional for *fritto misto*, I like to use beer batter – and prepare it several hours ahead; it gives such a light, crisp finish to the food. The following version, made with tender meats, offal and vegetables, is one I have used with great success.

Serves 6 to 8

Double recipe beer batter (see page 207)	*1 whole chicken breast, skinned and*
1 pair sweetbreads	*boned*
1 pair calves' brains	*2 veal kidneys*
2 or 3 firm courgettes	*1 cauliflower*
1 teaspoon salt	*Or 1 bunch broccoli*
1 tablespoon lemon juice	*Oil for deep-frying*
225 g. (½ lb.) veal scaloppine	*Flour*
225 g. (½ lb.) calves' liver	*4 lemons, quartered in wedges*

Make the beer batter and leave it in the refrigerator for 3 to 4 hours. (Do not add beaten egg whites until just before using.) Meanwhile, prepare the sweetbreads, brains and courgettes. First soak the sweetbreads and brains in ice water for 30 minutes. Peel off as much as possible of the covering membranes and dark thin veins from the brains.

Trim the courgettes, cut into 1-cm. ($\frac{1}{2}$-inch) strips, and put in a colander. Sprinkle with salt, as for fried courgettes, and set aside for about 1 hour to let the bitter juices drain out.

Put the sweetbreads and brains into a pan with 1 l. ($1\frac{3}{4}$ pts) water, 1 teaspoon salt, and 1 tablespoon lemon juice. Bring to a boil; reduce the heat and simmer for 10 minutes. Drain and immediately plunge the sweetbreads and brains into cold water to stop them from cooking. When cool enough to handle, drain and dry, then remove any remaining membrane, connecting tubes, and fat on the sweetbreads. Cut sweetbreads, brains, veal, liver and chicken breast into $3\frac{1}{2}$-cm. ($1\frac{1}{2}$-inch) pieces. Skin the kidneys; make a slit in the top and remove the hard core of fat and tubes, then cut into $3\frac{1}{2}$-cm. ($1\frac{1}{2}$-inch) pieces.

Wash the cauliflower or broccoli. Remove the flower heads, discarding the thick stalks of the cauliflower (the thick broccoli stems may be removed, reserved, then peeled, cut into julienne strips, and sautéed with other vegetables, as in the recipe on page 200). Break the heads of the cauliflower or broccoli into small flowerets; put in a pan; cover with lightly salted water; bring to a boil and boil for 3 minutes. Drain and plunge into cold water to stop them from cooking. Dry the parboiled flowerets well.

When ready to fry, remove the batter from the refrigerator; mix lightly with a wooden spatula, as some of the flour may have sunk to the bottom, then beat the egg whites until stiff but not dry with a wire whisk or an electric hand mixer and fold lightly into the batter. Preheat the oven to 130°C (250°F, gas mark $\frac{1}{2}$).

Put enough oil in a deep fryer to half fill it. Heat to 190°C (375°F). Have ready two baking trays lined with paper towels.

Dust the pieces of meat and chicken lightly with flour to prevent moisture or juices from seeping out. Dip the meats into the batter and turn until well coated. Lift them out with tongs; hold over the bowl for a moment to let excess batter drip off, then drop them into the hot oil, no more than 6 pieces at a time. Fry, turning them once or twice with tongs, until golden brown, about 4 minutes, then remove to the paper-lined baking trays to drain and keep warm in the oven. After frying the meats, dip the courgettes and flowerets into the batter and fry for 3 minutes.

Arrange the *fritto misto* on a platter lined with a plain white napkin and serve with wedges of lemon.

French Fried Onion Rings

Serves 4

3 large yellow onions, peeled   *Ice water*

BATTER

1 egg, beaten $\frac{1}{2}$ teaspoon salt
$\frac{1}{4}$ l. (8 fl. oz.) buttermilk $\frac{1}{2}$ teaspoon baking powder
130 g. (4$\frac{1}{2}$ oz.) flour   Oil for deep-frying

Slice the onions about 6 mm. ($\frac{1}{4}$ inch) thick, separate them into rings, and soak in ice water for 2 hours. Drain and dry thoroughly on paper towels.

To make the batter, mix the egg and buttermilk and then whisk in the flour, which has been sifted with the salt and baking powder, until smooth.

Heat the fat to 190°C (375°F) in a deep fryer; dip the onion rings into the batter and fry in the hot fat, a few at a time, until brown and crisp, about 4 to 5 minutes. Drain well on paper towels.

♕ Fruit Fritters

These are the dessert equivalent of the batter-dipped prawn, meat and vegetables, and they make a light delicious end to a meal. If you want a sauce for the fritters, serve them with *crème anglaise* (page 290) flavoured with 2 tablespoons of the spirit you used to marinate the fruit.

Serves 6 to 8

Oil for deep-frying   90 to 125 g. (3 to 4 oz.) stale
Flavoured fruit (for choices, see below)   macaroon crumbs or sponge-cake
Icing sugar   crumbs

BATTER

255 g. (9 oz.) flour $\frac{1}{4}$ l. (8 fl. oz.) light beer, at room
2 eggs, beaten   temperature
2 tablespoons melted butter   1 tablespoon kirsch or cognac
Pinch of salt

Sift the flour into a bowl and combine with the eggs, butter, salt and beer, beating with a wire whisk until smooth. Or whirl until smooth in an electric liquidizer. Mix in the kirsch or cognac. Let the batter stand 2 to 3 hours or longer before using.

When you are ready to fry, stir the batter with a spatula in case the flour has sunk to the bottom of the bowl. Heat the oil in a deep fryer to 190°C

(375°F). Roll fruit in crumbs, then dip into the batter and lower into the hot fat with tongs, a few pieces at a time. Fry until golden brown on all sides, about 4 to 5 minutes. Remove; drain on paper towels and serve hot, dusted with sugar.

VARIATIONS

Apricot Fritters. Drain 12 whole tinned apricots. Marinate them in 5 tablespoons kirsch for 1 hour. Roll in macaroon crumbs; dip in batter and fry.

Pineapple Fritters. Marinate 12 slices of tinned drained pineapple or fresh pineapple in 5 tablespoons kirsch for 1 hour. Coat with macaroon crumbs; dip in batter and fry.

Pear Fritters. Poach 6 small, peeled, cored, and halved pears in syrup (see directions for poached peaches, page 64) until just tender when pierced with a fork. Drain. Marinate for 30 minutes in kirsch or, preferably, *eau-de-vie de poire*. Coat with cake crumbs, pressing them in firmly; dip in batter and fry.

Apple Fritters. Peel, core, and quarter 4 apples and poach gently in syrup (see directions for poached peaches, page 64) until barely cooked through, not soft or mushy. Drain. Marinate for 30 minutes in calvados. Coat with cake crumbs; dip in batter and fry.

Breaded Foods

Prawn and Dill Croquettes

Croquettes are mixtures of finely chopped or ground meat, poultry, fish and vegetables, seasoned and bound together with a very thick white sauce, then shaped into balls, cylinders, or cones, rolled in fine bread crumbs and egg, and fried. The coating should cover the food completely, to protect it during the cooking and keep it soft and creamy and to prevent the fat from penetrating the interior and causing the croquette to burst open during the frying. Croquette mixtures are usually chilled, which makes them easier to shape and handle, and often chilled after coating, to help the coating adhere. Before frying, allow them to warm up at room temperature for an hour, or the inside may still be cold when the croquette is removed from the oil.

The trick in frying croquettes is to have the fat hot enough to form a quick, sealing crust immediately, keeping the inside moist.

While I seldom serve croquettes as a main dish, I find they do make very tasty little cocktail appetizers, or a simple starter.

Serves 4 to 6

3 tablespoons olive oil

60 g. (2 oz.) finely chopped onion

3 garlic cloves, finely chopped

3 tablespoons finely chopped green
pepper

3 tablespoons finely chopped celery

90 g. (3 oz.) peeled, seeded, and finely
chopped tomato

3 tablespoons chopped almonds

5 tablespoons finely chopped dill

$\frac{1}{4}$ teaspoon dried oregano

Salt, freshly ground black pepper

3 slices white bread, crusts removed

1$\frac{1}{2}$ dl. ($\frac{1}{4}$ pt) single cream

30 g. (1 oz.) butter

30 g. (1 oz.) flour

2 dl. ($\frac{1}{3}$ pt) warm milk

4$\frac{1}{2}$ dl. ($\frac{3}{4}$ pt) coarsely ground cooked
prawns

1 tablespoon dry sherry

150 g. (5 oz.) fine dry bread crumbs

2 eggs, beaten

Oil for deep-frying

Heat the olive oil in a frying pan; add the onion and garlic and sauté over medium heat until limp and golden. Add the green pepper, celery and tomato and sauté about 10 minutes, until softened. Stir in the almonds, dill and oregano; taste, and add as much salt and pepper as the mixture needs. Remove from the heat.

Soak the bread in the cream until soft; then squeeze dry and add to the mixture in the pan, mixing together well.

Melt the butter in a saucepan; add the flour and cook, stirring, over medium heat until smooth, golden and bubbling. Slowly mix in the warm milk, stirring continuously so the sauce does not lump, then cook slowly, stirring, for 10 minutes or until the sauce is smooth and very thick. Remove from the heat and mix in the onion mixture, prawns and sherry. Taste again and add salt and pepper if needed.

Spread the croquette mixture evenly in a flat baking dish and chill for 45 minutes, until firm enough to handle. Take large spoonfuls of the mixture and roll between the palms of your hands into balls about 3$\frac{1}{2}$ cm. (1$\frac{1}{2}$ inches) in diameter. Have the bread crumbs and eggs in separate pie plates. Dip the balls first in the bread crumbs, completely covering the surface, then in the egg, and then again in the bread crumbs, making sure the surface is completely coated. Chill for 30 minutes, then leave at room temperature for 1 hour before frying.

Preheat the oven to 130°C (250°F, gas mark $\frac{1}{2}$). Heat the oil to 190°C (375°F); drop in the croquettes, no more than 6 at a time, and fry until golden brown, about 3 minutes. You may use a frying basket or remove them with a skimmer. Remove and drain on paper towels and keep warm in a 130°C oven until all are cooked, then serve immediately.

🍲 Fried Fish

To deep-fry fish properly, without letting it get overly brown and overly cooked, is no mean task. It takes care and accurate timing. The fish should be no more than lightly browned. Overcooked fish may look beautifully brown and appetizing, but it will prove to be dry and dreary eating. Either fish fillets or cleaned small, whole fish, such as smelt and small whiting (with the backbone removed), can be fried. They may be first dipped in flour, beaten egg and cream and rolled in crumbs, or fillets can be dipped in the beer batter, like prawns. Measure the fish at the thickest point to determine the cooking time (10 minutes per measured $2\frac{1}{2}$ cm. or inch).

First, see that the fish is thoroughly dry. Dredge it with flour, dip it into beaten egg and cream (in the ratio of 1 egg to 1 tablespoon cream), and then roll it in crumbs – bread crumbs, cereal or biscuit crumbs, and cornmeal are all suitable. Completely cover the fish with the crumbs, pressing them in well. Heat the oil in the deep fryer to 190°C (375°F).

Lower the fish, a few pieces at a time, into the hot fat, using a slotted spoon, and cook for 10 minutes per measured $2\frac{1}{2}$ cm. or inch (see page 122). Immediately remove the fish to paper towels and drain. Season with salt and pepper. Let the fat return to the correct frying temperature between batches. Serve at once on a hot platter with a sprinkling of chopped parsley and wedges or slices of lemon or lime – the last gives a fine and rather different flavour. Accompany the fish with boiled or straw potatoes (see page 217), fried parsley and a tartare, rémoulade, or mustard sauce.

FRIED PARSLEY

Wash and dry 1 bunch of parsley. Be sure it is thoroughly dry before frying or the fat will splatter. Remove the heavy stalks from the sprigs and drop them, a handful at a time, into 185°C (365°F) oil. Step back as you do so, as the oil will hiss and sputter. When crisp, which happens almost immediately, in about 2 seconds, remove at once with a wire skimmer and drain on paper towels. The parsley should be crispy but not shrivelled.

Chicken Kiev

The Russian speciality called chicken Kiev has become very popular. The essence of the dish is that the boned chicken is rolled around a finger of butter so that when the chicken is cut into, the hot butter spurts out. The trick lies in having the butter frozen, so it doesn't ooze out during the frying, and the chicken very cold. Chicken Kiev is made with just the boned breast, as a general rule, but I like to leave the wing bone on, which forms a little handle. I also like to flavour the butter with chopped garlic and herbs, which make it much more flavourful, if not traditional.

Serves 6

90 g. (3 oz.) butter	*3 whole chicken breasts, with the*
2 garlic cloves, peeled and very finely	*wing on*
chopped	*125 g. (4 oz.) flour*
1 tablespoon chopped parsley	*2 eggs, beaten*
1 tablespoon chopped fresh basil	*60 to 90 g. (2 to 3 oz.) fine bread crumbs*
Or 1 teaspoon dried basil	*Oil for deep-frying*

Blend the butter with the garlic and herbs, either by beating them together with a wooden spatula or by putting everything in the food processor and processing until thoroughly mixed. Divide the seasoned butter into 6 equal pieces; shape them into long, tapered fingers and put in the freezer, covered with plastic wrap, until frozen hard.

Cut off the chicken wing tips, leaving the wing bone on. Skin and bone each breast (see page 175 for technique) and cut in half lengthwise, so you have 6 half breasts. Remove the meat about halfway up the wing bone, to make a little handle. Put the chicken breasts between sheets of waxed paper and flatten with a meat pounder (see page 144), pushing down and outwards as you pound. Be careful not to hit the bone or sever it from the breast. The chicken must be very thin, almost transparent. Put a finger of frozen butter in the centre of each pounded breast (on the inner, not the skin, surface) and roll the chicken around it, tucking in the ends, so the rolled-up breast makes a neat sausage-shaped package. The butter must be completely sealed in so that it cannot leak out during the cooking.

Dip the rolled breasts in flour, then in beaten egg, and finally roll in bread crumbs. Arrange on a baking tray covered with waxed paper; cover with plastic wrap and chill in the refrigerator for at least 4 hours. Or make them the day before you plan to serve them and chill until ready to fry.

Heat the oil in a deep fryer to 190°C (375°F). Fry the chicken rolls, 2 or 3 at a time, until golden brown, about 4 minutes. Drain on paper towels; put a paper frill on each wing bone and serve immediately.

Wiener Schnitzel
(Deep-Fried Veal Escalopes)

The famous Viennese dish of Wiener schnitzel is one of the few examples of
deep-fried veal escalopes, tender morsels which are more often sautéed.
There is another version, in which the veal is sautéed in butter, but this one
is better known.

Serves 4 to 6

125 g. (4 oz.) flour seasoned with
  2 teaspoons salt and ½ teaspoon
  freshly ground black pepper
90 to 125 g. (3 to 4 oz.) fine, dry bread
  crumbs

2 eggs, lightly beaten
Oil for deep-frying
12 large veal escalopes, about 680 g.
  ' (1½ lbs.), pounded thin
Lemon slices, chopped parsley

Put the seasoned flour on one sheet of waxed paper, the bread crumbs on
another, and the beaten egg in a baking dish. Dip each escalope into the flour,
then into the beaten egg, and finally into the bread crumbs. Arrange between
sheets of waxed paper on a baking tray and refrigerate for 20 minutes.

Either heat oil to 190°C (375°F) in a deep fryer, or heat 5 cm. (2 inches) of
oil to 190°C in a deep frying pan or electric frying pan. When hot, fry the
escalopes quickly, 2 at a time, until golden brown on both sides, about 2 to 3
minutes. Remove and drain on paper towels, then arrange on a hot platter.
Serve garnished with lemon slices and chopped parsley.

VARIATION

Serve each person 1 large escalope topped with a fried egg, an anchovy fillet,
and a slice of lemon.

French Fried Aubergine

Serves 4

680 g. (1½ lbs.) of aubergine
Oil for deep-frying
90 g. (3 oz.) flour

2 to 3 eggs, lightly beaten
125 g. (4 oz.) fine bread crumbs
Salt, freshly ground black pepper

Peel the aubergine. Cut into slices about 2 cm. (¾ inch) thick, then cut each
slice into strips 2 cm. (¾ inch) wide.

Heat the oil in a deep fryer to 190°C (375°F). Dip each aubergine strip first
into flour, then into the beaten egg, and finally into the crumbs. Fry, a few
strips at a time, in the hot fat until golden brown, about 4 minutes. Re-check
the heat of the fat after frying each batch.

As the aubergine strips cook, remove to drain on a baking tray lined with paper towels and keep warm in a 130°C (250°F, gas mark ½) oven until all are fried. Then season to taste with salt and pepper.

Uncoated Foods

♨ Perfect Chips (French Fries)

Serves 4

4 medium-to-large potatoes

Groundnut oil or rendered beef fat for deep-frying

Potatoes are best if peeled and cut just before you fry them. If you can't do that, put the cut potatoes into a bowl of cold water, take them out just before frying, spread them out on a double layer of paper towels or a terry towel, and dry thoroughly.

Peel the potatoes and cut them into long strips from 6 to 12 mm. (¼ to ½ inch) wide and thick. Have ready a baking tray lined with paper towels. Heat the fat in a deep fryer to 170°C (325°F) and, if you are using a basket, heat the basket in the fat. See that the potatoes are completely dry; lift out the basket; toss a handful of the potatoes into it and lower them slowly into the hot fat. Cook for 5 to 6 minutes, or until they get rather flabby-looking. They should not brown. During the cooking, lift the basket and shake the potatoes around once or twice to prevent them from sticking together.

Remove the potatoes as they are cooked to a baking tray lined with paper towels and leave at room temperature from 1 to 1½ hours, until you are ready to do your second frying. Then reheat the fat and basket to 190°C (375°F), toss the pre-fried potatoes back into the hot fat, a handful at a time, and fry for 2 or 3 minutes, or until they are as brown as you prefer. Be sure to bring the fat back to the correct temperature after each batch. Keep warm in a 130°C (250°F, gas mark ½) oven, on lined baking trays.

Season your chips with salt and freshly ground black pepper just before serving.

VARIATIONS

Shoestring Potatoes. Slice the potatoes thinner than for French fried potatoes and cut into long strips about as thick as a kitchen matchstick. Fry in deep fat heated to 190°C (375°F) for only 1 minute, until crisp and browned. Season and serve. (These are fried only once.)

Sliced or Waffle-Cut Potatoes. Slice the peeled potatoes about 3 mm.($\frac{1}{8}$ inch) thick, using a special vegetable slicer, such as a mandoline, which has plain and waffle-cut blades. Fry once only, in 190°C fat, for 2 to 3 minutes.

Wedges. Cut the potatoes into wedges, either peeled or with the well-scrubbed skins left on. Fry once, in 190°C fat, for 8 to 10 minutes.

Cubes. Peel the potatoes and cut into 12-mm. ($\frac{1}{2}$-inch) cubes. Fry once in 190°C fat, for 5 to 6 minutes.

Straw Potatoes
(Pommes Paille)

These are tiny, julienne-cut potatoes, which come out crisp, golden and very thin.

Serves 4

Peel and slice 4 or 5 large potatoes and cut the slices into very fine julienne strips, about 3 mm. ($\frac{1}{8}$ inch) thick. If you can, use a food processor with a fine shredding attachment, or the fine shredding disc of the vegetable slicer called a Mouli-julienne.

Heat oil in deep fryer to 185°C (365°F or 370°F); plunge the potato strips, a handful or two at a time, into the oil; and fry very briefly, less than a minute, until just golden and crisp. Remove with a skimmer, drain on paper towels, sprinkle with salt, and serve very hot.

Beignets Soufflés
(Soufflé Fritters)

Beignets are simply tablespoons of sweetened and flavoured cream puff dough (*pâte à choux*) fried in deep hot fat until they rise into air-filled puffs – the eggs in the dough are the leavening agent. This most versatile dough can also be baked (for cream puffs).

Serves 6

125 g. (4 oz.) unsalted butter, cut into pieces	140 g. (4½ oz.) plain flour
¼ l. (8 fl. oz.) water	4 eggs
⅛ teaspoon salt	2 tablespoons rum or brandy
½ teaspoon sugar	Oil for deep-frying
	Icing sugar

Combine the butter, water, salt and sugar in a heavy 2-litre (2-quart) saucepan over medium heat until the butter is melted and the water boiling. Remove the pan from the heat; dump in the flour all at once and beat vigorously with a wooden spatula until well blended. Put the pan over medium heat and beat the mixture with the spatula for about 1 minute, or until the mixture forms a mass that clings to the spatula and comes away from the sides and bottom of the pan.

Remove the pan from the heat and leave for 5 to 6 minutes (or, if you have an electric mixer, transfer the dough to the bowl of the mixer and put on the paddle attachment). The dough should have time to settle before the eggs are added.

Make a well in the centre of the dough with the spatula; drop in one egg and beat into the dough until thoroughly absorbed. Beat in the other eggs in the same way, one at a time, until the dough is smooth and glossy and the eggs completely absorbed. When adding the last egg, also beat in the rum or brandy. If you use an electric mixer, add the eggs one at a time, first at low speed, then, as the eggs become absorbed, at high speed. Beat only until dough is smooth and glossy – it should not be over-beaten.

Heat the oil in a deep fryer with a basket to 190°C (375°F). Drop the dough into the hot oil by tablespoons, a few at a time, and fry for about 4 minutes or just until the *beignets* puff up and brown. When one side browns, the *beignets* will turn themselves over. Drain on paper towels and sprinkle lightly with icing sugar, sifted over them through a fine sieve. Serve immediately with a sauce of raspberry purée (page 326) or *crème anglaise* (page 290).

Note. Cream puff dough is best used as soon as it is made. If you have to keep it, put it in a bowl and cover the bowl tightly with plastic wrap. If you store it in the refrigerator, remove and allow to come to room temperature 2 hours before using.

⌘ Raised Doughnuts

These are made with a yeast dough, which gives them a lovely lightness.

Makes 15 doughnuts

2 tablespoons warm water	*3 tablespoons melted butter*
1 teaspoon dried yeast	*370 g. (13 oz.) sifted flour*
100 g. (3½ oz.) sugar	*Groundnut oil or lard for deep-frying*
1 egg	*125 g. (4 oz.) icing sugar or castor*
¼ l. (8 fl. oz.) warm milk	*sugar for coating doughnuts*

Warm water from the hot-water tap can be used. Draw it off into a measuring cup and test the temperature with your meat thermometer; it should be between 43°C and 46°C (110°F and 115°F). If the water is too hot it will kill the yeast, if too cool, the yeast will not work properly.

Put the 2 tablespoons of warm water and the yeast into a large mixing bowl and stir. Add 2 teaspoons of the sugar and mix well. Leave for 10 to 15 minutes to give the yeast time to become frothy and bubbly.

Using your hands or two wooden spoons, stir in the egg, milk, 2 tablespoons melted butter, the remaining sugar and finally the flour. Continue to stir until the dough seems springy. Brush the top of the dough lightly with remaining melted butter and cover with waxed paper or foil. Place in a warm, draught-free spot (or in an oven heated only by the pilot light) to rise until doubled in bulk, about $1\frac{1}{2}$ hours. Or you may put the dough in the refrigerator overnight, where it will rise very slowly.

When risen, punch the dough down by hitting it with your fist – this deflates it. Turn it out onto a floured board. Divide in half. Roll out half the dough at one time to a thickness of 12 mm. ($\frac{1}{2}$ inch). Cut into doughnut shapes with a floured doughnut cutter and place them on a board or baking trays covered with waxed paper to rise until doubled in bulk, about 45 minutes to an hour.

Heat 10 cm. (4 inches) of oil or lard in a deep fryer, or an electric frying pan to 190°C (375°F). Put in the doughnuts, a few at a time, top sides down. Fry about half a minute, until brown on one side, then turn them with a skimmer and brown on the other side for half a minute. When nicely browned, remove and drain on paper towels. Be sure that the fat returns to the correct frying temperature after each batch or the doughnuts will absorb too much fat and become soggy.

While still warm, put the doughnuts in a large paper or plastic bag with the sugar and shake gently until coated. Serve warm.

Baking

One of the most vivid memories of my childhood is reading the story of King Alfred and how, during a lull in the battle, he sat by the fire in a peasant's hut watching the cakes that were being baked on hot stones. History tells us that he let the cakes burn, which proves he was no cook, but somehow this mental picture of that historic figure brooding over the cakes has always fascinated me. Who knows – it may well have influenced my choice of a career.

Nowadays baking is generally assumed to mean cooking in the oven, but that's only the half of it. We bake crêpes in a pan; we bake scones on a griddle or, as the Scots like to call it, a girdle. Our many flat breads and pancakes are reminders that we baked over heat before ovens were ever thought of. Mexican tortillas, Indian poori, the Chinese pancakes one has with Peking duck are griddle foods with a long and honourable history. Much later, when ovens came into existence, they were very chancy affairs – great caverns of brick built into the side of the fireplace into which hot coals were put and raked out when the oven had reached the required heat. The only way of testing the temperature was to put your hand inside and count up to a given number – and then the heat was apt to drop in the middle of baking and ruin whatever you were cooking.

Baking is many-faceted. If you stop to think, you realize that you use the oven many times during the day for a widely varied range of foods. For breakfast, you may heat coffeecake, bake shirred eggs. Later, you may bake bread or cakes, prepare a casserole or a stuffed fish for dinner, a pie, a soufflé, or a baked custard. It's all so easy with our modern temperature-regulated ovens equipped with timers and thermostats and well insulated. Of course, even with automatic controls, we still have to learn the right temperatures for various foods. We find out that puff pastry bakes best if started at rather high heat, then finished at a lower heat. We learn that some breads require high heat and that the majority of casseroles, vegetable dishes, and fruit dishes bake best at a moderate temperature of around 180°C (350°F, gas mark 4). Unlike surface cooking, you can't adjust quickly as you go along; you have to determine the degree of heat you will need beforehand.

What completely revolutionized baking as we know it was the discovery of leavening, in which heat combines with a rising agent, such as eggs, egg whites, yeast, baking powder, or baking soda, to make the food rise and expand. I wonder who first hit upon the miraculous leavening power of the egg? Long before baking powder was envisioned, the génoise and the other classic risen cakes depended for their lightness on eggs. Many of our cakes are entirely leavened by eggs. Some, like heavy, rich pound-cake, are leavened with whole eggs, beaten in one by one. For the génoise, whole eggs are beaten over heat, so they partially cook as the sugar is beaten in, and this initial beating gives the cake its magical lightness and unmatched flavour and texture. Then there is the angel food cake, leavened with whites alone, and other cakes in which the yolks and whites are added separately, at different stages.

One of the most spectacular examples of the leavening power of the egg is the soufflé, where the yolks go into the basic sauce mixture and the whites, beaten until light and firm and folded in at the last minute, elevate the solid mass to a light puffy cloud with an almost ethereal texture.

Then there is that other kitchen miracle – yeast – which has played a vital part in baking since the time of the ancient Egyptians. Our ancestors made their own yeast, using formulas that were part of their heritage. Until standard commercial yeast was introduced at the end of the nineteenth century, yeast was made from many things, among them potatoes, corn, and hops. One of these is still used – the sourdough of the pioneers, a yeast made from flour, water, sugar, salt and sometimes milk, which, as it ferments, gathers wild yeast cells from the air.

Finally came the artificial leaveners like baking powder and baking soda. These gave rise to a whole new range of quick breads which puffed and baked quickly at high temperatures and came out crisp on the outside, soft and rather crumbly inside, and our roster of cakes was increased by light, fluffy baking-powder cakes that rose faster than, and had a texture completely different from, the poundcake or génoise.

Baking is one of the most versatile cooking techniques we have – almost unlimited in its uses. Consider for a minute some of the forms it can take. For a start, let's take that old New England dish, baked beans, one of the simplest of all baked dishes. The beans, prepared on Saturday night for Sunday dinner, were placed in a crock with salt pork, onion, maple syrup or brown sugar and baked in the oven at a low, steady temperature overnight, sometimes for as long as 12 hours, until all the flavours had melded together. There are many peasant dishes from Europe that are made this way. One is the incomparable *tripes à la mode de Caen*, in which tripe, onions, garlic and white wine or cider are baked for 12 to 14 hours at a very low temperature in a pot sealed with a flour-and-water paste to lock in the steam and aromatic flavours. The longer it bakes, the more lip-smacking it becomes. Our modern crock-pot cookery is just a new-fangled version of this old technique.

The casseroles that have become such a familiar part of the American way of cooking are another type of baked dish. Casseroles have been rather looked down on in the last few years, probably because at one point we suffered through a proliferation of all kinds of bastardized versions made with tinned soups and other tinned ingredients and revoltingly topped with crushed cornflakes or potato crisps. Despite these lapses, casserole-cooking still remains one of the simplest and most satisfactory ways of turning out a good meal with a minimum of effort, or of using up leftovers that accumulate in the refrigerator. After all, when you come to think about it, all kinds of baked things, from stuffed vegetables to moulded and scalloped foods and gratins, are really casseroles. The only difference is the container and the name.

Next we have a loaf of good, honest homemade bread, baked at a high temperature that makes the bread rise and expand, sometimes to one-third more than the size at which it went into the oven, and browns and crisps the outside to a delicious crust.

Then there is the custard, baked in a dish or pan of hot water with damp rather than dry heat. The warm water creates a buffer of moisture around the delicate custard, allowing it to bake slowly to a firm creaminess without curdling or breaking down. The quiche, custard baked in a pastry shell, needs no such protection. The insulation of the pastry, the shallowness of the mixture, and the speed of the cooking are sufficient.

So while baking is one of the oldest of all cooking processes, it is also one of the most complex and scientific. In baking, you have to learn the rules and go by them.

🍳 Baked Potatoes

The simplest of all baking recipes, and one that illustrates perfectly the importance of the correct oven heat, is the baked potato. The potato bakes best at a high temperature, from 200°C to 230°C (400°F to 450°F, gas mark 6 to 8), and it should be the mealy type. With this type of potato, which is different from the waxier potatoes used for boiling, the starch expands under the intense heat and the potato becomes fluffy on the inside, with a nice crisp skin.

Preheat the oven to 220°C (425°F, gas mark 7). Scrub the skin of the potato well and either make a very thin slit around the centre of the skin with a sharp knife or prick it in two or three places with a fork. This gives the steam an escape route and prevents the skin from bursting during baking.

Put the potato on the oven rack in the centre of the preheated oven. Bake for 1½ hours. Then cover your hand with a cloth or oven mitt and gently squeeze the potato. If it feels soft and gives, it is baked. If not, give it a little while longer. Naturally, larger potatoes take longer to bake. When the potato feels soft, remove it from the oven and slit it open across the top at once to release the steam inside and keep the texture beautifully mealy and not soggy. Serve at once. Baked potatoes don't like to wait.

To savour a properly baked potato, don't smother it immediately with butter or soured cream. Just sprinkle it with salt and coarsely ground black pepper and the full taste and texture will come through. It should have a good potatoey flavour, a mealy texture, and a lovely earthy smell. If it is soggy and unpalatable, either it didn't bake long enough or you didn't let the steam escape properly.

VARIATIONS

Add butter to taste with the salt and pepper.

Add soured cream and chopped chives or crisp, crumbled bacon to taste with the salt and pepper.

Stuffed Baked Potato. Halve the baked potato lengthwise and scoop out the potato pulp into a hot bowl. For each baked potato, add salt and freshly ground black pepper to taste, 1 tablespoon grated Cheddar or Gruyère cheese and 1½ teaspoons single or double cream. Blend well, then heap back into the shells; dot each half with 1½ teaspoons butter cut into small pieces and sprinkle the tops with a little grated Parmesan cheese. Return to the oven to bake at 190°C (375°F, gas mark 5) until the tops are nicely browned, about

15 minutes. These stuffed baked potatoes are excellent with roasted or grilled meats, but rather rich, so you need serve nothing more than a simple green salad.

Potatoes Anna

Potatoes Anna, a French dish that has become quite the vogue, represents yet another way of baking potatoes. Sliced thin and well lubricated with butter, they form a kind of cake, crustily brown on the outside and meltingly tender inside.

Serves 6

6 medium baking potatoes
About 225 g. (8 oz.) butter, melted

Salt, freshly ground black pepper

Peel the potatoes and slice them into very thin, even rounds, 3 mm. ($\frac{1}{8}$ inch) thick. You can do this more easily if you use a mandoline, a vegetable slicer with an adjustable blade. As the potatoes are sliced, drop them into a large bowl of salted ice water until ready to use.

When ready to cook, preheat the oven to 200°C (400°F, gas mark 6).

The best thing to use for baking is a heavy 20-cm. (8-inch) cast-iron frying pan, 5 cm. (2 inches) deep. Lacking this, use a deep 20-cm. (8-inch) round pie dish or baking dish of the same dimensions. Brush the bottom and sides of the pan heavily with melted butter. Drain the potatoes and dry them thoroughly on a clean cloth or paper towels. They must be completely dry, as excess moisture would ruin the dish.

Arrange a layer of potatoes in the bottom of the pan: put one slice in the centre and arrange overlapping circles of potatoes around it, from centre to sides. Sprinkle the potatoes very lightly with salt and pepper and spoon a tablespoon or two of melted butter over them.

Continue to make layers of potatoes, seasoning each layer and spooning butter over it, until the pan is filled. Spoon another tablespoon or two of butter over the top.

Put the pan or dish on the centre shelf of the oven and a baking tray on the shelf below it to catch any butter that might bubble over. Bake for 30 to 45 minutes, until the potatoes are crisp and brown around the edges and tender when prodded with a fork or toothpick.

Remove the pan from the oven. Run a knife around the edge of the potatoes to loosen them. Put a large flat serving platter, big enough to hold the potato cake, on top of the pan and quickly invert it so the cake unmoulds itself on to the platter. To serve, cut into wedges. Serve potatoes Anna with steak, roast meats, or chicken.

♕ Crêpes

In my classes, I always start the students off with crêpes, because it is one of the most basic of cooking processes and demonstrates very graphically the change that takes place when a mixture is baked. The element of participation also brings the students together and they gain confidence from their newly found ability to make the batter, handle the pan, and turn out a perfect crêpe.

Until a year or two ago I always used the traditional French iron crêpe pan. In many ways, this pan is unbeatable. If it is properly seasoned and cared for, it will maintain a nice patina. You must never sink an iron crêpe pan in a bath of detergent or put it into the dishwasher. Merely rub it out with a little coarse salt and a paper towel if it should chance to stick, and keep it for crêpes alone. It will do yeoman duty for many years.

However, other types of pan are equally good for crêpes. Non-stick frying pans, which have become a regular part of our cooking lives in the last decade or so, work beautifully. They cannot take as intense a heat as iron and so do not heat or cook as fast, but I think they produce a tenderer, more supple crêpe. I find my non-stick aluminium omelet pan is ideal. It matters not one whit how often you wash it, or how many other things you cook in it, so it saves adding yet another specialized utensil to your kitchen. I am also prone to turn a crêpe over by flipping it, and it will slide with the greatest of ease in a non-stick pan. Of course, with this special lining you can't use a metal spatula; it must be one of wood or plastic. You should have no trouble with crêpes provided you use the right kind of pan, make a smooth batter, and practise until you have mastered the baking technique.

You need a pan about 20 to 23 cm. (8 to 9 inches) in diameter with sides sloping to a bottom 15 cm. (6 inches) in diameter, such as the French iron crêpe pan, the non-stick omelet pan, or a heavy frying pan of similar shape and material. Other necessities are a medium-sized mixing bowl, a wire whisk (or an electric hand mixer or liquidizer), a 60-ml. (2-oz.) ladle or dry measure (the kind that looks like a little pan and has a handle), a pastry brush, a small pan to hold the melted butter and either a thin-bladed, supple palette knife with a blade about $2\frac{1}{2}$ cm. (1 inch) wide and 20 cm. (8 inches) long for turning the crêpes or, if you are using a non-stick pan, a spatula of wood or plastic.

The first step is to make the crêpe batter. If you can, make it 2 or 3 hours ahead of time and let it rest, which enables the flour to expand and absorb the liquid. A batter that has rested will work better than one that is freshly made.

BATTER FOR 16 TO 18 15-CM. (6-INCH) CRÊPES

3 eggs
$\frac{1}{8}$ teaspoon salt
$2\frac{1}{2}$ to 3 dl. (8 to 10 fl. oz.) milk or beer
(use beer only for non-sweet or
savoury crêpes)

125 g. (4 oz.) plain flour
4 to 5 tablespoons melted butter

FOR DESSERT CRÊPES, ADD

3 tablespoons sugar

2 tablespoons cognac
Or 1 tablespoon vanilla essence

Break the eggs into the mixing bowl and beat until smooth with the wire whisk. Mix in the salt and $2\frac{1}{2}$ dl. (8 fl. oz.) of the milk or beer. Beer gives a nice lightness to the crêpes and the taste goes well with savoury fillings, but for dessert crêpes milk is preferable. Blend well. Stir in the flour with the whisk and, still stirring, add 2 tablespoons of the melted butter. Beat well until the batter is smooth, free of lumps, and has the consistency of double cream. Depending upon the dryness of the weather and, therefore, the flour, you may need to add the remaining 4 tablespoons liquid, but wait until the flour is thoroughly mixed in and then judge. It is better to underestimate the amount of liquid. You can always mix in more later if your batter seems too thick. Often you find that the batter thickens considerably after it has rested and needs to be thinned with a little more liquid.

If you are making dessert crêpes, add the sugar to the batter with the flour and stir in the cognac or vanilla when the batter is mixed.

A quicker and easier way of making the batter is to use an electric hand mixer instead of a whisk, or put all the ingredients in the liquidizer or food processor at one time and blend until smooth and well mixed.

Cover the bowl of batter with plastic wrap and let it rest at room temperature for 2 to 3 hours, or up to 12 hours in the refrigerator if you wish to make the batter well ahead of time.

When you are ready to bake the crêpes, assemble your equipment: a small pan containing the remaining melted butter, the pastry brush for brushing the crêpe pan, the crêpe pan, the ladle and palette knife, a plate to put the crêpes on, and some paper towels for wiping out the pan should it get too hot and the butter brown. Uncover the batter and beat with the whisk, as the flour will have settled. If the batter is thicker than double cream, add a little extra liquid.

Put a metal crêpe pan on medium-high heat, or a non-stick pan on medium heat. Let the pan get good and hot, then brush it with melted butter. The butter should sizzle but not brown or burn. If it does, the pan is too hot. Wipe it out with paper towels and cool it off by putting it on a cold burner or waving it in the air a few times. Then start again, reheating the pan and brushing it with butter.

The secret of a perfectly thin and tender crêpe is to use just enough batter to cover the bottom of the pan in a thin layer. When the butter sizzles, dip your ladle or measure into the batter and scoop up about 3 tablespoons.

Pour the batter into the pan with your left hand and, holding the handle of the pan with your right hand, raise the pan from the heat and tilt it so the batter quickly swirls around and runs over the bottom of the pan. If there is too much batter, pour the excess back into the bowl. If there is too little, and it does not completely cover the bottom of the pan, add a touch more.

Replace the pan on the heat and bake the crêpe for about 1 to 1½ minutes, until the surface is set and the crêpe moves slightly when you shake the pan. If you poured off excess batter, there will be a little tongue of crêpe on the side of the pan, which you should lop off with your palette knife. Now turn the crêpe. There are various ways to do this.

You can run the palette knife around the edges of the crêpe to loosen it, then slide the palette knife underneath, and *with a quick movement flip it over*, using your hand if needed. Or, if you are a hardy soul, you can tip and shake the pan until the crêpe hangs over the front edge a bit, *then pick it up with your fingers and turn it over* (if you do this quickly, you won't burn your fingers) *or use a palette knife and one hand.* Or, if you can flip a pancake, shake the pan once or twice to loosen the crêpe and then give the pan a quick jerk so the crêpe flips over of its own accord. If the crêpe does not lie completely flat in the pan, pat it down with your fingers. I find the flipping or hand-turning methods are safer and more professional. With a palette knife there is always the chance that you will break or cut the crêpe.

Return the pan to the heat to bake the second side, which will take only about half a minute, then turn the crêpe out by quickly inverting the pan over the plate. The second side will be less brown than the first side but that doesn't matter. This is the side on which you put the filling.

Continue to heat the pan, brush it with butter, and make crêpes until all the batter is gone. If you are using the crêpes right away, simply stack them on the plate. Should you wish to make them ahead of time, put greaseproof paper between the crêpes as you stack them and, when they are cool, cover the stack and the plate with plastic wrap and leave at room temperature or in the refrigerator until you are ready to use them. To store crêpes, put grease-proof paper between them, remove them from the plate when cool, wrap them in aluminium foil, and freeze them. If you have made batches of both sweet and savoury crêpes, identify them by writing 'sweet' or 'savoury' on the outside of the package so you don't get them mixed up.

It's a lot of fun to make crêpes. If you have never done it before, take some time to practise until you become deft at pouring in just the right amount of batter and turning the crêpes. Don't overbake crêpes or they will be crisp and difficult to roll. A crêpe should be rather pale and supple. If you are going to fill, roll and sauce the crêpes, don't worry if every one is not impeccable, for they are still perfectly usable.

For a main course, allow 2 to 3 filled crêpes per serving. For a dessert or starter, allow 2 crêpes per serving.

Chicken Crêpes

Serves 4 to 6

225 g. (8 oz.) white and dark meat from poached chicken, cut into 1-cm. (½-inch) cubes

4½ dl. (¾ pt) sauce suprême (page 287), made with chicken broth

12 savoury crêpes

4 tablespoons double cream

3 tablespoons grated Parmesan cheese

Mix the chicken cubes into the sauce and heat in a pan over very low heat until thoroughly warmed through. Do not overheat or the sauce will curdle. Rub a large baking dish with softened butter. Spread the crêpes flat on a board or the countertop, paler side up. *Place about 2 tablespoons of the filling on each crêpe, fairly near the edge closest to you; roll the crêpe up carefully and place it in*

the buttered dish, seam side down. Continue until you have used up all the crêpes and most of the chicken mixture, pushing the crêpes close together so they don't unroll. Put the remaining chicken and sauce back on the heat, stir in the double cream, and let it warm through. Pour this over the rolled crêpes and sprinkle with the Parmesan cheese.

Just before you are ready to serve, preheat the oven to 190°C (375°F, gas mark 5). Put the dish on the centre shelf of the oven and bake until the crêpes are heated through and the cheese melted, about 15 minutes. Serve the crêpes on hot plates, 2 or 3 per serving. As a main course, serve with a vegetable, such as broccoli, or a green salad and crisp French bread.

VARIATIONS

You can vary the fillings for the savoury crêpes, using different combinations of poultry, meat, or fish and sauces. Some fillings you might use are cooked prawns or crabmeat with the sauce suprême (made with milk or fish stock) or curry sauce; diced ham with the sauce suprême and a touch of sherry; sliced sautéed mushrooms and cubed cooked turkey with mornay sauce.

Quick Cannelloni. Spread the crêpes with a thin layer of fresh ricotta cheese; top with a tablespoon of poached, skinned and shredded Italian sweet or hot sausages, a sprinkling of grated Parmesan cheese and a little freshly ground black pepper. Roll up, and put into a baking dish. Cover the rolled crêpes with 3 dl. ($\frac{1}{2}$ pt) tomato sauce, sprinkle with grated Parmesan cheese, and heat as above.

Crêpes Directoire

There are many different types of dessert crêpes, ranging from the simplest of all – crêpes spread with fruit preserves, rolled, placed in a buttered frying pan, sprinkled lightly with sugar, and flamed with 1½ dl. (¼ pt) warmed cognac or whisky – to the ever-popular crêpes Suzette and crêpes soufflées, crêpes filled with a soufflé mixture and baked in the oven until the soufflé puffs up inside the crêpes. The following recipe is very easy and very good.

Serves 6

6 firm ripe bananas
12 dessert crêpes
2 tablespoons grated lemon zest (the
  yellow part of the rind)
1½ dl. (¼ pt) kirsch

4 tablespoons sugar
60 g. (2 oz.) butter
Juice of 1 orange
Grated zest of 1 orange

Bake the bananas in their skins in a 180°C (350°F, gas mark 4) oven for 20 to 25 minutes, until the skins are black. Split the skins, remove the bananas, and cut in half crosswise. Spread out the crêpes, pale side up, and arrange a half banana on each crêpe. Sprinkle each one with lemon zest and 1 teaspoon kirsch and roll up.

Melt 3 tablespoons of the sugar in a metal frying pan over medium heat until it becomes caramelized, or brown and bubbly. Stir in 2 tablespoons of the kirsch and then the butter, stirring rapidly so the butter and kirsch blend with the caramelized sugar, then add the orange juice and zest and stir to make a smooth sauce. Arrange the banana-filled crêpes in the pan, seam side down, and spoon the sauce over them. Turn off the heat. Heat the remaining kirsch in a small pan. Sprinkle the crêpes with the remaining tablespoon of sugar, light the kirsch with a match, and pour it flaming over the crêpes. Shake the pan until the flames die. Serve immediately.

Soufflés and Rolls

I have always said that the one thing that makes a soufflé fall is letting it know you are afraid of it. A soufflé is not the difficult, temperamental dish it is made out to be. I have let a completely mixed soufflé stand in the refrigerator for half an hour before putting it into the oven and I have even opened the oven door while it was baking without mishaps.

The secret of making a good soufflé lies in the egg whites. Provided they are beaten until they are full of little air bubbles and firm enough to stand in upright peaks, then folded into the soufflé base gently so that they do not lose that aeration, the soufflé will rise perfectly.

You may have been told that the only way to beat egg whites properly is in a large, unlined copper bowl with a big balloon whip. I don't agree. In my classes students beat the egg whites by hand in the copper bowl and by machine in the heavy-duty electric mixer and though there may be more initial expansion with the bowl and whip, it doesn't seem to make any noticeable difference in the volume of the finished soufflé. However, if you do beat egg whites in the mixer, or in any other non-copper bowl, you should add a pinch of cream of tartar to the egg whites when they have been beaten to the first, foamy stage. Cream of tartar supplies the acidity that unlined copper provides naturally, and it is this acidity that helps the whites to rise and to keep their stability after they have been beaten.

There are two other things to bear in mind if your beaten egg whites are to rise as they should. First, the whites should be at room temperature before beating. Second, there must not be so much as a speck of egg yolk in them, or any trace of grease on the bowl or beater.

To bake a soufflé, you don't have to invest in the classic, straight-sided porcelain soufflé dish, the kind that comes in sizes from $\frac{1}{2}$ litre ($\frac{3}{4}$ pint) to 3 litres ($2\frac{1}{2}$ quarts). There are other types of dish or mould that will do just as well. In one class we made soufflés in twelve different containers and they all worked. Metal charlotte moulds make superb soufflé dishes, and they have one very valuable attribute the classic type lacks – handles on the sides. You can lift them out of the oven easily by the handles, whereas a soufflé dish must be grasped awkwardly around the belly. Then there are the ovenproof glass soufflé dishes now on the market. To me, these are the ultimate in elegant containers, so beautiful to the eye. The thin glass conducts heat more rapidly than thicker porcelain, so if you use this kind of soufflé dish you should lower the oven temperature by 10 degrees centigrade (25 degrees Fahrenheit).

It is my contention that tying a collar of greaseproof paper or aluminium foil around a soufflé dish is unnecessary, unless you have added so many extra egg whites that there is a danger the soufflé might rise to spectacular heights and topple over. The standard soufflé contains only one additional white and can be counted on to support itself without assistance.

If you have a suitable, straight-sided $1\frac{1}{2}$-litre or $1\frac{1}{2}$-quart dish to bake a soufflé in, plus a 2-litre or 2-quart size for larger soufflés or those with more egg whites, you really don't need any other special equipment. For making the sauce you will use a 2- to $2\frac{1}{2}$-litre or quart saucepan, a wooden spatula, and a wire whisk. For separating the eggs, you will need a couple of small bowls. For beating the egg whites, you can use a copper bowl and balloon whip or an electric mixer, or a large bowl, about 25 cm. (10 inches) in diameter, of stainless steel, plastic, or ovenproof glass plus a big whisk or an electric hand beater. For folding in the egg whites, you will need a broad rubber or plastic spatula.

The most basic of all soufflés is the one with a béchamel sauce base, into which the yolks, seasonings, and flavouring ingredients are mixed and the beaten egg whites folded. This is the type used for almost all savoury soufflés and many dessert soufflés. I have chosen for our example a cheese soufflé, for others are merely variations, with different ingredients and flavourings.

☙ Cheese Soufflé

Serves 4

FOR A 1½-LITRE OR QUART SOUFFLÉ DISH OR MOULD

1 teaspoon butter	60 g. (2 oz.) grated sharp Cheddar
4 eggs	cheese
1 extra egg white	Or 125 g. (4 oz.) grated Parmesan
45 g. (1½ oz.) butter	cheese
3 tablespoons flour	Or 90 g. (3 oz.) grated Emmenthaler
¼ l. (8 fl. oz.) hot milk	or Gruyère cheese
1 teaspoon salt	Or 90 g. (3 oz.) crumbled Roquefort
¼ teaspoon freshly ground black pepper	cheese
Pinch of grated nutmeg	⅛ teaspoon cream of tartar (optional)

With your fingers, grease the bottom and sides of the soufflé dish or mould with 1 teaspoon butter. This will help the soufflé to rise and give it a nice shiny crust.

There are four steps in making a soufflé: separating the eggs, making the béchamel sauce base and adding the yolks and flavourings, beating the egg whites and folding the egg whites into the soufflé base.

Start by separating the eggs, which should be at room temperature. Have beside you two small bowls and the large bowl in which you will beat the egg whites. Crack the centre of the egg on the rim of one small bowl so the shell divides neatly into halves. Hold the egg over the bowl and tip it back and forth between the halves of the shell so the white slips into the bowl, leaving the yolk in the shell. When all the white is in the bowl, tip the egg yolk into the second small bowl and transfer the white to the bowl in which you will beat the whites. This is a precautionary measure. If by mischance a yolk should break and part of it mingle with the white, you only have to discard one egg white, not a whole batch. Continue this process until all the egg yolks are in one small bowl and all the egg whites have been transferred to the large beating bowl.

There is a safer way to separate eggs, and you should at least try it once to get the feel of the separating. Break the eggshell and tip the whole egg into the palm of your hand. Let the egg white run between your slightly parted fingers into the small bowl. Your hand is softer than an eggshell and there is less chance of the yolk breaking.

You'll have one extra yolk in this recipe – don't throw it away after it has been separated from the extra egg white. Store it in the refrigerator in a small screw-topped jar and use it for mayonnaise or hollandaise.

With the eggs separated, turn your attention to the sauce. Make a thick béchamel sauce as directed on page 285. Melt the butter in the saucepan over medium-low heat; stir in the flour; cook the roux until frothy and then mix in the hot milk. Stir and cook until it comes to the boiling point and thickens to a rather stiff sauce consistency. Season with the salt, pepper and nutmeg and remove from the heat. Stir the egg yolks into the sauce with a whisk or spatula until thoroughly mixed, and then mix in the cheese with the spatula.

Preheat the oven to 190°C (375°F, gas mark 5). Remove the top shelves. The soufflé will be baked in the centre of the oven and needs room to rise.

If you are beating the egg whites by hand, use the large balloon whip. Beat with a vertical circular motion, at first fairly slowly and then, as the whites become foamy, more rapidly, so as to incorporate as much air as possible into the whites. If you are not using a copper bowl, add the cream of tartar when the whites are foamy. Continue to beat rapidly until the whites are thick and stiff enough to hold their shape when the beater is lifted – they should just droop over in soft peaks. Do not overbeat until they are dry and stand stiffly upright, as for a meringue. When a recipe directs you to beat egg whites until 'stiff but not dry' or to the 'soft-peak stage', this is what is meant. If you are using an electric mixer or electric hand beater, watch the whites carefully as it is very easy to overbeat them.

The beaten egg whites must be folded into the soufflé mixture immediately, before they have a chance to subside. With the rubber spatula take up about one-quarter of the whites and mix into the cheese-sauce mixture in the pan, which lightens the rather heavy soufflé base.

Then tip the lightened cheese mixture into the bowl of egg whites and, with your rubber spatula, fold the egg whites lightly into it. *Cut down through the centre of the mixture with the edge of the spatula, then draw it towards the side of the bowl; pull it up*

and over and then cut down again. Continue to fold very rapidly and lightly for about a minute, turning the bowl as you do so, just until the cheese sauce has mixed with the egg whites. Don't over-fold, or the egg whites will deflate. There should still be little bits of unincorporated egg white visible. Immediately pour into the prepared soufflé dish and smooth the top with the rubber spatula. Put the dish in the centre of the preheated oven and bake for 30 to 35 minutes, until the soufflé has risen about 5 cm. (2 inches) above the rim of the dish and is browned on top. After 30 minutes the soufflé will be firm on the sides and still slightly creamy in the centre. If you like a firmer centre, bake the extra 5 minutes.

Serve the soufflé the minute you take it from the oven – soufflés can't wait. To serve, puncture the top of the soufflé with a serving spoon and fork, pull it gently apart, and spoon on to hot plates, giving each person some of the centre and some of the crusty brown exterior. All you need with this is a green salad.

For a larger soufflé, to serve 6, use a 2-litre or 2-quart dish or mould. Increase the quantities to 60 g. (2 oz.) each of butter and flour, 3½ dl. (12 fl. oz.) of milk, 6 egg yolks, 7 or 8 egg whites, and 150 g. (5 oz.) of cheese or other ingredients. Also increase seasoning to taste, and increase cooking time to 35 to 45 minutes.

VARIATIONS

For a spicier cheese soufflé, add to the seasonings a dash or two of Tabasco and 1 tablespoon Dijon mustard or 1 teaspoon dry mustard (don't add mustard and Tabasco if using Roquefort, which has a very strong flavour).

Instead of cheese, use 2 dl. (⅓ pt) of any of the following: finely ground chicken; finely ground ham plus 1 teaspoon dry mustard; well-drained, puréed, cooked spinach plus 2 teaspoons grated onion; puréed, cooked broccoli; tinned tuna, drained and flaked, plus 1 teaspoon lemon juice; poached, flaked finnan haddie.

Spinach Roll

A roll is really a fallen soufflé baked flat in a Swiss roll tin, and, according to the mixture involved, may be either savoury or sweet. The beaten egg whites cause the mixture to rise slightly during the baking, but after it is taken from the oven and turned out it quickly deflates. Rolls are delicate things and care must be taken not to break them when they are being rolled up. Spinach roll, filled with either creamed ham or scrambled eggs, makes an excellent brunch or luncheon dish.

Serves 8

FOR PREPARING THE SWISS-ROLL TIN

30 g. (1 oz.) butter
30 g. (1 oz.) freshly made white bread
* crumbs*

FOR THE ROLL

1½ kg. (3 lbs.) fresh spinach
* Or 3 packages frozen spinach*
1 teaspoon salt
½ teaspoon freshly ground black pepper
¼ teaspoon grated nutmeg

90 g. (3 oz.) butter, melted
4 eggs, separated
⅛ teaspoon cream of tartar (optional)
5 tablespoons grated Parmesan cheese

FOR THE FILLING

1 teaspoon Dijon mustard
2 tablespoons Madeira
3 dl. (½ pt) béchamel sauce (page 285)
* made with ham or chicken broth*

1½ dl. (¼ pt) double cream
225 g. (8 oz.) diced boiled or baked
* ham*

Butter a 38 × 28-cm. (15 × 11-inch) Swiss-roll tin, then line the tin with greaseproof paper, leaving an overhang of about 5 cm. (2 inches) at each end. Butter the greaseproof paper heavily and sprinkle the surface with the bread crumbs. Preheat the oven to 180°C (350°F, gas mark 4).

If you are using fresh spinach, wash it well and remove the heavy stems. Put into a large pot with only the water clinging to the leaves; cover and cook over high heat until the leaves have wilted down, turning the top leaves to the bottom with tongs or a wooden spoon. When wilted, drain very well, pressing out as much water as possible, then chop very fine. If you use frozen spinach, thaw it in a pan over low heat, drain well, and chop fine.

Put the spinach in a bowl and mix in the salt, pepper, nutmeg and melted butter. Beat in the 4 egg yolks, one by one, blending well. Beat the egg whites as for a soufflé, adding ⅛ teaspoon cream of tartar when they are at the foamy stage if you are not using a copper bowl.

Fold the stiffly beaten egg whites into the spinach mixture with a rubber spatula. It is not necessary to do this in two stages, and they should be more thoroughly incorporated than for a soufflé, with no bits of egg white showing. Do not overfold, however, or you will break down the air bubbles in the egg whites.

Spread the spinach mixture evenly in the prepared tin with a rubber spatula and sprinkle the top with 4 tablespoons of the grated cheese. Bake in the centre of the oven for 15 to 16 minutes, or until the top feels just firm when touched, but not dry or hard. The roll will have come away from the sides of the tin. Remove from the oven.

Butter a large sheet of greaseproof paper or aluminium foil. Very quickly invert the pan on to the paper or foil so the roll falls on to it, top side down. Carefully peel off the greaseproof paper adhering to the roll, loosening it, if necessary, with a small, sharp knife. If some of the surface sticks to the paper it is not too important, as the filling will go on this side.

Mix the Dijon mustard and Madeira into the béchamel sauce, then add the cream and stir over medium heat until heated through. Mix in the ham. *Spread some of this filling over the spinach roll, leaving about a 2½-cm. (1-inch) margin around the*

edge. Lift up the edge of the greaseproof paper or foil and gently roll up the roll. With the aid of the greaseproof paper, roll it on to a serving platter. Sprinkle the top with the remaining cheese and serve at once, slicing it 2 to 2½ cm. (¾ to 1 inch) thick. Leftover filling may be served on the side.

Grand Marnier Soufflé

This type of dessert soufflé is made without a béchamel base and with a great many eggs, to produce a very light, delicate and high-rising result. In this case. it is advisable to use a paper collar.

Serves 8

FOR PREPARING A 2-LITRE OR 2-QUART SOUFFLÉ DISH

1 tablespoon butter   *1 tablespoon sugar*

FOR THE SOUFFLÉ

8 eggs   *5 tablespoons Grand Marnier*
1 extra egg white   *Pinch of salt*
225 g. (8 oz.) sugar   *¼ teaspoon cream of tartar*
Grated zest (orange part of the rind)   *(optional)*
*   of 1 orange*

Take a piece of greaseproof paper or aluminium foil long enough to fit around the soufflé dish with a little overlap, fold it in half, and butter one side heavily. *Tie the greaseproof paper or foil around the soufflé dish, buttered side inward, so it rises about 8 to 10 cm. (3 to 4 inches) above the rim.* Butter the inside of the soufflé dish, sprinkle it with the sugar, and tilt the dish so the sugar rolls

around and coats the bottom and sides completely. Tip out any excess sugar. This helps the soufflé to rise and gives it a crusty, sugary exterior. The butter and sugar coating is standard for dessert soufflés. Preheat the oven to 190°C (375°F, gas mark 5) and remove the top shelves.

Separate the eggs, putting the whites in the bowl in which they will be beaten and the yolks in a large mixing bowl or the bowl of the electric mixer. Beat the yolks with a whisk, rotary or electric hand beater, or the whip attachment of the mixer, until the yolks are light and lemon-coloured. Gradually beat in 200 g. (7 oz.) of sugar and continue beating until the mixture is very thick, pale and ribbony, which means that when the beater is lifted the mixture falls from it in a thick, broad ribbon. Add the orange zest and Grand Marnier to the egg-and-sugar mixture and beat in.

Beat the egg whites, adding the salt (and cream of tartar if you are not using a copper bowl) when they are foamy. Beat until they reach the soft-peak stage, then gradually beat in the remaining sugar and continue to beat until the egg whites form stiff, glossy peaks. Fold one-quarter of the egg whites into the egg-and-sugar mixture to lighten it, then lightly fold in the rest of the whites, as for any soufflé (see page 234).

Pour the mixture into the prepared soufflé dish, smoothing the top with a rubber spatula, and bake in the centre of the preheated oven for 25 to

30 minutes, according to how cooked you like your soufflé. This type of soufflé is best if baked 25 minutes – the centre will still be slightly liquid and creamy and will form a little sauce for the crustier, firmer part of the soufflé.

Remove from the oven and untie the paper collar. Very gently peel it away from the risen soufflé, being careful not to puncture the crust or the soufflé will collapse. Serve immediately.

Chocolate Soufflé

Like the Grand Marnier soufflé, this is made without flour. It is much lighter and more delicate than a chocolate soufflé made with a béchamel base. The basic mixture may also be baked as a chocolate roll or 'fallen soufflé'.

Serves 6

FOR PREPARING A 1-LITRE OR 1-QUART SOUFFLÉ DISH

1 teaspoon butter	2 teaspoons sugar

FOR THE SOUFFLÉ

6 eggs	180 g. (6 oz.) semi-sweet chocolate
100 g. (3½ oz.) sugar	1 teaspoon vanilla essence
¼ teaspoon salt	¼ teaspoon cream of tartar (optional)

FOR THE WHIPPED CREAM

3 dl. (½ pt) chilled double cream	1 tablespoon cognac, Grand Marnier,
2 tablespoons sifted icing sugar	or dark rum
	Or 2 tablespoons kirsch

Butter the soufflé dish and sprinkle with sugar, as for previous soufflé.

Chill the bowl in which the cream will be whipped. Separate the eggs, putting the yolks in a mixing bowl and the whites in the bowl in which they will be beaten. Beat the yolks until light and lemon-coloured, then gradually beat in the sugar and salt until the mixture is very thick, pale yellow, and ribbony.

Meanwhile, melt the chocolate in the top of a double boiler over hot water or in a small pan in a 150°C (300°F, gas mark 2) oven.

Stir the chocolate and vanilla into the egg-and-sugar mixture and beat until well mixed. Preheat the oven to 190°C (375°F, gas mark 5).

Beat the egg whites until foamy; add the cream of tartar (unless you are using a copper bowl) and continue to beat until they hold soft, unwavering peaks. Fold into the chocolate mixture as for other soufflés, first folding in one-quarter of the egg whites to lighten the mixture and then lightly folding in the rest. Pour into the prepared soufflé dish and bake in the preheated oven for 45 minutes – this soufflé needs a longer baking time because of the density of the chocolate.

Just before the soufflé is ready to come out of the oven, put the chilled cream in a chilled bowl and beat with a rotary or electric beater until it has doubled in volume and holds its shape when the beater is lifted. Gently fold in the sugar and cognac, or other flavouring. Put in a serving bowl and serve with the soufflé as a sauce.

Chocolate Roll

Serves 10

For this, use the chocolate-soufflé mixture for the roll and the sweetened whipped cream as the filling.

Butter a 38×28-cm. (15×11-inch) Swiss-roll tin, then line the tin with greaseproof paper, leaving an overhang of about 5 cm. (2 inches) at each end. Butter the paper, to prevent the cake from sticking. Or, if you have kitchen parchment, line the pan with parchment, which does not need to be buttered. Preheat the oven to $180°C$ ($350°F$, gas mark 4).

Make the soufflé mixture as before, but fold in the egg whites rather more completely – it is not essential to have bits of unincorporated egg white, as this version of the soufflé is meant to fall. Spread the mixture evenly in the prepared tin, smoothing it with a rubber spatula so it is the same overall thickness. Bake on the centre shelf of the preheated oven for 15 minutes, or until the top feels firm and springy when touched.

Have ready a large sheet of greaseproof paper or aluminium foil sprinkled with cocoa or sifted icing sugar. Remove the Swiss-roll tin from the oven and, holding it carefully with oven mitts, very quickly invert the tin onto the paper or foil so the cake falls on to it, top side down. Carefully peel the paper or parchment from the cake, loosening it, if necessary, with a small, sharp knife. If some of the surface sticks, this is not too important as the filling will go on this side.

Let the cake cool, and then spread it with the whipped cream, not quite to the edges. Lift one long edge of the greaseproof or waxed paper or foil and raise it so the cake rolls inwards. Then, with the aid of the greaseproof paper, roll the cake on to a long narrow chocolate-roll board, or a flat serving tray. To serve, cut in diagonal slices.

VARIATION

Nut Roll. Substitute 125 g. (4 oz.) finely ground walnuts or hazelnuts for the chocolate, folding them into the egg-and-sugar mixture before folding in the egg whites.

Prune Soufflé

Another type of dessert soufflé is made with a fruit purée and nothing more except egg whites and sugar, beaten to stiff, glossy peaks, or the meringue stage.

Serves 6

FOR PREPARING A 1½-LITRE OR 1½-QUART SOUFFLÉ DISH

1 teaspoon butter   *2 teaspoons sugar*

FOR THE SOUFFLÉ

450 g. (1 lb.) pitted prunes, soaked for   *Pinch of salt*
1 to 2 weeks in port or madeira to   *¼ teaspoon cream of tartar (optional)*
cover   *75 g. (2½ oz.) sugar*
6 egg whites

Prepare the soufflé dish as for other dessert souffllés (see page 237). Preheat the oven to 200°C (400°F, gas mark 6).

Drain the prunes and purée them by putting them through a food mill, rubbing them through a fine sieve, or puréeing in a liquidizer or food processor.

Beat the egg whites until they are foamy; add the salt and cream of tartar (unless you are using a copper bowl) and continue beating until they hold soft peaks. Gradually beat in the sugar and continue to beat until the whites stand in stiff, glossy, upright peaks. Fold in the prune purée, incorporating it lightly but completely. Do not overfold. Turn into the prepared soufflé dish; smooth the top with a spatula and bake in the preheated oven for 25 to 30 minutes.

VARIATIONS

Apricot Soufflé. Soak 450 g. (1 pound) dried apricots in water or white wine to cover for 3 hours, then simmer in the water or wine with 75 g. (2½ oz.) sugar for 5 minutes. Cool. Purée the apricots, and use in place of the prunes.

Orange Soufflé. Substitute a 450-g. (1-pound) jar of orange marmalade for the prunes.

Other Fruit Soufflés. Substitute 4½ dl. (¾ pt) puréed fruit, such as raspberries, strawberries, or peaches.

Pastry

There are many types of pastry, starting with the simple shortcrust, which is merely flour sifted with salt into which butter is cut (with a pastry blender or two knives) or rubbed with the fingers and just enough water added to make a firm ball of dough. However, the pastry I teach in my classes is the French *pâte brisée*, or rich tart pastry, which is shorter – meaning that it will have a more brittle crumb – richer, and more versatile. It may be used unsweetened for pies and savoury quiches (the open-faced custard tart that originated with the classic quiche Lorraine and now has almost unlimited variations) and sweetened for dessert tarts.

For a flakier crust, suitable for meat pies or for cocktail or dessert turnovers, I find a simple, quick version of puff pastry works very well.

A third type of pastry is *pâte à choux*, or cream puff pastry which, as you have seen in a previous chapter, can not only be baked but also deep-fried. These three pastries will give you a good working knowledge of the pastry-making processes and a repertoire that should cover most of the pastry dishes you might want to begin with.

☺ Rich Tart Pastry
(Pâte Brisée)

This pastry can be prepared well in advance and refrigerated or frozen. The dough, formed into a ball, is wrapped airtight in greaseproof or waxed paper, plastic wrap, or aluminium foil, or it may be rolled out, fitted into a pie plate, covered, and stored either unbaked or partially or fully baked, according to your needs.

Two methods for making this pastry follow. One calls for mixing by hand or in an electric mixer with a paddle (not a beater) attachment, the other for almost-instant mixing in a food processor.

HAND OR MIXER METHOD FOR PÂTE BRISÉE

Makes enough pastry for a 23-cm. (9-inch) tart shell or about 8 5-cm. (2-inch) tartlets

200 g. (7 oz.) sifted flour

125 g. (4 oz.) unsalted butter, firmly chilled, cut into small pieces

1 egg yolk, slightly beaten with 2 tablespoons ice water

1 tablespoon lemon juice

¼ teaspoon salt

2 tablespoons sugar (optional, for dessert pastry only)

Put the flour in a mixing bowl; make a well in the centre and put the butter in the well. Work the butter and flour together quickly with the fingertips (do not let the warm palms of your hands come near pastry – they cause the butter to soften, melt and become very difficult to work with) until the mixture forms small, flaky granules, like oatmeal. Blend in the egg-yolk mixture, lemon juice, salt and sugar, if needed.

If you are using a mixer with a paddle attachment, the method is the same: first combine flour and butter and beat until mixture forms small, flaky granules, then add egg-yolk mixture, lemon juice, salt and sugar, if desired, and beat until pastry forms a ball on the paddle.

Cupping your hands tightly, gather the dough into a rough ball, pulling in any crumbs from the sides and bottom of the bowl. The dough should feel

moist but not sticky. If it seems too sticky, sprinkle with 2 to 3 teaspoons flour and blend in; if it feels dry, sprinkle with a few drops of water and knead in. *Break off small pieces, about 2 to 3 tablespoons each, and smear them across the board by pushing hard with the heel of your hand.* This process, called the *fraisage*, ensures the complete blending of the butter and flour. When all the dough has been worked this way, gather it together with a pastry scraper or spatula; form it into a ball; wrap in greaseproof paper, plastic wrap, or foil and chill for 30 minutes or until the dough is firm, but not so firm that it cracks at the edges when rolled out.

FOOD PROCESSOR METHOD FOR PÂTE BRISÉE

225 g. (9 oz.) flour
125 g. (4 oz.) butter, frozen, cut into
  small pieces
¼ teaspoon salt

1 tablespoon lemon juice
2 eggs
2 tablespoons sugar (optional, for
  dessert pastry only)

Put the metal chopping blade in place in the food processor beaker. Add the flour, frozen butter, and salt to the beaker. Process for 8 to 10 seconds, turning on and off, until the butter is cut into the flour and the mixture forms very small, flaky granules. Add the lemon juice and eggs to the beaker and process until a ball of dough forms on top of the blades, about 15 seconds. The dough should be damp but not sticky. If it seems too soft, sprinkle with 1 to

2 tablespoons flour and process for an additional 5 to 6 seconds, until well combined. If it feels too dry, sprinkle with a few drops of water and process to blend well.

Pastry made in the food processor needs no *fraisage*. Wrap the ball of dough in greaseproof paper, plastic wrap, or foil and chill until firm but still malleable.

ROLLING OUT THE PASTRY

When the pastry is chilled and firm but still malleable, it is ready to be rolled out. (For frozen dough, defrost in the refrigerator until it is the correct firmness, or defrost at room temperature and then refrigerate to firm if necessary. Do not keep in the freezer for longer than 3 to 4 weeks.) Roll out on as cool a surface as possible: a marble slab is ideal, but a countertop works almost as well, as long as it is in a cool part of the kitchen. If the dough gets too warm, the butter melts and the pastry becomes extremely difficult to work with. To prevent this, work as quickly as possible on a cool surface.

A good way to roll out a rich pastry such as this is between sheets of grease-proof or waxed paper: roll smoothly and evenly, and turn dough over often. With every turn, loosen the top paper to prevent it from sticking to the dough and wrinkling.

Or roll the pastry out on a lightly floured marble slab or other smooth surface. Rub the rolling pin lightly with flour and begin by flattening the ball of dough. Roll in one direction, not back and forth, smoothly, evenly and quickly, rotating the pastry a quarter turn each time and stopping just short of the edge so that you get a fairly even circle. While rolling, lift the pastry occasionally to see if it is sticking to the board; if it is, sprinkle the board lightly with flour. Also flour the rolling pin if the pastry is sticking to it. Roll the pastry out about 6 mm. ($\frac{1}{4}$ inch) thick, until you have a circle 28 to 30 cm. (11 to 12 inches) in diameter, or large enough to fit into a 23-cm. (9-inch) tart tin or a 23-cm. (9-inch) flan ring without skimping. There should be a little overlap. To check, hold the tin or ring over the rolled-out pastry and gauge with your eye. Use this method of gauging the size of your pastry whatever type of tin or flan form you are using – for a rectangular flan form, roll the pastry into a rectangle rather than a circle.

TO LINE A FLAN MOULD, PIE TIN, OR TART TIN

A flan mould (or form) is a bottomless piece of metal which may be round, square, or rectangular and it is ideal for baking open-faced tarts because after baking, the tart, mould and all, may be slipped on to a serving dish and the mould lifted off, leaving a perfectly shaped tart, a much more attractive form of presentation than if it were served from a pie plate. There are also heavy tinned tart tins with a fluted edge and removable bottom that serve much the same purpose. Again, the outer ring may be easily removed after baking. Flan moulds or forms come in tin, stainless steel, or other metals, in various sizes and shapes. The standard flan mould is $2\frac{1}{2}$ cm. (1 inch) deep, but you can sometimes find deeper ones, which are better for baking tarts or quiches with a liquid, custard filling. Flan moulds will last a long time and are well worth buying. If you have never tried one, look at the illustration and see how it works. As the flan mould has no bottom, it must be put on a baking sheet of heavy aluminium, or the heavier cast iron, open on at least one side so the baked pastry case may be easily slid from the sheet on to the serving dish.

The method for lining a flan mould, removable-bottom tart tin, or standard pie plate is much the same. If the dough has been rolled on a board, roll it loosely but carefully over the rolling pin, lift, then unroll carefully over the flan mould. Lift the edges of the dough and let it fall gently into place, patting it lightly into the bottom, without forcing or stretching it. If the pastry is stretched, it will shrink during baking. Press it snugly into the sides and trim edges with a sharp knife or scissors, allowing an overlap of about 6 mm. to 1 cm. ($\frac{1}{4}$ to $\frac{1}{2}$ inch) – you need the excess because the pastry will shrink. Crimp the edges of the pastry by pinching it between two fingers, making a firm edge.

If the dough has been rolled between sheets of greaseproof or waxed paper, remove the top sheet, slip one hand under the bottom sheet, and lift up the rolled dough, inverting it over the flan mould or tart tin. *Lift the edges of the dough and let it fall gently into place in the mould or tin without forcing or stretching it.* Peel off the greaseproof paper and let the dough sink into place in the mould, then pat it snugly into place.

Trim the edges by rolling your pin over the top or use scissors. Then with the flat of a paring knife, press the dough gently against the sides in an even pattern so it adheres.

When using a tart tin with a removable bottom, be sure the pastry is pushed well (without being stretched) into the fluted sides of the tin. Also be certain it is completely sealed and free of cracks or the filling will run out of the bottom. If a pie plate is used, let the dough flop over the rim, trim it, and crimp the top by pressing together thumb and finger, thus pinching the dough in the middle, at even intervals to give a scalloped pattern on the rim. Or flute the edges by pressing the back of the tines of a fork lightly into the dough.

Should the pastry break while you are lining the mould or tin (this can happen, as this short pastry is very fragile), don't worry. Just patch it by pressing the broken edges together with your fingertips. Patch any holes in the pastry with some of the trimmings.

If the pastry shell is to be baked and has become quite soft after rolling and fitting into the mould or tin, refrigerate or freeze it for 10 to 15 minutes, until firm.

TO BAKE A FLAN SHELL

Baking an unfilled flan shell is called 'baking blind'. There are various ways to do this: one method is to prick the dough well with a fork and bake the shell in a 220°C (425°F, gas mark 7) oven for 14 to 16 minutes, until the bottom is

set and the edges slightly browned. Or prick the dough lightly, line the shell with foil, shiny side down, pressing it well into the pastry, then bake the shell in a 220°C oven for 14 to 16 minutes. The third method, which gives a better-looking, better-textured shell, is to *line the shell with foil or greaseproof paper, weigh it down with raw rice or beans* (they may be kept in a jar and used repeatedly), and bake it in a 220°C oven for 14 to

16 minutes, until the bottom is set and the edges lightly browned.

After the initial baking, remove the shell from the oven, remove the lining if you have used one, brush the bottom with beaten egg yolk (or Dijon mustard for a savoury tart), and return to the oven for 2 minutes. This seals the bottom and prevents a soggy crust.

The timing of 14 to 16 minutes and the 2-minute period with the yolk glaze is for a partially baked shell; the pastry will finish cooking when it is baked with its filling. For a fully baked shell, bake it for 18 to 20 minutes, then put on the egg-yolk glaze and dry out for 2 minutes in the oven.

Dessert Tarts

Swiss Apple Tart

Serves 6 to 8

60 g. (2 oz.) unsalted butter
5 to 6 cooking apples (see page 357), peeled, cored, and thickly sliced
1 teaspoon vanilla essence
⅛ teaspoon mace
23-cm. (9-inch) pastry shell, partially baked in a 220°C (425°F, gas mark 7) oven for 10 minutes (see recipe and directions, opposite)

2 eggs
100 g. (3½ oz.) sugar
3 dl. (½ pt) double cream
1½ dl. (¼ pt) double cream, whipped just until stiff, and lightly flavoured with ⅛ teaspoon mace

Melt the butter in a heavy frying pan and cook the apples very gently in the butter until just tender, but not falling apart. Add the vanilla and mace. Carefully transfer the apples to the partially baked pastry shell, arranging the slices in an even layer. Beat the eggs and sugar together until light, creamy and lemon-coloured, then stir in the cream. Pour over the apples and bake in a 180°C (350°F, gas mark 4) oven until the custard has set and the crust is golden, about 30 minutes. Serve warm with mace-flavoured whipped cream.

Simple Strawberry Tart

Serves 6 to 8

1 recipe for pâte brisée (see page 242)
1 egg yolk, beaten
450 g. (1 lb.) perfect ripe strawberries,
  of more or less even size, washed and
  hulled

450-g. (1-lb.) jar red currant jelly
1 tablespoon kirsch
1½ dl. (¼ pt) double cream whipped just
  until stiff and flavoured with
  1 tablespoon kirsch

Roll out the pastry and fit it into a rectangular flan mould or a 23-cm. (9-inch) ring set on a baking tray (or use one with a removable bottom). Bake blind until it is browned and crisp, about 18 to 20 minutes. Brush with egg yolk and return to oven for 2 minutes to set the glaze. Cool.

Heat the currant jelly in a heavy saucepan over moderate heat until it comes to the boiling point; add the kirsch and let it cool slightly. Brush the bottom of the cooled flan shell with 1 or 2 tablespoons of this glaze.

Arrange the strawberries in the pastry shell, building from the sides towards the centre. You may make a double layer in the centre to give a feeling of elevation. Spoon the currant glaze over the berries. Serve the tart with kirsch-flavoured whipped cream.

Quiches

The French quiche is one of the most popular of culinary adoptions – and small wonder. While essentially a simple dish, it is infinitely accommodating, for the basis is nothing more than a custard tart to which different ingredients are added. A quiche can be served as a cocktail appetizer, a starter, a luncheon dish, or with a main course as a substitute for both the starch and the vegetable: a pea quiche with chicken; onion quiche with steak, roast beef or pork; spinach quiche with roast lamb.

For most quiches, a 23-cm. (9-inch) aluminium or ovenproof glass pie plate or a flan ring about 4 cm. (1½ inches) deep set on a baking tray is recommended for baking the shell. Rings 4 cm. (1½ inches) deep can be found in shops specializing in cookery equipment. I don't find rings shallower than that are satisfactory. To make small squares of quiche to serve as a cocktail appetizer, use a Swiss-roll tin, or a large, shallow, square tin. You can also make cocktail quiches in small tart tins, although this takes more time and work.

After years of sampling quiches, I have learned that the most common failing is a soggy crust. The secret of a crisp one is simple: the pastry shell is partially baked and then brushed with egg yolk and returned to the oven to dry. Some chefs use egg yolk, others prefer egg white or whole egg, and a new trick which lends excellent flavour is to use Dijon mustard, but the results are the same – a perfect, crisp, non-soggy crust.

To prevent any trouble in preparing quiches, follow these rules:

1. Partially bake the pastry shell in a 220°C (425°F, gas mark 7) oven for 14 to 16 minutes, until the bottom is set and the edges slightly brown. Remove from oven; remove the lining if one was used, brush with lightly beaten egg yolk, white, whole egg, or Dijon mustard, and return it to the oven for 2 minutes. This seals the crust and prevents it from soaking up the custard mixture and becoming soggy.

2. Do not pour the filling into the pastry shell until just before baking; this also prevents a soggy crust.

3. When baking in a heatproof glass pie plate, reduce heat by 10 degrees centigrade (25 degrees Fahrenheit) as glass conducts the heat more quickly than aluminium.

4. To test a quiche for doneness, shake the pan gently to see whether or not the custard is set (it should be just firm), or slide a knife tip into the custard at the centre – if it comes out clean (or almost clean), the quiche is cooked. Remember that the custard will continue to cook by internal heat after it is removed from the oven, so the very centre of the quiche should be slightly underdone.

5. Do not overcook or the custard will curdle and become watery. It is better to risk a quiche that is slightly underdone.

6. Allow the quiche to cool for a few minutes before serving (unless prepared in individual tart tins). This will give the custard time to settle and it will slice better.

♟ Classic Quiche Lorraine

Serves 4 to 6

6 to 8 thick rashers streaky (lean) bacon	3½ dl. (12 fl. oz.) single cream Or ¼ l. (8 fl. oz.) milk and ⅛ l. (4 fl. oz.) double cream
Partially baked 23-cm. (9-inch) pastry shell (see page 246)	Salt, freshly ground black pepper, freshly grated nutmeg
4 eggs	

Cook the bacon in a frying pan until it is cooked through but not crisp. Drain on paper towels. Cut the slices into small pieces and spread evenly in the partially baked pastry shell. Beat the eggs lightly and combine with the cream or milk and cream. Season to taste with salt, pepper and nutmeg. Pour the custard over the bacon. Bake in a 180°C (350°F, gas mark 4) oven for about 30 minutes or until the custard is set, puffed, and lightly browned. Serve hot, cut into wedges.

VARIATIONS

1. Substitute ¼ l. (8 fl. oz.) cream cheese or ¼ l. (8 fl. oz.) cottage cheese for milk. Beat the eggs with the remaining cream, combine with the cheese, and rub through a sieve or strainer before adding to the pastry shell. Bake as directed.

2. Instead of bacon, use about 180 g. (6 oz.) baked ham of good flavour, cut into small strips and distributed in the shell. Add the custard and bake as directed.

Chicken Quiche

Serves 4 to 6

2 whole eggs
2 egg yolks
2 dl. (⅓ pt) milk
2 dl. (⅓ pt) double cream
1 tablespoon chopped fresh tarragon
  Or ½ teaspoon dried tarragon

Salt, freshly ground pepper
225 g. (8 oz.) diced cooked chicken
  or turkey
Partially baked 23-cm. (9-inch) pastry
  shell (see page 246)

Beat the eggs and yolks lightly; blend with the milk and cream, season with tarragon, and salt and pepper to taste. Spread the chicken or turkey evenly in the pastry shell. Pour the custard over it. Bake in a 180°C (350°F, gas mark 4) oven about 30 minutes, until the custard is barely set and still a little creamy.

Spinach Quiche

Serves 4 to 6

680 g. (1½ lbs.) fresh spinach, cooked
  and drained
  Or 1 package frozen spinach, thawed
  and drained
⅛ teaspoon freshly grated nutmeg
1 tablespoon chopped fresh tarragon
  Or 1 teaspoon dried, crushed tarragon
1 tablespoon lemon juice

Salt, freshly ground black pepper
2 tablespoons chopped parsley
Partially baked 23-cm. (9-inch) pastry
  shell (see page 246)
60 g. (2 oz.) crumbled feta cheese
4 eggs
2 dl. (⅓ pt) double cream
1 dl. (3½ fl. oz.) plain yogurt

Cook the spinach as for spinach roll (page 236) and thoroughly drain off all liquid by squeezing small handfuls between the palms of your hands. Chop very fine.

Combine the spinach with the nutmeg, tarragon, lemon juice, salt and pepper to taste, and parsley and spread it in the bottom of the pastry shell. Sprinkle the cheese on top. Beat the eggs lightly; add the cream and yogurt and blend well. Pour over the spinach mixture. Bake in a 180°C (350°F, gas mark 4) oven for about 30 minutes, until the custard is just set. This is excellent as an accompaniment to roast lamb or chicken.

Swiss Onion Quiche

Serves 4 to 6

60 g. (2 oz.) unsalted butter	*2 whole eggs*
4 to 6 onions, peeled and thinly sliced	*2 egg yolks*
Salt, freshly ground black pepper	*3½ dl. (12 fl. oz.) double cream*
Partially baked 23-cm. (9-inch) pastry	*Or ¼ l. (8 fl. oz.) milk and ⅛ l.*
shell (see page 246)	*(4 fl. oz.) double cream*
125 g. (4 oz.) shredded Gruyère cheese	*⅛ teaspoon freshly grated nutmeg*

Melt the butter in a very heavy pan; add the onions; cover tightly and steam over medium-low heat until the onions are soft but not browned, shaking the pan occasionally. Season with salt and pepper to taste. Drain the onions; arrange in the pastry shell and sprinkle with the cheese. Beat the eggs, yolks, cream and nutmeg together and pour into the shell. Bake in a 180°C (350°F, gas mark 4) oven for about 30 minutes, until the custard is just set and puffed. This is an excellent accompaniment for steak, roast beef, or roast pork.

Puff Pastry

♟ Simple Puff Pastry

This type of pastry is made by rolling butter between layers of dough. When baked, it puffs up into a many-layered, light, flaky, and richly buttery pastry that is excellent for the top crust on meat or game pies, for tartlets, for meat baked *en croûte*, such as beef Wellington, or for cocktail appetizers. Any leftover scraps of dough can be rolled out and used for little turnovers of Roquefort cheese or other savoury fillings. Puff pastry freezes beautifully and will keep for six months to a year, if securely wrapped and airtight.

Makes about 1 kg. (2 pounds) pastry, or 2 23-cm. (9-inch) crusts

DOUGH MIXTURE

450 g. (16 oz.) plain flour   ½ teaspoon salt, mixed with 2 dl. (⅓ pt)
4 tablespoons vegetable oil   ice water

Reserve 75 g. (2½ oz.) of the flour. Stir the oil into the flour with a rubber spatula and mix thoroughly. Stir in the salt and water. Cut and press mixture firmly with a spatula and then the cupped fingers of one hand until it forms a mass. Lift the mixture from the bowl; sprinkle any remaining bits of flour with a few drops of ice water and gather them up and lightly press into the rest of the dough. The dough should be pliable but not damp or sticky. Sprinkle very lightly with flour. Wrap dough in waxed paper, then put in a plastic bag and refrigerate for 1 hour.

BUTTER MIXTURE

350 g. (12 oz.) unsalted butter, chilled   Reserved 75 g. (2½ oz.) flour

If working by hand, pound the butter with a rolling pin to make it softer and more pliable, then gather into a mass. Break off bits of about 2 to 3 tablespoons and smear across the work surface with the heel (not palm) of the hand, a process just like the *fraisage* described on page 243. Sprinkle the butter with flour, then gather the butter into a mass and knead it until it is smooth and completely mixed with the flour. Work quickly so that the mixture remains chilled but supple; if it melts because of the warmth of your hands, it becomes very difficult to work with and will have to be refrigerated until firmer. Gather into a mass.

If using an electric mixer, cut butter in six pieces, sprinkle with the flour, and work with the paddle at slow speed until it is thoroughly mixed, smooth, and supple, but still chilled. Gather into a mass.

Refrigerate uncovered for not more than 20 minutes.

MAKING THE PUFF PASTRY

Flour the work surface very lightly (again, as with all pastry, marble is best, but any cool surface will do). Lightly flour the dough, both top and bottom (whisk off any excess flour with a soft pastry brush), and your hands.

Push and pat the dough with the heels of your hands into a 40 × 20-cm. (16 × 8-inch) rectangle (to measure quickly, use a piece of paper cut to these dimensions). Lay the dough out lengthwise away from you. *Cut small*

pieces of the chilled butter and arrange them evenly spaced over two-thirds of the dough farthest from you, leaving a 1-cm. (½-inch) margin around the edge. Fold the unbuttered third of the dough over half the buttered dough, then fold the remaining buttered third over, just like folding a letter. Pinch the edges together to prevent possible leakage of butter. Rotate the dough a quarter turn clockwise, so the dough is once more lengthwise away from you. With a rolling pin, gently but firmly roll out to a 40 × 20-cm. (16 × 8-inch) rectangle. As you roll, try to keep the dough in as even a rectangle as possible: if the edges become ragged, even the sides with the side of the rolling pin. Roll across the width once or twice if necessary to widen it. Check to make sure the dough is not sticking to the work surface. If it is, either dust the work surface lightly with flour or brush the dough lightly with flour. Should the dough split and butter start to ooze out, dust the split area lightly with flour.

Now fold the top and bottom ends of the rectangle to meet in the centre, then fold these two halves together, as if you were closing the pages of a book. Wrap the dough in greaseproof paper, put into a plastic bag, and refrigerate for 1 hour.

You have now completed the first 'turn': rolling out the dough to a 40 × 20-cm. (16 × 8-inch) rectangle, bringing the ends to the centre, and folding them together. Do two more turns in the same way; chill for 1 hour after each turn. *After each, mark the number of turns you have made by making depressions on the dough with your fingers.* Each time start with the dough lengthwise on the work surface so the open ends of the 'book' are at top and bottom; roll into a 40 × 20-cm. (16 × 8-inch) rectangle; fold opposite ends to meet in the centre and then fold these two halves together. Should the dough be too cold and hard to roll easily after chilling, beat it firmly and evenly lengthwise and crosswise with the rolling pin to soften it a little. When the three turns have been completed, wrap the pastry well and refrigerate for 2 hours or until ready to use. It is now ready to be rolled out and used.

♨ Beefsteak and Kidney Pie

For this famous dish, the beef is best braised and then cooked in a pie dish under a puff-pastry crust.

Serves 6

1 kg. (2 lbs.) topside or rump steak, cut into 4-cm. (1½-inch) cubes
75 g. (2½ oz.) flour
1 teaspoon salt
½ teaspoon freshly ground black pepper
¾ teaspoon thyme
4 tablespoons chopped beef suet
2 medium onions, peeled and chopped

1 onion, stuck with 2 cloves
½ to ¾ l. (¾ to 1¼ pts) beef broth
3 veal kidneys
12 firm white mushroom caps
½ of the quick puff pastry (see previous recipe)
2 egg yolks, beaten

Put the beef, flour, salt, pepper and ½ teaspoon thyme into a plastic bag and shake until the beef is well covered with flour. Remove and shake off the excess. Render the beef suet over medium heat in a large, heavy frying pan with a cover and when the suet is melted and hot, add the meat cubes, a few at a time, and brown on all sides over high heat. Remove the cubes, reduce the heat, add the chopped onions, and sauté over medium heat until just limp. Replace the meat in the pan with the clove-stuck onion, the remaining thyme, and just enough beef broth to cover the meat. Cover and simmer for 1½ hours, or until the beef is tender when tested with a fork or knife point. Discard the clove-stuck onion and let the beef cool for 1 hour.

Clean the kidneys. Peel off the covering membrane and remove the white core in the centre with a small, sharp knife, making a slit in the top and then working around it. Slice the kidneys thin. Wipe the mushrooms with a damp cloth and slice them thin. Arrange layers of the cooled beef and onions, kidneys and mushrooms in a pie dish about 23 × 30 × 8 cm. (9 × 12 × 3 inches). Put in the centre of the dish an inverted ovenproof custard cup or egg cup that comes as high as the rim of the dish (this is to hold up the crust). Pour the juices from the braised beef into the dish and add just enough extra beef broth barely to cover the contents of the dish.

Roll out the puff pastry about 1 cm. ($\frac{3}{8}$ inch) thick and 4 cm. ($1\frac{1}{2}$ inches) larger than the dish. From this, cut off a strip $2\frac{1}{2}$ cm. (1 inch) wide and long enough to fit the circumference of the dish. Arrange this around the rim of the dish, dampen the top of the strip lightly with cold water (this makes it adhere to the top crust), and drape the remaining pastry over it to form the top crust. Press to seal the two edges together and trim off any pastry that overhangs the dish. Crimp the edge of the pastry by pressing it between thumb and forefinger. Cut a V-shaped slit in the centre of the top crust and place a small cone of waxed or greaseproof paper in it, to form a vent for the steam to escape. Roll out leftover pastry and cut into simple flowers and leaves with pastry cutters. Moisten the underside of the dough with cold water and lay on the crust as decoration. Brush top crust and decorations with beaten egg yolks, which give it a brown glaze when baked. Preheat the oven to 230°C (450°F, gas mark 8). Bake the pie at 230°C for 10 minutes, then reduce the heat to 190°C (375°F, gas mark 5) and bake 25 to 30 minutes longer.

Choux Pastry

♙ Cream Puffs with Chocolate Sauce

The name *choux*, or cabbage, for this pastry probably originated because when the little puffs rise, they resemble tiny cabbages. *Choux* pastry can be used for *beignets soufflés* (page 217) or, without the rum or brandy flavouring, it can be baked as little cream puffs, then filled with ice cream or whipped cream and served with a chocolate sauce. If the sugar is omitted from the following recipe, the puffs can be filled with a savoury mixture, such as creamed fish or mushrooms, and served as a hot first course or a cocktail appetizer. For cocktail appetizers, make bite-size puffs, using 1 teaspoon of the *choux* pastry instead of 1 tablespoon.

Makes 24 puffs, or enough for 8

CHOUX PASTRY

125 g. (4 oz.) butter, cut into pieces
$\frac{1}{4}$ l. (8 fl. oz.) water
$\frac{1}{8}$ teaspoon salt (for savoury puffs, use 1 teaspoon)
$\frac{1}{2}$ teaspoon sugar (omit for savoury puffs)
140 g. ($4\frac{1}{2}$ oz.) plain flour
4 eggs

GLAZE

1 egg beaten with 1 teaspoon water

CHOCOLATE SAUCE

350 g. (12 oz.) semi-sweet chocolate   1 tablespoon cognac or madeira or
60 g. (2 oz.) bitter chocolate   dark rum
¼ l. (8 fl. oz.) double cream

FILLING

4½ dl. (¾ pt) ice cream

Combine the butter, water, salt and sugar in a heavy 2-litre (2-quart) saucepan over medium heat and heat until the butter is melted and the water boiling. Remove the pan from the heat; dump in the flour and beat vigorously with a wooden spatula or spoon until well blended. Put pan over medium heat and beat the mixture with the spatula for about a minute or until it forms a thick mass that clings to the spatula and comes away from the sides of the pan. Remove the pan from the heat and leave for 5 to 6 minutes. Preheat the oven to 220°C (425°F, gas mark 7) and butter two baking trays.

Make a well in the centre of the dough and beat in the eggs, one at a time, beating thoroughly after each addition. When the eggs are absorbed and the pastry is smooth and glossy, drop small mounds of the *choux* pastry onto the buttered baking trays using either a tablespoon or a forcing bag fitted with a 2-cm. (¾-inch) plain nozzle, spacing the puffs 5 cm. (2 inches) apart to allow room for expansion.

If you use the forcing bag, turn the top back about 8 cm. (3 inches) to form a cuff, then fill the bag with the *choux* pastry, using a rubber spatula. Fold the top back again, then twist the bag tightly, forcing the pastry to the bottom. *Squeeze it on to the sheet, making a circular mound about 5 cm. (2 inches) in diameter at the base, tapering to about 2½ cm. (1 inch) at the top.*

If you use a tablespoon, push the pastry from the tablespoon on to the tray with another spoon.

Brush the tops of the puffs with the egg glaze, using a pastry brush, but don't allow any of the egg to drip on to the tray as it would set and prevent the puffs from rising. Put one baking tray on the upper shelf of the preheated oven and one on the lower, spacing them so one is not directly above the other, to allow for heat circulation. Bake for 10 to 15 minutes, or until the puffs are golden brown, puffed to twice their original size, and firm to the touch. To make sure they are baked, remove one puff and cut it open. If the inside is doughy, bake the puffs a minute or two longer. When puffs are baked, turn off the oven; remove the baking trays and pierce the side of each puff with a sharp knife to allow the steam to escape. Replace the trays in the oven for 10 minutes to allow the puffs to dry out, leaving the door ajar, then transfer the puffs to wire cake racks to cool.

Meanwhile, make the chocolate sauce. Either melt the chocolate in the top of a double boiler over hot water or put it in a small, heavy pan in a 150°C (300°F, gas mark 2) oven until it melts. Stir the cream into the melted chocolate and flavour with the cognac, madeira, or rum. Keep warm over hot water until ready to use.

When the puffs are cool, split them in half horizontally with a knife. Scrape out any moist paste inside with a small spoon, then put a scoop of the ice cream on the bottom of each puff and cover with the top. Serve immediately, with a bowl of the hot chocolate sauce to spoon over the puffs at the table.

Bread

In these days when commercially made bread often has the quality of a plastic sponge, many people have fortunately discovered the enjoyment of making their own, both for the comforting and rewarding experience breadmaking is, and even more for the pleasure of producing and eating a well-flavoured, beautifully textured loaf.

Before you start to make bread, there are a few things you should know. The first is that flours differ a great deal, not only in various locales, but also from one batch to another. Thus the balance of liquid to flour can be so changeable that an absolutely accurate measure cannot be given. You will have to learn to know your dough by the feel. Good dough should be firm, elastic and smooth and should blister easily on the surface when it has been well kneaded. Sticky, lumpy dough is not good and will never make a well-textured loaf.

Reactivating the yeast is a very important step in breadmaking. Dissolve the yeast in warm water, about 45°C or 110°F to 115°F (take the temperature the first time to get the feel of how hot this is – water from the hot tap is usually perfect), to start the fermentation. You can test the temperature with your sensitive meat thermometer. The bubbling of the mixture is proof that the yeast is active.

Risings are equally important. The double-in-bulk rule given in many recipes means that after the kneaded dough has been placed in a buttered bowl and set in a warm, draught-free place, the bulk should increase until it is double in volume. An oven is an excellent place for the rising – either a gas oven with the faint warmth given off by the pilot light or an electric oven that has been heated very slightly and then turned off. The place should be draught-free because the yeast must be pampered with constant warmth to keep it active. The rising time will differ for various types of breads. Some will rise in less than 1 hour, whereas others will take as long as $2\frac{1}{2}$ to 3 hours to double in bulk. Some recipes call for two risings, meaning that when the dough has risen once it is punched down and left to rise again before being shaped into loaves and given a third and final rising in the tin. Others need to rise only once before being shaped into loaves and put into the tin to rise again before baking. Rising bread should be covered with a towel or a sheet of polythene, unless otherwise noted, to prevent the surface from drying and cracking.

♨ Basic White Bread

This is my idea of a good, simple loaf of bread – firm, honest in flavour, tender to the bite yet with a slight chewiness in the crust. It is also excellent for toast. Once you have mastered the procedures given here, you can go on to more complex recipes without difficulty.

As I have said, there are many variables in breadmaking. As far as flours are concerned, for example, strong plain bread flour produces the best results in wheat breads. Compressed or cake yeast is becoming difficult to find and the dry variety is everywhere, so we'll use that. Water may be used for the liquid; the milk used in this recipe makes a richer bread. The amount of salt may be varied according to taste: my rule of thumb is 1 tablespoon for each 450 g. or pound of flour. Even the weather has an effect on breadmaking. The degree of humidity and warmth will govern the absorption quality of the flour and the action of the yeast.

Makes 1 large or 2 smaller loaves

7 g. ($\frac{1}{4}$ oz. or 2 teaspoons) dry yeast
4 tablespoons warm (45°C, 110°F to 115°F) water
2 teaspoons sugar
$\frac{1}{4}$ l. (8 fl. oz.) milk

1 tablespoon salt
45 g. ($1\frac{1}{2}$ oz.) butter
About 480 g.(17 oz.) strong plain flour
Egg wash: 1 egg white beaten slightly with 1 tablespoon water

In a small bowl mix the yeast and 4 tablespoons warm water; add the sugar, stir well, and set aside until the mixture swells and small bubbles appear on the surface – about 10 minutes. (If it doesn't froth at all, it means the yeast is not fresh.)

Heat the milk with the salt in a small saucepan and stir in the butter until it melts. Set aside to cool until it is no warmer than the yeast mixture. Put 255 g. (9 oz.) of the flour in a large mixing bowl and stir in the milk mixture. Beat well with a wooden spatula, add the yeast mixture, and continue beating the dough until it is smooth, adding an additional 150 g. (5 oz.) of flour to make a firm dough. Turn the dough out onto a floured work surface and begin the kneading process, which evenly distributes the fermenting yeast cells through the dough.

Knead for about 10 minutes, kneading in additional flour as necessary, until the dough is smooth and no longer sticky, and blisters form on the surface. There are several kneading methods, but the basic one is to *flour*

the dough and your hand lightly, then push the heel of your hand down into the dough and away from you. Fold the dough over, give it a quarter turn, and push down again. Repeat pushing, folding and turning until the motion becomes rhythmic. If you have a heavy-duty electric mixer with a dough-hook attachment, knead the dough with the hook and finish it off on the board. *To test whether the dough has been kneaded enough, make an indentation in it with your fingers; it should spring back.* If blisters form on the surface of the dough and break, this is another sign that the kneading is sufficient.

Butter a large bowl, transfer the dough to it, and turn the bowl until the dough is well coated with butter on all sides. Cover the dough with a tea towel and let it rise in a warm, draught-free place for 1 to 1½ hours, until it is double in bulk.

To test further if the dough has risen properly, make an indentation in it with two fingers: if the dough does not spring back, then it is ready.

Butter a 23 × 13 × 8-cm. (9 × 5 × 3-inch) bread tin, or two tins that are about 20 × 10 × 5 cm. (8 × 4 × 2 inches). Punch the dough down with your fist to deflate it; transfer it to a floured board and knead well for about 3 minutes. Pat it into a smooth round or oval shape and let it rest for 4 to 5 minutes. *Then form into 1 large or 2 small loaves, by shaping the dough into an oval the length of your bread tin, then gently stretching, rounding, and plumping it in the palms of your hands,* tucking the edges underneath and pinching them together. Lift carefully; drop the dough into the tin or tins

and smooth out. Cover the dough with a towel and let it rise again in a warm, draught-free place for about 45 minutes to 1 hour, until it is double in bulk.

Preheat the oven to 200°C (400°F, gas mark 6). Brush the egg wash over the top of the dough. Bake in the centre of the oven for 20 minutes; reduce the heat to 180°C (350°F, gas mark 4) and bake for 20 to 25 minutes longer, until the crust is well browned and the bread sounds hollow when removed from the tin and tapped on the bottom with the knuckles. If you like a crusty loaf, remove it from the tin about 5 to 10 minutes before the end of the baking time and let it finish baking on the oven rack. It will get brown and crusty all over. Remove the bread from the oven and let it cool on a rack before slicing. The bread may be stored in a plastic bag in the refrigerator after it has cooled (if you seal it in a bag before it is completely cooled, the crust will become soft); it will keep about a week. It also freezes well if wrapped tightly in plastic wrap and sealed in a plastic bag and can be kept for up to 3 months.

Batter Bread

Batter breads are extremely popular with people who feel that kneading is too much work. There's nothing complicated or arduous about making a real loaf, but if you want to start modestly, begin with batter breads and work up to the others.

Makes 1 large round loaf

14 g. (½ oz.) dry yeast

4½ dl. (¾ pt) warm 45°C (110°F to 115°F) water

5 tablespoons non-fat dry milk

2 tablespoons sugar

30 g. (1 oz.) butter

2 teaspoons salt

2 garlic cloves, finely chopped (optional)

510 g. (18 oz.) strong plain flour

Egg wash: 1 egg white lightly beaten with 1 tablespoon water

3 to 4 tablespoons sesame seeds

Add the yeast to the water in a large mixing bowl and leave it to become frothy. Add the dry milk, sugar, butter, salt, optional garlic and half the flour. Beat the batter by hand or with an electric mixer at medium speed for 2 minutes. Stir in the remaining flour by hand and stir the mixture well to make a soft dough. Cover it with a damp towel and let it rise in a warm, draught-free place for about 40 minutes or until it is double in bulk.

Preheat the oven to 190°C (375°F, gas mark 5). Uncover the risen dough and stir it vigorously for 1 minute. Butter a 1½-litre (1½-quart) straight-sided casserole or soufflé dish and put in the batter. Brush the top with the egg wash and sprinkle with sesame seeds. Bake the bread in the centre of the oven for about 1 hour, or until it is delicately browned and sounds hollow when rapped with the knuckles. Remove from the casserole or dish and serve warm, cut into wedges.

♔ Corn Bread

There are innumerable recipes for corn bread, which is leavened by baking powder. This one, which is very moist and rich, happens to be my favourite.

Serves 6

75 g. (2½ oz.) flour

255 g. (9 oz.) yellow cornmeal

1 teaspoon salt

1 teaspoon sugar

3 teaspoons baking powder

3 eggs, well beaten

¼ l. (8 fl. oz.) milk

4 tablespoons cream

5 tablespoons melted butter

Preheat the oven to 200°C (400°F, gas mark 6). Butter a 20 × 28-cm. (8 × 11-inch) baking tin. Sift the flour, cornmeal, salt, sugar, and baking powder into a large bowl, to mix the ingredients thoroughly and distribute the baking powder evenly. Beat in the eggs and milk with a wooden spoon until well mixed. Beat in the cream and, lastly, the melted butter. Pour into the buttered tin and bake for 18 to 20 minutes. While still hot, cut into squares and serve wrapped in a napkin.

Cakes

In cake baking, it is very important to use the size of tin specified in the recipe. Most recipes call for a round or square 20-cm. or 23-cm. (8-inch or 9-inch) tin, 4 or 5 cm. (1½ or 2 inches) deep. There are, of course, other sizes and types, such as the flat Swiss-roll tin, the deep rectangular bread tin, the deep, round tube tin, and the ring mould in which a savarin is baked, but the 20- or 23-cm. (8- or 9-inch) tins are those you will find you need most often. Keep tins of different sizes separate and check them before you bake. If you use a tin that is too small for the recipe the batter is likely to overflow during baking, while with a too-large tin the cake may bake too rapidly.

Whatever you bake in or on, whether it is a cake tin, Swiss-roll tin, a pie plate, or a baking tray, it should be made of heavy-duty aluminium, not a flimsy material that would warp or buckle with the heat. Keep your tins clean. Burned tins or those darkened with grease may make a batter scorch or overbake, as dark surfaces conduct more heat than light ones. Some aluminium cake tins and baking trays have a non-stick coating, which works extremely well and enables you to remove the baked cake or biscuits from the nonstick coating with a minimum of effort. Otherwise, you should prepare your tin according to the type of cake you are baking. For the majority of cakes the inside of the tin should be buttered, or buttered and floured, or buttered and lined with buttered greaseproof paper cut to fit the tin. To do this, place the tin bottom side down on the paper, trace around it with a pencil, and then cut out the shape. If you are using more than one layer-cake tin, fold the greaseproof paper in layers and trace and cut out all the liners at one time. An extremely valuable baking accessory that not too many people seem to know about is cooking parchment or kitchen parchment, which is sold in sheets and rolls. Cooking parchment doesn't need greasing, won't discolour or scorch, and is easy to cut and fit into the tin. Using a forcing bag with one of its various-shaped nozzles you can pipe sticky things like meringues onto a parchment-lined baking tray and be confident that you'll be able to get them off without any problem.

If you are baking more than one cake, or cake layer, in the oven, don't put the tins directly above each other. Stagger them on the oven racks so that the hot air can circulate around them, and keep the tins about 5 cm. (2 inches) away from the back and sides of the oven where the heat tends to be more intense or your cake may bake more on one side than the other. If you are baking only one cake, put it in the centre of the oven. Unless the heat is right, the cake won't bake properly. It is heat that makes the leavening expand and 'sets' the cake when it has expanded. A cake with a gummy texture or a soggy bottom is an indication that the heat was too low.

An inexpensive essential is a flour sifter, the kind you operate by squeezing the handle. For cakes, flour is practically always sifted.

Apart from your basic cake tins and baking trays, scales and sifter, the only equipment you will need in addition to the normal kitchen complement of mixing bowls, beaters, whisks, spatulas, and rolling pin and board are a couple of wire cake racks, for cooling the cakes, and a set of biscuit cutters.

A final tip. Your cake will be easier to mix, lighter and better-textured if you have all your ingredients at room temperature. This is particularly important when you are using eggs, for both yolks and whites will have greater volume if they are allowed to warm up before being beaten.

♟ 1-2-3-4 Cake

This layer cake was a standard in our house. The recipe is a very old one that people could keep in their heads because of the utter simplicity of the formula that gave the cake its name – 1 cup (8 fl. oz.) of butter, 2 cups of sugar, 3 cups of flour and 4 eggs. Here baking powder is the leavening agent, so this is a very easy cake to make. You might like to try mixing it the first time with your hands, which will give you a good idea of the basic techniques of beating and folding. If you don't want to use your hands to mix the cake, use a whisk, a rotary hand beater, or an electric beater or mixer to cream the butter and sugar and to beat in the egg yolks, milk, flour, and vanilla. Fold in the egg whites by hand.

Makes 1 3-layer cake

FOR PREPARING 3 23-CM. (9-INCH) LAYER-CAKE TINS, 4 CM. (1½ INCHES) DEEP

1 tablespoon softened butter   2 tablespoons flour

FOR THE CAKE

300 g. (10 oz.) sifted plain flour   400 g. (14 oz.) sugar
4 teaspoons baking powder   4 eggs, at room temperature
½ teaspoon salt   ¼ l. (8 fl. oz.) milk, at room temperature
225 g. (8 oz.) unsalted butter, at room   1 to 1½ teaspoons vanilla essence
   temperature

FOR THE FILLING AND TOPPING

2 dl. (⅓ pt) strained orange juice   150 g. (5 oz.) sugar
2 tablespoons lemon juice   1 tablespoon finely grated orange rind

Preheat the oven to 180°C (350°F, gas mark 4). Butter the bottom and sides of each layer-cake tin with the softened butter, using your hands, then sprinkle the flour inside and shake this around so you get a thin coating on the butter. *Tip out any excess.*

Now to sift your flour. Lay a large piece of greaseproof paper on the scale, hold a sifter directly over it, scoop flour from the package into the sifter, and sift the flour directly on to the paper. When you have 300 g. (10 oz.) of sifted flour on the paper tip it into a mixing bowl, then put the baking powder and salt in the sifter, holding it over the mixing bowl, and sift it over the flour. Then mix the baking powder and salt lightly with the flour, using your hands.

Next, put the butter into a second, large mixing bowl. If it is very firm (it shouldn't be, if you have left it out of the refrigerator), squeeze it through your fingers until it softens up. When it is soft enough to work, *form your right hand into a big fork, as it were, and cream the butter – which means that you beat it firmly and quickly with your hand, beating and aerating it, until it becomes light, creamy, and fluffy. Then whirl your fingers around like*

a whisk so the butter forms a circle in the bowl. Gradually cream the 400 g. (14 oz.) of sugar into the butter with the same fork-like motion, beating until the mixture is very light and fluffy. As the sugar blends in it will change the colour of the butter to a much lighter colour, almost white.

Now wash and dry your hands thoroughly and separate the eggs, as you would for a soufflé, letting the whites slip through your slightly parted fingers into a small bowl and dropping the yolks into a second, larger bowl. Beat the yolks for a few minutes with a whisk until they are well blended. Then, again with your hand, beat them very thoroughly into the butter-sugar mixture. Now beat in the milk alternately with the sifted flour – first one, then the other – this time keeping your fingers close together as if your hand were a wooden spatula. Beat, beat, beat until the batter is well mixed, then add the vanilla and beat that in for a minute or two.

Put the egg whites in your beating bowl and beat them with a large whisk or an electric hand beater until they mount first to soft, drooping peaks and then to firm, glossy peaks. Do not overbeat until they are stiff and dry. Tip the beaten whites onto the cake batter and fold them in with your hand. *Slightly cup your hand and use the side like a spatula to cut down through the whites*

and batter to the bottom of the bowl and then flop them over with your cupped hand, rotating the bowl with your other hand as you do so – exactly the technique you use when folding egg whites into a soufflé mixture with a rubber spatula. Repeat this very lightly and quickly until the whites and batter are thoroughly folded and blended. Once you have mastered this hand technique you can use it for a soufflé, too.

Again using your hand like a spatula, pour and scrape the batter into the three prepared tins, dividing it equally between them. Give the filled tins a little knock on the countertop to level the batter. Put the three tins in the centre of the oven, or, if you have to use more than one rack, stagger them on the two middle racks of the oven so they do not overlap. Bake for 25 minutes, then touch the centre of each cake lightly with your fingertip. If it springs back, it is done. Remove the tins from the oven and put them on wire cake racks to cool for a few minutes, then loosen the layers by running the flat of a knife blade around the sides of the tins, put a rack on top of each tin, and invert so the cake comes out onto the rack, top side down. Then reverse the layers so they are top side up.

Mix the orange juice, lemon juice, sugar and orange rind together and drizzle the mixture over the still-warm cake layers, being careful not to let it all soak into one spot; then pile the layers on top of each other. The juice mixture will give the cake a lovely, fresh, fruity flavour and it is not rich like an icing. Leave the cake to cool.

☕ Savarin with Apricot Glaze

A savarin is a rich spongy cake leavened by yeast and baked in a ring mould. The technique is different from that of other cakes and the soft, sticky dough requires quite a lot of beating by hand. The cake is not sweet and is usually saturated with a rum syrup or, in this case, coated with an apricot glaze.

TO PREPARE THE 2-LITRE (3½-PINT) RING MOULD

2 teaspoons soft butter

FOR THE SAVARIN

1½ dl. (¼ pt) lukewarm milk   *4 eggs*
*   45°C (110°F to 115°F)*   *½ teaspoon salt*
7 g. (¼ oz., or 2 teaspoons) dry yeast   *150 g. (5 oz.) softened butter, cut into*
1 tablespoon sugar   *small pieces*
255 g. (9 oz.) plain flour

FOR THE GLAZE AND FILLING

450-g. (1-lb.) jar pure apricot jam   *225 g. (½ lb.) strawberries, washed,*
*   (without added pectin)*   *hulled, and lightly sugared*
3 dl. (½ pt) sweetened whipped cream

Butter the inside of the ring mould well and set aside.

Pour the milk into a cup and test the temperature with a meat thermometer. Sprinkle the yeast into the milk, add a pinch of sugar, and stir. Leave it until it proofs (becomes frothy), which shows that the yeast is working.

Sift the flour (using the technique described for the previous cake) into a large mixing bowl or the bowl of an electric mixer. Beat the eggs slightly with a fork or whisk and add to the flour with the salt, the rest of the sugar, and the yeast mixture. Beat with a wooden spoon or spatula, or the dough-hook attachment of the electric mixer, until it forms a soft, sticky dough. You may have to add a little more milk to get the right consistency.

When thoroughly mixed, beat for 2 minutes with your hands, pulling the dough up and letting it drop back into the bowl, until it becomes elastic, smooth, and no longer sticky. Cover the bowl with a towel and let the dough stand in a warm place (on top of the cooker, or in the oven, heated by the pilot light) for 45 minutes, or until doubled in bulk.

Deflate the risen dough by gathering it from the sides of the bowl towards the centre. Then beat the pieces of softened butter into the dough with your hands or a wooden spatula, beating for about 4 minutes. Use the same beating technique you used when making the 1-2-3-4 cake.

Turn the dough into the buttered ring mould and let it stand in a warm place, uncovered, until the dough has risen to the top of the mould, about 1 hour or more. Meanwhile, preheat the oven to 230°C (450°F, gas mark 8).

Put the mould in the centre of the oven and bake the cake for 10 minutes, then reduce the heat to 180°C (350°F, gas mark 4) and continue baking until nicely browned, about 20 minutes longer. Test by inserting a cake tester or skewer into the cake; if it comes out clean, the cake is baked.

Take the mould from the oven and put a wire rack on top of it. Invert so the savarin comes out onto the rack. Let it cool slightly while making the glaze.

Put the apricot jam (be sure to use pure jam, without added pectin, or the jam won't melt properly) into a small, heavy saucepan and stir over medium heat until the jam comes to a boil. Reduce the heat and cook for 2 minutes, stirring, until liquid. Rub through a fine sieve with a wooden spatula, then put the savarin on a plate and pour the apricot glaze over it. Allow the savarin to cool. Just before serving, fill the centre with sugared strawberries and top with whipped cream.

🍳 Génoise

This light cake, leavened entirely by eggs, is of Italian origin but French by adoption. Mostly it is used as a layer cake, with a butter-cream filling and icing, but it can also be baked flat in a Swiss-roll tin, filled with a fruit-flavoured Bavarian cream and rolled, or used as a base for trifle (see page 339).

FOR PREPARING 2 23-CM. (9-INCH) ROUND LAYER-CAKE TINS, 4 CM. (1½ INCHES) DEEP

1 tablespoon soft butter	2 tablespoons flour

FOR THE GÉNOISE

125 g. (4 oz.) unsalted butter	140 g. (4½ oz.) fine plain flour
6 large eggs	½ teaspoon salt
200 g. (7 oz.) castor sugar	1 teaspoon vanilla essence

FOR THE BUTTER CREAM
Makes ½ l. (¾ pt)

2 egg yolks	1½ dl. (¼ pt) single cream
4 tablespoons sugar	½ teaspoon vanilla essence
⅛ teaspoon salt	225 g. (8 oz.) unsalted butter

First, prepare the tins. Put one tin on a double sheet of greaseproof paper or kitchen parchment and trace the diameter of the bottom with a pencil. Cut out the circles, which will be used to line the tins. Grease the bottom and sides of each tin with butter, then put a greaseproof-paper circle in the bottom of each tin and butter the paper. Put a tablespoon of flour in each tin. Toss it around until the greased tins are lightly coated with flour, then shake out the excess. Set the tins aside. If you use parchment, there is no need to butter and flour the paper.

For this cake, the butter must be melted and clarified and only the clear yellow part of the melted butter used. Melt the butter in a small saucepan over low heat until the clear yellow fat and the whey (the whitish, curdlike substance that sinks to the bottom) separate. Put the pan of melted butter in the refrigerator to chill until the fat solidifies on top, then remove it from the moist whey underneath. Reheat the solidified fat until it melts and leave to cool until just tepid. You should have 125 ml. (4 fl. oz.) clarified butter. Preheat the oven to 180°C (350°F, gas mark 4).

Combine the eggs and sugar in the top of a double boiler over hot (not boiling) water, which should not touch the bottom of the upper pan. Set the double boiler over low heat (the water must not even simmer) and beat the eggs and sugar for about 15 minutes with a whisk or an electric hand beater until the mixture is very thick, pale in colour, and falls in a thick ribbon when the beater is lifted. Remove the top of the double boiler from the water and put the contents into a mixing bowl.

Sift the flour through a sifter, letting it fall lightly on to a sheet of grease-proof paper on kitchen scales. When you have 140 g. (4½ oz.) flour, put it back in the sifter with the salt and sift twice again, letting the flour fall on a large piece of greaseproof paper.

Sprinkle one-quarter of the sifted flour over the egg-sugar mixture and quickly fold in with a rubber spatula, rotating the bowl as you do so, using the same folding technique as for a soufflé or the 1-2-3-4 cake. Add the rest of the flour and the clarified melted butter and vanilla in the same way, a third at a time, rotating the bowl as you fold. (If you have an electric mixer, put the egg-sugar mixture into the bowl and beat in the flour, butter, and vanilla at low speed, using the beater attachment. Add all the flour, butter and vanilla at one time and beat just until mixed. Do not overbeat.)

Immediately turn the batter into the prepared tins, smoothing the tops lightly with a rubber spatula. Tap the tins lightly on the countertop to settle the batter. Bake in the centre of the preheated oven for 25 to 35 minutes, or until the top of the cake springs back lightly when touched with a fingertip. Remove the tins from the oven and cool on wire racks for 15 minutes, then hold the racks over the tins and quickly reverse them, turning the cakes out onto the racks. If the greaseproof paper sticks to the cake, remove it. Again reverse the cakes so the top side is uppermost. Cool for 1½ to 2 hours on the racks, meanwhile preparing the butter cream.

To make the butter cream, first make a *crème anglaise* or custard with the egg yolks, sugar, salt, single cream and vanilla, as directed on page 290. Cool the custard. Put the butter into a bowl and beat with a whisk, rotary beater, or electric hand beater until very thick, light and creamy. Beat this vigorously, a little at a time, into the cooled custard. Chill slightly before using. If the mixture separates, heat it gently in the top of a double boiler over hot water, beating until re-emulsified.

Sandwich the génoise layers with the chilled butter cream and spread a layer of butter cream on the top, if you wish. Or sift icing sugar over the top. If you don't fill and ice the cake, cool it and wrap in plastic wrap and foil to keep it from drying out. It will keep under refrigeration for several days, or it may be frozen and kept in the freezer for several months.

Cookies

·······················

There are all types and shapes of American cookies, or biscuits. Easiest to make are the bar type, for which ingredients are simply mixed, spread on a tin, and baked. Rolled cookies are made from a stiff, chilled dough, rolled until thin between sheets of greaseproof paper or on a lightly floured board, and cut out with cookie or biscuit cutters. Dropped cookies are pushed from a spoon on to the baking tray with the aid of another spoon. These cookies are usually thick and round, with a soft centre, and as they spread more than the other types it is important to leave plenty of space – about 5 cm. (2 inches) – between them. Pressed cookies are pushed through a cookie press with a shaping tip. Moulded or shaped cookies are made with chilled dough and are either shaped into balls and flattened or moulded into all kinds of different shapes, such as crescents and rings. Refrigerator cookies are made from dough shaped into a roll, chilled thoroughly and then sliced thin with a sharp knife. The following cookies belong to the bar, rolled and dropped types.

For baking cookies, you need large flat tins without sides or with very shallow sides, known as baking trays, from which the cookies can be removed easily after baking. Swiss-roll tins can also be used. Large tins are better than small ones, but the tin shouldn't be so large that it impedes the circulation of the hot air in the oven – there should be at least 5 or 8 cm. (2 or 3 inches) between the tin and the oven sides.

As you usually bake more than one tray of cookies and cookies bake fast, you can set up an assembly-line system. Put the first tray of cookies on the lower rack of the oven and when they are almost baked move this tray to the top rack to finish baking and slide another tray on to the lower rack. In this way the cookies bake evenly. However, if you are baking meringue-type cookies, bake only one tray at a time as the cookies might fall if the oven door is opened and they are exposed to the cold air.

Scotch Shortbread

This is a very rich, short, buttery type of bar cookie. The dough can either be pressed into 20-cm (8-inch) pie plates and marked in wedges with a knife so it can be broken into pieces after baking, or patted out on baking trays and cut into fingers.

Makes about 5 dozen

350 g. (12 oz.) unsalted butter   400 g. (14 oz.) sifted plain flour
200 g. (7 oz.) sugar

Preheat the oven to 150°C (300°F, gas mark 2).

Beat the butter in a bowl with a wooden spatula or an electric hand beater until creamy and fluffy, then gradually beat in the sugar and continue beating until very light and thick. Mix in the flour until thoroughly incorporated, then turn the dough out on to a lightly floured board and knead the dough, as you would knead bread; until it is very smooth and forms a ball that breaks slightly when the thumb is run from the centre to the edge. Divide the dough in half. Put each half on an ungreased baking tray, flatten it with your palms, and then pat the dough out about 1 cm. (½ inch) thick. Trim the edges of the dough with a knife and cut it into fingers about 1 cm. (½ inch) wide and 9 cm. (3½ inches) long. Prick the surface well to prevent it from blistering during baking.

Bake the shortbread until it turns a very pale brown around the edges, about 30 minutes. Remove from the oven and cool slightly, then remove the shortbread with a palette knife to a rack to cool completely. Store in an airtight tin, or place in freezer bags and seal. Shortbread may be eaten fresh, but is best if allowed to age for a week in a cool place.

☃ Sand Tarts

One of the most popular kinds of rolled cookie is sand tarts. Make sure the dough is thoroughly chilled before rolling.

Makes about 2½ dozen

FOR THE COOKIES

125 g. (4 oz.) unsalted butter	1 egg
200 g. (7 oz.) sugar	200 g. (7 oz.) fine plain flour
¼ teaspoon salt	½ teaspoon vanilla essence

FOR THE TOPPING

2 egg whites	½ teaspoon ground cinnamon
2 tablespoons sugar	

Beat the butter in a bowl until creamy and fluffy, then beat in the sugar, salt and egg and continue to beat until very light, fluffy and pale. Beat in the sifted flour and the vanilla until thoroughly combined. When the dough is well blended, form it into a ball, wrap in waxed or greaseproof paper, and chill in the refrigerator for at least 3 hours.

Roll out the dough between sheets of greaseproof paper until very thin, about 5mm., less than ¼ inch, and cut into 8- or 9-cm. (3- or 3½-inch) rounds with a plain or fluted biscuit cutter. Preheat the oven to 190°C (375°F, gas mark 5).

Butter 3 baking trays. Arrange the cookies on the trays, lifting them from the paper with a flexible, thin-bladed palette knife. Beat the egg whites lightly with a fork and, using a pastry brush, brush the tops of the cookies with the beaten egg white. Sprinkle the tops with the sugar and cinnamon, to taste. Do not overdo either sugar or cinnamon.

Bake the cookies until they turn a deep yellow around the edges, 10 to 12 minutes. Remove from the oven and cool slightly, then remove from the trays with a palette knife and put on wire racks to cool. These cookies are better used within a week, but they will stay crisp 3 or 4 weeks if stored in an airtight tin in a cool place.

♨ Meringue Kisses

These are dropped cookies made with a meringue mixture and are therefore very sticky. Preferably they should be baked on a tray lined with cooking parchment. If you don't have parchment, the trays should be both buttered and floured.

Makes 5 dozen

3 egg whites	200 g. (7 oz.) castor sugar
½ teaspoon cream of tartar	1 teaspoon vanilla essence

These meringues are most easily made in an electric mixer or with an electric hand beater. If you don't have either one, beat in a large bowl with a wire whisk. Prepare 3 baking trays, either by lining them with parchment or by buttering them well, then dusting them lightly with flour.

Beat the egg whites in a bowl until foamy, add the cream of tartar, and beat until white, fluffy, and just beginning to hold their shape when the beater is lifted. Gradually beat in the sugar, 3 or 4 tablespoons at a time, adding the flavouring when half the sugar has been added. Beat until the sugar is dissolved and the whites are smooth, glossy and stand in stiff, upright peaks – the meringue stage. Preheat the oven to 140°C (275°F, gas mark 1).

Take up a teaspoon of the meringue mixture and push from the tip of the teaspoon with the back of another teaspoon on to the prepared baking tray. Space the meringues at least 2½ cm. (1 inch) apart to allow for expansion. Bake one tray at a time on the centre shelf of the oven for about 20 minutes, or until the meringues are set and very lightly coloured. Remove from the oven and cool slightly, then remove them from the trays to a wire rack to cool, sliding a flexible palette knife under them. Cool completely. Store in an airtight container between sheets of greaseproof paper or aluminium foil.

Casseroles
and Other Baked Dishes

Gratin of Greens

Serves 6 to 8

1 kg. (2 lbs.) fresh spinach
2 dl. (⅓ pt) olive oil
1 kg. (2 lbs.) Swiss chard
1 kg. (2 lbs.) courgettes
Salt

180 g. (6 oz.) cooked rice
3 garlic cloves, finely chopped
6 eggs
30 g. (1 oz.) fine bread crumbs

Wash the spinach well. Remove the coarse stalks; dry the leaves thoroughly and chop rather fine. Cook in 2 tablespoons oil in a heavy frying pan over medium heat until just wilted. Drain and put into a large bowl. Wash, dry, and chop the chard and cook in 2 tablespoons oil in the same pan until wilted. Drain and add to the spinach. Wash, dry, trim and dice the unpeeled courgettes; add about 4 more tablespoons oil to the pan; and sauté them, tossing well until just tender. Add to the spinach and chard, season with salt to taste, and mix in the rice and garlic. Combine well and transfer to a well-oiled, heavy 2-litre (2-quart) baking dish. Spoon 3 to 4 tablespoons oil over the top and bake in a 150°C (300°F, gas mark 2) oven for 20 minutes. Beat the eggs well; pour them over the vegetable mixture; sprinkle the top with crumbs; return to the oven and bake until the eggs are just set, about 10 to 15 minutes. Eat warm or cold. This makes an excellent luncheon or supper dish.

Scalloped Oysters

One of the most popular of all baked oyster dishes, this is a traditional feature of the American Thanksgiving or Christmas dinner menu. It can also be served as the hot dish for a supper of cold turkey or ham, or as a luncheon main dish.

Serves 4 to 6

125 g. (4 oz.) butter
90 to 125 g. (3 to 4 oz.) freshly rolled
   cream-cracker crumbs

1½ dl. (¼ pt) liquid from oysters
7½ dl. (1¼ pts) oysters
Salt, freshly ground black pepper,
   Tabasco   *(continued)*

1½ dl. (¼ pt) double cream
30 g. (1 oz.) fine bread crumbs

Melt half the butter in a pan and brush a little of it on the bottom and sides of a 1½-litre (1½-quart) baking dish. Reserve the rest of this melted butter for sautéing the bread crumbs. Cut the other 60 g. (2 oz.) into small pieces.

Cover the bottom of the dish with a layer of cracker crumbs (to make the crumbs, put crackers in a plastic bag and crush coarsely with a rolling pin). Arrange on them a layer of half the oysters, then another layer of cracker crumbs. Dot with half the pieces of butter and sprinkle lightly with salt and pepper and a dash or two of Tabasco. Make another layer of oysters and another layer of crumbs; dot again with butter and sprinkle with salt, pepper and Tabasco. Pour the liquid from the oysters and the double cream over the top. Lightly sauté the bread crumbs in the remaining melted butter until golden, tossing and turning them well. Sprinkle over the top of the oyster mixture. Bake in a 200°C (400°F, gas mark 6) oven for 25 minutes. Serve hot.

Stuffed Aubergine

Hollowed out, stuffed and baked vegetables represent one of the best ways to use up leftovers – cold meat, cooked rice or other grains, a few mushrooms, some bread crumbs, whatever you have around. Half the fun is making up your own combinations. Good candidates for stuffing are aubergine, courgettes, green peppers, onions and tomatoes. When baking aubergine or courgettes, there should always be some water in the dish to create steam and keep the shell soft.

Serves 4 to 8

4 medium aubergines
45 g. (1½ oz.) butter
4 tablespoons oil
1 large onion, finely chopped
2 garlic cloves, finely chopped
180 g. (6 oz.) cooked rice or cooked cracked wheat
225 to 350 g. (½ to ¾ lb.) finely ground cold lamb

4 tablespoons chopped parsley
60 g. (2 oz.) chopped walnuts or whole pine nuts
2 tablespoons tomato paste or ketchup
Salt, freshly ground black pepper
2 eggs, well beaten
30 g. (1 oz.) fine bread crumbs

Trim off the stem end and the brown part of the rounded end of the aubergines and wash and dry them. Halve the aubergines lengthwise and cut around the inside with a sharp knife or grapefruit knife, about 1 cm. (⅜ inch) from the skin, then scoop out the pulp with a spoon, leaving a 1-cm. ($\frac{3}{8}$-inch) layer around the sides and bottom of the shell. Chop the pulp and set aside. Preheat the oven to 180°C (350°F, gas mark 4).

Heat the butter and 2 tablespoons oil in a frying pan and sauté the onion and garlic over medium heat until limp and golden. Add the aubergine pulp and sauté for 5 minutes, until it has cooked down and some of the liquid has evaporated. Stir in the rice or cracked wheat, lamb, parsley, nuts, tomato paste or ketchup and season with salt and pepper to taste. Blend well, stir in the beaten eggs, and cook over low heat for 2 minutes. Fill the aubergine shells with this mixture; spoon a little of the remaining oil over the filling and sprinkle the tops with the bread crumbs. Arrange the stuffed shells in a large baking dish or pan and add about $1\frac{1}{2}$ cm. ($\frac{1}{2}$ inch) hot water.

Bake for 40 minutes. If the stuffing seems to be getting too dry on top (it should be brown but not too crisp), baste it with a little oil or with melted butter. Serve half an aubergine as a starter or a main course at luncheon or two halves as a dinner main course.

Celery and Walnut Ring

You can serve this ring hot, filling the centre with creamed mushrooms, chicken, shrimp, crabmeat, lobster, or sweetbreads; or cold, with shellfish or chicken salad.

Serves 6 to 8

75 g. ($2\frac{1}{2}$ oz.) very finely chopped or ground celery

2 tablespoons finely chopped parsley

100 g. ($3\frac{1}{2}$ oz.) finely chopped or ground walnuts

5 tablespoons very finely chopped or ground onion

5 tablespoons very finely chopped or ground green pepper

60 g. (2 oz.) fine bread crumbs

3 large eggs, slightly beaten

3 tablespoons melted butter

$1\frac{1}{2}$ teaspoons salt

$\frac{3}{4}$ teaspoon freshly ground black pepper

$3\frac{1}{2}$ dl. (12 fl. oz.) milk

Either chop the vegetables and nuts by hand or, if you have a liquidizer or food processor, process them until you have a more finely ground texture.

Combine the celery, parsley, nuts, onion, green pepper, crumbs, eggs, butter, salt, pepper and milk and mix together thoroughly. Heavily butter a 1½-l. (2½-pt) ring mould and pour the mixture into it.

Preheat the oven to 180°C (350°F, gas mark 4).

Put the ring mould into a large tin, such as a roasting tin, and place on the centre shelf of the oven. Pour into the tin enough hot water to come about halfway up the mould (this prevents the ring from drying out as it bakes) and bake for 1 hour.

Remove from the oven and let the ring mould stand in the hot water for 10 minutes before unmoulding. To unmould, loosen the baked mixture from the edges of the mould by running a thin-bladed knife or palette knife around it; put a round serving platter on top of the mould and invert. Fill the centre with desired creamed filling and serve at once. Or cool, cover with plastic wrap, and chill in the refrigerator. When ready to serve, unmould in the same way.

Lentil Casserole with Sausage

Lentils are nutritious, delicious, and too often ignored. They combine extremely well with any kind of pork product. You can vary this casserole by substituting for the sausages such meats as well-browned pork chops; braised pork tenderloin, cut into thick slices; quartered roast duck; braised lamb shanks.

Serves 6

370 g. (13 oz.) lentils	*60 g. (2 oz.) butter*
1 onion, stuck with 2 cloves	*60 g. (2 oz.) finely chopped onion*
1 bay leaf	*Salt, freshly ground black pepper*
1 tablespoon salt	*3 dl. (½ pt) dry red wine*
12 Italian sausages, either sweet or hot	

Cover the lentils with water, add the clove-stuck onion and bay leaf, and simmer until just tender, adding the salt when the lentils are almost cooked. Drain. Preheat the oven to 180°C (350°F, gas mark 4).

While the lentils are cooking, prick the skins of the sausages well and poach in water to cover for 5 minutes (see page 38). Drain. Melt the butter in a frying pan and sauté the onion until just limp and golden. Butter a 2½-litre (2-quart) baking dish or casserole. Arrange half the sausages in the bottom, cover with half the lentils and half the sautéed onion, and sprinkle lightly with salt and pepper. Make another layer of lentils, then top with sausages and the rest of the onion. Pour in the wine and bake for 25 to 35 minutes or until the top sausages are nicely browned.

VARIATION

If you prefer, you can use 6 knockwurst in place of the Italian sausages. Before adding to the casserole, split them in half lengthwise and sauté in butter or bacon fat until browned on both sides.

Corned Beef Hash Ring

This is a rather more elegant way of serving corned beef hash, good for a luncheon party. You can use the leftover corned beef and potatoes from the recipe on page 24.

Serves 4

1 large onion, finely chopped
30 g. (1 oz.) butter
180 g. (6 oz.) finely chopped cold
  corned beef

450 g. (1 lb.) finely chopped boiled
  potatoes
Salt, freshly ground black pepper
4 to 8 tablespoons double cream

TO FILL THE RING

280 g. (10 oz.) sliced or quartered hard-boiled eggs (about 4 to 5 eggs) mixed with 3 dl. (½ pt) béchamel sauce.

Sauté the onion in the butter until just golden and limp. Mix with the chopped meat and potatoes and season to taste with salt and pepper. Add enough cream barely to moisten the mixture.

Preheat the oven to 180°C (350°F, gas mark 4). Butter a 1½ l.- (2½ pt-) ring mould and pack the corned beef hash into it. Bake for about 45 minutes. Allow to stand for a few minutes after removing from the oven, then loosen around the edges with a knife, put a serving platter on top of the mould, and invert the mould. Fill the centre with the creamed eggs.

Casserole of Turkey with Rice

A good finale for the leftover Christmas turkey, stuffing, and ham.

Serves 4 to 6

75 g. (2½ oz.) unsalted butter

2 medium onions, peeled and chopped

225 g. (8 oz.) firm white mushrooms, sliced

225 g. (8 oz.) diced cold turkey

90 g. (3 oz.) diced baked ham

125 g. (4 oz.) crumbled leftover bread stuffing

2 tablespoons chopped parsley

¼ teaspoon dried thyme

Salt, freshly ground black pepper

1 tablespoon curry powder

225 g. (8 oz.) uncooked rice

4½ dl. (¾ pt) hot chicken or turkey broth

Melt 60g. (2 oz.) of the butter in a frying pan, add the onions, and sauté over medium heat until limp and golden. Add the mushrooms and sauté for 2 or 3 minutes, until just cooked through. Combine the vegetables in a casserole with the turkey, ham, stuffing, parsley and thyme. Mix well, taste, then add salt and pepper – the amount will depend on the seasoning in the stuffing. Preheat the oven to 190°C (375°F, gas mark 5).

Melt the remaining butter in the pan, add the curry powder and the rice, and sauté lightly over medium heat until the rice is just translucent (curry powder should always be cooked in fat to take away the raw taste before being added to a dish). Add to the casserole; pour in the hot broth; cover the casserole and bake until the rice is tender and the liquid absorbed, about 25 to 30 minutes. If the rice does not seem quite tender, add a little more heated broth and continue cooking.

Baked Fish

Baking is an excellent way to cook a whole fish, and if you stuff it the fish will go even farther. Have the fish gutted and the scales and fins removed, but the head and tail left on – the fish will look better and stay moister and juicier. If the fish is to be stuffed, also have the backbone removed. Good choices for baking are cod, haddock, sea bass, red snapper and grey mullet. A whole fish weighing from 4 to 6 pounds will easily serve 4.

For stuffings, you can choose one with a bread crumb base, a vegetable stuffing, or one containing shellfish such as oysters or crabmeat. To my taste, a simple vegetable stuffing is best.

The baking temperature, time, and method are the same whether the fish is baked stuffed or unstuffed.

🍲 Stuffed, Baked Fish

Serves 4

1 fish weighing about 2½ kg. (5 lbs.),
  backbone removed
2 medium onions, thinly sliced
4 or 5 ripe tomatoes, thinly sliced
30 to 45 g. (1 to 1½ oz.) butter, cut
  into small pieces

60 g. (2 oz.) chopped parsley
1½ teaspoons salt
½ teaspoon freshly ground black pepper

Preheat the oven to 230°C (450°F, gas mark 8). Line a baking dish large enough to hold the fish with a double layer of heavy-duty aluminium foil (this makes it easy to lift the fish out and transfer it to a platter after baking). Butter the foil well.

Wash the fish well, dry it, and stuff with alternating layers of the sliced vegetables, dotting each layer with pieces of butter and sprinkling with chopped parsley. Salt and pepper the filling well. Close the opening with small skewers or toothpicks. Measure the fish at its thickest point, from back to belly. Rub the skin of the fish with butter, salt and pepper it, and place in the foil-lined baking pan. Bake for 10 minutes per measured inch – it should take about 30 to 35 minutes. Test with a fork or toothpick; the fish is done when the flesh flakes.

Transfer to a hot platter and remove the skewers. Decorate with lemon wedges and watercress and serve with small boiled potatoes.

VARIATION

Baked, Stuffed Fish Steaks. Substitute 2 large fish steaks for the whole fish; sandwich the stuffing between them and bake as before, allowing 10 minutes per measured 2½ cm. or inch of thickness of the combined steaks.

Baked Fish Fillets or Fish Steaks

Arrange fish fillets or steaks in a foil-lined baking dish or a foil-lined grill pan. Brush with the basting mixture given for grilled fish fillets (page 120) and bake for 10 minutes per measured 2½ cm. or inch of thickness in a preheated 230°C (450°F, gas mark 8) oven, basting once or twice during cooking.

Thickeners
and Liaisons

'Liaison' is a very useful word that explains a lot – in the language of cooking, the language of love and the language of diplomacy. In each case it means very much the same thing: a bond or relationship that in cooking binds the solids and liquids in a sauce, in love binds two people together and in diplomacy binds countries.

In cooking, the most basic and most valuable of liaisons is the roux, the mixture of fat and flour that thickens a sauce. In a great many French recipes you find the instruction 'first make a roux'. You may not have realized it, but when as a child you watched gravy being made in the tin in which meat had been roasted, this was exactly what was happening. First some of the fat was poured off, then flour was added and cooked over low heat in the remaining fat to make a roux, with all those little bits of browned goodness scraped up in the process. Finally, hot stock was mixed in to make a brown gravy. The flour was what brought and held everything together, forming a liaison between the fat and the liquid.

This, in a rather more refined and classic form, is what happens when you make one of the great French mother sauces (so called because so many other sauces spring from them) such as a béchamel sauce or white sauce, or a sauce Espagnole or brown sauce. In each case, butter and flour are cooked together until completely amalgamated and frothy. However, the roux for a béchamel is cooked only until it is a light golden colour, while for a brown sauce it is cooked until it turns a rich nut-brown, which colours the sauce and gives a more pronounced flavour.

The trouble with the sauces many people make is that the flour in the roux is not cooked long enough, which gives the sauce an unpleasant raw-flour taste. The flour must be stirred and cooked in the fat until it is smooth, golden, and lightly frothing in little bubbles before the liquid is added. Forty-five grams ($1\frac{1}{2}$ ounces) of butter and 3 tablespoons of flour will make a thick roux that will take about $\frac{1}{4}$ litre (8 fl. oz.) of liquid and give you a heavy, stiff sauce of the type used as a base for a soufflé. Thirty grams (1 oz.) of butter and 2 tablespoons of flour to about $\frac{1}{4}$ litre (8 fl. oz.) of liquid will make a medium roux and a medium sauce, the kind we call a cream sauce or a white sauce. When you make a sauce, it is better to make it too thick than too thin. It's an easy matter to thin it down by adding more liquid, but if you have to thicken it, you'll need to add another type of liaison called *beurre manié*, which I'll tell you about in a minute.

To make a good béchamel sauce takes time and care. I remember visiting a cooking class in London, given by one of my colleagues, where nine girls were being taught béchamel. This was a repeat performance, as the one they had made the previous week had been very poor. Their teacher, a Frenchwoman, showed them how, after the liaison had taken place and the sauce had thickened, the sauce should be simmered very gently while occasionally a pat of butter was stirred in – not enough to cause the sauce to separate or become very fatty, just enough to enrich it and give it a beautiful glossy finish. This gives you a much richer white sauce, and while you don't have to do it, especially if you are going to add other enrichments or flavourings to your basic sauce, you might try it sometime and discover the difference it makes. You'll also find that some of the older French cookbooks will tell you to simmer a béchamel as much as 45 or 50 minutes, which might seem a hell of a long stretch, but again it does make a difference to the texture and flavour.

Once you know how to make a béchamel and a brown sauce, recipes for which I will give you later, you'll have a whole repertoire of other sauces at your fingertips. The addition of cream makes a béchamel a velouté sauce; with cream and egg yolks it becomes a sauce suprême; with cheese it is a mornay; with white wine and fish stock as the liquid you have a white wine sauce for fish. From the basic brown sauce springs a sauce Bordelaise, a sauce diable, a sauce piquante, a Madeira sauce and many other brown sauces for meat, poultry, game, fish, or vegetables.

The other type of butter and flour liaison evolved by the French, *beurre manié*, is made quite differently. Instead of being cooked together at the beginning, the equal quantities of butter and flour are worked together with a fork or your fingers until they form a thick paste, with the flour completely absorbed by the butter. The paste is rolled into tiny balls, or patted out and cut into squares, and these little pieces are used to thicken a liquid at the end of the cooking time. The mixture, called *beurre manié* because the butter is manipulated or kneaded with the flour, is something you can make up ahead of time and store in the refrigerator for 2 or 3 weeks and bring out whenever you find your sauce is too thin or your soup or stew needs thickening.

Say you have made a stew and it seems a little too thin. You remove the meat and vegetables, bring the liquid to a boil, and then drop in your little balls of *beurre manié*, one or two at a time, cooking and stirring constantly until the liquid is thickened to your liking. The *beurre manié* has to break up, allowing the flour to cook and expand in the liquid, so it takes a little while before you can judge how much you will need to get the right thickness. It's better to underestimate at the beginning, as you can always add more. Once the liquid has thickened, taste it. If there is a floury taste, let it simmer gently for a few more minutes. Then return your meat and vegetables to the pan and let them reheat. *Beurre manié* is also an easy way to thicken a soup to just the consistency you want, or you may use it to thicken a sauce that is too thin.

While butter and flour is the classic, and to my mind the best, liaison, occasionally you'll find a recipe where flour alone is used. The flour is mixed to a heavy paste with water or milk, stirred into simmering liquid, and cooked until thickened. Should this lump, as it is inclined to do, it must be beaten vigorously with a wooden spoon or wire whisk until the lumps disappear or, if that doesn't work, the sauce must be rubbed through a fine strainer.

The Chinese thicken their fast-cooking sauces with cornflour, adding it in the same way as the flour, after mixing it to a paste with water. Cornflour does not require long cooking and it makes a sauce very smooth. While it is a serviceable liaison, it has, to my mind, one great drawback. As it thickens, it gives the dish a translucent glaze that I find aesthetically displeasing. My great bone of contention with many Chinese chefs is that they overdo the cornflour and their dishes have a sticky, glazed look instead of being smooth, velvety and glossy. Nor do I like pies or fruit desserts in which cornflour has been used to thicken the juices. They look like cheap bakery products to me.

There are other starches that are mixed with water and used for thickening, usually at the last minute because, like cornflour, they don't need the long cooking that flour does. Arrowroot, potato flour and rice flour serve this purpose, but as their thickening power is greater than that of flour, you use proportionately less. One teaspoon of potato flour or arrowroot, or 2 teaspoons of cornflour or rice flour, have the thickening power of 1 tablespoon of flour.

Arrowroot, more delicate in texture than cornflour, is often used to thicken desserts as well as sauces. Potato flour is frequently resorted to by chefs and cooks to thicken a sauce that has thinned out or shows signs of separating after cooking. It cooks clear quickly, has no raw taste, and gives a rather glossy finish. Rice flour, which also cooks clear and is almost tasteless, is often used to thicken vegetable soups. While these starches are easy to use and have their place in cooking, I do not care for the rather shiny, artificial-looking finish they give a dish. I prefer to stick with the roux and *beurre manié*.

There are, of course, other thickeners, like ground nuts, grated potato or mashed potato, bread or cake crumbs, that you find indicated in various recipes. These, naturally, give a very different texture and result. Bread sauce for poultry and game isn't a smooth, velvety kind of sauce; it has a thick, almost porridgelike consistency, but it is nevertheless delicious. A traditional thickener for certain brown sauces is the blood of an animal or bird. In old recipes for *coq au vin*, beef *bourguignon*, *civet* of hare, and other French dishes, blood was added at the last minute and brought to a boil to both thicken and give great colour to the sauce. *Boudin noir*, or black pudding, is made from pigs' blood. Certain butchers sell pig and beef blood, but it isn't something you are likely to encounter at your local supermarket.

Finally, there is that masterpiece of nature, the egg. In the preceding chapter on baking we discussed the miraculous leavening power of eggs. They have an equally miraculous thickening power as a liaison. Egg yolks are the liaison with milk or cream that thickens a custard; stirred into chicken broth they produce the velvety *avgolemono*, or Greek egg-lemon soup, and in combination with double cream they turn pan juices into an exquisitely, delicately thickened sauce. Probably the most common use of the egg yolk in the kitchen is in the making of the two other mother sauces, hollandaise and mayonnaise. These are known as emulsified sauces because the butter or oil is beaten into the egg yolks in such a way that the egg absorbs and holds the fat in a thick emulsion.

Making mayonnaise and hollandaise is not complicated, but it must be done slowly and with great care and patience and the ingredients must be at the right temperature, otherwise the yolks will curdle and the sauce will break or separate, at which point you must start over with a fresh egg yolk.

In the old days (and even now) people made mayonnaise with a fork or a whisk, beating the egg yolks by hand and then beating in the oil, drop by drop. There is no doubt that to make mayonnaise by hand is a praiseworthy accomplishment, but now that we have perfected electric appliances that do the same job in a great deal less time, I think that anyone who spurns the modern methods is either a fanatic or a masochist. I have come to adopt the food processor or liquidizer method of making mayonnaise. It is unbelievably speedy and enables one to use the whole egg, not just the yolk. The terrific centrifugal power that emulsifies mayonnaise in a matter of seconds produces a stabler and firmer sauce than the old hand method and I, for one, am all for this type of operation. I have yet to tell the difference between a mayonnaise made by hand and one made in the food processor. I'll bet that the great chefs, like Escoffier and Carême, would have used one had it been around in their day.

Roux-Thickened Sauces

♔ Basic White Sauce
(Béchamel Sauce)

This is the most valuable and versatile of all the sauces. It can be used, in its many variations, for fish and shellfish, poultry, meat, vegetables, crêpes, pasta, eggs and for dishes that are to be gratinéed, or browned under the grill. A thin white sauce 15 g. (½ oz.) butter and 1 tablespoon flour to ¼ l. (8 fl. oz.) liquid is the base for certain cream soups. A thick white sauce (45 g. or 1½ oz. butter and 3 tablespoons flour to ¼ l. or 8 fl. oz.) is the base for soufflés. Very thick white sauces act as the binding agent for croquettes and mousses. In each case, the method is the same, only the proportions of butter and flour to liquid differ.

According to the recipe you are following, or the food for which the sauce is to be used, the liquid may be any of the following, or a combination of two (usually broth and milk or cream): milk; cream; chicken or turkey broth; veal, beef, lamb, pork or ham broth; game broth; fish or shellfish broth; mushroom or other vegetable broth; dry white wine or dry vermouth combined with broth.

Makes ¼ litre (8 fl. oz.) medium white sauce (béchamel)

30 g. (1 oz.) unsalted butter	Salt, freshly ground black pepper,
2 tablespoons flour	nutmeg
¼ l. (8 fl. oz.) heated milk or broth, or other specified liquid	

Melt the butter over low heat in a heavy-bottomed 1½-litre (1½-quart) saucepan. This can be of any suitable material such as stainless steel with an aluminium core, enamelled cast iron, lined copper or heatproof porcelain.

Uncoated iron and aluminium are not recommended as they may discolour a white sauce that contains wine or egg yolks.

Mix the flour into the melted butter with a wooden spatula or spoon and cook slowly, stirring all the time, for 2 or 3 minutes, or until the roux of butter and flour is well blended and frothy. This initial cooking removes the starchy taste of the flour. Gradually stir in the hot liquid – when the liquid is hot there is less likelihood of the sauce lumping, but you should also stir vigorously while adding it to thoroughly mix the liquid and the roux. Or you may, if you prefer, remove the pan from the heat while adding the liquid, which makes it easier to control the thickening of the sauce as the flour absorbs the liquid. Return to the heat as soon as the liquid is mixed in.

Increase the heat to medium and cook, stirring all the time with a wooden spatula or a wire whisk, until the sauce is smooth, thick, and at the boiling point. Let the sauce simmer, stirring, for 3 or 4 minutes, then season to taste with salt, pepper and nutmeg. Many people tell you to use white pepper in a white sauce, but I am against this. The flavour of black pepper is so much better. If you do see a fleck or two of black in the sauce, so what? I also think a little touch of freshly grated (not ready-ground) nutmeg improves the flavour of a white sauce, but this is for you to decide.

The sauce is now ready to be used, or ready for the enrichments and flavourings that turn it into a sauce of another name. If you are not using it right away, butter a piece of greaseproof paper large enough to fit inside the pan and lay it on the surface of the sauce, buttered side down, to prevent a skin from forming.

HOW TO COPE WITH MISHAPS

If your sauce should lump, don't despair. Force it through a fine sieve to remove lumps, return to the pan, and reheat.

If your sauce is too thin (which may happen if you have to remove lumps), make *beurre manié* by working together equal quantities of butter and flour – 2 teaspoons of each. Roll into tiny balls, bring the sauce to a boil, drop one or two of the balls into the sauce, and beat them in with a wire whisk, stirring until the sauce thickens. Do not add them all at once, wait and see how thick the sauce becomes before adding more – the amount of thickening depends on how thin your sauce was.

If your sauce is too thick (a medium white sauce should be of a good, thick coating consistency, not stiff and pasty, but not so thin that it slides off the spatula), add a little extra liquid, a tablespoon at a time, until thinned to the right consistency.

VARIATIONS

Sauce Velouté. Enrich the finished sauce by adding $1\frac{1}{2}$ dl. ($\frac{1}{4}$ pt) double cream. Simmer a few minutes to blend. Just before using the sauce, beat in a further enrichment of 45 g. ($1\frac{1}{2}$ oz.) butter, one third at a time.

Sauce Suprême. Use chicken or veal stock as the liquid. Enrich the finished sauce with cream and egg yolks. Lightly beat 3 egg yolks and mix with $\frac{1}{4}$ l. (8 fl. oz.) double cream. Stir a little of the hot béchamel sauce into the mixture, to warm and temper the yolks (prepare them for the shock of heat), then stir the yolk mixture into the sauce. Reheat, but do not let the sauce get too hot or boil or the yolks will curdle.

White Wine Sauce for Fish. Use 2 dl. ($\frac{1}{3}$ pt) fish stock and 4 tablespoons dry white wine for the liquid. Beat 2 egg yolks lightly and mix in $1\frac{1}{2}$ dl. ($\frac{1}{4}$ pt) double cream. Blend into the finished sauce, as for sauce suprême.

Sauce Mornay. Stir 30 to 60 g. (1 to 2 oz.) grated Parmesan cheese into the finished sauce and 15 or 30 g. ($\frac{1}{2}$ or 1 oz.) butter, 15 g. ($\frac{1}{2}$ oz.) at a time. Simmer 3 or 4 minutes. This is a favourite sauce for vegetables, pasta, fish and shellfish dishes, and for dishes that are gratinéed under the grill. If the sauce is for a gratinéed dish, use the smaller quantity of cheese and omit the final butter enrichment. Then sprinkle the sauced dish with grated Parmesan cheese before putting it under the grill.

Cheese Sauce. This is a sharper and spicier version of sauce mornay, and a favourite sauce for vegetables. Stir 60 g. (2 oz.) grated sharp Cheddar cheese (or, if you prefer, grated Swiss Gruyère or Emmenthaler cheese) and a dash of Tabasco or dry mustard into the finished sauce. Heat only until the cheese melts into the sauce, or it may become stringy from overheating.

Tarragon Sauce. Use chicken broth for the liquid. Add 2 tablespoons chopped fresh tarragon or 2 teaspoons dried tarragon and an enrichment of 2 eggs and $1\frac{1}{2}$ dl. ($\frac{1}{4}$ pt) double cream, as for white wine sauce. Serve with poached or roast chicken.

French Curry Sauce. This is not a true curry sauce, but a mildly curry-flavoured white sauce. Cook 2 teaspoons good-quality curry powder in the butter for 2 minutes before adding the flour (this precooking in butter takes away the acrid rawness of the curry powder), then make the sauce in the usual way. Use for chicken, turkey, veal and egg dishes and for savoury crêpes.

Mustard Sauce. Stir 2 tablespoons Dijon mustard into the finished sauce. Simmer for 2 to 3 minutes. This makes a fairly hot sauce, excellent with grilled fish and strong-flavoured oily fish such as herring and mackerel. For milder sauce, add less mustard.

Horseradish Sauce. Stir 1 to 2 tablespoons drained bottled horseradish, or to taste, into the finished sauce. Or use fresh-grated horseradish to taste and 1 tablespoon lemon juice. Serve with boiled beef.

Caper Sauce. Add 3 tablespoons bottled capers and 1 tablespoon liquid from the bottle to the finished sauce. Caper sauce is traditional with boiled leg of mutton or lamb and poached fish.

Egg Sauce. Peel and slice 2 hard-boiled eggs and add to the finished sauce. This is another traditional sauce for poached fish, especially salmon.

Parsley or Dill Sauce. Stir 4 tablespoons finely chopped parsley or 1 tablespoon finely chopped fresh dill and a few drops of lemon juice into the finished sauce. Serve with fish, chicken, or veal.

♔ Basic Brown Sauce

There are various ways of making the classic French brown sauce, most of them quite time-consuming and requiring many different ingredients and long simmering. One method is first to make a brown roux by cooking the butter and flour very slowly over low heat in a heavy frying pan until the roux turns a delicate nut-brown, then mixing this roux into brown stock or beef broth. This would appear to be simplicity itself, but I have found that once a roux has been browned, the parched starch granules in the flour no longer expand as they do in a white roux and a lot more of the roux is needed to thicken the liquid.

After working out various methods over the years, I have settled on two brown sauces that work well for me. One is made with a white roux and beef broth, to which I add a drop or two of homemade caramel colouring (similar to the commercial gravy browner) or, if I have any on hand, some *glace de viande*, to colour the sauce a rich, deep brown. Or, if I am in a rush and don't have homemade beef broth on hand, I make a quick brown sauce by simmering tinned beef bouillon with red wine and seasonings, to give it a good flavour, and then thickening it with *beurre manié*.

Makes ¼ litre (8 fl. oz.) basic brown sauce

30 g. (1 oz.) unsalted butter	*1 or 2 drops of caramel colouring*
2 tablespoons flour	*(see below)*
¼ l. (8 fl. oz.) brown stock or beef broth	*Or ½ teaspoon glace de viande*
Salt, freshly ground black pepper	*(see page 32)*

Make a roux of the butter and flour, cook until frothy, and then stir in the liquid and simmer as for basic white sauce. Season the sauce to taste with salt and pepper. Stir in just enough caramel colouring to turn the sauce a rich brown or stir in *glace de viande* and simmer for 2 or 3 minutes. If you are not using the sauce right away or are adding other flavourings, lay a piece of buttered greaseproof paper on the surface to prevent a skin from forming.

CARAMEL COLOURING

Heat 400 g. (14 oz.) sugar over low heat in a heavy metal frying pan until the sugar melts and begins to bubble and turn a very dark brown. Stirring constantly with a long-handled wooden spoon, add ¼ l. (8 fl. oz.) water. Stand back as you pour in the water; the liquid sugar will hiss, bubble up, and may splash on you. Cook the mixture over low heat until it begins to smoke and turn very black and gives off a strong, caramelized smell. What you are really doing is burning it. Add 4½ dl. (¾ pt) water and simmer until blended, about 2 to 3 minutes, then strain and bottle the liquid, which will be thick and syrupy. Store in the refrigerator; it will keep indefinitely.

Note. Never use tin-lined copper when making caramel, as the great heat of the caramelized sugar will melt the tin lining.

Quick Brown Sauce

Makes 3½ dl. (12 fl. oz.) brown sauce

45 g. (1½ oz.) unsalted butter
3 shallots or spring onions, finely chopped
¼ l. (8 fl. oz.) dry red wine
300-g. (10½-oz.) tin beef bouillon (not consommé)

Pinch of dried thyme
45 g. (1½ oz.) soft butter
3 tablespoons flour
Salt, freshly ground black pepper

Melt the butter in a heavy-bottomed 1½-litre (1½-quart) saucepan; add the shallots or spring onions and sauté over medium heat until limp and golden. Stir in the wine and bouillon and bring to a boil. Season with the thyme and cook over high heat until the liquid is reduced almost by half. While the liquid is reducing, work the butter and flour together to a paste with your fingers and then roll it into tiny balls. Drop the *beurre manié* balls, one or two at a time, into the boiling liquid, and cook, stirring constantly with a wooden spatula or a whisk, until the sauce is thickened to your liking. Don't add all the *beurre manié* at once as it will take a little time to break up and thicken the liquid. Forty-five g. (1½ oz.) butter and 3 tablespoons of flour will thicken 3½ dl. (12 fl. oz.) liquid, the same proportions as a roux. Season to taste with salt and pepper, then put the sauce through a strainer to eliminate the bits of cooked shallot or onion.

VARIATIONS

Sauce Bordelaise. Put 6 chopped shallots or spring onions, 1 teaspoon dried thyme, and ¼ l. (8 fl. oz.) dry red wine into a pan; bring to a boil and cook down over high heat until reduced to 5 tablespoons. Strain this into $\frac{1}{4}$ l. (8 fl. oz.) of brown sauce; add 1 tablespoon cognac and simmer for 3 minutes. Stir in 1 tablespoon chopped parsley. Serve with steaks, roast beef, or roast lamb. Makes $3\frac{1}{2}$ dl. (12 fl. oz.).

Madeira Sauce. Combine $\frac{1}{4}$ l. (8 fl. oz.) brown sauce and 5 tablespoons Madeira; bring to a boil, then reduce the heat and simmer until reduced to $\frac{1}{4}$ l. (8 fl. oz.). For sauce Périgueux, add 2 tablespoons finely chopped black truffle to the sauce. Serve either sauce with roast fillet of beef, or the Madeira sauce with ham or chicken livers. Makes $\frac{1}{4}$ l. (8 fl. oz.).

Sauce Diable. Boil $1\frac{1}{2}$ dl. ($\frac{1}{4}$ pt) tarragon vinegar, 2 dl. ($\frac{1}{3}$ pt) dry white wine, 1 finely chopped shallot, and 1 teaspoon dried tarragon until reduced by half. Combine with $3\frac{1}{2}$ dl. (12 fl. oz.) brown sauce, a dash of Tabasco, and 2 teaspoons dry mustard. Simmer for 3 minutes. Add several grinds of black pepper (the sauce should be very spicy) and strain. Serve with grilled, flank steak, grilled chicken, or devilled beef bones. For sauce piquante, add 1 tablespoon chopped capers and 1 tablespoon finely chopped sour pickle to the sauce diable. Serve with roast pork, pork chops, or boiled beef. Makes $4\frac{1}{2}$ dl. ($\frac{3}{4}$ pt).

Orange Sauce for Roast Duck. Combine $3\frac{1}{2}$ dl. (12 fl. oz.) brown sauce with 5 tablespoons undiluted frozen orange juice, 2 tablespoons orange rind (the orange part only, no white pith) cut into very fine julienne strips, and 1 tablespoon lemon juice. Simmer 5 minutes, then add 1 tablespoon Grand Marnier, Cointreau, or cognac. Just before serving, add 125 g. (4 oz.) orange sections and heat through. Makes 6 dl. (1 pt).

Egg-Yolk-Thickened Sauces

♔ Custard Sauce
(Crème Anglaise)

The French may call it *crème anglaise*, but this egg-yolk-thickened dessert sauce was known as 'boiled custard' to early American cooks, although boiled it is certainly not and never should be. A custard is a delicate thing that should always be approached with respect. It is absolutely essential to have the right implements. Choose a heavy-bottomed saucepan of enamelled cast iron, stainless steel with an aluminium core, or lined copper. Or use a double boiler. The glass type is the best, although those with earthenware tops and metal bottoms are also good (the drawback being that you can't see if the water starts to boil in the bottom). You will also need a wire whisk or electric hand mixer and a wooden spatula.

This simple, basic custard may be used as a sauce for fruit, fritters, or soufflés and as a base for desserts such as Bavarian cream and ice cream.

Makes 6 dl. (1 pt) custard sauce (crème anglaise)

4 egg yolks (preferably from large eggs)
4 tablespoons sugar
Pinch of salt
¼ l. (8 fl. oz.) milk

¼ l. (8 fl. oz.) double cream
2 teaspoons vanilla essence
Or a 4-cm. (1½-inch) piece vanilla bean

Combine the egg yolks, sugar and salt in a 1½-litre (1½-quart) saucepan or the top of a double boiler. Beat with a wire whisk or electric hand mixer until well mixed, pale and creamy.

Put the milk and cream in another heavy-bottomed saucepan and heat them just to the boiling point – until tiny bubbles appear around the edge – stirring occasionally to make sure the liquid does not scorch on the bottom of the pan. (If you are using a vanilla bean, heat it in the liquid and remove before adding the liquid to the egg mixture.)

Slowly pour the hot liquid into the egg mixture in a thin stream, stirring constantly. Put the saucepan over medium-low heat, or put the top of the double boiler over simmering, not boiling, water. The water should not touch the pan but be about 1 cm. (½ inch) below it. Cook, stirring constantly with an electric beater turned to low or with a wooden spatula all over the bottom and sides of the pan, until the custard thickens to a light, creamy consistency that just coats the spatula. The custard must not overheat or approach the simmering point, or it will curdle and there is no way to save a curdled custard. Timing cannot be estimated; it may take 20 to 25 minutes, depending on the thickening power of the egg yolks, and whether you use a saucepan or the double boiler, which takes longer but is safer.

Remove the custard from the heat. Stir in the vanilla essence and any desired liqueur flavouring, such as those given below. If you are serving the custard hot, let stand over warm water, covered, until ready to use. To serve cold, pour into a cold bowl and cool. When cool, cover the bowl with plastic wrap and refrigerate.

VARIATIONS

Coffee Flavour. Dissolve 1 tablespoon instant coffee in the hot liquid before adding to the egg mixture.

Chocolate Flavour. Dissolve 30 or 60 g. (1 or 2 ounces) of semi-sweet chocolate in the hot liquid before adding to the egg mixture, and reduce the vanilla essence to 1 teaspoon.

Liqueur Flavour. Add 1 tablespoon rum, cognac, or flavoured liqueur to the finished custard with the vanilla essence.

Note. Some cookbooks recommend that you mix 1 teaspoon arrowroot or cornflour with the egg yolks and sugar to stabilize the yolks and help the custard to thicken. While I don't think this is necessary, if you haven't had good luck with your first custard, by all means try it.

Emulsified Sauces
....

♔ Hollandaise Sauce

This rich, suave butter and egg sauce which tastes so elegant with freshly cooked asparagus, artichokes, poached fish, or eggs Benedict takes care and patience unless you make it in a liquidizer or food processor, in which case it is practically foolproof. When you make hollandaise by hand, over direct heat or hot water, you have to be very careful that the sauce doesn't overheat or you'll end up with scrambled eggs.

Hand Method

Makes ¼ litre (8 fl. oz.) hollandaise sauce

3 egg yolks	1 tablespoon lemon juice
½ teaspoon salt	125 g. (4 oz.) butter, cut into small
Pinch of cayenne pepper	pieces
Or dash of Tabasco	

To make your sauce, use a small, heavy saucepan (enamelled cast iron is ideal) or the top of a double boiler over but not touching hot (not boiling) water. If you use the saucepan, make the sauce over low heat.

Put the egg yolks, salt, pepper or Tabasco and lemon juice in the pan over low heat. Beat with a wire whisk or electric hand mixer until the eggs and seasonings are well blended and the egg yolks have thickened to the consistency of double cream. You should be able to see the bottom of the pan between strokes. The egg yolks must be beaten until thick or they will not absorb and hold the butter properly and the sauce will not thicken as it should.

Have the pieces of butter at your elbow, on a warm plate. The minute the yolks are thick, drop one piece of butter into them and stir rapidly with a wire whisk in a circular motion until it has been absorbed by the eggs. Then stir in another piece. Continue to add the butter, one piece at a time, each time stirring until absorbed, until you have a sauce of a consistency that coats the whisk heavily.

If by any chance the sauce seems to be thickening too fast, add a tablespoon of cold water to slow the process. If it is too thin, you are adding the butter too quickly.

As soon as the sauce is made, remove it from the heat and serve. If you have to keep it for a short time, cover the pan with plastic wrap and let it stand over warm water, then reheat slowly over the water until the sauce is just warm. Hollandaise should not be served hot. However, it is my contention that hollandaise should be served freshly made and not reheated, because there is always the chance that the warm sauce will develop bacteria.

COPING WITH MISHAPS

Should your sauce break and curdle because you have let it get too hot, try stirring a tablespoon of hot water or an ice cube into it, which often works. If it doesn't, start over again with a clean pan and 1 egg yolk. Beat the yolk until thick and then gradually beat in the curdled sauce until it smooths out (this is the same technique you use for saving a curdled mayonnaise).

Liquidizer Method

Makes 2 dl. (⅓ pt) hollandaise sauce

4 egg yolks	1 tablespoon lemon juice
½ teaspoon salt	125 g. (4 oz.) butter
Dash of Tabasco	

Combine the egg yolks, seasonings, and lemon juice in the container of a liquidizer and turn the liquidizer on and off, at high or 'blend' setting, to just blend the mixture. Heat the butter until it is bubbling and very hot, but not browned. Remove the insert from the lid of the liquidizer, turn the liquidizer to high or 'blend', and pour in the hot butter in a thin, continuous stream – do not pour too fast or the eggs will not absorb the butter properly. When the butter is absorbed and the sauce thick, turn off the machine. If the sauce should start curdling while you are adding the butter, pour 1 tablespoon hot water into the sauce while the liquidizer is running.

Food Processor Method

Makes 2 dl. ($\frac{1}{3}$ pt) hollandaise sauce

4 egg yolks
2 tablespoons lemon juice
$\frac{1}{2}$ teaspoon salt

Dash of Tabasco
125 g. (4 oz.) unsalted butter,
    melted and hot

With the metal blade in place, add egg yolks, lemon juice, salt and Tabasco to the beaker. Process for 3 seconds and, still processing, pour in bubbling melted butter. It is essential that the butter be bubbling hot or the sauce will not thicken.

VARIATIONS

Béarnaise Sauce. Put 1 tablespoon finely chopped shallots or spring onions, 1 tablespoon chopped fresh tarragon or 1 teaspoon dried tarragon, 1 teaspoon chopped parsley, 4 tablespoons white wine, and 4 tablespoons white wine vinegar into a small pan; bring to a boil and boil until it is reduced practically to a glaze – about 2 tablespoons. Cool. Press this through a strainer into the beaten egg yolks before starting to add the butter. Serve with steak, grilled liver, chicken, or fish.

Tomato Hollandaise (Sauce Choron). Add 1 or 2 tablespoons tomato paste to Béarnaise sauce. Serve with steaks, fish, or chicken.

Mustard Hollandaise. Add 1 or 2 teaspoons Dijon mustard or 1 teaspoon hot dry English mustard to the seasonings for the hollandaise. Serve with steak or fish.

Sauce Mousseline. Fold 3 dl. ($\frac{1}{2}$ pt) whipped cream into the finished sauce. Serve with fish, asparagus, or soufflés.

Anchovy Hollandaise. Add 4 very finely chopped anchovy fillets, 1 finely chopped or crushed garlic clove, and 1 teaspoon capers to the finished sauce. Serve with steak.

☺ Mayonnaise

I learned to make mayonnaise when I was just about tall enough to reach the work table. I would stir the mixture constantly with a fork in a deep plate to the slow drip, drip from the oil cruet. Later, I made the sauce with a Dover beater (now called a rotary beater), which was to me a much trickier process than the slow, sure, productive technique of the fork. Nowadays I prefer to make mayonnaise in a food processor or liquidizer. Or, if a large quantity is needed, I use an electric mixer with a whisk attachment. I start the mixer on a rather slow speed and increase it as the mixture becomes a true emulsion.

I have always, since childhood, preferred mayonnaise made with a good, fruity olive oil. However, I'm aware that many people do not like the definite flavour of olive oil and would rather have a bland and tasteless oil, in which case I consider groundnut oil as good as anything else.

In making mayonnaise, it is imperative that both the eggs and the oil be at room temperature. Often mayonnaise made with refrigerated eggs and warm oil will curdle. Here, then, is the traditional way of making mayonnaise by hand.

Hand Method

Makes 4½ dl. (¾ pt) mayonnaise

2 egg yolks (from large or extra-large eggs)

1 teaspoon salt

½ teaspoon dry or Dijon mustard

3½ dl. (12 fl. oz.) good, fruity olive oil
Or half olive oil and half groundnut oil

1 tablespoon lemon juice
Or white wine vinegar

Put the egg yolks, salt and mustard into a mixing bowl and beat with a wire whisk or electric hand mixer until the yolks become thick and sticky. Begin adding the oil, drop by drop, beating it in thoroughly after each addition.

As the mayonnaise begins to thicken, stiffen, and become light in colour, which means it has emulsified, you can beat in the remaining oil more rapidly, but be sure it is all incorporated before adding the next batch. When thick and stiff, beat in the lemon juice or vinegar, which gives a nice tartness and thins it out slightly.

Transfer the mayonnaise to a bowl or jar, cover and refrigerate. You can safely keep it for a week under refrigeration.

COPING WITH MISHAPS

Should the mayonnaise start to curdle, this indicates you have added the oil too fast. Start over again in a clean bowl. Beat 1 egg yolk until thick, then beat in a few drops of oil. Gradually beat in the curdled mixture until it becomes thick and smooth. This method also works if the mayonnaise does not thicken properly but remains liquid.

Liquidizer Method

The main difference between the hand and the liquidizer method is that with the liquidizer you use whole eggs and add the lemon juice to them. Because of the great speed of the machine, the mayonnaise will begin to stiffen almost immediately and you can add the oil more quickly.

Makes 4½ dl. (¾ pt) mayonnaise

2 whole eggs

1 teaspoon salt

½ teaspoon dry or Dijon mustard

Dash of Tabasco (optional)

1 tablespoon lemon juice

Or white wine vinegar

3½ dl. (12 fl. oz.) olive oil

Or half olive oil and half groundnut oil

Put the eggs, salt, mustard, Tabasco (if used) and lemon juice or vinegar in the container of the liquidizer. Blend at 'blend' or high-speed setting for no more than 5 seconds, remove the cover insert, and, with the machine running, dribble in the oil in a slow, thin, steady stream, adding it more quickly as the sauce emulsifies. Blend only until smooth and thick; do not overblend.

Food Processor Method

Makes 4½ dl. (¾ pt) mayonnaise

1 whole egg

1 tablespoon vinegar or lemon juice

1 teaspoon salt

¼ teaspoon freshly ground pepper

3½ dl. (12 fl. oz.) oil

With the metal blade in place, add the egg, vinegar, salt, and pepper to the beaker. Process until blended, about 2 to 3 seconds. Continue processing and gradually pour oil through feed tube, slowly at first. As mayonnaise thickens, the sound of the machine will become deeper.

Taste for additional vinegar or lemon juice, salt and pepper. Transfer to a covered container and refrigerate until needed. This mayonnaise will hold for a week to 10 days in the refrigerator.

If mayonnaise should separate, pour the separated mixture into a liquid measuring jug. Using the metal blade and a clean beaker, add 2 egg yolks, and process, pouring the separated mixture through the feed tube very slowly. The mayonnaise will rebind.

VARIATIONS

Sauce Verte. Chop 30 g. (1 oz.) very dry raw spinach until it is practically a purée (or purée in a liquidizer or food processor). Add to 3 dl. (½ pt) mayonnaise with 1 tablespoon finely chopped fresh tarragon, 2 tablespoons finely chopped parsley, 1 tablespoon finely chopped capers, and, if you can get it, 1 tablespoon finely chopped fresh chervil. You can substitute finely chopped fresh dill for the tarragon and capers, if you serve the sauce with fish. Or you can use finely chopped watercress leaves in the mixture. This sauce is especially good with cold fish and shellfish, such as poached salmon, trout in aspic, or cold prawns. Sauce verte does not keep very well.

Mustard Mayonnaise. Add 1 tablespoon Dijon mustard or 1 teaspoon dry mustard to each 2 dl. ($\frac{1}{3}$ pt) of mayonnaise. This is an excellent sauce for prawns, for celeriac salad, or for cold meats such as roast pork.

Soured Cream Mayonnaise. Combine equal quantities of mayonnaise and soured cream. Use for shellfish or poultry salads or for coleslaw.

Tartare Sauce. Mix $1\frac{1}{2}$ tablespoons finely chopped onion, 2 teaspoons chopped parsley, 1 teaspoon lemon juice, and 1 tablespoon finely chopped dill pickle into 2 dl. ($\frac{1}{3}$ pt) mayonnaise. This is just about the most popular sauce for fried fish and shellfish. It is also good with baked fish.

Rémoulade Sauce. Mix 1 finely chopped hard-boiled egg, 2 tablespoons finely chopped capers, 1 tablespoon finely chopped parsley, a squeeze of lemon juice, and salt and pepper to taste into 3 dl. ($\frac{1}{2}$ pt) mayonnaise. You may also add $\frac{1}{2}$ teaspoon anchovy paste and omit the salt. This is perfection with crabmeat, raw scallops, lobster, or prawns, as a starter, and also with cold chicken or on hard-boiled eggs.

Thousand Island Dressing. Mix 1 tablespoon finely chopped onion, 3 tablespoons chili sauce, 1 finely chopped hard-boiled egg, and salt and pepper to taste into 3 dl. ($\frac{1}{2}$ pt) mayonnaise. Allow to stand 1 hour. Serve with salads of crabmeat, avocado, hearts of palm.

Russian Dressing. Mix 1 teaspoon dry mustard, 2 tablespoons finely chopped onion, 2 teaspoons Worcestershire sauce, and 2 tablespoons red or black caviar (*not* the best quality) into 3 dl. ($\frac{1}{2}$ pt) mayonnaise. If you don't want to use caviar, add 1 tablespoon chili sauce, but caviar makes it an authentic Russian dressing. Great with cold meats and for cold meat sandwiches.

Tomato Mayonnaise. Peel, seed (see page 401), and finely chop 2 ripe tomatoes and mix into 3 dl. ($\frac{1}{2}$ pt) mayonnaise with $1\frac{1}{2}$ tablespoons chopped fresh basil or 1 teaspoon dried basil. If you can't get really ripe tomatoes, substitute 2 tablespoons tomato paste or strained chili sauce, but the tomatoes give the best flavour. Serve with crabmeat or lobster salad, or on sliced tomatoes.

Tuna Mayonnaise for Cold Roast Veal. Combine 125 g. (4 oz.) drained and flaked French or Italian white-meat tuna fish (packed in olive oil) with 6 to 8 finely chopped anchovy fillets, 4 tablespoons drained and rinsed capers, $\frac{1}{4}$ to $\frac{1}{2}$ teaspoon finely chopped garlic (to taste), and 3 dl. ($\frac{1}{2}$ pt) mayonnaise. Add salt and freshly ground black pepper to taste. Let the sauce mellow for 3 to

4 hours before serving. Thinly slice cold roast leg or shoulder of veal and cover each slice with a thin layer of the tuna mayonnaise, which gives you a short-cut version of the classic Italian *vitello tonnato*.

Smoked Salmon Mayonnaise for Cold Roast Veal. Combine 125 g. (4 oz.) finely slivered smoked salmon with 4 tablespoons drained and rinsed capers, 4 tablespoons finely chopped onion, 4 tablespoons finely cut fresh dill, 4 tablespoons finely chopped parsley and 3 dl. ($\frac{1}{2}$ pt) mayonnaise. Season to taste with salt and freshly ground black pepper. Mellow the sauce for 2 to 3 hours before serving. Serve with thinly sliced cold roast leg or shoulder of veal.

Greek Garlic Sauce
(Skordalia)

Skordalia is basically a mayonnaise with a great deal of garlic, further thickened by finely ground almonds (you can make these by chopping blanched almonds in a liquidizer or food processor until they are pulverized to the consistency of very fine bread crumbs). Traditionally, the sauce is made with a mortar and pestle. First the whole garlic cloves are ground to a paste with the pestle, then raw egg yolks are pounded into the garlic with the pestle until thick and sticky, then the olive oil is pounded in drop by drop until it forms a mayonnaise. (This is also the way *aïoli*, the garlic mayonnaise of Provence, is made and it is a long and arduous business.) The other ingredients are then mixed into the mayonnaise.

I find it much easier to be less traditional and make the sauce in a liquidizer or food processor. It is delicious with hot or cold poached fish, with fried fish, as a dip for prawns, raw vegetables, or artichokes, and as a sauce for rather bland vegetables such as cauliflower and boiled potatoes.

Makes about 4$\frac{1}{2}$ dl. ($\frac{3}{4}$ pt) sauce

4 to 6 garlic cloves, very finely
  chopped
2 whole eggs
3 or 4 tablespoons lemon juice
1 teaspoon salt

$\frac{1}{4}$ l. (8 fl. oz.) olive oil
  Or half olive oil and half groundnut oil
60 g. (2 oz.) finely ground
  blanched almonds
1 tablespoon finely chopped parsley

Put the chopped garlic (the amount depends on your taste), the eggs, 2 tablespoons lemon juice and the salt into the liquidizer or processor, blend or process until just mixed, and then add the oil in a thin, steady stream, according to the directions for liquidizer or food-processor mayonnaise (page 296). Remove to a bowl and stir in the ground almonds and remaining lemon juice, to taste. Mix in the parsley and chill before serving.

VARIATIONS

1. For a thicker sauce, stir in 60 g. (2 oz.) fresh white bread crumbs with ground almonds.

2. Instead of ground almonds, mix 225 g. (8 oz.) plain mashed potatoes (with no butter or milk added) into the sauce. After the mayonnaise is made, put the potatoes into the liquidizer or processor and blend with the mayonnaise until just combined.

Bread-thickened Sauce

Bread Sauce

This is the traditional sauce for roast turkey and game birds, such as pheasants. Bread crumbs, the thickening agent, give the sauce its almost porridgelike consistency.

Makes about 6 dl. (1 pt)

1 onion, peeled and stuck with	*125 g. (4 oz.) fresh white bread crumbs,*
* 2 cloves*	* made from unsweetened, day-old bread*
6 dl. (1 pt) milk	*30 g. (1 oz.) unsalted butter*
1 bay leaf	*Salt, freshly ground black pepper*

Put the onion, milk, and bay leaf into a 2-litre (2-quart) saucepan and bring slowly to a boil, being careful not to let the milk stick to the bottom and scorch. Remove the pan from the heat, cover with the lid, and leave to steep for 15 minutes, until the onion and bay leaf flavour the milk. Stir in the bread crumbs and the butter and cook the sauce over very low heat, stirring occasionally, for 15 minutes or until the bread crumbs have expanded to make a very thick sauce. Season to taste with salt and pepper. Remove the onion and bay leaf before serving.

Soups

Like sauces, soups may be thickened by a roux or *beurre manié*, by egg yolks, or by various other starches. You'll also find soups, especially those of Spain and Mexico, in which ground almonds or hazelnuts are the thickening agents.

Then, of course, many vegetable and dried legume soups are thickened by the natural starchiness of potatoes, split peas, or dried beans. Another natural thickener is puréed avocado, much used for cold liquidizer soups.

Cream of Mushroom Soup

Serves 6

450 g. (1 lb.) mushrooms
1 l. (1¾ pts) chicken broth
30 g. (1 oz.) butter
3 tablespoons flour
4½ dl. (¾ pt) double cream

2 tablespoons sherry or cognac
  (optional)
1½ teaspoons salt, or to taste
¼ teaspoon Tabasco

Wipe the mushrooms with a damp cloth and break off the stems. Simmer the stems in the chicken broth for 35 to 40 minutes, or until the mushroom flavour has thoroughly permeated the broth. Strain the broth through a sieve and return to the pan. Discard the stems. Mix the butter and flour to a paste and roll into tiny balls. Bring the broth to a boil; drop in the balls of *beurre manié* and beat in with a whisk until the *beurre manié* is absorbed and the broth slightly thickened. Slice the mushroom caps thin and add them to the thickened broth. Simmer for 8 to 10 minutes. Meanwhile, heat the cream in another pan, stirring, until just at the simmering point. Add the sherry or cognac to the mushroom broth and then stir in the cream. Add salt to taste and the Tabasco. Reheat the soup until hot, but not boiling, and serve in heated soup plates or cups.

Egg-Lemon Soup
(Soupa Avgolemono)

This famous Greek egg-lemon soup is kin to the equally well-known, basic egg-lemon sauce for vegetables, meat, and fish.

Serves 6

2 l. (3½ pts) double chicken broth
  (see page 28)
125 g. (4 oz.) long-grain rice
Salt to taste

2 whole eggs
2 egg yolks
1½ dl. (¼ pt) lemon juice

Bring the broth to a boil in a pan and add the rice. Simmer until the rice is tender, about 15 to 20 minutes. Taste, and add salt if needed (this depends on how seasoned the broth is).

Beat the eggs and egg yolks together in a bowl with a whisk or rotary beater until light and frothy. Slowly beat in the lemon juice. Add a cup of the hot broth to the mixture, little by little, beating it in until well blended, then slowly add the mixture to the pan, stirring constantly. Heat through, stirring, but do not allow to overheat or come to a simmer or the eggs will curdle. The soup should be lightly and delicately thickened, of a thin custardlike consistency.

Cold Spinach and Seafood Soup

An unusual combination with a lovely, fresh taste, this refreshing soup is excellent for a summer luncheon or dinner party. The thickening is supplied by instant mashed potatoes.

Serves 8 to 10

1½ kg. (3 lbs.) fresh spinach
2 l. (3½ pts) strong chicken stock
  (see page 28)
Juice of 1 lemon
1 tablespoon chopped fresh tarragon
  Or 1 teaspoon dried tarragon
1 garlic clove, peeled and finely chopped
Salt, freshly ground black pepper

180 g. (6 oz.) mashed potatoes (made
  with instant mashed potatoes,
  according to package directions)
225 g. (8 oz.) finely chopped cooked
  prawns, crabmeat, or lobster
8 to 10 tablespoons soured cream or
  crème fraîche (see below)
2 to 3 tablespoons chopped parsley

Wash the spinach well in cold water to get rid of all the sand. Break off the heavy stems and put the spinach in a large pot with only the water clinging to the leaves. Cover the pot and cook over high heat until the spinach has just wilted down, turning it with tongs so the top leaves fall to the bottom. Remove, drain well, and press to remove excess liquid. Chop as fine as possible. Combine in a large bowl with the stock, lemon juice, tarragon, garlic and salt and pepper to taste. Beat in just enough mashed potato to give a smooth but light consistency. Chill well, taste, and correct the seasoning, if necessary. Serve in chilled bowls and sprinkle the top of each serving with chopped shellfish, a tablespoon of soured cream or *crème fraîche*, and a teaspoon of parsley.

CRÈME FRAÎCHE

Buttermilk, like yogurt, has been thickened by warmth and a bacterial culture. It can also be used, in turn, to thicken double cream, producing a reasonable approximation of the French *crème fraîche*, a matured cream thickened by lactic acids and natural fermentation.

Combine $4\frac{1}{2}$ dl. ($\frac{3}{4}$ pt) cream and 5 tablespoons buttermilk in a jar. Cover and shake the jar, as if you were shaking a cocktail, for 2 minutes. Let the jar stand at room temperature for at least 8 hours, or overnight, until the cream has thickened. This will keep under refrigeration for a week.

Non-cooking

Several years ago a young man I know came out with a book for children called *The No-Cook Cookbook*, and if you think that is a contradiction in terms, just stop for a minute and consider how many of the dishes we eat are actually uncooked. It's amazing how much can be done without resorting to the cooker or oven. Given all our vegetables, fruits, salad greens, cheeses and breads, the range of dishes that may be eaten *au naturel* is impressive.

For a beginning, let's take that old favourite, steak tartare. All right, so it does require a little muscle, a little effort, to do the chopping and blending, but it is a no-cook process. If you have that latest kitchen miracle worker, the food processor, it's no trouble to chop the beef with onion, maybe a little garlic, capers, anchovies (if you like them), season it, form it into little mounds, top them with an egg yolk and garnish with chopped onion or chopped parsley. Again, let me repeat that modern equipment can produce just as perfect food as the old, time-consuming hand methods. I've tried just about everything both ways and I can assure you that there is no difference.

Then there's the delicious Middle Eastern raw lamb dish, *kibbeh nayé*, which again can be done completely in the food processor, and the Italian *carpaccio*, slices of raw beef pounded paper-thin and served with a mustard mayonnaise.

One of the more interesting of the world's fish dishes is seviche, from Latin America. Tender raw fillets of fish, little scallops, or raw crabmeat are covered with lime juice which 'cooks' them by the action of the acid in the citrus, turning the translucent flesh opaque. Now that can't really be called cooking. Scandinavia has *gravad laks*, raw salmon cured with salt, sugar and dill until the flesh becomes beautifully, fragrantly edible. The Japanese, of course, eat a lot of raw fish in the form of *sushi* and *sashimi*, which takes a deft hand, a sharp knife, and the very freshest of firm-fleshed fish. The French latched on to this idea and came up with salmon tartare, raw salmon chopped, seasoned, and served in the same manner as steak tartare.

If you look through cookbooks, you'll find many soups that involve absolutely no cooking, from the Spanish gazpacho and the Turkish soup of cucumber and yogurt to liquidizer soups made with raw or tinned vegetables and buttermilk or yogurt. Tinned goods are very handy for no-cook dishes. One of my favourite quick soups is made with condensed tomato soup, soured cream, onion and basil, shaken up like a cocktail.

Raw fruits are among the best and easiest of all desserts. All you have to do is flavour them with a little liqueur or serve them with whipped cream, soured cream, or the version of *crème fraîche* given on page 301.

Turning to the vegetable world, we have a vast assortment of things that are eaten raw, either freshly tossed in salads or after they have marinated in a vinaigrette sauce – among them mushrooms, tomatoes, cucumbers, avocados, courgettes, celery, onions, radishes, mangetout, carrots, fennel and green peppers.

First, let's consider the basic dressing for any salad, a sauce vinaigrette, the universal mixture of oil, vinegar and seasonings that is widely (and incorrectly) known as French dressing.

Green Salad

♕ Basic Vinaigrette Sauce

You can't make a good salad without a good vinaigrette sauce. A true vinaigrette is as simple as one, two, three – oil, vinegar, salt and pepper – and the success depends on the quality of the ingredients.

First, a good oil, preferably a rich, fruity, and flavourful olive oil. Other oils don't have enough flavour to make a good vinaigrette.

Second, a vinegar that is not sharp or acid, either red or white wine vinegar (white tends to be milder). There are some fine imported French wine vinegars available. If you can't find a good wine vinegar, use cider vinegar or lemon juice. I don't recommend that you buy a herb-flavoured vinegar – if you want a herb flavour in your salad it's better to use real herbs, fresh or dried.

Third, salt and pepper. I like to use coarse salt for salads, as for other cooking, because it has more flavour and guts than iodized table salt, and a better texture. Freshly ground black peppercorns have more spiciness and taste than ready-ground pepper which, as far as I'm concerned, is worse than useless.

As to proportions, after years of experimenting I find that I prefer to use 3 or 4 parts of oil to 1 of vinegar, depending on the heaviness of the oil and the sharpness of the vinegar. This is something you must learn to adjust so there is a perfect balance. Start with less vinegar than you think you will need, then taste and see if you need more. You can always add, but you can't subtract.

For a green salad for 4

1 teaspoon coarse salt	1½ to 2 tablespoons wine vinegar
½ teaspoon freshly ground black pepper	6 tablespoons fruity olive oil

Blend the ingredients together with a wooden spatula or a fork, using 1½ tablespoons vinegar. Then taste, and add more if you feel the dressing needs it. This makes about 1½ dl. (¼ pt).

Never add sugar to a vinaigrette. If the vinegar is mild, as it should be, no sweetening is necessary. Always mix your vinaigrette just before you intend to use it. The fresher it is, the better. Don't follow the reprehensible practice of making the vinaigrette days ahead and keeping it in a jar in the refrigerator. For that matter, don't store oil in the refrigerator. It gets cloudy, thick and sluggish. If you are afraid of opened oil going rancid in hot weather, buy a small quantity at a time and use it up quickly.

VARIATIONS

Garlic. If you like garlic flavour in a salad, either crush a clove of garlic and rub it into the salt you are using for your dressing or impale the crushed clove on a toothpick, put it in the vinaigrette, and remove it just before tossing the salad. Or adopt the French way of giving salad a garlic flavour. Rub the crushed clove on a small cube of dry bread (called a *chapon*), toss the bread with the salad, and let some garlic-lover eat it. Never, ever, use garlic salt or garlic powder; the flavour is ersatz and disagreeable and will ruin your salad.

Mustard. There are times when mustard is needed in a vinaigrette – for instance, when you are dressing a vegetable that needs some extra punchiness, such as the coarse, bitter greens like endive, or French beans. Use either the French-style Dijon mustard or dry, hot mustard and adjust the amount to the salad. First blend the mustard (about $\frac{1}{2}$ teaspoon) with the salt, pepper, and vinegar, then mix in the oil.

Herbs. The outstanding salad herbs are tarragon, chervil, parsley, chives and, if you are using tomatoes, basil. Dill goes well with cucumber salads or tomato salads, but is rather limited as a regular salad herb. Use either 1 tablespoon chopped fresh herbs or 1 teaspoon dried herbs, crushed in the palm of your hand with your thumb, to $1\frac{1}{2}$ to 2 dl. ($\frac{1}{4}$ to $\frac{1}{3}$ pt) of vinaigrette. Don't throw a bouquet of herbs into your dressing – they will just cancel each other out. One herb, possibly with parsley as a companion, is ample.

CHOOSING AND PREPARING GREENS FOR SALAD

Too many simple green salads suffer from a lack of imagination. (You'll find a detailed list of salad greens on page 370.) Select from such leafy types as butterhead, Webb's, cos, celtuce, chicory, watercress, corn salad, dandelion greens, rocket, endive and tender young leaves of spinach and sorrel. Finely shredded cabbage and Chinese cabbage can also be used in salad. Pick one type of green or a combination – but consider their texture and nature. Delicate butterhead lettuce or corn salad would be overpowered by coarse, tough greens such as endive.

Wash the greens ahead of time. The reason salads are limp, soggy, and insipid is because the greens are not thoroughly dried and crisped before being tossed. Separate the leaves and wash the greens carefully, removing all sand and dirt. Discard wilted or discoloured leaves. Shake off excess water, or spin dry in a salad dryer, if you have one. Then roll the washed greens loosely in several thicknesses of paper towels or in a clean tea towel; put them in plastic bags and store in the vegetable crisper section or on the bottom shelf of the refrigerator for 12 to 24 hours. Don't put them in a part of the refrigerator that gets too cold, or they may freeze and become unusable.

How much salad should you calculate per serving? That's hard to say, but it is my feeling that you should allow about $4\frac{1}{2}$ dl. ($\frac{3}{4}$ pint) of loosely packed greens per person, or slightly less if you are putting other ingredients in your salad.

Prepare the salad at the last minute so it will stay fresh and crisp. Break or tear (do not cut) large leaves into bite-size pieces with your hands, leaving

smaller ones whole. Put the greens in the salad bowl, pour some of the vinaigrette sauce over them, and toss gently, with salad tossers or your hands. Add more vinaigrette as needed, until each leaf is lightly coated. I like to use my hands to toss. It's a good practice for a beginner because your hands will tell you when the greens are coated with just enough dressing. Don't drown your salads. Serve at once. You can vary your plain tossed green salad by adding other vegetables.

Here are some suggestions:
1. Sliced raw mushrooms
2. Slices or cubes of avocado and chopped chives
3. Finely cut celery and thin strips of green pepper, topped with onion rings
4. Sliced radishes, sliced cucumber and chopped spring onions
5. Onion rings or finely chopped raw onions or spring onions
6. Thin shreds of cooked or tinned beetroot in a salad of bitter or peppery greens, such as endive, chicory, rocket or watercress.

I'm not an advocate of adding tomatoes to a green salad, except for whole cherry tomatoes. The flavours are complementary, but the addition of slices or wedges of tomato tends to make the salad watery. If you like tomatoes as a salad, have a platter of sliced tomatoes vinaigrette.

Vegetables Vinaigrette

Salads of vegetables, cooked, tinned or raw, served with a vinaigrette sauce, are more commonly known as vegetables vinaigrette. They can be served alone as a salad or starter, or as part of an hors d'oeuvre selection, along with other vegetables vinaigrette, tinned, fresh, and cured fish and shellfish, pâtés, ham and sliced sausages such as salami and mortadella. Some vegetables benefit from being marinated first for an hour or two.

Fresh Mushroom Salad

Serves 6 to 8

1 kg. (2 lbs.) very firm mushrooms
1½ dl. (¼ pt) vinaigrette sauce
  (see page 304)

1½ tablespoons chopped fresh tarragon
  Or 1½ teaspoons dried tarragon
2 tablespoons finely chopped parsley

Contrary to what you are often told, white, cultivated mushrooms don't need washing. Just wipe them with a damp cloth or dampened paper towels.

Wipe the mushrooms, break off the stems and reserve them for some other use (they can be chopped and cooked down in butter until all the liquid evaporates, then used for an omelet filling or swirled into scrambled eggs). Slice large mushroom caps lengthwise about ¾ cm. (¼ inch) thick. Small mushrooms may be left whole, or halved. Put the mushrooms into a mixing bowl, add the vinaigrette sauce and tarragon, and toss well. Let the salad stand for 1 or 2 hours. To serve, put into a serving bowl or dish, add additional oil and vinegar, if needed, and sprinkle with the parsley.

VARIATION

Use chopped fresh dill instead of tarragon. This gives the salad another dimension that is extraordinarily agreeable.

Cucumber Salad

Serves 4

2 large or 3 medium cucumbers
2 teaspoons salt
1½ dl. (¼ pt) vinaigrette sauce
  (see page 304)

2 tablespoons chopped fresh dill
  or parsley

Peel the cucumbers with a paring knife or vegetable peeler, cut them in half lengthwise, and remove the seeds with a spoon. Slice the cucumbers thin, put them in a colander or sieve and sprinkle them with the salt. Let them drain in the sink or over a bowl for 1 to 2 hours or until the bitter juices have been drawn out by the salt and the slices are limp. Rinse them quickly with cold water, pat dry on paper towels, and toss them with the vinaigrette sauce. Add the dill or parsley and toss again, lightly. Serve on lettuce leaves as a salad or starter.

VARIATION

Instead of vinaigrette sauce, dress the wilted cucumber with $1\frac{1}{2}$ to 3 dl. ($\frac{1}{4}$ to $\frac{1}{2}$ pt) soured cream or yogurt mixed with 1 tablespoon lemon juice, and toss with the dill or parsley.

Tomato Salad

Really ripe tomatoes usually need no peeling, but if the skin is thick and coarse, they are better peeled. To peel, drop the tomatoes into a bowl; pour boiling water over them to cover; leave for 30 seconds, then remove by piercing the core of the tomato with a fork or knife point and lifting it out of the bowl. Cut out the core and remove the skin, which will slip off easily. No salt, vinegar, or oil should touch the sliced tomatoes until they are ready to be eaten. Tomatoes that are left to stand in a vinaigrette sauce become slimy and gooey. I also feel that tomatoes should not be chilled before serving; they taste better at room temperature.

Serves 6 to 8

6 firm ripe tomatoes, cored and peeled (if necessary)

$1\frac{1}{2}$ dl. ($\frac{1}{4}$ pt) vinaigrette sauce (see page 304)

1 tablespoon chopped parsley, preferably Italian

1 tablespoon chopped fresh basil or dill

Slice the tomatoes thin and arrange them on a serving platter or in a glass or earthenware salad bowl. Just before serving, pour the vinaigrette sauce over them and sprinkle with the chopped herbs.

VARIATIONS

1. Add 2 tablespoons finely chopped spring onions.
2. Use chopped chives instead of basil or dill.
3. Add 1 small garlic clove, peeled and very finely chopped.

Other Vegetables

Other raw or tinned vegetables that may be dressed with a well-seasoned or a herbed vinaigrette sauce, in the proportions of $1\frac{1}{2}$ dl. ($\frac{1}{4}$ pt) vinaigrette to 1 l. ($1\frac{3}{4}$ pts) vegetable, are:

FRESH VEGETABLES

Broad Beans. Use a basil-flavoured vinaigrette.

Cabbage, Green or Red, Shredded. Use a mustard-flavoured vinaigrette and 1 teaspoon celery seed.

Carrots, Grated. Use a basic vinaigrette.

Cauliflower, Thinly Sliced. Use a basic vinaigrette.

Celery, Thinly Sliced. Use a mustard-flavoured vinaigrette.

Onions, Thinly Sliced. Crisp in ice water for several hours. Drain, dry, and dress with a basic vinaigrette flavoured with 1 small garlic clove, peeled and very finely chopped.

Sweet Green or Red Peppers, Peeled and Thinly Shredded. Use a basic vinaigrette. (For directions for removing skins, see page 126.)

TINNED VEGETABLES

Drain the tinned vegetables, rinsing them if they are in a thick fluid, like kidney beans and cannellini (white beans), and arrange on a platter or in a bowl.

Artichoke Bottoms or Hearts. Use a basic vinaigrette.

Asparagus Tips or Spears. Use a tarragon-flavoured vinaigrette.

Whole French Beans. Use a basic vinaigrette. They may also be combined with thin rings of white onion and chopped parsley.

Kidney Beans. Use a basic vinaigrette and thinly sliced white onion.

Cannellini Beans. Use a basic vinaigrette.

Beetroot, Whole or Sliced. Use a basic vinaigrette.

Whole-Kernel Corn. Use a basil-flavoured vinaigrette.

Celeriac, Sliced. Use a basic vinaigrette.

Celery Hearts. Use a basic vinaigrette and drape with anchovy fillets.

Hearts of Palm. Use a basic vinaigrette. They may also be combined with anchovy fillets and sliced boiled potato.

Mayonnaise-Dressed Vegetables

Celeriac Rémoulade

Celeriac is a knobby root vegetable that is most generally used for a purée (see page 61), or sliced in fine julienne and combined with a spicy mayonnaise. There are two schools of thought about the preparation of celeriac. Some blanch the celeriac for a minute or two in boiling water before slicing it. Personally, I prefer to peel it and slice it raw, using a mandoline slicer, a

Mouli-julienne, or the coarse shredding attachment of a food processor. If you have none of these aids, slice thin and then cut into fine julienne with a sharp knife. Celeriac rémoulade is usually served as a starter, either alone or as part of the hors d'oeuvre selection.

Serves 4

½ kg. (1 lb.) celeriac, peeled and cut into
  fine julienne strips
2 dl. (⅓ pt) mayonnaise (see page 294)
1 tablespoon Dijon mustard

1 tablespoon Dusseldorf mustard
  Or 1½ teaspoons English mustard
Salt

Put the celeriac strips in a mixing bowl. Blend the mayonnaise and mustards (for a spicier sauce, use English mustard), mix with the celeriac, and let it mellow for 1 hour. Taste for seasoning and add salt if necessary. Serve as a starter, on lettuce leaves. It also makes a good accompaniment to thinly sliced, dry (ready-to-eat) sausages like salami and cervelat.

My Favourite Coleslaw

Coleslaw must be one of the oldest and certainly one of the most popular American dishes. There are innumerable ways of making it, some with a boiled dressing, others with a very spicy vinaigrette, but to my mind it is best when simply tossed with homemade mayonnaise and soured cream.

Serves 6 to 8

1 firm white cabbage, weighing
  1 to 1½ kg. (2 to 3 lbs.)
2 dl. (⅓ pt) homemade mayonnaise
  (see page 294)

2 dl. (⅓ pt) soured cream
1 teaspoon salt
½ teaspoon freshly ground black pepper

Wash and dry the cabbage, then trim it, cutting off the stalk end and removing discoloured or limp outer leaves. Cut into quarters, lengthwise; cut out the hard core at the bottom with a small sharp knife; then put the cabbage on a board and cut the quarters into thin shreds with a large sharp knife, cutting down through the rounded side. Put the shreds into cold water and leave for 1 hour to crisp. Drain well and combine with the mayonnaise, soured cream, salt and pepper. Toss well and let stand for 30 minutes, or longer if you like a wilted slaw.

VARIATIONS

1. For a sweet-and-sour slaw, mix together 2 tablespoons sugar, 4 tablespoons cider vinegar, 1 teaspoon dry mustard (or to taste) and ¼ teaspoon Tabasco.

Mix into the mayonnaise, soured cream and seasonings before combining with the cabbage.

2. For a spicy slaw, add 1 tablespoon freshly grated horseradish or drained bottled horseradish to the mayonnaise mixture.

Composed Salads

These salads are composed in two senses of the word: composed of a variety of ingredients and allowed to compose or rest themselves, rather than being agitated like a tossed salad. Composed salads can encompass anything from a modest mixture of different vegetables to an elaborate combination of greens, vegetables, fish and shellfish, meat, poultry and fruit that is a main dish in itself – and almost a work of art. Arrangement is one of the secrets of a perfect composed salad. There should be a blend of colours, tastes and textures. The ingredients should be attractively cut and the salad beautifully arranged on a large platter or in a bowl so that it becomes almost a centrepiece for the table.

While a very simple composed salad, such as one of butterhead lettuce and raw mushrooms, may be served with meat or poultry, the majority are eaten alone, either as a starter, or as a main course with French bread or rolls. More substantial composed salads of cold cooked meats and fish, such as beef salad or lobster salad, are generally served as a main course. The following composed salads are made chiefly with raw or tinned ingredients.

Salade Niçoise

This Provençal salad is one of the best of all luncheon dishes. You can vary it to taste, adding other vegetables of your choice. The only constants are the tuna fish, anchovies, hard-boiled eggs, tomatoes and tiny black olives. You can also serve small helpings of this salad as a starter, as they do in Provence.

Serves 4 to 6

1 head butterhead or cos lettuce,
   washed, dried, and crisped
2 200-g. (7-oz.) tins white-meat tuna
   fish drained
20 to 30 anchovy fillets, drained on
   paper towels
4 to 6 ripe tomatoes, cored and quartered

4 to 6 hard-boiled eggs, quartered
60 g. (2 oz.) small black olives,
   preferably Niçoise olives
1 tablespoon chopped fresh basil
   Or 1 teaspoon dried basil
2 dl. (⅓ pt) vinaigrette sauce
   (see page 304)

OPTIONAL INGREDIENTS

60 g. (2 oz.) finely chopped yellow onion
   Or 1 red Italian onion, sliced into
   thin rings
4 tablespoons pimiento strips

1 green pepper, sliced into thin rings
90 g. (3 oz.) tinned drained artichoke
   hearts

Cover a large platter or line a large salad bowl with the lettuce leaves. Place the tuna fish in the centre and surround it with the anchovy fillets. Arrange the tomatoes and eggs around the edge of the platter or bowl and sprinkle the olives on top. Add any of the optional ingredients – onion is good in a salade Niçoise, and so are green pepper rings. Sprinkle the salad with the basil. When you are ready to serve, pour the vinaigrette sauce over the salad at the table and toss lightly. Serve with French bread.

VARIATIONS

Certain cooked vegetables may also be added to the salad, such as tiny, boiled new potatoes or sliced boiled potatoes, French beans cooked until just bitey-crisp, or cooked artichoke hearts rather than tinned. Little croutons of bread, sautéed until golden brown in oil with a garlic clove, are another good addition.

Tomato, Onion, and Avocado Salad

Basically a variation on the simple tomato salad, this combines three ingredients with complementary flavours and textures, and so becomes a composed salad.

Serves 6

6 firm ripe tomatoes
1 large red Italian onion
1 ripe avocado
1 to 2 tablespoons chopped parsley

1 tablespoon chopped fresh basil,
   if available
1½ dl. (¼ pt) vinaigrette sauce
   (see page 304)

If the tomatoes have coarse, thick skins, peel them (see page 309). Otherwise, remove the core with a small, sharp knife and slice them thin. Peel and thinly slice the onion. Halve the avocado lengthwise; remove the stone; peel and slice into 1-cm. ($\frac{1}{2}$-inch)-wide strips. Do not peel and slice until just before serving, as avocado darkens quickly when exposed to the air. (If the avocado is fully ripe and easily separated from the skin, you may find it easier to first slice the avocado with the skin on and then peel it off with your fingers.) Arrange alternating slices of tomato, onion and avocado on a platter and sprinkle with the chopped herbs. Pour the vinaigrette sauce over them and serve.

Health Salad

This delicious and attractive salad of raw vegetables is often served in health-food restaurants, hence the name. To shred the vegetables, use a food processor or Mouli-julienne with a coarse shredding attachment, the coarse side of a grater, or cut into fine shreds by hand.

Serves 6

1 head lettuce of your choice, washed, drained, and crisped

180 g. (6 oz.) freshly shredded raw carrots

180 g. (6 oz.) freshly shredded raw young beetroot

90 g. (3 oz.) freshly shredded Japanese radish (daikon) or icicle radish

150 g. (5 oz.) freshly shredded raw, young, white turnips

1 small cucumber (peeled if waxed), seeded and shredded

6 quartered tomatoes

6 sticks celery, cut into julienne strips

1$\frac{1}{2}$ to 2 dl. ($\frac{1}{4}$ to $\frac{1}{3}$ pt) vinaigrette sauce (see page 304)

OPTIONAL INGREDIENTS

180 g. (6 oz.) of any of the following: raw young green peas, thinly sliced mangetout, sliced raw mushrooms

Arrange the lettuce leaves on a platter or in a shallow bowl. Heap shredded and julienne vegetables in individual mounds to make an appealing colour pattern and arrange the tomatoes around the edges. Serve the vinaigrette sauce in a separate bowl, so the guests can help themselves to their choice of vegetables and add vinaigrette to taste.

Avocado, Onion and Grapefruit Salad

Serves 4

1 *large avocado*
1 *large grapefruit*
1 *red Italian onion*

1 *head lettuce, washed, dried and crisped*
1½ *dl. (¼ pt) vinaigrette sauce*
  (see page 304)

Halve the avocado lengthwise; remove the stone; peel and cut into crescent-shaped strips, about 1 cm. (½ inch) wide. Remove the peel and pith from the grapefruit by cutting it off in a long spiral, around the fruit, with a sharp knife (hold the grapefruit over a bowl to catch the juice). Then remove whole sections, one by one, by cutting downwards on either side of the membrane surrounding them. Peel the onion and slice thin. Arrange the lettuce leaves on a platter or in a bowl, then put alternating slices of avocado, onion and grapefruit on top of them. Dress with the vinaigrette sauce.

Note. Oranges can be peeled, sectioned and used in the same way.

Gruyère Cheese Salad

An excellent salad to take on a picnic, as it improves with keeping.

Serves 6

1 *kg. (2 lbs.) Gruyère cheese, finely*
  shredded
225 *g. (8 oz.) finely sliced spring onions*
125 *g. (4 oz.) sliced stuffed green olives*

2 *dl. (⅓ pt) vinaigrette sauce (see page*
  304) flavoured with 1 tablespoon
  Dijon mustard
Salad greens

Combine the cheese, onions and olives; add the vinaigrette sauce and toss until well combined. Let the salad stand at least 30 minutes to mellow the flavours, then arrange it in a bowl lined with salad greens. If you wish, garnish the top with a few more sliced onions and olives – about 2 tablespoons of each. Serve with French bread or rolls.

White Bean and Tuna Fish Salad

A delicious summer salad for a buffet or a luncheon main dish that may be made either with cooked white beans or tinned Italian cannellini beans.

Serves 6

*1½ l. (2½ pts) cooked white beans
 (see page 58)
 Or 3 570-g. (20-oz.) tins cannellini
 beans*
*2 dl. (⅓ pt) vinaigrette sauce (see
 page 304) flavoured with 1 tablespoon
 chopped fresh or 1 teaspoon dried basil*

*125 g. (4 oz.) finely chopped onion
2 200-g. (7-oz.) tins white-meat
 tuna fish, drained and flaked
1 tablespoon chopped fresh basil
4 tablespoons chopped parsley
Additional oil and vinegar if necessary*

If you use the tinned beans, after draining them, rinse them well under cold running water in a colander to get rid of the thick, gummy liquid that clings to them. Shake well to free of excess water, then put the tinned or the freshly cooked beans into a serving bowl or dish. Pour the vinaigrette sauce over the beans, letting it run through to coat them, then toss very lightly to distribute the vinaigrette – don't toss too much or the beans will break up. Put the onion and tuna fish on top of the beans. Sprinkle with the basil and parsley. Just before serving, add a little more oil and vinegar, if the salad seems to need it, and toss lightly to combine ingredients.

VARIATIONS

1. Add 60 g. (2 oz.) small black olives and 6 chopped anchovy fillets with the onion and tuna fish.
2. Use tinned salmon, or boneless, skinless tinned sardines instead of tuna fish.
3. Omit the tuna fish. Serve bean salad in tomato shells, as a starter. To prepare the shells, slice off about 1 cm. (½ inch) of the top, scoop out all the seeds and pulp, and turn the hollow shells upside down to drain.

Tabbouleh

This Middle Eastern salad is immensely refreshing on a hot day and especially good with grilled chicken or kebabs. Be sure to use the fine grade of bulghur (cracked wheat); the others are too coarse for this salad. You can buy it in Middle Eastern groceries or health-food stores.

Serves 4 to 5

*90 g. (3 oz.) fine bulghur
 (cracked wheat)*

*3 medium-sized ripe tomatoes, peeled,
 seeded, and finely chopped*

125 g. (4 oz.) finely chopped parsley
125 g. (4 oz.) finely chopped spring
  onions
5 tablespoons lemon juice
Salt
5 tablespoons olive oil

4 tablespoons finely chopped fresh mint
  leaves
Or 2½ tablespoons dried mint,
    crushed with your fingers
Butterhead or cos lettuce leaves

Soak the bulghur in cold water to cover for 30 minutes. Drain in a sieve, lined with butter muslin to prevent the fine grains from falling through, then twist the muslin into a bag and wring out the remaining moisture from the bulghur. Put the bulghur on a clean dry tea towel, pat out flat, and leave until fairly dry. Then place the bulghur in a large bowl; add the tomatoes, parsley, onions, lemon juice and salt to taste. Mix gently but thoroughly, using your hands or wooden spoons. Just before serving, mix in the oil and fresh or dried mint. Taste, and correct seasoning if necessary. Serve on lettuce leaves.

Guacamole

There are innumerable versions of this Mexican sauce-cum-salad, which seems to have become American by adoption, and I'm going to give you my favourite, with variations.

Buy avocados that are ripe and soft enough to be easily mashable, but not so ripe that they have turned dark. Avocados discolour very quickly when cut and exposed to air. Use a stainless-steel knife, make the guacamole a short time before you plan to serve it, and keep it tightly covered with plastic wrap. Putting the avocado stone in the centre of the guacamole helps to prevent darkening and so does the acidity of lime juice.

Makes about 4 cups

1 to 2 tinned, peeled mild green chilies
  Or 1 tinned hot jalapeño
    or serrano chili

2 large, fully ripe avocados
2 tablespoons lime juice
Salt

Split the tinned chilies, scrape out and discard the tiny seeds, which are very hot, then chop the flesh very fine. Jalapeño and serrano chilies are hotter than those sold as 'peeled green chilies', so use less. Never touch your fingers to your eyes when working with chilies, as the juice is highly irritating, and wash your hands well with soap and water afterwards.

Halve the avocados, remove the pits, and scoop the pulp into a bowl with a spoon. Mash until smooth with a fork. Mix in the chopped chili, lime juice and salt to taste. The mixture should be spicy, not bland. Put the avocado stone in the centre; if you are not serving it right away cover the bowl tightly with plastic wrap until ready to use. Serve as a dip with tortilla chips, as a salad on lettuce leaves, or as a sauce for Mexican foods, such as tacos. It is also delicious on top of hamburgers or charcoal-grilled steaks or as a sauce for fried chicken which has had a little chili powder added to the flour coating.

VARIATIONS

1. For a more traditional guacamole, add 1 peeled, seeded, and finely chopped tomato, 60 g. (2 oz.) finely chopped white onion, and 1 tablespoon finely chopped cilantro, or fresh coriander (sold as Chinese parsley in Oriental markets).
2. Add 60 g. (2 oz.) of any of the following: crisply cooked, crumbled bacon; chopped roasted peanuts or chopped salted almonds; thin strips of well-flavoured cooked ham.

Soups

California Gazpacho

The Spanish gazpacho has become one of the most universally popular uncooked cold soups and, as was to be expected, variations have proliferated. Traditionally, the soup is a combination of puréed raw vegetables, garlic, bread crumbs, oil, vinegar, water and seasonings – served well chilled with an ice cube in the plate and a garnish, passed in separate bowls, of the same vegetables, finely chopped, and sometimes small croutons. This version has more texture and needs no vegetable garnish.

Serves 6

1½ kg. (3 lbs.) ripe tomatoes	4½ dl. (¾ pt) chilled tomato juice
2 cucumbers	5 tablespoons olive oil
60 g. (2 oz.) finely chopped green pepper	3 tablespoons wine vinegar
60 g. (2 oz.) finely chopped onion	¼ teaspoon Tabasco
2 garlic cloves, very finely chopped	Salt, freshly ground black pepper
	6 cubes tomato juice, frozen in ice cube trays

CROUTONS

60 g. (2 oz.) 6-mm. (¼-inch) cubes of white bread	2 to 3 tablespoons olive oil
	1 garlic clove, finely chopped

Peel and seed the tomatoes and chop fine, saving as much of the juice as possible. Peel cucumbers, split lengthwise, scoop out seeds with a teaspoon, and chop fine. Combine tomatoes and their juice, cucumbers, green pepper, onion, garlic, tomato juice, oil, vinegar, Tabasco and salt and pepper to taste in a large mixing bowl. Stir well, cover with plastic wrap, and chill until very cold, 3 or 4 hours.

Sauté the bread cubes in the olive oil with the garlic over medium-high heat until lightly browned on all sides, tossing them well. Do not let the bread or garlic burn. Remove to paper towels to drain and cool.

Taste the gazpacho for seasoning and add more salt, pepper, Tabasco and garlic, if needed. Serve in chilled bowls or soup plates with a tomato-juice cube in each and pass the croutons in a bowl.

Turkish Cucumber and Yogurt Soup

Serves 4 to 6

1 large or 2 small cucumbers	*7 dl. (1¼ pts) yogurt*
Salt, freshly ground black pepper	*3 tablespoons finely chopped fresh mint*
2 to 3 garlic cloves, peeled	*Or 1 tablespoon dried mint, crushed*

Peel the cucumber and either shred or dice fine. If diced, sprinkle lightly with salt and put in a colander over a bowl to drain for 30 minutes (shredding will remove most of the water from the cucumber), then taste. If salty, rinse with cold water, then drain.

Crush the garlic cloves to a paste with ¼ teaspoon salt with a mortar and pestle, mix in 3 tablespoons of the yogurt, then mix the garlic paste into the rest of the yogurt. Beat the yogurt with an electric hand mixer or rotary beater, which will liquidize it slightly (or whirl it briefly in the liquidizer). Mix in the cucumber and mint. Taste and add more salt, if needed, and 1 teaspoon pepper. If the soup seems rather thick, thin with a little cold water to the desired consistency, but do not make it too liquid. Serve in chilled soup cups.

VARIATION

For the Iranian version of this soup, omit the mint and add 60 g. (2 oz.) seedless raisins, 1 tablespoon finely chopped fresh dill and, just before serving, 2 chopped hard-boiled eggs.

Quick Iced Tomato Soup

This very easy tomato soup can be made as quickly, and in the same fashion, as a cocktail.

Serves 4

300-g. (10½-oz.) tin condensed tomato
  soup
3½ dl. (12 fl. oz.) soured cream or yogurt
1 tablespoon chopped fresh basil
  Or 1 teaspoon dried basil
1 tablespoon grated onion

½ teaspoon salt
½ teaspoon freshly ground black pepper
6 or 7 ice cubes
1 tablespoon chopped parsley or
  hard-boiled egg

Just before you are ready to serve, combine all the ingredients, including the ice cubes, in a large cocktail shaker, a screw-top jar, or a plastic container with a tight-fitting lid and shake vigorously until well blended and chilled. Pour into chilled cups and garnish with chopped parsley or chopped hard-boiled egg. The soup can also be mixed in a liquidizer.

Cold Avocado and Buttermilk Soup

Serves 4

1 large ripe avocado
2 tablespoons grated onion
1 tablespoon fresh chopped tarragon
  Or 1 teaspoon dried tarragon

1 teaspoon salt
½ teaspoon freshly ground black pepper
7 dl. (1¼ pts) buttermilk

Split the avocado lengthwise; remove the stone and scoop out the pulp. Put the avocado pulp in a liquidizer with the other ingredients and whirl until smooth. If you don't have a liquidizer, put the avocado pulp through a stainless-steel sieve or food mill and combine with the remaining ingredients.

Meat

Kibbeh Nayé

This delicious Middle Eastern dish of ground raw lamb, cracked wheat and onions is even easier to make if you have a food processor. It does everything from chopping the onions to grinding the lamb and mixing all together in a matter of minutes.

Serves 6

680 g. (1½ lbs.) leg or shoulder of lamb
225 g. (8 oz.) fine bulghur
  (cracked wheat)
3 medium-sized onions,
  peeled and grated or
  finely chopped

1 or 2 ice cubes
1½ to 2 teaspoons salt
1 teaspoon freshly ground black pepper
½ teaspoon allspice
Shredded spring onions, radishes,
  cherry tomatoes

If you are using a food processor, trim the lamb of all fat and tendons; cut it into cubes; put into the processor and mince until fairly fine. Otherwise, have the butcher trim the lamb and put it through the meat grinder twice. The lamb must be used while very fresh.

Soak the bulghur in cold water to cover for 1 hour, then drain it through a butter muslin-lined sieve and squeeze the muslin well with your hands to remove all excess water. Spread the soaked bulghur on a clean tea towel and pat dry. Put the bulghur, lamb, grated or chopped onion, ice cubes, salt, pepper and allspice into a bowl and blend the mixture well with your hands. The ice cubes keep the mixture cold and fresh and add moisture. When well blended, taste and add any necessary seasoning. Remove and discard any fragments of ice. If you use a food processor, add the soaked bulghur, onion and seasonings to the ground lamb and process until well mixed. Omit ice cubes.

Spread the *kibbeh* flat on a chilled serving platter and decorate with shredded spring onions and radish, putting a few cherry tomatoes around the edge for more colour. Serve immediately as a cocktail spread with thinly sliced French bread or the flat, round Arab bread called pita.

♨ Steak Tartare

Probably the most famous of all raw meat dishes, steak tartare requires beef that is very tender and absolutely fresh.

Serves 6

1 kg. (2 lbs.) beef fillet, sirloin, or
   topside with no fat
2 medium onions, peeled and finely
   chopped
60 g. (2 oz.) capers
2 teaspoons Dijon mustard
2 egg yolks

5 tablespoons cognac
4 tablespoons chopped parsley
2 teaspoons salt
1 teaspoon freshly ground black pepper
Tabasco
6 anchovy fillets (optional)

GARNISH

1 tablespoon chopped parsley

6 egg yolks (optional)

The best steak tartare is made of chopped (not minced) fillet. Cut the meat into finger strips and then chop it very fine, using a heavy chef's knife. If this seems too arduous, buy sirloin or topside and have it minced twice.

If you have a food processor, cut the meat into cubes and put into the processor with the onions, roughly cut up, capers, mustard, cognac, parsley, salt, pepper, Tabasco and anchovy fillets. Do not add egg yolks. Process until the meat is finely ground and well mixed with the other ingredients.

If you do not have a food processor, combine the chopped or ground meat with the onions, capers, mustard, egg yolks, cognac, parsley, salt, pepper and Tabasco to taste. You may, if you wish, add finely chopped anchovy fillets (in which case, reduce the salt, as anchovies are very salty), or serve the whole anchovy fillets on the side. Mix everything together very well and taste for seasoning.

Steak tartare can be served in a bowl, sprinkled with the parsley, or formed into 6 mounds and placed on serving plates with a hollow made in the top of each mound. Drop a raw egg yolk into every mound (to be mixed into the beef by each person) and garnish with chopped parsley. Serve as a light main course for luncheon with toast fingers on the side, or as a snack.

For cocktail food, form the mixture into balls about 2 cm. ($\frac{3}{4}$ inch) in diameter, roll them in chopped parsley or chopped hazelnuts, and pile them in a mound, to be speared with toothpicks.

Marinated Raw Beef

While almost everyone knows the delights of steak tartare, few know the pleasures of sliced raw beef as an hors d'oeuvre. Ask the butcher to slice the beef with his meat slicer.

Serves 6
680 g. (1½ lbs.) fat-free fillet of beef, sliced paper-thin

MARINADE

1½ dl. (¼ pt) olive oil

4 tablespoons wine vinegar

4 tablespoons soy sauce (preferably
  Chinese or Japanese)

4 tablespoons cognac

1½ teaspoons salt

1 teaspoon freshly ground black pepper

1 teaspoon dried thyme

1 large onion, peeled and very finely
  chopped

2 garlic cloves, peeled and very finely
  chopped

GARNISH

6 thin slices of lemon

2 tablespoons chopped parsley

Arrange the beef in a serving dish. Combine the marinade ingredients and pour them over the beef. Marinate for 4 to 6 hours, turning the beef several times. Serve garnished with lemon slices and chopped parsley.

VARIATION

For the Italian raw beef dish, *carpaccio*, put the beef slices between sheets of greaseproof paper and pound until practically transparent with a meat pounder. Serve 2 or 3 slices of the raw beef to each person as a starter, with mustard mayonnaise (see page 297), flavoured with 1 very finely chopped garlic clove and 1 tablespoon chopped parsley, crusty French or Italian bread and red wine.

Fish

Seviche

This spicy Latin-American dish of pickled fish 'cooked' in lime juice is delicious served with cocktails or as a starter.

Serves 4 to 6

680 g. (1½ lbs.) firm sole fillets, cut
  into thin strips about 1 cm. (½ inch)
  wide

2 dl. (⅓ pt) fresh lime juice

1½ dl. (¼ pt) olive oil

4 tablespoons finely chopped spring onion

4 tablespoons finely chopped parsley

1 garlic clove, finely chopped

2 tablespoons finely chopped, tinned,
  peeled mild green chilies

1½ teaspoons salt

1 teaspoon freshly ground black pepper

Dash of Tabasco

1 tablespoon chopped fresh coriander
  (cilantro or Chinese parsley)

Arrange the fish strips in a baking dish and pour the lime juice over them. Refrigerate for 4 hours, by which time the citrus juice will have turned the fish opaque and made it firm. Drain off the lime juice; combine the remaining ingredients (except the fresh coriander) and pour over the fish, tossing the pieces lightly in the mixture. Chill for $\frac{1}{2}$ hour, then sprinkle with the chopped coriander and serve.

VARIATIONS

1. Substitute tiny raw scallops, raw crabmeat, or raw red snapper fillets for the sole.
2. Add slices of avocado and whole-kernel corn (either tinned or sliced from freshly cooked ears) to the sauce.

Gravad Laks

For this dish, native to Scandinavia, the raw salmon is cured with salt and sugar, a process that, like the action of lime or lemon juice on fish, 'cooks' the flesh and gives it a most exciting and interesting flavour.

Serves 6 to 8

1½ kg. (3 lbs.) centre cut of fresh salmon	1 to 2 tablespoons coarsely ground peppercorns
125 to 150 g. (4 to 5 oz.) coarse salt	Large bunch of fresh dill
4 tablespoons sugar	

SWEET MUSTARD SAUCE

4 tablespoons seasoned German mustard (not hot, but very spicy)	2 tablespoons wine vinegar
1 teaspoon dry mustard	5 tablespoons vegetable oil
3 tablespoons sugar	3 tablespoons finely chopped dill

When you buy the salmon, tell the fishmonger to leave the skin on but to split the salmon lengthwise and remove the backbone and the little bones surrounding it. This will give you two pieces of boneless salmon.

Place one half, skin side down, in a large dish or casserole in which it can lie flat. Combine the salt, sugar and peppercorns and rub the flesh of the salmon very well with this mixture. Place the dill on top. Rub the rest of the salt-sugar-peppercorn mixture into the flesh of the second piece of salmon and place over the dill, skin side up, re-forming the salmon shape. Cover salmon with foil, then put a board or large plate on top and weigh this down with tinned goods. Refrigerate for 36 to 48 hours, turning the salmon over each day so that it cures evenly, and basting with the liquid that accumulates from the curing process. Each time, weigh it down again.

About 4 hours before the fish is done, make the sweet mustard sauce. To make the sauce, put the mustards, sugar, vinegar and oil in a small bowl and beat well with a whisk until it has the consistency of a thin mayonnaise (the mustard thickens the liquid). Mix in the dill and refrigerate for 3 or 4 hours before serving to let the flavours mellow.

At the end of the curing time, remove the fish from the liquid, scrape away the dill and seasonings, and dry it well on paper towels. To serve, place on a carving board (I like to put a bouquet of dill at one end, parsley at the other, as a garnish) and slice thick on the diagonal, detaching the flesh from the skin as you do so. Serve with the sweet mustard sauce and buttered rye bread as a starter or a main course for luncheon or supper, or with other fish dishes on a cold buffet.

Fruit

Of all the desserts in the spectrum of cuisines, I find those made with fruit the most rewarding. If you are serving fresh fruit at the end of a meal, only the freshest and ripest are worthy of your attention. Give them a sprinkling of sugar if they are not sweet enough in themselves, but keep the preparation simple. A little macerating, or steeping, in fruit juice or a liqueur of a complementary flavour, a spoonful or two of raspberry purée, a touch of whipped cream or *crème fraîche* (see page 301) are all that good fruit needs.

Strawberries Romanov

If there is one satisfactory version of strawberries Romanov, there are twenty-five. The classic is probably that of the great Escoffier. As served at the Carlton in his day, it was a simple but extraordinarily good dish notable for the interesting contrast of flavours.

Serves 4

Wash and hull 450 grams (1 pound) large, ripe strawberries. Put them into a bowl and sprinkle them with sugar, if necessary. Add 2 dl. ($\frac{1}{3}$ pt) freshly squeezed orange juice and 5 tablespoons orange-flavoured liqueur and let the strawberries macerate for 1 hour. Transfer the berries to a chilled serving dish, draining off some of the liquid. Whip $3\frac{1}{2}$ dl. (12 fl. oz.) double cream and sweeten it with 2 tablespoons sugar. Spread the cream over the berries and decorate the dish with candied violets.

Strawberries with Raspberry Purée

Serves 4

Thaw 2 packages frozen raspberries and pour off three-quarters of the syrup. Using a wooden spatula or spoon, force the raspberries and the remaining syrup through a fine sieve. Discard the seeds.

Wash and hull 450 grams (1 pound) large, ripe strawberries and pile them pyramid fashion in a serving dish. Sprinkle them very lightly with sugar and spoon over them some of the syrup from the frozen raspberries. Spoon raspberry purée over the strawberries and top with macaroon crumbs or finely chopped pistachio nuts. Serve the dessert with a bowl of sweetened whipped cream flavoured with Madeira or *eau-de-vie de framboise*.

Sugared Peaches

Few things in the food world equal the flavour of a ripe peach. To ripen them, keep them out of the refrigerator in a plastic bag in a dark place for a day or two; ór put them in a paper bag with a ripe apple, make a hole in the bag, and store it in a dark place. When peaches are really ripe you can peel them the way Spanish and Portuguese waiters do: rub each peach with the dull side of a table knife without breaking the skin. This loosens the skin so that, with practice, it can be removed in one piece with a squeeze of the hand, a spectacular trick.

Depending on size, allow 1 to 3 peaches for each serving. Slice the peaches at the last possible moment to prevent them from discolouring. Add sugar to taste; the amount will vary greatly with the acidity of the peach. Some peaches require a mere sprinkling; others require no sugar at all. Several sugars can be used – icing sugar, castor sugar, brown sugar, Demerara sugar, or Barbados sugar. Single cream, soured cream and *crème fraîche* are natural companions to peaches. We lack true *crème fraîche* but a fairly good substitute can be made with double cream and buttermilk (see recipe on page 301).

Peaches with Raspberry Purée

Serves 8

Peel and halve 8 peaches and arrange them in a serving dish. Sprinkle them with 2 tablespoons sugar and 1 tablespoon lemon juice, or more to taste. Spoon raspberry purée (page 326) over the peaches and serve them with single cream or kirsch-flavoured whipped cream.

Raspberry purée may also be spooned over peeled and sliced peaches. Serve with double cream or *crème fraîche* (see page 301).

Sugared Raspberries

Ripe raspberries have an exquisite bouquet, a subtle flavour, and a silky texture that make them ambrosial whether served with just a dusting of sugar, with sugar and double cream, or with a touch of crème de cassis, the liqueur made from black currants. I also like them with sugar and crisp, toasted, sliced almonds, which provide a bold contrast of textures and flavours. Madeira enhances raspberries too, as does *eau-de-vie de framboise* if it is incorporated in whipped cream or *crème anglaise*. Straight kirsch or *framboise*, on the other hand, is perhaps too harsh for raspberries and overshadows their delicacy. If you use these fruit brandies, first heat them to evaporate the alcohol.

Raspberry Fool

Serves 4

Purée 450 g. (1 pound) raspberries by forcing them through a fine sieve or the fine disc of a food mill. Sweeten the purée to taste. (Two packages of frozen raspberries, with some of the syrup poured off, flavoured with several drops of lemon juice, may be substituted.) Combine the purée with 2 dl. ($\frac{1}{3}$ pt) double cream, whipped not too stiff (see page 334), or with $3\frac{1}{2}$ dl. (12 fl. oz.) soured cream. The purée may also be combined with yogurt, which might require additional sugaring of the berries. Serve the dessert very cold in small glasses with thin butter cookies or fingers of shortbread.

Pineapple with Raspberries

Raspberries and pineapple have a great affinity for each other, and they are combined to wonderful effect in this recipe.

Serves 4 to 6

Cut about $2\frac{1}{2}$ cm. (1 inch) from the top of a large, ripe pineapple and reserve it. Remove the pulp from the shell by cutting around the inside edge with a long-bladed, sharp knife and then slicing down towards the centre. Scoop out the loosened pulp with a spoon. Discard the less tender pulp and the core. Sprinkle the pulp with 3 tablespoons sugar and, if desired, 4 tablespoons *eau-de-vie de framboise* and chill it for 2 hours. Make alternating layers of the pineapple and fresh raspberries, sugared, in the pineapple shell and replace the top. Stand the pineapple on a serving platter and surround it with fresh raspberries sprinkled with icing sugar and garnish with a few pistachio nuts, finely chopped. Serve the fruit directly from the shell.

Sugared Oranges

Sometimes people forget how satisfying good oranges can be when served as a dessert.

For each serving peel 1 or $1\frac{1}{2}$ oranges very carefully with a sharp knife, removing all the white pith, and cut them into 1-cm. ($\frac{3}{8}$-inch) slices. Sugar them lightly, sprinkle them with orange-flavoured liqueur, and chill them.

In Spain and Mexico the oranges are peeled and sliced as above and arranged in layers in a serving dish. Each layer is sprinkled with icing sugar and cinnamon. Extra orange juice is sometimes added.

Melon with Port

Cantaloupe, honeydew, or Ogen melons are all perfect for this dish. Be sure the melons are fully ripe and sweet. Cut them into halves or slices, depending on type and size, and make 2 or 3 gashes in the flesh of each piece with a spoon. Add 4 tablespoons of port to each piece and let it stand half an hour to mellow. Serve a half cantaloupe or Ogen melon or a slice of larger melon per person.

Drunken Watermelon

Cut a deep plug about 5 cm. (2 inches) square out of the top of a ripe watermelon. Remove the plug and slowly pour in as much light rum, brandy, or champagne as the melon will absorb. Replace the plug and seal with masking tape. Refrigerate the melon for 24 hours, turning it 4 or 5 times to allow the liquor or wine to seep through the pulp. Serve in slices, like ordinary watermelon.

Coeur à la Crème

Cream cheese and fresh fruit are good companions. This is the classic French dessert, for which fresh cream cheese is drained in little heart-shaped moulds or baskets.

Serves 6

450 g. (1 lb.) cream cheese
2 dl. ($\frac{1}{3}$ pt) soured cream

450 g. (1 lb.) fresh strawberries,
washed and hulled

Blend the cream cheese and soured cream together with a fork to a smooth paste. If the mixture seems too firm, add a little double cream. It should be soft, but not sloppy.

Line one large or two small, heart-shaped porcelain moulds or straw or reed baskets (the type sold in kitchen shops for this dessert) with muslin. Press the cheese mixture into the mould or moulds and place them on a rack over a bowl in the refrigerator. Let them stand for several hours, until the liquid part has drained off and dripped through and the cheese mixture is firm. If you don't have any suitable moulds, the cheese can be drained through a muslin-lined sieve.

When ready to serve, unmould the dessert by inverting it into a flat serving dish. Remove the muslin and surround with fresh strawberries. Or tip the cheese out of the muslin-lined sieve and form into a mound on the plate. Serve with more strawberries (or homemade strawberry jam) and slices of French bread or brioche bread.

Chilling
and Freezing

A very different, but extremely useful and necessary aspect of cooking is chilling and freezing, the action of extreme cold on such foods as aspics, jellies, and creams in order to shape and solidify them.

I have always been struck by the expression 'congealed salad', which is much used in certain parts of the American South to refer to gelatin salads. This rather unappetizing phrase defines exactly what the application of cold does – causes the contents to congeal and become firm yet delicate, fragile yet shapely. The process applies to many dishes that contain gelatin, such as mousses, Bavarian creams, charlotte russes, soufflés glacés, and to certain desserts thickened with eggs and cream or cornflour – custards and blancmanges, for example; all these dishes depend on chilling for their final texture and edibility.

In its simplest form, chilling plays a great part in retaining texture and flavour. We chill lettuce to keep it crisp and refreshing; we chill cold soups to give them a velvety smoothness; we chill pâtés to make them firm and easy to slice, or marinated seafood and vegetables to let them absorb and blend with the spicy flavours. While we are on the subject of chilling, I'd like to stress that there are times when chilling can damage flavour. If roast meats and poultry have been cooked to eat cold, they will taste far more delicious, juicy and flavourful if they are cooled at room temperature and eaten just tepid (slightly above room temperature) instead of being chilled in the refrigerator. A roast chicken with crisp, buttery skin and moist flesh, a squab, a joint of beef or pork will have a better taste and texture if cooled this way.

Another interesting aspect of cooling or chilling food is cooling with pressure, which you do when making a pâté or terrine, or cold boiled beef or tongue. When cooling a pâté, you take a board or plate that fits inside the mould or dish and press it down with weights from a scale or tinned goods so that as the meat mixture cools and settles, the excess fat is forced out and it becomes firmer. For cold beef or tongue, or jellied chicken, the hot meat is put into a bowl or mould and weighted down in the same way until it congeals and sets. This makes it more solid and easier to slice and the slight jelly that forms around the edge looks very attractive when the food is unmoulded onto a platter.

An extension of these 'set' dishes are aspics, one of the glories of *haute cuisine*. Aspics date back to those prerefrigeration days when a means had to be found of keeping cold, cooked foods succulent and unspoiled. Even today, aspic is used to protect the tender, moist flesh of a dish like poached salmon that may have to stand on a buffet table for hours. Sealed in its aspic coat, it won't dry out, but stays fresh and flavourful.

I once knew someone in New York who taught nothing but aspics. She did a certain amount of catering in that field as well, for she was a specialist in clarifying, moulding, decorating, and chilling the most exquisite dishes ever put on a table. That's an art in itself and one that few people can master. Anyone can whip up a wine jelly or a fruit gelatin, but to produce a perfect, firm, and shimmering aspic is a feat.

The most extreme application of cold is freezing, on which we depend for the success of frozen mousse, sherbet, ice cream, or any one of a number of frozen desserts. Whereas in the old days one had to make ice cream in a hand-cranked freezer or embed moulded mixtures in salt and ice and freeze them for hours, today, with freezers that go as low as $-29°C$ or $20°F$ below zero, electric ice cream makers and *sorbétières*, it is a very easy process indeed.

Frozen dishes, by the way, taste better if the mousse or ice cream or sherbet is removed from the freezer to the refrigerator and allowed to soften a little before you serve it. It improves both the texture and the flavour and is certainly pleasanter for the palate than the assault of something icy and hard as a rock.

Mousses

A cold mousse is one of the best examples of 'cooking' through the action of chilling temperatures. The most basic type of mousse is a combination of minced or puréed food mixed with gelatin for firmness and whipped cream for an airy, velvety smoothness, put into a mould, and chilled until firm and set. There are, of course, variations on this formula. Some savoury mousses, like the ham mousse on page 336, have as a base a thick egg-and-cream-enriched béchamel sauce and do not include whipped cream. Or soured cream, cream cheese, or mayonnaise may replace all or part of the whipped cream. However, it is the mousses made with whipped cream, which doubles in volume when beaten, that have the lightest, softest and creamiest texture.

Cold mousses, sweet or savoury, are usually moulded, chilled, and then turned out on to a chilled platter for serving. Metal moulds, which chill fast and well, are the easiest to use. Before adding the mousse mixture you should brush the inside of the mould with vegetable oil, which will prevent the mousse from sticking to the mould when it is turned out.

♔ Roquefort Mousse with Seafood Salad

Serves 6 to 8

4 tablespoons strained lemon juice

1 tablespoon unflavoured gelatin

¼ l. (8 fl. oz.) boiling water

125 g. (4 oz.) Roquefort cheese, left at room temperature for 1 hour

180 g. (6 oz.) peeled and grated cucumber

4 tablespoons finely chopped parsley

2 tablespoons finely chopped tinned pimiento

1 tablespoon finely chopped capers

1 teaspoon grated onion

1 teaspoon salt

½ teaspoon or more freshly ground black pepper

¼ l. (8 fl. oz.) chilled double cream

350 to 450 g. (12 to 16 oz.) shellfish salad

GARNISH

Chopped parsley or parsley sprigs

Before you start the recipe, put the bowl in which you will whip the cream into the refrigerator or freezer – beating the chilled cream in a chilled bowl prevents it from breaking down. Brush the inside of a 1½-litre (2½-pint) ring mould with 1 tablespoon vegetable oil, using a pastry brush. Coat the bottom and sides thoroughly, then turn the mould upside down on paper towels to drain off the excess oil.

Put the lemon juice into a bowl and sprinkle the gelatin on top. When softened, add the boiling water and stir until the gelatin is completely dissolved.

Put the cheese into a mixing bowl and mash with a wooden spoon or a fork until smooth. After grating the cucumber, wrap it in a tea towel and squeeze out all the water, then spread it out on a clean tea towel or paper towels and pat dry – excess water in the mousse might prevent it from setting properly.

Combine the cheese, cucumber, 4 tablespoons parsley, pimiento, capers, onion, salt and pepper; mix well and taste for seasoning. Adjust the pepper to taste – you probably will not need any more salt because of the sharpness of the Roquefort cheese. If you have a food processor, you can mash the cheese and combine with the other ingredients in the processor, using the steel blades.

Combine the cheese-and-gelatin mixture and mix until smooth (this can also be done in the processor). Put into the refrigerator for 20 minutes, or until the mixture is slightly thickened – the whipped cream should be folded in when the gelatin has thickened to the point where it will support the air bubbles in the cream.

Take the cream and bowl from the refrigerator; pour the cream into the bowl and beat, using a whisk, a rotary beater, an electric hand beater, or, if you have an electric mixer, the whip attachment. Whip the cream until it has doubled in volume and is just firm enough to hold soft peaks when the beater is lifted from the bowl. Remove the cheese-and-gelatin mixture from the refrigerator and lightly but thoroughly fold the whipped cream into it with a rubber spatula, using the technique with which you fold egg whites into a soufflé (see page 234). Pour the mousse mixture into the prepared ring mould, cover the top with plastic wrap, and chill in the refrigerator for 4 hours, or until the surface is firm when pressed with a finger. Also chill a round serving platter large enough to hold the mousse.

To unmould, remove platter and mould from the refrigerator. Run a thin-bladed knife or palette knife blade around the edges of the mousse to loosen it from the sides of the mould. Tilt the mould to one side and rap sharply with your hand to shake the mousse free; then tip the rounded part of the mould quickly in and out of hot water to free the top of the mousse. Place the platter on the bottom of the mould, next to the mousse and, holding platter and mould firmly, invert them, giving a sharp shake downwards as you do so to release the mousse. Lift off the mould. If the mousse does not come out of the mould, either dip again briefly in hot water, or rub the top with a tea towel wrung out in very hot water. Return the unmoulded mousse to the refrigerator for another 10 minutes to firm up, then fill the centre with 225 to

280 g. (8 to 10 oz.) of the shellfish salad. Sprinkle the salad with a little chopped parsley. You can also put sprigs of parsley or a ring of chopped parsley around the base of the mousse, if you wish.

SHELLFISH SALAD

Combine 350 to 450 g. (12 to 16 oz.) cooked lobster chunks, or whole prawns, or crabmeat (or a combination of the three) with 1½ dl. (¼ pt) tarragon-flavoured vinaigrette dressing (see page 306). Heap in the centre of the mousse (serve excess salad separately, in a bowl) and sprinkle with 1 tablespoon chopped parsley.

Frozen Lemon Mousse

This very simple form of frozen dessert mousse is made with a thick, cooked lemon curd, lightened by whipped cream, that can also be used, unfrozen, as a filling for a Swiss roll. As this mixture is not quite as firm as one containing gelatin, it is advisable not to unmould it.

Serves 6

125 g. (4 oz.) butter	*280 g. (10 oz.) sugar*
Grated rind of 1 large lemon (the yellow part only)	*3 egg yolks*
	3 whole eggs
Juice of 3 large lemons	*¼ l. (8 fl. oz.) chilled double cream*
¼ teaspoon salt	

Chill the bowl in which you will whip the cream in the refrigerator or freezer. Chill a 1½-litre (2½-pint) metal charlotte mould.

Melt the butter in the top of a double boiler over hot water (the water should not touch the upper pan but come about 1 cm. (½ inch) below it). Mix in the lemon rind and juice, salt and sugar. Beat the egg yolks and eggs together with a whisk and add to the ingredients in the pan. Cook over hot water (which should not be allowed to boil), beating constantly with a whisk, until the mixture is smooth, glossy, and very thick. Remove from the heat and cool.

When the lemon curd is cold, whip the cream in the chilled bowl with a whisk, rotary beater, or electric hand beater, or in an electric mixer with a whip attachment, until doubled in volume and firm enough to hold soft peaks when the beater is lifted. Fold the whipped cream into the lemon curd with a rubber spatula until thoroughly combined. Pour into the metal mould, cover the top with plastic wrap, and freeze until firm and set, about 6 hours. Serve from the mould.

Cold Ham Mousse

Another variation on the mousse theme, with a béchamel sauce base, this is an easy and good way to use up leftover cooked ham. You might serve it for a summer luncheon party or as part of a cold buffet.

Serves 6

60 g. (2 oz.) unsalted butter	*1¼ dl. (4 fl. oz.) double cream*
4 tablespoons flour	*1 tablespoon unflavoured gelatin*
¼ l. (8 fl. oz.) milk	*1¼ dl. (4 fl. oz.) cold water*
Salt	*1¼ dl. (4 fl. oz.) hot chicken broth or*
⅛ teaspoon cayenne pepper	*ham broth*
½ teaspoon grated nutmeg	*350 g. (12 oz.) very finely ground*
4 tablespoons cognac	*cooked ham*
2 egg yolks	

CUCUMBER GARNISH

2 medium cucumbers, peeled, seeded,	*2 tablespoons sugar*
and very thinly sliced	*3 tablespoons chopped parsley*
3 tablespoons white wine vinegar	*2 teaspoons chopped fresh dill*

Prepare a 1-l. (1¾-pt) ring mould by brushing it with 1 tablespoon vegetable oil, then turning it upside down on paper towels to drain off the excess oil.

Melt the butter in a saucepan, blend in the flour, and cook over medium heat, stirring, until golden and bubbling. Slowly mix the milk into this roux, and continue to stir, over low heat, until very thick and smooth. Season to taste with salt (be sparing if the ham is salty), the pepper and the nutmeg. Stir in the cognac. Mix the egg yolks and cream in a small bowl with a fork, then stir a little of the hot sauce into them to warm up the yolks. Stir into the sauce in the pan and cook over low heat, stirring, until blended. Do not let the sauce get too hot or boil, or the eggs will curdle. Remove pan from the heat.

Sprinkle the gelatin on the cold water. When softened, stir into the hot broth until thoroughly dissolved. Blend this into the sauce, then thoroughly mix in the ground ham. Fill the prepared mould with the ham mousse, smoothing it evenly with a rubber spatula. Cover the mould with plastic wrap and chill in the refrigerator until firm and set, about 2 to 3 hours.

Meanwhile, put the cucumbers into a bowl. Stir the vinegar and sugar until the sugar dissolves; mix with the parsley and dill; pour over the cucumbers and mix. Leave to marinate until the mousse is set.

When ready to serve, remove the plastic wrap from the mould; loosen the edges with a knife or spatula, dip the top of the mould in hot water for a second or two to release it, then invert on to a serving platter, as for Roquefort mousse (see page 333). Drain the marinated cucumbers. Put them in the centre of the moulded ring.

Soufflé Glacé Benedictine

A soufflé glacé, which can be either chilled or frozen (when frozen, it does not contain gelatin), has very little in common with an oven-baked soufflé, apart from name and appearance. In fact, if you analyse it, a soufflé glacé is merely another, fancier form of mousse. The illusion that the soufflé has, by some magic, risen in the refrigerator, is produced by containing the mousse within a paper collar that comes some 8 or 10 cm. (3 or 4 inches) above the rim of the dish and is removed before serving.

Serves 8

10 eggs, separated
280 g. (10 oz.) sugar
3 tablespoons unflavoured gelatin
1½ dl. (¼ pt) cold water
4½ dl. (¾ pt) chilled double cream

1½ dl. (¼ pt) Benedictine or other liqueur
¼ teaspoon cream of tartar
60 g. (2 oz.) finely crushed almond macaroons

First, prepare a 1½-litre (2½-pint) soufflé dish. Take a piece of greaseproof or waxed paper or aluminium foil long enough to fit around the soufflé dish with about 2½ cm. (1 inch) of overlap and fold it in half. Brush one side of the paper or foil with vegetable oil (this prevents the soufflé mixture from sticking when the collar is removed). Wrap the collar around the soufflé dish so that it extends 8 or 10 cm. (3 or 4 inches) above the rim, oiled side inward, and tie securely around the dish with string (see illustration, page 238).

Combine the egg yolks and sugar in the top of a double boiler and beat over hot water (which should not boil or touch the bottom of the pan) until the mixture is warmed and thick. Meanwhile, sprinkle the gelatin on the cold water to soften. When softened, stir into the hot egg/sugar mixture until completely dissolved.

Whip the cream in a chilled bowl until it has doubled in volume and holds soft peaks when the beater is removed. Put into the refrigerator until ready to use.

Put the top of the double boiler containing the egg/sugar mixture over a bowl of ice cubes and beat it over the ice until the mixture is cold. Then beat in the Benedictine. Fold the whipped cream into the mixture, before it starts to set.

Put 10 egg whites in a bowl with the cream of tartar, or in the bowl of the electric mixer, and beat with a whisk or the mixer until stiff but not dry, as for a soufflé. The cream of tartar helps the egg whites to mount, but if you are beating them in an unlined copper bowl, cream of tartar is not necessary. Lightly but thoroughly fold the beaten egg whites into the mousse mixture and then carefully pour into the prepared soufflé dish, so that it mounts inside the collar. Smooth the top with a rubber spatula.

Chill in the refrigerator until set and firm, about 4 to 6 hours. To serve, untie the string and very carefully peel off the collar without disturbing the moulded mousse. Sprinkle the top with the crushed macaroons. If you are not serving the dessert right away, replace in the refrigerator to keep firm until ready to use, which should be within an hour or two.

VARIATION

Instead of Benedictine, use a coffee-flavoured liqueur, such as Tia Maria, and decorate the top with macaroon crumbs and the little sweets that look like coffee beans.

Chilled Custards

♙ Orange Bavarian Cream

The Bavarian cream or *bavarois* is a rich but delicate mousselike dessert usually made by combining *crème anglaise* with gelatin, whipped cream and any desired flavourings – one of the pleasantest is orange.

Serves 8

CRÈME ANGLAISE

8 egg yolks	¼ l. (8 fl. oz.) milk
150 g. (5 oz.) sugar	¼ l. (8 fl. oz.) double cream
⅛ teaspoon salt	1 teaspoon vanilla essence

FLAVOURING

1 tablespoon unflavoured gelatin	2 tablespoons Grand Marnier
4 tablespoons strained orange juice	¼ l. (8 fl. oz.) chilled double cream
2 tablespoons finely grated orange zest (the orange part of the rind)	

The Bavarian cream may be chilled in a mould, in the same way as a mousse, or spooned into individual glass serving dishes or one large glass serving bowl, which is easier and equally attractive.

Put the bowl in which you will whip the cream into the refrigerator or freezer to chill.

Prepare the *crème anglaise* according to the directions on page 290, using the proportions given above. Sprinkle the gelatin on the orange juice to soften it.

Immediately after the *crème anglaise* is made, pour it into a bowl and blend in the softened gelatin. The gelatin must be thoroughly dissolved in and distributed through the hot custard, otherwise you will get hard little lumps of gelatin in your Bavarian cream. Add the orange zest and Grand Marnier and stir until well mixed. Cool the custard, then lay a piece of plastic wrap on the surface to prevent a skin from forming, and chill in the refrigerator until it is thick and just at the point of setting.

Whip the cream in the chilled bowl until it holds soft peaks when the beater is lifted – do not let it get too stiff. Fold lightly but thoroughly into the chilled custard mixture with a rubber spatula.

Spoon into 8 individual glass serving dishes or 1 large glass serving bowl and chill until set and firm, about 6 to 8 hours for the large bowl, about 1 to 2 hours for individual dishes. You may, if you wish, decorate the top with peeled orange segments (see page 315) and rosettes of whipped cream piped through a forcing bag with a rosette nozzle.

Trifle

This most delectable of desserts is very easy to make and quite spectacular on a buffet table or for a summer dinner party. As it is very rich, it will serve a lot of people.

Serves 8 to 10

23-cm. (9-inch) *génoise (see page 268)*   6 dl. (1 pt) chilled *crème anglaise*
   or sponge-cake layer   *(see page 290)*
   Or 10 to 12 sponge fingers   ¼ l. (8 fl. oz.) chilled double cream
1½ dl. (¼ pt) or less cream (sweet) sherry   2 tablespoons fine sugar
1½ dl. (¼ pt) raspberry jam   1 tablespoon cognac
   Or 2 dl. (⅓ pt) raspberry purée
     (see page 326)

GARNISH

30 g. (1 oz.) chopped pistachio nuts   4 to 6 pieces of angelica
30 g. (1 oz.) glacé cherries

You will need a crystal serving bowl or soufflé dish, 23 cm. (9 inches) in diameter – the crystal dish is more effective, as you can see the different layers. Put the cake layer or the sponge fingers on the bottom and sprinkle liberally with the sherry. Use just enough to dampen and flavour the cake, but not enough to make it soggy. Let the cake stand 15 minutes.

Spread the cake or sponge fingers with a 1-cm. ($\frac{3}{8}$-inch)-thick layer of raspberry jam, or with the raspberry purée. (The purée is not as concentrated as the jam and also has a more delicious flavour and texture.) Cover with the *crème anglaise* and chill for 3 or 4 hours.

Just before serving, whip the cream in a chilled bowl until it stands in soft peaks, then beat in the sugar and cognac. Cover the surface of the custard with the cream, smoothing it evenly with a rubber spatula. Sprinkle chopped pistachio nuts over the top and decorate with glacé cherries and angelica or other decoration of your choice. Serve chilled, but do not let it stand in the refrigerator for more than 30 minutes or it will become soggy.

Chilled Soups

Chilled Minted Pea Soup

This soup is made with dried split peas, which may or may not need soaking, according to the type you buy. Check the package directions as to the length of cooking time required.

Serves 8

280 g. (10 oz.) dried, green split peas	Salt, freshly ground black pepper
2 to 3 l. (1$\frac{3}{4}$ to 2$\frac{1}{2}$ qts) chicken broth	6 tablespoons soured cream
2 garlic cloves, crushed	2 tablespoons chopped fresh mint

Soak or preboil the peas according to package directions. Drain and put in a deep pot with 2 l. (1$\frac{3}{4}$ qts) chicken broth and the garlic. Bring to the boil; reduce the heat and simmer, covered, until the peas are completely cooked. Strain the peas, reserving the broth. Purée the peas by putting them through a food mill, whirling them in a liquidizer, or processing them in a food processor, then measure the purée and combine it with an equal amount of chicken broth. Taste, correct the seasoning, adding salt and freshly ground black pepper as needed, and chill.

When you are ready to serve, stir in the soured cream and serve in chilled soup cups; sprinkle with the chopped fresh mint.

Chilled Avocado Soup

Serves 4

1 large ripe avocado
3½ dl. (12 fl. oz.) hot chicken broth
1 tablespoon chopped fresh tarragon
  Or 1 teaspoon dried tarragon

¼ teaspoon Tabasco
1 tablespoon lemon juice
1½ dl. (¼ pt) double cream
1½ dl. (¼ pt) soured cream

GARNISH

1 tablespoon chopped fresh tarragon or chives

Cut the avocado in half lengthwise; remove the stone and either peel off the skin (if the avocado is really ripe, it should come off easily), or scoop the avocado pulp out with a spoon. Put the avocado into a liquidizer with the chicken broth and seasonings and whirl until smooth. Chill well in a covered bowl. Just before serving, mix with the double cream and soured cream and chill again, briefly. Serve in chilled soup cups, topped with a sprinkling of chopped tarragon or chives.

Gelatin Moulds and Aspics

♨ Cucumber and Carrot Ring with Crabmeat

This is a very simple jellied salad, the kind popular for buffets and luncheons. You can fill the centre with crabmeat or with prawns or lobster meat.

Serves 4 to 6

1½ dl. (¼ pt) cold water
2 tablespoons unflavoured gelatin
3½ dl. (12 fl. oz.) boiling water
2 tablespoons lemon juice
2 dl. (⅓ pt) white wine
1 teaspoon salt
¼ teaspoon Tabasco
180 g. (6 oz.) peeled, seeded, and
  grated cucumber

60 g. (2 oz.) grated carrot
2 tablespoons chopped parsley
225 to 350 g. (8 to 12 oz.) crabmeat
1 head of butterhead lettuce or other
  salad greens, washed and chilled
3 hard-boiled eggs, peeled and sliced
2 dl. (⅓ pt) mayonnaise (see page 294)

Put the cold water into a bowl. Sprinkle the gelatin on top of the water. When the gelatin has softened, pour in the boiling water and stir until thoroughly dissolved. Add the lemon juice, wine, salt and Tabasco and cool in the refrigerator until the gelatin is thick and syrupy, but not set.

Squeeze the grated cucumber in a tea towel to get rid of the excess water. Rinse a 1½-l. (2½-pt) ring mould with cold water and shake out the excess (for gelatin moulds, the ring should be rinsed with water rather than brushed with oil, which would cloud the surface of the clear gelatin).

Mix the cucumber, carrot and parsley into the syrupy gelatin mixture and spoon into the prepared ring mould. Cover the top with plastic wrap and chill until set and firm, about 3 hours. Also chill a round platter large enough to hold the unmoulded ring.

To unmould, run a thin knife blade or palette knife around the edge of the mould, put a plate over the bottom of the mould, and invert quickly. If the mould does not release, rub the top with a cloth wrung out in very hot water, then, holding mould and plate, give it a sharp shake. Return to the refrigerator until ready to serve, or to set, if the top of the mould has been softened by the heat of the towel.

To serve, pile crabmeat in the centre of the ring, passing any excess in a separate bowl, and garnish the edges of the platter with lettuce leaves and slices of hard-boiled egg. Pass mayonnaise separately to dress the crabmeat.

Jellied Veal

This recipe for a jellied veal that can double as a mock brawn is one I have used most of my life for picnics, on the hors d'oeuvre table, and for supper. It originated with a most remarkable cook who worked for a family I knew years ago. This is my adaptation of one of her specialities.

Serves 8 to 10

1½ kg. (3 lbs.) veal shin	1 bay leaf
1 kg. (2 lbs.) veal neck	1 teaspoon dried basil
1 tablespoon salt	Or several leaves fresh basil
3 peeled garlic cloves	2 tablespoons Worcestershire sauce
1 onion, stuck with 2 cloves	½ teaspoon Tabasco
3 or 4 sprigs of parsley	6 to 8 hard-boiled eggs

Put the veal shin and neck in a deep pot with the salt, garlic, onion, parsley, bay leaf, basil and water barely to cover. Bring to a boil and boil rapidly for 5 minutes, skimming off the scum that rises to the surface. Reduce the heat; cover the pot and simmer the veal for 2 hours, or until the meat is very tender but not overcooked. Remove the veal from the pot and take all the meat from the bones. Return the bones to the pot with the Worcestershire sauce and Tabasco and simmer the broth briskly for 15 minutes. Strain the broth through a double thickness of butter muslin or a linen towel into a clean pot. Cut the meat into small pieces and add them to the strained broth. Bring to a boil, then taste and season with salt and pepper, if needed. Remove from the heat.

Peel and slice the eggs. Rinse a 2-litre (3½-pint) metal melon mould or ring mould with cold water. Put in a layer of the veal and broth, then a layer of sliced egg, and continue making layers until all the veal and eggs have been used, finishing with a layer of veal and enough broth to cover. Cover the mould with foil and chill for at least 8 hours. Unmould the jellied veal according to the directions for the previous recipe. Cut into fairly thick slices and serve with a vinaigrette sauce (see page 304).

Cold Poached Salmon in Red Wine Aspic

A whole poached salmon in aspic is a glorious sight on a buffet table. You should get fish bones and heads to provide a strong, concentrated, flavourful stock with natural gelatin, and clarify it for your aspic. This recipe is rather unusual in that red wine is used in the poaching court bouillon, rather than the usual white.

Serves 12

COURT BOUILLON

1 to 1½ kg. (2 to 3 lbs.) fish bones and heads	1½ tablespoons salt
	1 tablespoon thyme
2 l. (3½ pts) water	2 bay leaves
2 to 2¼ l. (3½ to 4 pts) red wine	1 carrot, scraped
1 onion, peeled and stuck with 2 cloves	1 lemon, sliced
	1½ dl. (¼ pt) red wine vinegar

SALMON AND ASPIC

3-kg. (6- to 7-lb.) salmon	3 tablespoons unflavoured gelatin
2 egg whites, lightly beaten	4 tablespoons cold water

DECORATION

Thin slices of lemon, tarragon leaves, cucumber slices, sprigs of dill

Cook the fish bones and heads in the water until they practically fall apart, 1 hour or more. Strain this fish stock and transfer it to a fish poacher with a rack, or a pan large enough to hold the salmon. Add the remaining court bouillon ingredients, bring to a boil, reduce the heat, and simmer for 10 minutes.

Measure the salmon at its thickest point, from belly to backbone, to determine the cooking time (10 minutes per measured $2\frac{1}{2}$ cm. or inch). Put it on the rack of the fish poacher or on a large piece of heavy-duty foil; lower it into the simmering liquid and poach at a simmer for the necessary time. Test for doneness with a fork or toothpick. If the flesh flakes easily, it is done. Transfer to a platter and cool completely. When cool, carefully peel off and discard all the skin; put the fish on a board or serving platter, cover with plastic wrap and chill while making the aspic.

Boil the poaching liquid rapidly until reduced to about $1\frac{3}{4}$ l. (3 pts), then strain it through several thicknesses of butter muslin into a deep pan and clarify with the beaten egg whites (see description of technique on page 29). Strain the clarified stock through a sieve lined with a linen towel or several thicknesses of butter muslin into a pan. Reheat the liquid.

Sprinkle the gelatin on the 4 tablespoons cold water to soften, then stir it into the hot, clarified liquid until dissolved. Let the aspic mixture cool, then stir over a bowl of ice cubes until it starts to get syrupy. Remove the salmon from the refrigerator, take off the plastic wrap, and coat the flesh on the best-looking side of the salmon with a thin coat of the syrupy aspic, pouring it over with a large spoon. Chill the fish until the aspic sets, then give it another coat and again chill until set. You may find when working with aspic that it gets too cold and sets. In this case, you have to melt it over low heat and chill again until it starts to get syrupy. Decorate the fish with thin slices of lemon or cucumber arranged in overlapping rows to look like fish scales and with sprays of tarragon leaves or sprigs of dill. Dip the decorations in aspic first so they will adhere to the coating. Then, very carefully, apply a final coat of aspic over the decorations and chill until set. Remove any aspic that ran on to the board or platter.

To serve, garnish the board or platter with tomato shells (see page 316) filled with Russian salad (cold, diced cooked vegetables bound with mayonnaise) and tuck sprigs of parsley or watercress in between. Leftover aspic can be chopped fine on a sheet of greaseproof or waxed paper and scattered around the fish. You might also serve a cucumber salad if you didn't use cucumbers for decoration.

Sherry and Grapefruit Jelly

This is a very easy and pleasant dessert to serve after a rich main course.

Serves 8

2 tablespoons plain gelatin
150 g. (5 oz.) sugar
3½ dl. (12 fl. oz.) water
2 tablespoons lime juice
1½ dl. (¼ pt) medium sherry
1 tablespoon angostura bitters
4½ dl. (¾ pt) grapefruit juice

125 g. (4 oz.) grapefruit sections
   (for technique, see page 315)
4 teaspoons grated orange zest (the
   orange part of the rind)
2 dl. (⅓ pt) chilled double cream
2 tablespoons sweet sherry

Mix the gelatin and sugar in a small, heavy saucepan; add the water and stir over low heat until the gelatin and sugar are completely dissolved. Remove from the heat and stir in the lime juice, sherry, bitters and grapefruit juice. Pour into 8 individual moulds or 1 large 1½-l. (2½-pt) mould. Chill until firm. Unmould on to chilled plates or a platter, as for other gelatin moulds (see page 334); garnish with the grapefruit sections and sprinkle with the orange zest. Whip the cream in a chilled bowl until it just holds its shape, then add the sweet sherry and whip until doubled in volume. Serve the sherry-flavoured cream with the jelly.

Pâté

Veal and Ham Pâté

This is a rather different pâté because it is made with whole pieces of meat, rather than the usual minced-meat mixture, or forcemeat. A pâté is baked in an oval or a long, deep, rectangular dish (known as a terrine), which is lined with very thin strips of bacon to lubricate the meat and prevent it from drying out during cooking. The classic terrine, which may be made of glazed earthenware, ovenproof porcelain, or enamelled cast iron, has a cover and comes in a range of sizes. If you don't own a terrine, you can make this recipe in a 23-cm. (9-inch) pan of glass or metal, the kind you would use for bread, and cover it with heavy-duty aluminium foil.

Serves 10 to 12

½ kg. (1 lb.) bacon

1 kg. (2 lbs.) veal scaloppine, pounded
   until very thin

800 g. (1¾ lbs.) thinly sliced gammon

About 1 tablespoon salt

1 teaspoon freshly ground black pepper

10 shallots, peeled and finely chopped

60 g. (2 oz.) finely chopped parsley

1 teaspoon dried thyme

1 bay leaf

1½ dl. (¼ pt) dry white wine

Line a 23-cm. (9-inch) oval or rectangular terrine or bread tin with the bacon, draping the strips across the bottom and up the sides, first crosswise and then lengthwise. Leave overhangs at the top to cover the pâté.

Before putting in the meat, check to see how salty the gammon is. Sauté a small piece in a tablespoon of butter in a frying pan and taste. The amount of salt used for seasoning depends on the saltiness of the meat.

Preheat the oven to 170°C (325°F, gas mark 3).

Beginning and ending with veal, alternate layers of scaloppine and layers of gammon in the lined tin, sprinkling each layer with salt, pepper, shallots, parsley and thyme. Drape the ends of the bacon slices over the mixture. If they don't cover completely, add a few more strips, placing them down the length of the meat, and fold the ends over these strips. Arrange the bay leaf on top of the slices and pour the white wine over all.

Put the cover on the terrine or cover the top of the bread tin with a double layer of heavy-duty foil, tucking it around the sides of the tin. Put the terrine or tin on a baking tray (to catch any overflow of juices that might bubble out during the baking) and bake in the centre of the oven for 2 to 2½ hours, or until the fat and juices bubbling up around the sides of the tin are clear. Remove cover or foil and check after 2 hours. If the juices are cloudy, more cooking is needed.

When the pâté is cooked, remove it from the oven, uncover, and cool for about 20 minutes. It should then be weighted down, which firms the texture and forces out excess juices from the meat, and refrigerated until cold. For this you will need something flat and heavy that will fit inside the tin, such as a piece of board or plywood, cut to size and weighted down with tinned goods, or a foil-covered brick. Pâté should be weighted for 12 hours before unmoulding.

When the pâté is cold and firm, remove the board and weights and refrigerate, covered with the lid or with foil, until ready to serve. Do not store a pâté for more than 3 or 4 days in the refrigerator, as the juices are apt to sour. If you wish to store it for longer, remove excess liquid or jelly and cover the top of the pâté with a layer of melted pork fat to seal it. Most pâtés do not freeze well; they lose texture and flavour.

To serve, unmould by inverting the pâté on to a serving dish and cut into slices about 1 cm. ($\frac{3}{8}$ inch) thick. The fat should be left on and removed at the table.

Ice Cream

I well remember the simple homemade ice creams of my childhood. They were turned by hand in a freezer packed with cracked ice and rock salt – a strenuous task, particularly towards the end when the cream froze solid and turning the handle required a fair amount of brute force. Nowadays electric ice-cream freezers have made the whole business effortless, and if you are a lover of ice cream, it's well worth buying one. Some people make ice cream in refrigerator ice trays, but it is my feeling that the finished product seldom equals that made in an ice-cream freezer, which churns the mixture to a perfect, smooth creaminess.

There are different kinds of ice creams. Those with a base of custard, often called French ice cream, have a distinctly different taste and texture from the ice creams made of single or double cream.

⛾ Basic Vanilla Ice Cream

This is the simplest of all ice creams to make. For a rich ice cream, use double cream instead of single.

Makes about 1½ litres (2½ pints)

1 l. (1¾ pts) single or double cream
150 g. (5 oz.) sugar
1½ teaspoons pure vanilla essence
  Or a 5-cm. (2-inch) piece of vanilla
    bean

Cracked ice and rock salt
Or coarse salt for freezing

Stir the cream and sugar together for 5 or 6 minutes to dissolve the sugar. Add the vanilla essence or slit the vanilla bean lengthwise with a sharp paring knife and scrape the tiny black seeds inside into the cream.

Pour the mixture into the can of an electric or hand-operated ice-cream freezer (the can should be about three-quarters full, to allow for expansion), put in the dasher, and cover the can tightly with the lid. Lower it into the freezer and pack the freezer with alternating layers of cracked ice and rock salt or coarse salt in the proportions of about 150 g. (5 oz.) salt to 680 g. (1½ lbs.) ice, or whatever proportions are recommended by the freezer manufacturer. Connect the dasher to the crank or shaft mechanism, according to manufacturer's directions, and turn the mixture by hand or electrically, again following operating directions, until the ice cream is frozen. With a hand-operated freezer this will be at the point when the crank can barely be moved. With a machine, the motor will slow down or stop. When operating by hand, do not stop turning until the mixture is frozen, or the ice cream may be lumpy.

When the ice cream is frozen, disconnect the mechanism, remove the can, and wipe it carefully to remove any salt. Remove the lid and dasher, press the ice cream down firmly with a spoon, and cover the can again, plugging the hole in the top of the can where the dasher was with a piece of aluminium foil (this prevents salt from seeping through). Drain the water from the freezer, replace the can, and repack with more ice and salt until ready to serve, which will keep it firm. The ice cream may be kept this way for up to 4 hours. If you are going to serve it right away, it need not be repacked.

VARIATIONS

Banana Ice Cream. Peel and remove strings from 5 or 6 very ripe bananas. Crush them well with a fork and combine them with 200 g. (7 oz.) sugar, 1 tablespoon vanilla essence, 1½ tablespoons lime or lemon juice and ⅛ teaspoon salt. Stir this mixture into 1 l. (1¾ pts) double cream and freeze as for basic vanilla ice cream.

Ginger Ice Cream. Follow the recipe for basic vanilla ice cream, but use half the amount of vanilla and add 150 g. (5 oz.) finely cut preserved ginger and 5 tablespoons of the syrup in which the ginger is packed. Combine well and freeze.

Cassis Ice Cream. Follow the recipe for basic vanilla ice cream but use only $\frac{3}{4}$ teaspoon vanilla essence. Add 2 dl. ($\frac{1}{3}$ pt) cassis syrup or crème de cassis liqueur (made from black currants) and 225 g. ($\frac{1}{2}$ lb.) sieved black currant jam (rubbed through a strainer with a wooden spoon). Mix well and freeze. Serve this with additional cassis syrup or crème de cassis blended with raspberry purée (see page 326), if you wish. In peach season, this ice cream can be served with halved or sliced, sugared peaches in addition to the raspberry and cassis purée.

French Vanilla Ice Cream

Makes about 2 litres (3$\frac{1}{2}$ pints)

6 *egg yolks*	1 *l.* (1$\frac{3}{4}$ *pts*) *double cream*
200 *g.* (7 *oz.*) *sugar*	1$\frac{1}{2}$ *to* 2 *tablespoons pure vanilla*
$\frac{1}{8}$ *teaspoon salt*	*essence*
4$\frac{1}{2}$ *dl.* ($\frac{3}{4}$ *pt*) *milk*	*Or* 7 *cm.* (2$\frac{1}{2}$ *inches*) *of vanilla bean*

The first step is to make a *crème anglaise* or custard. Combine the egg yolks, sugar and salt in a heavy, 3-litre (2$\frac{1}{2}$-quart), enamelled cast-iron saucepan or the top of a double boiler and beat together with a wire whisk, rotary or electric beater, or wooden spatula until well mixed, pale and creamy. Meanwhile, in another pan, heat the milk until little bubbles appear around the edges of the pan. Gradually pour the hot milk into the egg mixture, stirring constantly. Cook over medium heat or hot water (if using the double boiler), stirring constantly, until the custard thickens sufficiently to coat lightly a wooden spatula or spoon. Remove from the heat and cool. Stir in the double cream and the vanilla essence or seeds scraped from the vanilla bean. Freeze as for basic vanilla ice cream (see previous recipe).

VARIATIONS

Lemon Ice Cream. Before freezing, add 1$\frac{1}{2}$ dl. ($\frac{1}{4}$ pt) lemon juice and 3 tablespoons grated lemon zest (the yellow part of the lemon rind) to the ice cream. Serve topped with chopped pistachio nuts.

Strawberry Ice Cream. When the ice cream is half frozen (after about 15 minutes in a hand-cranked freezer, or 10 minutes in an electric freezer), add 225 g. ($\frac{1}{2}$ lb.) fresh, crushed strawberries and 1 tablespoon lemon juice. Stir well and continue freezing.

Peach Ice Cream. When half frozen, add 350 g. (12 oz.) sliced, sugared peaches and 1 tablespoon lemon juice. Stir well and continue freezing.

Note. When you remove the lid and add any of the above ingredients, be very careful not to let any of the salt mixture drip into the ice cream.

Ice-Tray Apricot Ice Cream

If you are making ice cream in an ice tray, I find it advisable to use a slightly different mixture and to whip the cream, the result of which is nearer a frozen cream or a very rich, creamy version of sherbet. As it is very difficult to get luscious, ripe apricots these days, I make this ice cream with apricot jam, which works beautifully.

Serves 6

450-g. (1-lb.) jar pure apricot jam	*5 tablespoons sugar*
¼ l. (8 fl. oz.) water	*3½ dl. (12 fl. oz.) double cream*

Rub the jam through a strainer with a wooden spoon or put through a food mill.

Boil the water and sugar together for 5 minutes to make a simple syrup, then cool until cold. Combine the apricot purée and the syrup, mixing well.

Whip the double cream in a chilled bowl with a rotary beater or electric hand mixer (or in the bowl of an electric mixer) until it has doubled in volume and holds its shape when the beater is lifted. Fold the cream thoroughly into the apricot mixture with a rubber spatula, then pour the mixture into refrigerator ice trays and put in the coldest part of the freezing compartment or freezer until frozen around the edges and mushy in the centre. Remove, turn into a bowl, and beat with a wooden spatula until smooth. Return the trays to the freezer. Repeat this beating process 1 or 2 times, then return to the freezer and freeze until hard. The beating process keeps the ice cream from forming crystals and makes it smooth.

Sherbet

Sherbets, or *sorbets*, as the French call them, and *granités* are water ices made with a simple syrup, or sugar, and flavourings – fruit juice, coffee, champagne and puréed fruit are the most usual. The main difference seems to be that while the sherbet may contain other ingredients such as beaten egg whites or milk (for a milk sherbet), the *granité* is simply frozen liquid and has a more crystalline, grainy texture. Ice-tray freezing works well for sherbets and *granités*, provided they are taken out of the freezer and beaten smooth 2 or 3 times while still mushy. Sherbet may also be turned in an ice cream freezer until it is just softly frozen, not hard like ice cream. Before serving a sherbet, remove it from the freezing compartment to the refrigerator to soften a little.

The freezing time for sherbet or *granité* depends on how often you beat it and how cold your freezer or freezing compartment is – to speed the process, set it at the lowest possible temperature.

♟ Strawberry Sorbet

Serves 8

680 g. (1½ lbs.) fresh strawberries
  Or 3 packages frozen strawberries
400 g. (14 oz.) sugar
  Or 200 g. (7 oz.) sugar if using
    frozen strawberries

3½ dl. (12 fl. oz.) orange juice
2 dl. (⅓ pt) lemon juice
5 tablespoons Grand Marnier

Wash and hull the fresh strawberries or slightly thaw the frozen strawberries. Combine the strawberries, sugar, and fruit juices in a bowl and let stand 2 to 3 hours for the strawberries to absorb the flavours. Put the mixture through a food mill, rub through a sieve, or purée in a liquidizer or food processor. Stir the Grand Marnier into the purée and pour it into refrigerator ice trays. Freeze until about 2½ cm. (1 inch) of the mixture has frozen around the sides of the trays, then remove; turn the mixture into a bowl and beat until smooth. Return to the trays and freeze until firm. For a more delicate *sorbet*, beat the mixture twice, freezing between beatings until just solid around the edges.

Lemon Granité

Serves 4

100 g. (3½ oz.) sugar
¼ l. (8 fl. oz.) water

5 to 8 tablespoons-lemon juice

Boil the sugar and water together for 5 minutes to make a simple syrup. Cool completely, then mix in the lemon juice – the amount depends on how tart you like your *granité*. Pour into ice trays and freeze as for strawberry *sorbet* (see previous recipe), removing and beating once or twice. Serve in sherbet glasses.

VARIATION

Coffee Granité. Combine 8 tablespoons Italian-roast coffee, ground for espresso (or instant espresso), 2 to 4 teaspoons sugar to taste (according to how sweet you like your *granité*), and 1 litre (1¾ pints) boiling water in a glass or pottery coffee maker. Leave to steep for 30 to 40 minutes. Cool completely, then pour into ice trays (if you use coffee ground for filtering, strain it through a paper filter cone to remove the grounds). Freeze, beating twice. Serve in sherbet glasses topped, if you wish, with a spoonful of whipped cream.

Cooking Terms and Methods
The Concordance
Carving

Cooking Terms and Methods

I have never thought that the glossary of terms given in most cookbooks was particularly helpful. Processes such as clarifying or folding are defined in the abstract, without relating them to the recipes. To me, you learn a technique by doing it, not by reading a definition. Therefore, in the list that follows you'll find, instead of a definition, a page reference to the place in the text where that particular term or technique is first described and fully demonstrated, so you can turn there, immediately get your hands in, and learn all about it as you cook.

Avocado, slicing, 314

Barding with fat: beef fillet, 77; pheasant, 97

Basting, 69, 81

Beans, soaking: quick method, 58; overnight, 157

Biscuit crumbs, making, 274

Blanching, 23

Boiling: shellfish, 42; pasta, 46; rice, 50; eggs, 57; vegetables, 59

Bread crumbs, sautéing in butter, 274

Butter: flavoured, 112; clarified, 361

Buttered greaseproof or waxed paper, to prevent skin forming on sauce, 286

Caramel: for colouring stock, 33; for colouring sauce, 289

Caramelizing: crème brûlée, 130; onions, 156; sugar, 289

Chicken: disjointing, 172; boning breasts, 175

Chicory, cleaning and trimming, 198

Chopping, 12

Clarifying: stock, 29; butter, 361

Collar: for hot soufflé, 238; for cold soufflé, 337

Courgette, salting, 199

Court bouillon: for fish, 39, 40; for vegetables, 62

Creaming butter and sugar: with hands, 264; with beater, 271

Double boiler, how to use, 291

Dressing a salad, 307

Drying out potatoes, 56

Eggs, separating, 265

Egg whites, beating: soft peaks, 265; stiff peaks, 265; folding in, 265; meringue, 272

Egg yolks, tempering, 287

Flaming (flambéing), 96, 128, 168, 175

Flattening meat or chicken fillets, 144

Flour: dusting with, 144; sifting, 264

Folding, 234

'Frenching' rib chops, 100

Glazing: ham, 82; turnips, 198; fruit tart, 248; cake, 268

Gratinéing, 105

Julienning, 12, 134

Kneading, 259

Larding fresh ham, 80

Marinating: venison, 100; flank steak, 110; kebabs, 118; beef, 147; halibut, 122

Mirepoix, 134

Mushrooms, cleaning and slicing, 196

Pan-frying, 163

Parboiling, 23

Pastry: rolling out, 244; lining pan, 245; crimping, 246

Peeling: band from potatoes, to stop bursting, 35; garlic, 73; onions, 79; peppers, 126; tomatoes, 309; avocados, 314; oranges and grapefruit, 315

Piping cream puffs, 256

Poaching: sausages, 38; whole fish, 40; fish fillets, 41; eggs, 56; vegetables, 62; fruit, 63

Puréeing: vegetables, 60; fruit, 326

Rabbit, disjointing, 178

Reducing, 29

Rendering fat, 78; from goose, 93

Roux, 281, 285

Searing, 69

Sharpening knives, 14

Shelling prawns, 124, 207

Shredding vegetables, 314

Skimming: fat from cool broth, 28; fat from hot broth, 28

Slicing, 11

Steaming: beefsteak and kidney pudding, 35; mussels, 45; rice, 50; cracked wheat, 53

Straining stock, 29

Stuffing: cabbage leaves, 34; chicken, 87; poussins, 88; turkey, 89; goose, 93; breast of veal, 141; veal birds, 144

Thickening: with *beurre manié*, 283; with flour-and-liquid paste, 283; with cornflour, 283; with arrowroot, potato flour, rice flour, 283; with egg yolks, 284, 287, 290–99

Tomato(es): peeling and seeding, 401

Trussing poultry, 84–5

Unmoulding mousse, 336

Whipping cream, 335

Yeast: using dried, 257, 258

The Concordance

APPLES   For cooking, one needs tart apples such as Bramley's Seedlings or Lord Derby, which are firm, well-textured, and flavourful, with a good bouquet and excellent texture. Apples are good stewed for apple sauce (see page 65), baked, sautéed (see page 201), as fritters (see page 211), and, of course, there's nothing like them for flans (see page 247), pies, certain cakes and fruit stuffings for poultry (see page 93), and with certain game birds (see page 158). For eating apples, Cox's Orange Pippin, Worcester Pearmain and Granny Smiths are the most generally available, but look for other firm, juicy varieties, particularly in farm markets in the autumn.

APRICOTS   One of the finest fruits when fully ripe. They should be tender to the touch, sweet to the tongue, and full of flavour, but are seldom found that way in the markets today because they are picked too green. You may be better off using dried apricots and reconstituting them by bringing them to a boil in water and letting them stand. They have a fine flavour. A good brand of tinned apricots can be substituted in some dishes, such as fritters (see page 211).

ARTICHOKES   For most purposes, the large green globe artichokes are best. Choose big ones with firm heads and tight leaves. Tinges of brown on the leaves are frost marks. These do not affect the flavour, only the appearance. To cook, break or cut off the stalk and pull off the small hard leaves around the base. Slice off 6 mm. ($\frac{1}{4}$ inch) of the prickly top with a sharp knife, then snip off the prickly tips of the remaining leaves with sharp scissors. Boil uncovered in plenty of salted water with a slice of lemon and 2 garlic cloves. Allow 40 minutes for large artichokes, less for the small ones. They are done when a leaf pulls out easily. Drain upside down, on paper towels. Serve hot with melted butter or hollandaise sauce, or cold with vinaigrette sauce. Artichokes can also be steamed, braised, or stuffed and baked. To remove the unpalatable choke (the fuzzy core), spread the leaves, pull out the tight centre cone of pale leaves, and scrape the choke from the artichoke bottom with a teaspoon. Very tiny, immature artichokes in which the choke has not developed may be eaten raw or sautéed whole.

ASPARAGUS   Asparagus is most plentiful and inexpensive in the early summer. Most fresh asparagus needs no peeling, unless the stalks are very thick and woody. Merely break off the tough lower part of the stalk where the tender spear begins. There are many ways of cooking asparagus. My favourite is to lay it flat in a frying pan and boil very rapidly in salted water (see page 59). Serve hot with melted butter or hollandaise or cold with vinaigrette sauce or mustard mayonnaise. Young asparagus may be eaten raw. Frozen asparagus is limp, tasteless and not worth buying. Tinned asparagus tastes like an entirely different vegetable – either you enjoy it as a salad or you hate it.

AUBERGINES   Versatile vegetables, by themselves and in combination with others, aubergines vary in size and colour, from the large bell-shaped purple aubergines and white aubergines (the latter more or less curiosities) to small, thin, elongated purple ones about 10 to 15 cm. (4 to 6 inches) long. Buy aubergines that are firm to the touch, with smooth, unblemished skins. If aubergine is to be cooked for a short time, it is best to peel, salt and drain it, to draw out the water and bitter juices. If it is to be cooked for a long time, peeling is not necessary and salting is a matter of taste, as the liquid will evaporate in cooking. Aubergine may be sliced with the skin on and grilled (see page 126); or sautéed, cut into strips, and deep fried (see page 215); combined with other vegetables in a mélange such as ratatouille (see page 153); stuffed and baked (see page 274); or used in various casseroles and dishes, especially Middle Eastern, Oriental, French and Italian.

AVOCADOS   One of the pleasantest fruits. A ripe avocado will be yielding to the touch, soft but not mushy, with buttery-tender green flesh. If the flesh is dark or brown, the avocado is overripe. If firm when bought, avocados will ripen if left in a dark place for a day or two. Avocados are usually served in their natural state, peeled and cut up in salads (see page 307), split and stuffed with shellfish or other salads, mashed with a fork or in a liquidizer to a soft purée (see guacamole, page 317), or blended in cold soups (see page 320). They may also be stuffed and baked. In Central and South America they are blended with sugar and lime juice for a dessert. When cut and exposed to air, avocados discolour quickly so serve as soon as possible after cutting. To keep a leftover piece, rub cut surfaces with lemon juice and cover tightly with plastic wrap. Some say that leaving the stone in puréed avocado prevents discolouration.

BAKING SODA   Baking soda or bicarbonate of soda is a leavening agent mostly used for doughs mixed with sour milk, buttermilk, orange juice and treacle, which have a rather high acid content. It is a valuable leavener, but take care not to use too much or it will adversely affect the taste and colour of the finished product.

BANANAS   Considered a great source of potassium, if that means anything to you and your diet. Never refrigerate bananas. If you buy them yellow and firm, they will ripen quite quickly at room temperature. The riper they become, the more brown-speckled the skin and the more intense the flavour. For desserts, bananas are used whole, sliced, or puréed. Good grilled (see page 128); baked (see crêpes directoire, page 231); sautéed (see page 201); in pies; puréed for soufflés, ice cream (see page 348); and, of course, sliced raw and eaten with cream. In season all year, widely available.

BEANS Available both fresh and dried.

Broad beans. A bean with a thick, fleshy pod, varying in size from $1\frac{1}{2}$ to $2\frac{1}{2}$ cm. (half an inch to an inch) in diameter. Shell and cook in boiling salted water to cover until just tender, about 10 to 20 minutes, according to size. Cool slightly, slip off the heavy skin, and serve with butter, or with oil, garlic and a touch of lemon juice.

French beans. Look for those that are firm, crisp and small. They should snap when you break them – and don't be afraid to test one in the market. French beans no longer need stringing. Just trim off the ends and cook whole in rapidly boiling salted water to cover until crisply tender – there should always be some bite left in them. Very young tender beans can be simply sautéed in a little butter. It's a good idea to cook more beans than you need and save some to have cold in vinaigrette (coated with the sauce, they last several days). Frozen green beans are acceptable, and tinned ones, rinsed off, are possible at a pinch.

Dried beans. All dried beans require either overnight soaking or the following quick treatment: Cover the beans with enough water to come $2\frac{1}{2}$ cm. (1 inch) above the top, bring to a boil, and boil 2 minutes. Turn off the heat and let stand in the water for 1 hour – no longer. Add salt, seasonings, extra water, if needed, bring to a boil again, and simmer until just tender, but not mushy. Drain and use for various recipes, such as baked beans, bean casseroles, bean salad (see page 59) and white bean and tuna fish salad (see page 316).

BEETROOT One of the few vegetables that is equally good tinned or fresh. Fresh beetroot bought in the market should be small and firm (large ones tend to be woody and tasteless), with the tops still on. (For cooking the tops, see 'Greens Primarily for Cooking'.) Never peel fresh beetroot before cooking, or they'll bleed to death. Cut off the stem $2\frac{1}{2}$ cm. (an inch) above the bulb and leave the roots on. Boil in salted water to cover until tender. Small beetroot will take 25 to 30 minutes, larger ones 35 to 40 minutes. Drain and cool a little until you can peel them by slipping off the skins. Leave whole if small, or slice or cut into thin julienne strips. Serve hot with butter or cold in salads, especially salads of slightly bitter greens such as endive or chicory that welcome the sweetness of the beetroot. Tiny baby beetroot take less cooking time and are usually served whole. Beetroot may also be wrapped in foil and baked in a 170°C (325°F, gas mark 3) oven for about the same length of time as for boiling. Test with a fork.

BLACKBERRIES The little wild blackberries that trail through the woods are full of flavour, though hard to pick, and make delicious pies, jams and jellies. Large cultivated blackberries are somewhat seedy but heavenly with sugar and cream, baked in pies, or puréed for sauce.

BROCCOLI In season most of the year. Don't be deceived just because it looks green. If the stems are thick and woody and the buds beginning to open, it is old. Look for tender young buds, tiny and tightly packed. I like to cook the buds, or flowerets, separately from the stems, cutting or breaking them off and cooking them in boiling salted water to cover until crisply tender, about 10 to 12 minutes, or steaming them. Serve dressed with butter, with hollandaise, or with olive oil and garlic, or chill and use in salads. For another meal, save the stems, peel, cut into fine julienne strips, blanch for 2 minutes in boiling water, drain, and sauté in butter for 2 to 3 minutes, until crisply tender. Also good combined with swede and turnip (see three-vegetable sauté, page 200). Broccoli also makes a lovely purée. Frozen broccoli, if not overcooked, merely blanched briefly in boiling water, is quite acceptable.

BROCCOLI RABE OR RAPE A more vigorously flavoured member of the broccoli family, with longer, thinner stems, small leaves, and tiny, open yellow buds, all of which can be eaten. The flavour is strong, slightly bitter, and the vegetable, boiled and puréed in a food mill or a food processor, is an interesting departure from the usual purée. Cook in plenty of boiling salted water for 10 to 12 minutes, or until crispy tender, drain, and serve whole or finely chopped with garlic and olive oil, or cold with vinaigrette sauce. Or chop coarsely, put into a frying pan with hot oil and a few garlic cloves, and steam until tender, covered, over low heat in just the water clinging to the leaves.

BRUSSELS SPROUTS A much maligned member of the cabbage family, probably because they are invariably served overcooked, soggy, and not fit for human consumption. Look for small, compact heads, not the large, loose ones. As with most vegetables, the smallest are the best. Trim off the stems and any discoloured leaves, and wash. May be served raw if tiny, tender and crisp, or sautéed (see page 194). Small frozen Brussels sprouts are good if blanched briefly in boiling salted water. They need minimum cooking. Tinned ones are to be avoided at all costs.

BUTTER

Salt butter. Even though the salt does help to preserve the flavour and quality, it is highly possible and fairly common to find strong-tasting, even rancid salt butter in stores. Buy in small quantities and, if the butter doesn't taste right, switch to another brand. If you buy in quantity, freeze the butter you are not using immediately.

Unsalted butter. Commonly referred to as sweet butter, it is more perishable than salt butter, but more delicate in flavour and by far the more desirable for cooking, especially for baking. Keep butter you are using in a covered container in the refrigerator away from strong-flavoured foods, or it will absorb the flavours very quickly. Freeze what you aren't using. One uses sweet butter for flavour, so keep it pure.

Clarified butter. Something you make, rather than buy. Melt sweet butter in a heavy pan over low heat, to prevent it from browning. The white froth that rises to the top should be skimmed off with a spoon, and the clear yellow 'clarified' liquid butter carefully poured off into a container, leaving the white curdlike dregs in the pan. Clarified butter will remain fresh for 2 or 3 weeks, so you may make it in quantity and use as needed. Use it for sautéing when you need high heat, and for delicate cakes such as génoise (see page 268).

CABBAGES   You'll often find in the markets not only the familiar green-to-white cabbages, but also red cabbages and the curly leafed savoy cabbages, which have a looser head. Both the green and red cabbages should have firm heads and fresh, unwilted leaves. The leaves of savoy cabbages should be crisp and dark green. Heads vary from $\frac{1}{2}$ to $2\frac{1}{2}$ kg. (1 to 5 pounds). If you use only part, cover the rest tightly with plastic wrap and refrigerate. Trim off the stalk and any discoloured or limp outer leaves. Cut into wedges, remove the hard core with a large sharp knife, and shred. Soak the shreds well in cold water for an hour to crisp. Drain well for coleslaw. To cook, shred or cut into wedges and either boil in plenty of salted water until crisply tender (about 5 to 8 minutes for shredded cabbage, 10 to 12 minutes for wedges) or braise. Blanched individual cabbage leaves may be stuffed and rolled (see *poule au pot*, page 33). For stuffing and cooking whole, savoy cabbage is best, as the leaves are easy to separate for stuffing (blanch the head first to soften them). Cabbage is a great friend of boiled dinners (see boiled corned beef and cabbage, page 24) and a classic combination with pork, ham, sausages and sautéed game birds, such as pheasant (see page 179). Braise red cabbage with apples, or with chestnuts (see page 161). Raw cabbage is used for coleslaw and other salads, with red and green sometimes combined for colour.

CARROTS   For best flavour, look for small young carrots, those sold in bunches with the feathery tops on. Old carrots have a woody core. Large carrots, which are what you find most of the time, should be soaked in water before preparing, to crisp them. To cook, trim the ends, scrape the carrots, then boil in salted water to cover, anywhere from 7 or 8 to about 20 minutes, depending on the size and the way you have cut them. Small carrots may be left whole; large ones can be sliced or cut into fine julienne strips. Don't overcook. Carrots may be roasted (see page 102), sautéed (see page 194), or poached *à la Grecque* (see page 62), and are excellent puréed, especially in combination with puréed potatoes (see page 61). They, of course, are delicious eaten raw, crisp and chilled. Tinned carrots are not very good – and why use them when carrots come fresh in the market all year?

CAULIFLOWER   Look for heads with firm, tightly packed buds that are snowy white, not yellow or discoloured. Wash well, cut off the heavy stem end and green leaves. Cook whole, stem down, or broken into flowerets, in lots of boiling salted water: 12 to 20 minutes for a whole head, depending on size, 5 or 6 minutes for flowerets. Do not overcook until dark and mushy. Serve dressed with butter, or cover with béchamel sauce, grated cheese, browned bread crumbs and bake until the cheese melts and the top browns. Cauliflower may be puréed after boiling, or sautéed after being parboiled, then sliced or chopped (see page 195). Flowerets may be cooked à la Grecque (see page 62) or used raw as a vegetable hors d'oeuvre, with a dip. Frozen cauliflower is acceptable, but I don't really recommend it.

CELERIAC   Also called celery root or knob celery. A large, knobby, brownish root vegetable. Cook in boiling salted water until tender, peel and purée (see page 61). Also good braised. Celeriac may be peeled raw (rub with lemon to prevent discolouring), cut into very fine julienne, and mixed with mustard mayonnaise for celeriac rémoulade (see page 310), a fine hors d'oeuvre. Difficult to find in some markets.

CELERY   Buy the green celery; it is tastier and crisper. Wash well to get rid of dirt at the base of the stalks and trim off the bottom and leafy tops (save tops for flavouring soups or stocks, or use in salads). Remove the coarse outer stalks; use for stock or mirepoix for braised meat (see page 140). Celery, to my mind, is better sautéed (see page 195) than boiled. The inner stalks, known as the heart, are delicious split and braised (see page 159). The tiny leafy stalks in the centre are good as a raw vegetable hors d'oeuvre or in salads. Tinned celery hearts are quite acceptable for braising and need only to be heated through.

CHEESE   Among the enormous and constantly growing range in the market today are some old faithfuls we cannot cook without. Cheese, whether for cooking, eating, or both, should be kept in the refrigerator (the warmer, not the colder part) tightly covered in plastic wrap or foil, or in plastic bags. If a cheese is to be eaten, remove and bring to room temperature an hour before serving.

Cheddar. This firm cheese can be sharp, medium sharp, or bland. Sharp is best for cooking. Be sure it is natural Cheddar, please, not processed. Buy mature Cheddar – it has the most flavour. Cheddar keeps well, and if you buy a whole wheel, it will last you several months. Grate or shred for soufflés (see page 233), cheese sauce (see page 287), or omelets (see page 193), or as a topping for baked dishes, or use for toasted cheese sandwiches and Welsh rabbit. And, of course, eat with salad or fruit, especially apples. **Cottage cheese.** In its many variations, the fresh soft cheese favoured by dieters. Try to find a natural cottage cheese, without preservatives (health-food stores have them). **Ricotta,** a very soft, light and creamy fresh cheese, is mostly used for Italian dishes such as lasagne and cannelloni, for cheesecake or cheese pie and other desserts.

Cream cheese. Soft fresh cheese mixed with cream to a smooth consistency, for cheesecakes, cheese pie, *coeur à la crème* (see page 329), salad dressings. It is bland and very receptive to strong flavourings such as chives, onions, and anchovies. Eat it with fruit, or with jam for breakfast or tea.

Gruyère. A cooking and table cheese with a fine-grained, rather firm texture and a few holes or eyes. Nutty aroma and flavour. Not to be confused with **Emmenthaler,** a similar Swiss cheese that has much larger eyes. The best comes from Switzerland, other versions from France, Austria and Finland. Sold by the piece. Never buy the processed Gruyère – it will not do the job at all. Used extensively in cooking because of its superb melting qualities. The only suitable cheese for fondue, and perfect for topping casseroles and gratinéed dishes, such as onion soup (see page 43), for soufflés (see page 233), quiches (see page 251) and other custardy dishes. A salad of Gruyère and olives (see page 315) makes a lovely summer lunch. Also to be eaten with salad and fruit, especially pears. Keeps well, wrapped in foil or plastic wrap. Should a slight mould form, cut it off; it will not affect the cheese.

Mozzarella. The Italian mozzarella is a super melting cheese which in its best version comes in bell-shaped pieces. Absolute hell to slice but essential for pizza, lasagne, aubergine Parmigiana and veal Parmigiana.

Parmesan or Parmigiana. A rock-hard, very pungent, sharp and slightly salty grating cheese, the very essence of Italian cooking. The ground version of Parmesan sold in jars is third rate and should be shunned save for emergencies. Imported Italian Parmesan, sold by the piece and, in some cheese stores, grated, is very expensive. Don't buy more than you need. Keeps well wrapped in foil or plastic, and may be grated in the food processor or liquidizer or on the finest side of a hand grater. Used more extensively than almost any other cheese, as a topping for pasta and gratinéed dishes, for soufflés (see page 233), quiches and other egg and cheese dishes, for Mornay sauce (see page 287), risotto (see page 51) and gnocchi (see page 55). A less costly substitute for Parmesan is **asiago**, a hard Italian skim-milk cheese with a sharp, piquant flavour.

CHERRIES For cooking, buy the tart Kentish cherries. They are best for poaching, pies, or as a garnish for meats and poultry. The large, lusciously sweet White Hearts and Bigarreaux are used for open-face flans and other desserts and, of course, eaten raw.

CHICKEN Fresh chickens are infinitely preferable to frozen. Some are of higher quality than others. If chicken is wrapped in polyethylene, remove it. Wrap loosely in greaseproof paper and refrigerate. Cook fresh chicken within 3 days. Estimate about 350 g. ($\frac{3}{4}$ pound) of chicken per serving, to allow for the bone.

Grilling chickens. Small birds, weighing around 1 kg. ($1\frac{1}{2}$ to $2\frac{1}{2}$ pounds),

should be split in two lengthwise by you or your butcher. Be sure to cut out
the backbone (see illustration, page 173) and the part that goes over the
fence last so the chicken will lie flat in the pan. Marinate before grilling, if
you wish, in red wine, oil, and garlic, or teriyaki marinade (see page 111).
Or push flavoured butter under the skin (see page 112).

Frying chickens. Birds weighing around $1\frac{1}{2}$ kg. or 3 to $3\frac{1}{2}$ pounds. The way
they are raised and fed affects the flavour and texture so shop around until
you find those most satisfactory to your palate. Use for fried chicken, for
sautés (see pages 172 and 174), fricassees, or for braised dishes such as *coq
au vin* (see page 155). Whole fryers may be roasted (see page 84) or
poached (see page 33). If, like me, you are a lover of dark meat, you'll buy
your frying or sautéing chicken in parts and get only legs and thighs. The
chicken-in-parts business has done us all a great service. The breasts may
be boned and sautéed (see page 174), deep-fried (see page 214), or
poached, chilled and glazed with aspic, and the less-expensive wings and
thighs used for sautés, fricassees, and casseroles.

Boiling fowl. The mature, fairly good-sized birds that give rich flavour to
our chicken stock have worked hard for a living producing eggs and need
long, slow cooking to achieve tenderness. The poached flesh is excellent for
chicken hash, creamed chicken and chicken à la king. Usually an
economical buy if you can find them. Nowadays we are more often forced
to buy expensive roasting chicken for stock and poached chicken dishes
such as *poule au pot* (see page 33).

Roasting chickens. Usually run $1\frac{1}{2}$ kg. to $2\frac{1}{2}$ kg. (3 to 5 pounds). They
should be plump and tender with a good amount, but not an overbundance,
of fat. It is difficult to find roasters larger than $2\frac{1}{2}$ kg. (5 pounds), but
occasionally you can find them in the frozen-poultry section, or frozen 4- to
$4\frac{1}{2}$ kg. (8- to 9-pound) capons (the desexed male birds), which are expensive
but beautifully meaty and tender. Chickens may be roasted stuffed (see page
86) or unstuffed (see page 84).

Poussins. Tiny birds weighing about 450 g. (1 pound). Serve 1 to a person.
Best split and grilled (see page 112) or stuffed and roasted (see page 87).

CHOCOLATE Most recipes call for bitter or semi-sweet chocolate and
occasionally for sweet. Shop around for uncommon brands (some shops
stock good imported cooking chocolate) and make a taste comparison with
the supermarket variety – there is often a vast difference. To melt
chocolate, put it in the top of a double boiler over hot water, or in a pan set
in a second pan of hot water, or in a dish in a 150°C (300°F, gas mark 2)
oven. If it seems to tighten up when melted, stir in a small amount (1 to
2 tablespoons) of hydrogenated vegetable fat to reliquefy. Chocolate keeps
well, if tightly covered with plastic wrap. If it 'blooms' (gets dusty-looking

on the outside), that is because of exposure to air; it doesn't mean the chocolate is stale.

CORN Naturally, the shorter the time from field to pot, the better the eating. Whenever possible, buy freshly picked corn and cook as soon as you can. Never buy corn with coarse, dry kernels. To check, peel down the husk and silk at the top (you can also spot any worm damage). To my way of thinking, corn on the cob should be put into cold water, just brought to a boil, without cooking further, and served at once with lots of butter, salt and pepper. Corn is often cut from the cob and sautéed, sometimes combined with other vegetables, such as chopped sautéed onion, green pepper, or cooked broad beans. Both frozen and tinned whole-kernel corn are most acceptable and can be used in many dishes.

CORNMEAL There are two grades of cornmeal, one quite coarse, the other rather fine. The coarse is best for polenta and cornmeal mush (see page 54) and the fine for corn bread (see page 261). Also excellent used like bread crumbs for breading sautéed fish, or for thickening casseroles.

CRACKED WHEAT A coarsely ground wheat, sold in health-food stores and in Middle Eastern stores, usually under the names bulghur or burghul. A nutritious alternative to rice, with a nutty texture and flavour. Fine-grade cracked wheat is best for uncooked dishes where the grain is merely soaked, such as *tabbouleh* (see page 316) and *kibbeh* (see page 321), medium and coarse grades for pilaf (see page 53) and cooked dishes. Also used in porridge and, in small amounts, in some breads, as a substitute for other ingredients.

CREAM Dairies in various parts of the country differ greatly in what they have to offer. The most commonly found forms of cream are:

Single cream. A very light cream with a lower butterfat content than double cream, which means it will not whip. Works well in sauces and soups and with fruits.

Double cream. This is the heaviest cream available, and may be whipped and used as a topping for desserts, or in mousses and other chilled or frozen desserts, such as orange Bavarian cream (see page 338). Unwhipped, it is often added to soups and sauces as an enrichment.

Soured cream. A cultivated product, rather thick in texture and slightly acid in flavour. Excellent on fruits and baked potatoes and in some soups, and good mixed half and half with mayonnaise for salads or coleslaw (see page 311). Traditional in Central European and Russian cooking, including such recipes as beef Stroganoff. If used in sauces, it should be stirred in slowly and with great care, and never allowed to come to the boiling point, or it will break and curdle.

Crème fraîche. Another cultivated cream, the famous French *crème fraîche* is high in butterfat. It makes a beautiful topping for fruits and desserts, and adds new quality to many sauces. It may be stirred into sauces such as béchamel, suprême and sauces for braised veal or fish, as an additional thickener. For a homemade approximation of *crème fraîche*, see page 301.

CUCUMBERS   Cucumbers range in size from the minute gherkins of late autumn, used for pickling, to the long, thin, bright green Chinese or English cucumber. Slice paper-thin and eat in sandwiches or salads or marinate in vinaigrette sauce. To cook cucumbers, peel, seed, cut into strips or oval lozenges, and poach briefly in salted water to cover, just until translucent. Serve with butter. Or blanch for 1 minute in plenty of boiling salted water, drain, and sauté quickly in butter, adding seasonings and perhaps a little cream. Cucumbers also make a delicious soup (see page 319).

DUCKS   Available both fresh and frozen. Frozen duck should be thawed before use (see page 95). Thawed ducks are pretty wet. Dry them well inside and out by rolling them in and stuffing them with paper towels. If you have an electric fan, blow it on the duck for a little while to help dry it out. Ducks vary in weight from $2\frac{1}{2}$ to $3\frac{1}{2}$ kg. (5 to 8 pounds), and have a thick layer of fat under the skin and not very much meat, so a $2\frac{1}{2}$-kg. (5-pound) duck will serve 4 only scantily. It is not too extravagant to gauge half a duck per person, whether you roast it (see page 95), grill it (see page 114), or braise it (see page 157). Be sure to prick the skin of grilling ducks well during roasting or grilling to let the fat drain out, and don't whatever you do, overcook the meat or it will be dry and tasteless. Don't discard the duck liver, either. This is a great delicacy. If you don't cook it with the duck, accumulate livers in the freezer until you have enough for a pâté or terrine, or some other duck liver dish.

Wild duck. A very different bird, with no thick layer of fat. While the breast is usually well-meated, the legs and thighs are less tender. Roast (see page 98) to taste, but don't overcook. Wild ducks are really hell to pluck. Try to find an accommodating butcher or, if you live in a community where duck hunting is common, someone who makes a business of plucking ducks during the season. Wild ducks weigh only $\frac{1}{2}$ to 1 kg. (1 to 2 lbs.). A small duck, such as teal, will serve 1; a large duck, 2.

EGGS   For the most part, the eggs we buy are produced on poultry farms, graded, packed and shipped to market. In country districts, or in some markets and health-food stores, you will be able to buy eggs from free-range (as opposed to battery-fed) hens. These tend to be richer in flavour and darker in yolk – and more expensive. Egg sizes range from the very small pullet eggs, not widely available, to small, medium, large and extra large. Despite what some people may tell you, there is absolutely no difference, in flavour or nutrition, between white eggs and brown eggs. Pick the colour that appeals to you. Unless a recipe specifies a certain size of egg, you can take it for granted that it should be the large size. Naturally, the fresher the egg when you use it, the better. It has been my experience that most supermarkets have a quick turnover of eggs, more so than the local grocery store where they may be left on the shelf for a longer time. Store eggs in the refrigerator, but don't let them hang around for months, getting stale and absorbing food odours and flavours. Buy them by the half dozen and use them up, unless you are a great egg eater.

For most recipes, it is better to remove the eggs from the refrigerator 30 minutes to an hour before using, to come to room temperature. Room-temperature eggs beat better and have greater volume. For mayonnaise, there's the likelihood that the sauce will curdle unless the egg yolks and oil are the same temperature. When separating eggs, be careful not to get whites in the yolks or vice versa, especially important for soufflés, where the oiliness of the yolks can prevent the whites' beating to their greatest volume (see page 233 for separating technique). If you need only whites for a recipe, store the yolks in a tightly covered jar in the refrigerator, or freeze them, first labelling the jar so you know how many are in the container. Egg whites freeze well. Put them in $\frac{1}{4}$ l. ($\frac{1}{2}$ pt) containers (8 to 11 egg whites, or 12 to 14 egg yolks, according to size, equal $\frac{1}{4}$ l. or $\frac{1}{2}$ pt). Use the egg whites for meringues (see page 272), certain cakes such as angel food, or for clarifying stock (see page 29); the egg yolks for emulsified sauces such as mayonnaise (see page 294), hollandaise, and Béarnaise (see pages 292–4), to enrich sauces (see page 287), and in rich custards such as crème brûlée (see page 130). For scrambling and omelets, beat eggs with a little water to lighten them.

FENNEL There are two kinds of fennel. One, correctly called Florence fennel, is cultivated and sold commercially. The other, less well known, is wild fennel. Florence fennel, a bulbous plant of broad, fleshy ribs with a strong anise flavour, is a cousin of celery. The rather feathery, dill-like leaves are sometimes used as a seasoning. The bulb may be halved or quartered and braised (see page 159); sliced or quartered and included in vegetable mixtures, such as ratatouille; poached *à la Grecque* (see page 62); or sliced and used raw, like celery, in salads and as a vegetable hors d'oeuvre. Wild fennel grows quite tall and the long stalks are dried and used as a flavouring. A dried fennel stalk may be thrust through a loin of pork before roasting, or a whole grilled fish may be placed over a bed of fennel stalks and flambéed with cognac – it takes on the taste of the burning fennel. You can buy packaged stalks imported from France.

FISH Many varieties of fish are caught around our shores and in our waters. Although it is harder to get a good selection of fish inland than in the coastal regions, you should always be able to find some of the more popular prolific types, either fresh or frozen. Whole fish should look and smell fresh and have bright eyes, shiny scales, and flesh that springs back when pressed with a finger. After buying, wrap fish in greaseproof paper or place in a covered dish and refrigerate. Cook as soon as possible. Estimate 150 to 225 g. ($\frac{1}{3}$ to $\frac{1}{2}$ pound) boneless fish per serving or 450 g. (1 pound) of whole fish, to allow for head, tail and bone.

Cod. A fish with rather coarse white flesh, less expensive than many others. Fresh cod can be bought whole, in steaks, and in fillets. Whole cod run from $2\frac{1}{2}$ or 3 kg. (5 to 6 pounds) to large specimens of 14 or 18 kg. (30 or 40 pounds). Cod may be poached, grilled, baked, and sautéed,. and is excellent cold. **Salt cod** is much used all over the world, especially by the Italians and Portuguese. The hard, dried, salted fillets must be soaked overnight in cold water to soften them and remove the salt, then drained, covered with fresh water, and simmered until tender, about 15 minutes. Serve with melted butter or béchamel sauce; or use in codfish cakes, soufflés, in a salad with potatoes, onions and vinaigrette sauce, or in other codfish dishes.

Haddock. Another coarsely textured fish, similar to cod, with excellent flavour. At its best poached or baked whole. Fillets must be handled carefully as they tend to break easily. Poach, grill, sauté, or bake them in aluminium-foil packages. Haddock takes kindly to strong flavours, such as onions, garlic and tomato mixtures. **Smoked haddock,** commonly known as finnan haddie, is a great breakfast favourite. Poach in milk and serve with parsley butter or béchamel sauce, or grill. Also good flaked and used for fish cakes and soufflés, like salt cod.

Halibut. A white-fleshed flat fish with a rather coarse texture and a pleasant but slightly bland flavour, which, to my mind, needs dressing up. It is very friendly to strong seasonings such as garlic, onion, capers, to herbs like rosemary and thyme, to olive oil and tomato sauce, and is excellent prepared in the Italian manner. Halibut comes in sizes from 3 to $3\frac{1}{2}$ kg. (6 to 8 pounds), known as chicken halibut, up to 45 kg. (100 pounds) or more. Usually cut into steaks. Steaks from halibut, cut $2\frac{1}{2}$ to 5 cm. (1 to 2 inches) thick, may be poached (see page 39), sautéed (see page 187), baked, or grilled (see page 121). Leftover halibut is delicious cold with vinaigrette sauce or mustard mayonnaise.

Salmon. A splendid though expensive fish, in fairly good supply throughout the country, either fresh or frozen. Fresh salmon in season is extraordinarily good, with rich but delicate flesh. When it is not available, frozen is quite acceptable. Whole salmon or large cuts of salmon may be poached (see page 39) and served hot with hollandaise, cold with mayonnaise, or glazed with aspic (see page 343). They can also be stuffed and baked, like other large fish. Salmon steaks are good almost any way – poached, grilled (see page 121), sautéed (see page 187), or baked. One of the more unusual ways to prepare salmon is to pickle it with salt and sugar for the Scandinavian *gravad laks* (see page 324). Salmon smokes and tins extremely well. The best smoked salmon comes from Scotland and Nova Scotia. Smoked salmon is a very elegant first course, sliced paper-thin and dressed with oil, lemon juice, capers and freshly ground pepper, but try it sometime slivered in a risotto (see page 51) or a quiche. Both choice and inferior cuts of salmon are tinned, so shop carefully. Only the best grades are worth the money tinned salmon costs these days.

Trout. An adaptable fish with delicate flesh. Large sea trout may be prepared like salmon. The small trout, usually served whole, with head and tail on, are handy little fish, for one is usually just enough for a serving. Brown or river trout and the fresh and frozen rainbow trout widely available throughout the country can be cooked in all manner of ways – poached, sautéed (see page 186), deep-fried, stuffed and baked, grilled in the oven or over charcoal, or poached, chilled, and glazed with aspic. Live trout, fresh from the stream or the tank, may be tossed straight into the pot and cooked *au bleu* (the skin turns blue and the fish curls up).

Fish fillets. Fillets are easy to prepare and satisfy those who shun fish with bones. Fillets come both fresh and frozen, varying from 1 cm. to 4 or 5 cm. ($\frac{1}{2}$ to $1\frac{1}{2}$ or 2 inches) in thickness, depending on the type and size of fish they are taken from. A tremendous amount of fish is filleted – cod, haddock, hake, plaice, sole, brill, turbot and many others. Lemon sole and plaice fillets break easily and are best poached (see page 41) or marinated for seviche (see page 323). Fillets of Dover sole and flounder can be stuffed and rolled for paupiettes; flounder or haddock fillets can be deep-fried (see page 213). Flounder, plaice and sole can be baked, grilled, sautéed, or fried. Haddock and cod, coarser in texture, lend themselves to any style of cooking.

FLOUR   There are many different types of flour on the market today, some generally available, others mainly sold by mail order or in health-food stores. Always use the flour specified in a recipe, if it is a type other than plain. Substitutions can ruin a recipe.

Plain flour. The most commonly used flour for cooking, for everything from sauces to cakes and cookies. It is a mixture of hard-wheat (high-gluten) and soft-wheat (low-gluten) flours and now comes both bleached and unbleached. I much prefer the unbleached, which retains more of the natural qualities and nutrition of the wheat, for breadmaking.

Strong or bread flour. A high-gluten flour used for certain breads. It makes a loaf with a firmer, tougher texture, similar to French and Italian breads. Use only if specified in a recipe.

Self-raising flour. Flour to which baking powder and salt have been added. Use only in recipes calling for this type of flour. Because it contains baking powder, which with age loses its leavening power, self-raising flour does not have a long shelf life.

Stone-ground flours. Flours from mills that grind the old-fashioned way, with millstones, rather than with modern steel rollers. They do not keep as well as commercial plain flour and should be stored in a cool place, or the refrigerator.

Wholemeal and wheatmeal flour. Wholemeal flour comes in different grinds, some coarser than others. Wholemeal flour is a whole-kernel flour that still retains the wheat germ, which white flour does not.

GEESE   Available both fresh and frozen. Fresh are at their best from October to February. Geese weigh from 3 to $5\frac{1}{2}$ kg. (6 to 12 pounds) and are the bearers of a good deal of fat. A 3-kg. (6-pound) goose will serve 4. A $3\frac{1}{2}$-kg. (8-pound) goose will serve 6 to 8. Geese are best stuffed with a fruit, crumb and chestnut stuffing (see page 93). Goose fat is useful in many types of cooking, particularly for sautéing potatoes.

GINGER   In its various forms, a spicy, sometimes fiery, accent for dishes – a major spice. Ground ginger, the least pungent, goes into spice cakes and gingerbread, and a touch adds an interesting fillip to codfish cakes. Fresh ginger root, subtler in flavour, enhances many marinades, such as teriyaki (see page 111) and most Oriental dishes. Look for young, plump, juicy ginger root. As it ages, it dries out and becomes woody, stringy and much hotter. Ginger root can be kept for quite a long time in the refrigerator if peeled and put into a small jar of vodka. The vodka, tasteless itself, takes on a spicy ginger flavour and can be used for seasoning. If you cut a piece of ginger root, wrap it tightly in plastic wrap and refrigerate. Candied ginger can often be substituted for ginger root if the sugar is washed off. Finely chopped, it is good for such things as teriyaki marinade, fruit compotes and syrups. Preserved ginger, in syrup, can also be used for fruit compotes and for ginger-flavoured ice cream (see page 349). Avoid dried ginger root, sometimes found in jars on the spice shelves of supermarkets – it is virtually useless.

GREENS FOR SALADS   Wash and dry thoroughly before using (see page 306), wrap loosely in paper towels, put into a plastic bag, and refrigerate. Before washing head lettuce cut out the core. Hold head, core side up, under running water; leaves will then separate easily. Salad spinners with a centrifugal action are good for drying lettuce. Use faded outer leaves of lettuce in stuffings for turkey, chicken and meat to add moisture and texture.

Round lettuce. Pale-green, deliciously tender head lettuce. Use in salads or as a garnish. Small leaves may be left whole, the larger ones broken with the fingers. Add coarse outer leaves, not good for salads, to soup stocks. Whole heads may be braised (see page 160).

Chicory. A small elongated lettuce with a tight head, blanched for marketing and carefully packed, so it requires little cleaning. Usually it is sufficient to wipe it off with a damp cloth and remove any discoloured outer leaves. Crisp in texture with a delicately bitter flavour. One of the choicest and most expensive salad greens. However, the heads have no waste and go a long way. Use leaves whole, shred, or cut into julienne strips or rings. The sweetness of chopped beetroot is almost a must with chicory salads. Separated leaves may be stuffed with various hors d'oeuvre mixtures. Braises or sautés beautifully.

Corn salad. A less common type of green with small tongue-shaped leaves, usually sold with roots attached. Flavour is tangy and 'wild'. Best combined with blander greens. Difficult to find in shops, but easy to grow.

Cos lettuce. Head lettuce with long, crisp leaves shading from bright green to yellow. Excellent texture and flavour. Recommended for salads that need a lot of tossing, such as Caesar salad, as it does not wilt. Break large leaves into pieces, leave small ones whole. Coarse outer leaves may be added to soups or shredded, blanched, drained, and added to a cheese soufflé mixture, to give a crunchy texture.

Dandelion greens. Commercially grown or wild dandelion leaves are excellent in salads, with a refreshingly bitter taste. Use alone or with other greens. Pick wild dandelions before the flowers form, dig up the root, and use the tender inner leaves.

Endive. A robust, crisp salad green with a slightly bitter tang. Best combined with other greens. Use the curly leaves for garnishing. May be braised.

Rocket. Small, flat-leafed greens with a bitter, slightly peppery flavour and rather coarse texture. Usually sold with the roots on. Wash thoroughly. Easy to grow from seed.

Watercress. Sold in bunches. Look for those with crisp, bright green leaves, not limp or yellowed. The small leaves have a refreshing bite and are usually mixed with other greens in salads. Watercress wilts quickly when dressed. A big bowl of plain watercress is good to munch on with steaks or chops. Or roll sprigs in soft white, buttered homemade bread for a lovely sandwich.

GREENS PRIMARILY FOR COOKING The leafy green tops of beetroot, kale, spinach, Swiss and rhubarb chard, and dandelion greens are all good cooked. Remove damaged or discoloured leaves and heavy stems and wash thoroughly. Boil, steam, or sauté. Cooking time depends on the age and coarseness of the different greens. Heavy, coarse greens like kale take longest to cook. A $\frac{1}{2}$ kg. or pound of greens will serve 2.

Beetroot greens. Wash, put into a heavy pan with just the water clinging to the leaves. Sprinkle lightly with salt. Cover and cook over medium heat about 5 minutes or until just wilted – the leaves will lose most of their water, reduce in bulk, and become limp. Turn once or twice with a wooden spoon or spatula so top leaves fall to the bottom during cooking. If water evaporates too fast and leaves show signs of sticking, add a very little boiling water. Drain, leave whole or chop, dress with butter, and serve with lemon wedges.

Chard. Swiss chard has green leaves and long white ribs. The less common rhubarb chard has red ribs and reddish-green leaves. Cook the leaves like beetroot greens, about 10 minutes. Cook the white or red ribs as a separate vegetable, like asparagus, in boiling salted water to cover until just tender. Serve hot with melted butter or hollandaise, or cold with a vinaigrette sauce.

Dandelion greens. Delicious sautéed with bacon. Fry squares of bacon in a heavy frying pan until the fat has been drawn out, add the washed and dried dandelion greens, and toss in the fat with the bacon, a little chopped garlic, finely chopped fresh mint and a touch of wine vinegar until wilted, about 5 minutes.

Kale. A heavy, coarse green with curly leaves. Best cooked in water to cover with a piece of ham or bacon for 1 hour. Drain and serve.

Spinach. A very versatile vegetable, with many uses in cooking. Buy fresh, loose spinach with crisp, undamaged leaves. Wash well in several changes of water to remove all the sand, and pull off the heavy stems. May be cooked in just the water that clings to the leaves, like beetroot greens, for about 5 minutes until wilted, or sautéed in oil (see page 197). Plainly cooked spinach may be puréed (try combining it with a purée of cooked watercress), or drained very well and chopped fine to use in spinach roll (see page 236), soufflés, crêpes, stuffings, quiche, or omelet fillings. Frozen spinach is an acceptable substitute, but it holds a great deal of water and yields less than fresh.

HERBS   With the vastly increased use of fresh herbs in cooking, herb-growing has become more popular and it is easier than ever before to find herbs, both cut and potted, in vegetable stores and supermarkets. There is no doubt that the herbs you grow and dry yourself are vastly superior to the packaged ones. If you do buy dried herbs, shop around for a good brand. Some companies powder their herbs too much. Look for large leaves with a strong perfume, such as the dried herbs from Provence, sold in many speciality shops. Dried herbs lose their potency very fast. Always keep them in a dark place, away from heat, and replace them frequently. Most dried herbs are improved by crushing, either in a mortar and pestle or in the palm of your hand with your thumb, before being added to a dish. Soaking them in a little wine also helps to release the flavour. When substituting dried herbs for fresh, the standard ratio is 1 teaspoon dried herb for 1 tablespoon chopped fresh herb. Some of the more essential kitchen herbs are:

Basil. The sweet basil used for cooking (there are also ornamental basils) is an annual that grows abundantly, with a deliciously pungent leaf. There are two types: the large-leafed basil and the tiny-leafed bush basil. Basil is the definitive herb for tomatoes, whether they are sliced as a salad (see pages 306 and 309), turned into tomato sauce (see page 49), or used in sautéed courgettes (see page 199) or salade Niçoise (see page 312). Ground with oil, garlic and pine nuts, it makes that most glorious of pasta sauces – the Italian pesto. Chopped fresh basil leaves give lovely flavour to a green salad. Basil is easy to grow on your windowsill.

Bay leaf. The dried leaf of the bay tree is essential in a bouquet garni and for flavouring stocks, court bouillon, marinades for game and meat, stews, and many meat dishes. It can also impart an unusual and interesting flavour to custard and some sauces. The imported Mediterranean bay leaf has the best and most lasting flavour.

Bouquet garni. Not a single herb, but a little bundle of herbs that flavour stocks and stews. Bay leaf, thyme and parsley are the usual assortment, tied with string to a stick of celery or a leek which holds them firmly together so the bouquet can be easily removed after cooking. Or the flavourings, perhaps with the addition of an onion and a clove or two, may be tied in a muslin bag. Sometimes a sprig of rosemary is included.

Chives. This slender green member of the onion family (see page 390) is one of the favourite herbs for salads, sauces, or garnishes for soups and vegetable dishes and is part of the classic fines herbes trio for an omelet (see page 193). Often mixed into cream cheese or cottage cheese, or the horseradish cream that goes with roast beef. Chives should be finely cut, not chopped, as their moist tubular stalks bruise easily. A hardy perennial for garden or flowerpot.

Coriander. Also known as Chinese parsley and, in Spanish, cilantro. Fresh coriander has pale-green leaves, rather like those of continental or Italian parsley. Much used in Chinese, Indian, and Latin-American cooking, coriander has had quite a vogue in the last few years, although some people find the strange, strong, distinctive flavour unpalatable. This is one herb you either love or loathe. Guacamole (see page 317) and seviche (see page 323) are dishes that depend for their flavour on freshly chopped coriander, which is more often sprinkled over food as a seasoning and garnish than cooked in a dish. Chinese, Indian and Greek shops have coriander. This is one herb that is always sold with the roots on. Do not remove. To keep, wrap, roots and all, in damp paper towels and store in a plastic bag or a covered glass jar in the refrigerator. Do not wash until ready to use. Coriander is easy to grow, but goes to seed quickly in hot weather. The dried seeds, which have an entirely different flavour, are much used in curries, and are excellent with pork and chicken.

Dill. Very popular in Scandinavian, Russian and Central European cookery. The dill sold in markets is mostly raised in hothouses. The branches are about 20 cm. (8 inches) long, extremely feathery, and highly aromatic. Garden dill goes to seed fast, especially in the summer. Dried dill seeds are a standby for pickles − in fact, for most of us, our first acquaintance with dill was the ubiquitous dill pickle. Finely chopped fresh dill leaves are good with fish, veal, chicken, vegetables such as sauerkraut, cabbage and boiled new potatoes, in cucumber salad (see page 308), soured-cream sauces, and soups. A whole bunch of dill is part of the curing ingredients for the Scandinavian *gravad laks* (see page 324). In most cases, dried dill weed, although not as flavourful as fresh dill, is an acceptable substitute.

Mint. Popularized in the form of mint sauce (see page 74) with roast lamb, which to my mind smothers the good flavour of the meat, mint, both fresh and dried, is used with great imagination in Middle Eastern dishes such as *tabbouleh* (see page 316) and cucumber and yogurt soup (see page 319). Mint is chopped and added as a flavouring and a garnish, rather than cooked. Use it in some salads, with cooked dandelion greens, on new potatoes and peas. An easily grown perennial − beware, it spreads like mad.

Parsley. Probably the most widely used of all fresh herbs − and the most easily available. There are 2 kinds, the familiar curly parsley that garnishes practically every platter, and the continental flat-leaf parsley, not as useful as a garnish (it wilts easily) but infinitely better for cooking, with a subtler, more refined flavour. Curly parsley is delicious fried in hot fat (see page 213) as a garnish for fish. Parsley belongs in a bouquet garni, in stocks, soups, stews, almost everything from salads to a chicken sauté. Parsley butter, like other herb or flavoured butters (see page 109), can be made in quantity, frozen, and put on cooked vegetables, a grilled steak, or grilled fish. Parsley keeps well in a plastic bag in the vegetable compartment of the refrigerator. A sturdy biennial, it will flourish in the garden for 2 years, then disappear.

Rosemary. A marvellously fragrant perennial that grows wild in great bushes in Europe, especially the south of France. Quite easy to grow and very ornamental, but best potted in cold climates as it cannot survive an icy winter. The sweet-and-bitter pungency of rosemary does marvels for roast lamb (see page 73), beef, chicken and turkey, but it is a powerful herb and must be handled with caution and never overused. The needlelike leaves are as good dried as fresh (or even better), but must be crushed before using.

Sage. Dried sage is most often used in sausage and in poultry stuffings, but a little can enhance pork, duck, goose and some beef dishes. Use sage with discretion; it can be unpleasant if overdone.

Tarragon. One of the most highly prized members of the family of herbs; French tarragon being considered the choicest. The pungent but light anise flavour of the long pointed leaves is highly complementary to sautéed chicken (see page 173) or rabbit (see page 178), roast chicken, veal, fish, poultry stuffings and egg dishes. A lovely salad herb, and the essential flavouring for Béarnaise sauce (see page 294). Always cut, rather than chop, the leaves. Tarragon is a perennial, usually grown from plants rather than seeds. After a few years, it will lose its flavour and have to be replaced.

Thyme. Next to parsley, the most useful of the kitchen herbs for stocks, soups, stews, marinades, bouquet garni, poultry stuffings, brown sauce, braised dishes such as shoulder of veal (see page 140), or a roast loin of pork (see page 79). There are very few savoury dishes that can't benefit from a touch of thyme, including beefsteak and kidney pudding (see page 35). There are various kinds of thyme, all easily grown as perennials in the garden or in pots. English and French thyme, very similar in flavour, are preferred for cooking. Lemon thyme has a distinct and pleasant lemony tang.

HORSERADISH A pungent root that carries a tremendously hot message. Freshly grated and combined with vinegar, or with soured or whipped cream, it is one of the greatest accompaniments for hot or cold roast or boiled beef. Also good with steak, ham, oysters, smoked trout. Excellent combined with applesauce and served with roast pork. Widely available ready-prepared in jars, but best if you buy the root and grate it fresh. Country markets and stores in Jewish neighbourhoods often carry horseradish root.

JERUSALEM ARTICHOKES These are no relation to globe artichokes but are another vegetable entirely, kin to the sunflower. They look like small, knobby new potatoes. Scrubbed, they may be boiled in their jackets in salted water to cover for 8 to 10 minutes or until just tender, peeled, sliced and dressed with butter, or puréed. Also good as a soup, or pickled. Sliced raw and used in salads they add an excellent, crisp texture.

KOHLRABI A small pale-green, slightly knobby, turnip-shaped root vegetable. Sometimes called cabbage turnip but with the virtues of neither. Not one of my favourites. Both tops and bulbous root may be eaten. The root is the better part. Buy small or medium kohlrabi. Remove tops, peel bulb, and slice thin. Put in a pan with a small quantity of salted water, cover, and steam gently until tender, about 25 minutes. Drain, dress with butter and season with salt and pepper to taste.

LARD Lard, the rendered fat of the pig, has fallen from favour of late. However, good lard, especially the pure and delicate leaf lard rendered from kidney fat, is excellent for baking, frying and sautéing. Pastry made with leaf lard is even shorter than pastry made with butter. An interesting fat for the kitchen.

LEMONS Brilliant yellow citrus fruit, irreplaceable in cooking. Fresh lemons, available all year, easily outdistance the artificial lemon juice and flavourings. The juice is an essential flavouring for hollandaise (see page 292), mayonnaise (see page 294), egg-lemon soup (see page 300), for pies, soufflés, cakes, ice cream and sherbet (see page 351). A squeeze of lemon in the butter for vegetables gives a zesty tang. In marinades for meat, game, or fish, the acidity of lemon juice is a tenderizer. Lemon juice or a cut lemon rubbed in the cavity of poultry or game birds freshens the meat and improves the taste. Lemon is used widely as a garnish and condiment for caviar, fish, all shellfish, veal and beef. The lemon zest, the yellow part of the rind, is added to many dishes, from frozen lemon mousse (see page 335) to Viennese goulash (see page 149), and it is an important part of the Italian garnish called *gremolata* (see page 154). To remove zest without pith, use a special tool called a zester, or a grater, or strip it off with a potato peeler and shred fine with a knife.

LIMES   Like the lemon, the green-skinned, green-fleshed lime is immensely valuable in cooking, for baking, marinades, as a flavouring for chicken, duck, or fish. Lime juice 'cooks' raw fish for seviche (see page 323). Tough of skin, the lime is best juiced with a small metal hand squeezer of the type used in bars.

MANDARINS   The mandarin, which originated in China, is a type of small orange with a soft, loose skin that peels easily. Tangerines belong to this family, as do satsumas, the type of mandarin orange found in tins, and hybrids such as the tangelo (a grapefruit-tangerine cross) and the temple orange (an orange-tangerine cross). Mandarin oranges and tangerines have a bouquet and flavour slightly different from a true orange and are excellent eating fruits. Mandarins make delicious sherbet. Tangerines can be made into jams and chutneys, and the sections are often used in salads. As with other citrus fruit, pick tangerines and mandarins that are heavy in the hand, which means they are full of juice.

MEAT   We have two categories of shops where we buy meats. One is the small private butcher, who cuts meats to order, and the other is the supermarket, which deals primarily with packaged, ready-cut meats, although many do have a butcher on the premises who will, on request, cut meat for you and order special cuts.

To buy packaged meats requires a working knowledge of the cuts most suitable for the various cooking processes and the difference between the more expensive and less expensive cuts (for instance, if you are making braised beef, you have a choice between the very lean topside or silverside and the fatter but less costly chuck). Once you know your cuts, you can start experimenting and use parts of the animal you never thought of before.

When buying meat cuts with a good deal of bone, estimate 450 g. (1 pound) per person. For cuts with a small amount of bone, 250 to 350 g.

($\frac{1}{2}$ to $\frac{3}{4}$ pound). And for boneless beef, 225 g. (8 ounces) is a generous serving, 150 to 180 g. (5 to 6 ounces) normal.

I personally feel that uncooked meat should be kept in the refrigerator no longer than 4 or 5 days. It should not be wrapped airtight, but have an opening at the end so the meat can breathe. Minced meat is best cooked the day of purchase because bacteria grow easily. Certainly it should never be kept in the refrigerator for more than 24 hours. Wrap like other meat. The freezer can be a great boon. When there are specials on meat, you can stock up on various cuts and refer to them as you would a library of books, knowing there is always something to cook in an emergency. I find the commercially flash-frozen meats to be equally as good as fresh, but on the other hand I have eaten a good deal of meat that has lost its savour and texture because it was carelessly wrapped and tossed into the freezer. If you freeze meat, wrap it well and tightly and store at a temperature of 0° or below.

Beef If you follow the chart above, you will learn a great deal about beef cuts and how to cook them. We will start at the head, wherein lies the **tongue,** excellent boiled and served hot with a sauce, cold in a salad, or thinly sliced for sandwiches. Then we go to the **shoulder** or **chuck** section. The individual cuts are blade steak and chuck steak. They may be bought bone in or boned and are braised (see page 137), stewed, pot roasted, and minced for hamburger. Cuts with a lot of bone can be used for stock and the boiled meat saved for hash. The rack of the **rib** section, from which we get rib joints usually contains 7 ribs. The 3 closest to the chuck are the least desirable because of excess fat. The next 4 ribs are the choicest and usually sell for a premium price. A rib steak or boneless rib eye steak cut from the ribs can be grilled or sautéed – pick one that is not too fatty. Under the rib cage is the **heart,** which can be stuffed and braised, or cut up and stewed. Stuffed heart is pretty good eating, but I prefer to use the smaller, tenderer veal or pork hearts.

Next to the rib is the **loin,** first the short loin, which furnishes the most expensive steaks, and then the sirloin. Lining the bone is the fillet, a boneless, fat-covered strip of meat that rates as the most expensive of all cuts but has practically no waste when trimmed. With the tiny tip removed it becomes a luxury joint that needs to be barded with fat or marinated before roasting (see page 77). Beef fillet is exceedingly tender but, for my taste, greatly in need of flavour enhancing. The fillet is also cut into steaks for sautéing or grilling. A châteaubriand is cut on the diagonal from the thickest part. Smaller steaks cut $2\frac{1}{2}$ cm. (an inch) or more thick are known as fillet steaks or tournedos. The most misunderstood term of all, filet mignon, rightly refers only to the tip of the fillet. Steaks cut from the smaller end of the loin, nearest the ribs, are first the porterhouse steak, which has none of the fillet; then the T-bone, which has a small amount of fillet.

The sirloin, which lies between the porterhouse and the rump, is not quite as tender because it includes the hip, a working part of the animal, but it is still excellent eating. Sirloin steaks contain different sizes and shapes of marrowbone and are good buys and should be grilled. Top sirloin steaks are cut from the largest part of the sirloin, a continuation of the top loin. The sirloin tip, a triangular, boneless piece trimmed from the base of the sirloin (technically, it is the part of the round nearest the sirloin), is usually sold as a joint or cut into steaks for sautéing or cubes for shashlik (see page 119) and kebabs. It costs less than the better-known cuts though, naturally, it isn't as tender.

Next comes the **rump,** sold as a joint or as steaks. Many people prefer the chewier but good-flavoured rump to the tenderer cuts. The **round,** the meat from the hind leg, is divided into the topside and silverside, the topside being the choicest quality. Though less tender than loin or rump, topside may be roasted if barded with fat, cooked quickly to the rare stage – this is the cut sold as roast beef in delicatessens – but it is more often braised (see page 148). Minced round, especially topside, makes good, lean hamburgers (see page 169).

The leg bone contains a great deal of marrow. Sometimes it is sold with the knuckle for soup bones, or it may be sawed into pieces and used for marrow-bones and *pot-au-feu* (see page 30). **Oxtail,** a very bony cut that yields a thick, gelatinous, flavourful broth, is excellent braised (see page 150).

Below the loin and the ribs are two pieces of rather flat, long-grained meat. The one closest to the loin is the **flank.** Flank steak, formerly considered only worthy of braising, makes perfect London grill (see page 110), especially if marinated first, then cooked very fast and close to the heat; a teriyaki marinade (see page 111) is particularly good. Next to the flank is the **plate** or **thin rib,** a less tender cut often used for boiling in conjunction with other cuts. Then comes **brisket,** much favoured for boiled beef. There is a fairly heavy coating of fat on either side, but the meat itself is juicy and full of flavour. Brisket is good braised (see page 146) and is considered the best cut for corned beef (see page 24). Now we come to the **shank** or **shin** of beef, the lower part of the fore or hind legs, cut in crosswise pieces. It has a great deal of gelatinous fibre and is an excellent cut for soup or stock (see page 30). Less tender than brisket for boiled beef, but very flavourful.

The offal and lesser-known cuts that are found in certain shops should not be ignored. They are usually a good buy. **Skirt steak,** for instance, similar in texture to flank, is very often rolled up and braised or, if you care to try, marinate and grill it like flank. Butt is a triangular piece of meat found between the sirloin and the short loin. One end is very tender and can be grilled; the other is much less so and should be braised or grilled. If it isn't labelled, ask your butcher to identify it. **Beef kidneys** are larger and less tender than veal or lamb kidneys. Never try to grill or sauté them, only braise. I always soak them in milk for 2 hours before using them, to draw out some of their strong flavour. **Ox liver** used to be extremely coarse and heavy and was shunned by most people. Now, with smaller cattle and shorter grazing and fattening time, ox liver is much more acceptable. Best braised or simmered in wine, but may be sautéed if it is sliced very thin and cooked very quickly (see page 170). **Tripe,** the lining of the stomach, varies in textures from that of a Turkish towel to a large honeycomb. Honeycomb tripe is considered the best. Although tripe is partially cooked before being sold, it still needs quite a lot of simmering to make it tender. Braise, stew, or pre-cook and grill. **Testicles** have a rich, heavy flavour and are regarded by some people as a great delicacy. They must be peeled and sliced before being grilled or sautéed.

Lamb. Good lamb with pinkish-red flesh and rather flaky, creamy-coloured fat is available throughout the country. In some areas and markets you may be able to buy the head, which should be split and either roasted or braised. **Lambs' brains,** while less well known than calves' brains, are equally good and may be prepared in the same ways, as may the very small **tongues,** which, if properly seasoned, make tasty and inexpensive morsels.

Neck is a good cut for stews and similar dishes. Sometimes it is included with the **shoulder,** a cut usually boned, rolled and tied for roasting, braising (see page 153), or poaching. Many people consider roast shoulder of lamb to have an even more delicious flavour than the leg. Middleneck chops are extremely bony, but well flavoured. Don't try to sauté them; grill or braise. The **rib** section is used in a variety of ways. The whole rack of ribs is a popular joint (sometimes 2 racks are tied together to make a crown joint). The ribs are cut into thick chops – when the rib bones are scraped to look fancy, they are known as Frenched chops. Best end of neck rib chops can be grilled (see page 115) or braised (see page 153). For a special dinner, the eye section may be removed from the rack, cut into thick slices, known as noisettes, and sautéed. Next to the ribs is the **loin,** the choicest part of the lamb. Here, as in beef, the bone becomes a T-bone, with meat on both sides of the bone: the tiny fillet, which is hardly ever removed, and the top loin. This part of the lamb is sometimes cut as a double loin, known as a saddle, and sometimes tied with the kidneys in. A whole saddle and the 2 legs as one piece is called a baron and is sometimes roasted for a large dinner party. Loin chops are grilled or braised, like rib chops. I find the flavour of **lamb kidneys** is better if they are soaked in milk for an hour or so before being grilled, braised, or used in steak and kidney pudding (see page 35).

The most commonly used cut of lamb is the **leg,** which can weigh anywhere from 2 to 3 kg. (4 to 6 pounds) according to the size of the animal. In many shops you can buy half a leg, either the knuckle (leg) end or the fillet or butt end, the part that is next to the loin. For roasting, I prefer not to have the knuckle bone cracked or the chump chops removed, as is so often done. A good butcher will remove the fell, the thin papery covering, from the leg. If he doesn't, remove it yourself (see page 72). A leg may be roasted (see page 72), braised, poached, or sliced for lamb steaks. Boned and cubed leg of lamb is the standard cut for shish kebab (see page 118), and the minced meat (or minced shoulder) makes the Middle Eastern dish *kibbeh* (see page 321).

Lambs' liver, while as delicate as calves' liver, is less appreciated and therefore less expensive. Cook in the same ways – sauté, grill, or roast whole. The humblest of the cuts is the **breast** . If not too fatty, it may be grilled to crispness over charcoal or under the grill and makes delicious eating, almost like spare ribs. The breast may also be stuffed and braised, stewed, or poached and devilled (see page 185). Lambs' **sweetbreads** from the neck, near the shank, are less common than calves' sweetbreads, and lend themselves to the same styles of cooking. Tiny, tender lamb **hearts** may be cubed and grilled like kebabs, or braised.

Pork. The pig is by far my favourite meat-yielding animal, for he is edible from snout to tail and provides an enormous variety of eating. Unfortunately, like many humans, the pig has been put on a diet within the last 10 years – and we have suffered because of it. The meat is less streaked with fat and less juicy and tender than before. Let's hope that the streamlined porker will not last forever.

We start with the **head,** the basis of brawn or headcheese, a highly gelatinous mixture of bits and pieces of meat from that area, which is one of the more popular cold meats. The **tongue** is of medium size, and 1 person could eat 1 or possibly 2 at a sitting. Tongue is often braised, sometimes boiled with sauerkraut. The **brains,** less often seen than calves' brains, may be prepared in the same way. **Pig's ears** have a chewy, gelatinous texture for which one has to develop a taste. I like them parboiled, crumbed and either sautéed or fried, or stuffed and braised.

Behind the head comes the **shoulder** and **fatback,** the plain white fat sold for larding meat, for barding (see page 78), and for lining moulds for pâtés. Below the fatback and before the loin comes the **spare rib** or **shoulder butt,** used fresh for braising, roasting and boiling, and also one of the choicest smoked cuts.

The **loin** is one of the best cuts. It extends from the shoulder to the leg and includes the rib and loin sections and the fillet. Rib chops are smaller and less choice than the loin chops, which contain a good piece of the fillet and are grilled, sautéed (see page 184), and braised. **Loin chops** cut extra thick may be split and stuffed before braising. The succulent fillet is sometimes removed and sold separately for sautéing, braising, or grilling. The loin is the most popular joint (see page 79), and the best for roasting is the **centre cut,** which contains part of the rib and part of the loin. It is also the most costly. The two end cuts of the loin are the blade end or rib end (sometimes cut into pieces and sold as thick, meaty ribs) and the sirloin end, the part next to the leg. The loin cuts may be roasted with the bone, or boned, rolled, and tied. For a crown roast, 2 loin roasts are tied together. Boned loin is also good for braising. Below the loin, more or less in the centre of the pig but extending right through, is the belly which is boned from the rib cage and smoked for **bacon** or salted for salt pork. Some is put down in a brine, or pickle, and sold as pickled pork. The **spareribs** themselves are roasted (see page 83), braised, or grilled. The **heart** is mostly stuffed and braised. The **tail** is a much neglected little delicacy that is sometimes cut deep into the animal, poached, and barbecued, or cut short with only a small bit of bone and boiled with sauerkraut.

The hind legs of the pig are sold as fresh hams or smoked hams, either whole or separated into the fillet end, that closest to the loin, and the knuckle end, closest to the foot. I prefer the knuckle end; it slices better. Fresh ham takes to roasting (see page 80) or to braising. Steaks from 1 to 5 cm. ($\frac{1}{2}$ inch to 2 inches) thick may be cut from the leg and boiled, sautéed, or braised. **Pork kidneys,** though rather hard to find, are tender and sweet and, to my taste, quite as good as other kidneys. Soak in milk for an hour before cooking. **Pork liver** can be sautéed, but is more often minced for pâtés and terrines because of its high fat content and excellent flavour. The front section of the pig includes the **shoulder** and **hand.** The hand may be cut in the shape of a ham, and is often smoked and sold as a picnic ham. It is excellent fresh, braised, boiled, or roasted. While the hand has a different bone structure from ham and is less simple to carve, the meat is well flavoured and it is a good, economical buy. If the hand is cut short, a piece of the leg about 2 or 3 inches long is removed. This is the **hock,** which contains some very edible meat covered by a thin layer of fat and skin. When boiled or braised (see page 154), hocks make a delectable dish, and the gelatin in the skin helps to thicken the liquid. Pork hocks are often lightly smoked and may be treated like smoked ham and served hot or cold. In some shops you will find **pigs' trotters,** cut long or short. Pork meat and other bits of the pig are, of course, turned into various kinds of sausage. Even the blood goes into the making of black pudding.

Veal. The best veal is pinkish-white, an indication that it is very young. Most of the veal sold is admittedly costly but worth the money. Because of its youth, veal has very little fat and needs some moisture in cooking. Usually it is better braised than roasted or grilled. This is also one of the most gelatinous of the meat animals, and the bones and bony cuts are ideal for stocks, aspics and meat jellies.

The **head** is a great delicacy; in France it is boiled and served as *tête de veau vinaigrette*. The small and extremely tender **tongue** is delectable braised, especially in the Italian manner, with tomato sauce, and is often incorporated into terrines and pâtés. **Calves' brains,** by far the best of the animal brains, are usually blanched about 15 minutes in slightly acidulated water, then sautéed, but they are also extremely good poached, sliced and served cold with vinaigrette sauce.

Bony veal **neck** is used extensively for stock (see page 30). The pieces of meat from the bones make lovely jellied veal (see page 30). Veal **shoulder** is generally boned and braised (see page 139). Eat hot or press under a heavy weight and serve cold, with the natural jelly around it. Use boned, cubed shoulder meat for stews and braised dishes. Middle neck cutlets, while not the most desirable, braise successfully. I don't recommend sautéing them. Veal **loin** and **saddle** (the saddle comprises the 2 loins and part of the legs) is the tenderest part of the animal. A rolled and tied saddle, boned or bone in, sometimes with the kidneys included, is a luxurious and spectacular joint for a special dinner party. A joint of best end of neck cutlets is called a rack. A loin may be roasted whole, with or without the bone, or cut into thick chops for sautéing or braising (see page 144). If the chops are grilled, baste well with butter or oil to prevent the meat from drying out. The **kidneys** are very delicate and lend themselves to grilling, (see page 117), braising, and sautéing (see page 182). Never overcook or they will toughen. Kidneys should still be slightly pink in the centre. **Rump** of veal is an excellent joint for roasting and for making escalopes.

The **leg** is prepared in many different ways. It may be roasted (usually after being boned and tied), or braised, or sliced into veal cutlets. Steaks may be cut across the leg, either bone out or with the tiny round bone left in. Smaller, thinner pieces of veal leg, cut as scaloppine or veal escalopes and pounded thin, are usually sautéed (see page 181) or braised as veal birds (see page 144), although they are occasionally deep-fried, as Wiener schnitzel (see page 215). The **breast,** boned or bone in, is an excellent cut for stuffing and braising (see page 141) and for stews. There's a famous Italian dish, *cima di vitello*, for which the stuffed breast is wrapped in a cloth and poached, then braised and eaten cold. The breast meat has a rather long grain and an interesting texture. The bones from both the leg and the breast are much valued for stocks, as is the highly gelatinous **knuckle.** The **shin** or **shank**, which adjoins the breast, is commonly braised for such dishes as the Italian *osso buco*, or it may be used, like the neck, for jellied veal, once a very popular summer dish. Although **calves' feet** are pretty hard to come by these days, if you find them they make a delicious dish when poached and served with a sauce poulette, hollandaise, or Béarnaise. Highly gelatinous, the feet are much sought after for stock.

Calves' liver and sweetbreads are the most delicious and prized of all. Veal sweetbreads may be blanched in boiling water for 12 minutes. They are then plunged into ice water and, when cool enough to handle, excess fatty pieces are removed. Sweetbreads are often placed in between 2 plates and weighted down before cooking. The liver may be sliced thick and grilled rare (see page 117); sliced thin and sautéed quickly; rolled, tied, barded with bacon, and roasted rare, to be served with mustard sauce; or cut into pieces and deep-fried, along with kidneys, brains and thin pieces of veal, for an Italian *fritto misto* (see page 208). Veal **hearts**, which weigh about 450 g. (a pound), lend themselves to braising. Minced veal goes into certain sausages, such as bockwurst and bratwurst, and is important in the making of pâtés and terrines. Because of its lack of fat, it makes a very dry meat loaf unless combined with fattier meats such as pork and beef.

MELONS Some of the members of this large family are seasonal. Others are widely grown and can be found in the markets throughout the year. Melons are one of the hardest fruits to pick out. If you have a trustworthy fruit dealer, ask him to select a melon for you; he should know more about judging ripeness than you. If the melon you buy is less than ripe, leave it at room temperature until it ripens. A ripe melon will keep for a week in the refrigerator, 2 to 4 days if cut and tightly covered with plastic wrap. Leave the seeds in a cut piece; it helps to keep the flesh moist.

Cantaloupes. Melons with webbed skin and orange flesh. Extremely sweet and pungent at their best, tasteless at their worst. While not as desirable as other melons, cantaloupes are the most easily found. Halve and eat for breakfast, as a dessert, or cut into balls for a fruit compote.

Charentais. Small round melons with a yellow-green skin and faintly scented orange flesh.

Honeydews. White-skinned, green-fleshed melons that nine times out of ten are quite dull. The tenth time they can come right out and surprise you. Good used in combination with other varieties in a melon-ball compote.

Ogens. Yellow to orange skinned melons with faint green stripes. The flesh is pale yellow and sweet.

Watermelons. Round or oblong in shape, brilliant green on the outside and pure watermelon pink on the inside, these are the quintessential American melons, with a luscious, liquid sweetness that is positively addictive. Pick one up and thump it with your knuckles. If it sounds hollow and resounding, it is probably full of juice. Best eaten very cold on a hot day. Good for sherbet. The leftover rind makes highly prized watermelon pickles. To gild the lily (or watermelon), fill it with liquor for drunken watermelon (see page 329).

MUSHROOMS Cultivated mushrooms need no peeling and usually no washing – just a wipe with a damp cloth. Should mushrooms look dusty or dirty, toss under running water in a colander and dry well before cooking. Sauté sliced or whole mushrooms quickly over fairly high heat in butter, or butter and oil, seasoning them with salt and pepper. Use alone, or combine with other vegetables, such as green beans or turnips (see page 196). Cook mushrooms soon after buying; they discolour and shrivel if stored more than a few days. Discoloured mushrooms (often sold off at a lower price in markets) may be made into duxelles, a delicious mushroom paste. Chop very fine, stems and all, squeeze dry in a towel, and sauté slowly in butter (225 g. or ½ pound for 1 kg. or 2 pounds mushrooms) with a finely chopped shallot or garlic clove, stirring occasionally, until dry and dark in colour. Season with salt and pepper. Duxelles will keep for a week or two in the refrigerator or may be frozen in small quantities. Add some to scrambled eggs, omelets, vegetables, sauces, stuffings, or spread on toast as an appetizer with drinks. Use raw firm mushroom caps for salads (see page 308), grill (see page 125), or cook à la Grecque (see page 62).

Dried mushrooms, imported from Europe and the Orient, are wild, not cultivated, varieties, with a totally different taste. Soak in warm water, or in wine, to rehydrate, then drain and chop or slice. They don't have the texture of fresh mushrooms but bring delicious flavour to stews, soups and certain meat dishes.

MUSTARD A universal and widely used spice of varying degrees of hotness and pungency. Available in two forms: dry mustard or mustard powder and prepared mustard of different types, strengths, and flavours. Most of the good prepared mustards, like the Dijon mustards, come from France. Some contain coarsely ground mustard seeds; others are perfumed with herbs such as tarragon, dill, or thyme, spiced with green peppercorns, or mixed with wine. These mustards are delicious with meats, in certain sauces, and for dishes where mustard is the main flavouring, like the classic French *lapin à la moutarde*. Sometimes kidneys or liver are coated with mustard before being grilled. German mustards mostly ally a little sweetness to their bite and are excellent with pork, ham and sausage dishes. Use dry or prepared mustards to flavour sauces, dressings, mayonnaise.

NECTARINES Fruits that look like fuzzless peaches, with golden flesh and a lovely aroma that sometimes belies their flavour and ripeness. Look for well-fleshed fruits, not too hard, or they will take a long time to ripen. Best eaten as a dessert fruit, with no accompaniments.

NUTS Today, most nuts sold for cooking purposes, such as baking, stuffings, and garnishing, are already shelled. They come either whole and blanched (with the skins removed) or unblanched, sliced, chopped, or broken into pieces. In supermarkets, nuts are sold in glassine or cellophane bags or vacuum cans, but if you use a lot of nuts and can locate a store where they are sold in bulk, you can save an amazing amount of money. Why pay for packaging? Bulk nuts (or any nuts apart from those in the shell or in sealed vacuum tins) keep better if put in plastic bags and stored in the freezer. Exposure to heat turns the oil in nuts rancid. Distributors of nuts always keep them at freezing temperatures because they hold better, so unless you are using them right away I strongly recommend that you store them in the freezer. Thaw at room temperature before using. You can chop whole nuts by hand with a chef's knife, but it is infinitely faster and easier to chop or grind them in a food processor or liquidizer, if you own one.

Almonds. The nuts we use most in cooking and as a garnish for sautéed fish (see page 187) and vegetables – either the long Jordan almonds or the California almonds, which are interchangeable. You can buy almonds unblanched or blanched and whole, thinly sliced, slivered, or chopped, and toasted. To blanch almonds in the skin, plunge them into boiling water, remove after thirty seconds, and when cool, rub the skins off between thumb and forefinger. Unless a recipe requires pure white, blanched almonds, I think a little toasting for 10 minutes or so in a 180°C (350°F, gas mark 4) oven, either before or after cutting, improves the flavour of almonds – and most other nuts. Should a dish require a strong almond flavour, intensify it with one or two drops of almond essence.

Brazil nuts. These very large nuts are sold whole or sliced, and semi-blanched (with part of the brown skin on). Blanch if you wish. To slice them yourself, soak whole nuts in boiling water for 30 minutes to soften them up. Also improved by toasting at 180°C (350°F, gas mark 4), for 15 to 20 minutes.

Filberts or hazelnuts (two names, but the same nut). These have heavy skins, and I strongly advise blanching them, or rubbing them vigorously between towels – it is amazing how much skin will come off. Available whole, sliced, or chopped, and also improved by a slight toasting.

Peanuts. Need no blanching since the skins rub off easily. Unless you buy raw peanuts, they are already roasted and need no further toasting. Be careful when chopping them in a liquidizer or food processor not to overdo it, or they will turn into peanut butter. If that should happen, add a little salt and oil and enjoy your own good homemade product.

Pine nuts. The tiny kernels of certain pine cones, they are probably the least known of all nuts. The thin, tapering pignolia nut is sold shelled and blanched. A very oily, delicately flavoured nut, it is improved by toasting for 10 minutes at 180°C (350°F, gas mark 4). May be used in stuffings for poultry (see page 89) and vegetables (see page 274), and in casseroles and various other dishes.

Pistachio nuts. The most distinctive because instead of being white-meated, like other nuts, they are pale to medium green in their natural state (avoid those that have been dyed red). More often used for decoration, because of their lovely colour, than as an ingredient, although there are several cakes and a pistachio bread that include them in the batter. When bought shelled, they are usually salted, but the small amount of salt can usually be rubbed off and what remains is hardly noticeable. Pistachios are fairly easy to shell, because the nuts crack on one side during the roasting process. Extremely expensive but cheaper bought in bulk.

Walnuts. Usually bought shelled, in halves or broken into pieces. The contours of walnuts make them hard to blanch, but it can be done. Toasting at 180°C (350°F, gas mark 4), for 15 to 20 minutes gives walnuts a different and better flavour. Next to almonds, the most popular nut for pastries, breads, cakes, cookies and as a garnish for vegetables (see page 199) and fish. Salted and toasted they are a popular and addictive snack or cocktail nibble.

OIL   A kitchen staple that varies enormously in quality, taste, and price. The finest oil, to my mind, is olive oil. One finds eight or ten different qualities, from the very rich first pressing, called 'virgin olive oil', down to the low-quality oil made from the final pressing of fruit and cracked stones. The best and most flavourful, fruity olive oil comes from Provence, in the south of France. After this I would rate the better Italian and Greek oils and then the Spanish and North African. Buy the best you can afford and store it carefully. Olive oil should not be kept in the refrigerator (when refrigerated it turns thick and cloudy); if the weather is warm or the oil is left open for a long time, it can turn rancid, so buy in small quantities unless you are a liberal user. The vegetable oils (corn, soyabean, groundnut) are mostly flavourless and odourless – to my mind too tasteless for salads, but practical, inexpensive, and highly efficient for deep-frying, sautéing, mayonnaise, marinades and general cooking. Groundnut oil is my preference. Two other oils which have come into great favour in the last few years are safflower and sunflower oil. Both are very light, flavourless, and acceptable for frying, sautéing, baking and certain pastries.

ONIONS   The members of this family see more service in the kitchen than any other vegetable. They range from the dry yellow, white and red onions to small brown shallots, spring onions, leeks, garlic and chives. When bought, dry onions, garlic and shallots should be hard and firm, with no soft spots or green sprouting tops. Buy as needed and store in a cool, dry place. Refrigerate spring onions, leeks and chives.

Yellow globe onions. Sometimes called Spanish onions. General-purpose onions with brownish-yellow skin, either large or medium size. Excellent raw, baked, boiled, braised (see page 162), deep-fried (see page 210), or in soup (see page 43). Used in many dishes, chopped or sliced.

Large white onions. Sometimes called Bermuda onions, though they no longer come from that island. Mild and sweet, excellent deep-fried or for salads.

Small white onions. About 4 to 5 cm. (1½ to 2 inches) in diameter. Fairly mild. Excellent whole in stews and braised dishes, such as *coq au vin* (see page 155) and *boeuf à la mode* (see page 146). Smaller ones may be prepared *à la Grecque* (see page 62). If dropped in boiling water for 3 to 4 minutes, the skins will peel off easily. Tinned white onions are acceptable, if not overcooked.

Pearl onions or pickling onions. Very tiny white onions, usually pickled but also good for garnishing dishes.

Red or Italian onions. Exceptionally sweet and decorative onions, delicious raw in sandwiches and salads (see avocado, onion and grapefruit salad, page 315).

Spring onions. Fresh young onions with a white bulb and leafy green top, harvested while immature. Those with thin white bulbs are to be preferred to the rounder, thicker ones. Trim off the root end, all but 2½ to 5 cm. (an inch or two) of the green tops, and the outer layer of skin before using. Cook quickly in boiling salted water to cover, like asparagus, and serve with hollandaise, or cook *à la Grecque* (see page 62). Chop and sauté for use in various dishes. May be used in place of shallots. Eat raw in vegetable hors d'oeuvres and salads.

Leeks. Somewhat similar in appearance to spring onions, but much larger, with darker, coarser green tops. Known in France as 'poor man's asparagus'. Trim off root end and all but about 2½ cm. (an inch) of the green top, wash thoroughly, running water between the leaves (slit the top, if necessary) to remove the gritty sand lurking between them. Widely used as a flavouring, an aromatic vegetable in soups, stews, and braised dishes, traditional in *pot-au-feu* (see page 30). Good poached *à la Grecque* (see page 62), braised, or boiled and served with vinaigrette sauce.

Shallots. Sometimes called the aristocrat of the onion family, these small bulbs of cloves covered with papery brown skin have a subtle flavour, more pungent than onion, more delicate than garlic. A little goes quite a long way. Chopped and sautéed, they are an important flavouring for many dishes, from sauces such as Béarnaise, Bordelaise and diable (see Thickeners and Liaisons chapter) to sautéed chicken (see page 174). Much used in French cooking.

Garlic. The most pungent member of the family. Widely used in soups, sauces, salads, braised dishes, sautés and as a seasoning for joints, such as leg of lamb (see page 72) or pork loin (see page 79). Always use cloves of garlic, never garlic powder or garlic salt, which have an ersatz flavour. Look for full, firm, heavy heads and buy garlic loose, not packaged. The packaged kind is frequently old and stale. Buy only as much as needed and use quickly. To peel, either drop in boiling water for 5 seconds to loosen the skin, or bruise the clove slightly with the flat of a large knife blade, which splits the skin. Chopping garlic with a touch of salt prevents it from sticking to the knife blade. In sautéing, do not let garlic brown or burn or it will turn bitter. Garlic cloves cooked whole in their husks, either in liquid or in a sauté, add flavour but lose their strong pungency and become delicate, mild and buttery-soft. Squeeze the garlic out of the husk after cooking.

Chives. Herbs that are also members of the onion family, with a delicate onion flavour. Sold cut or in pots – the more you cut chives, the better they grow. The blue chive flowers have an intense onion flavour and can be tossed in salads. Chop chives and use in fines herbes mixtures for omelets (see page·193), in scrambled eggs, cold soups, salads, herbed mayonnaise and dressings, on sliced tomatoes, or anywhere their bright colour and zippy flavour are appropriate.

ORANGES Smooth-skinned oranges, the Spanish or Valencia type, are most favoured for juice. Navel oranges have a more brilliant colour than Valencias and usually a thicker, pithier skin. They are better for slicing, sectioning, and general cooking, extremely good for candying and glazing, or for eating out of hand. Try to find oranges that are not waxed. Pick those that are not over-ripe or scarred or have soft spots. They should be firm and heavy in the hand, which means that they are full of juice (this applies to all citrus fruits). Combine oranges with onions for a salad. Use the juice and/or grated rind as a flavouring for soufflés (see page 238), sauces, glazes, frozen desserts, Bavarian cream (see page 338), the fruit for open-face tarts. Section or slice oranges for fruit salads, compotes.

PAPAYAS A tropical fruit with brilliant orange flesh, round black seeds, and an extremely delicate, unusual flavour and texture. Known as pawpaw in the West Indies, where it is also cooked, when green and unripe, as a vegetable. Fully ripened, soft-skinned papayas are the best buy. Serve chilled, halved and seeded, with a wedge of lime, or as a first course with prosciutto, like melon. Delicious in fruit salads or, puréed in a liquidizer or food processor, for ice cream and sherbet.

PAPRIKA Paprika can easily fool you – it looks like red pepper, but it's not. Nor was it created to garnish food and look pretty, as some people think. Paprika is a spice in its own right. The finest comes from Hungary, where it is much used in dishes such as paprikash and goulash (see Viennese goulash, a slightly different version, on page 149), in sauces, and in salad dressings. There is also. a paprika from Spain. coarser in texture and flavour, that I favour a great deal for Spanish recipes. The spice is ground from a variety of capsicum peppers, some of which are sweet, others hot – in some cases, almost as hot as cayenne pepper, from another capsicum variety. A very perishable, heat-sensitive spice, paprika should be kept in a tin, never a glass bottle or shaker, preferably in the refrigerator. If you are purchasing paprika in bulk from a spice shop, you may be asked if you want the sweet or the hot variety – sweet paprika is what is called for in most recipes, unless otherwise specified.

PARSNIPS   A much maligned creamy-coloured root vegetable, long and tapering in shape. Sweetish in flavour and extremely good boiled, puréed, and mixed with plenty of butter and a little madeira (see page 62). Can be used, sparingly, in soups, stews and boiled dinners, or in the *mirepoix* for braised meats. Look for firm, good-sized roots. In season all winter long.

PASTA   Pasta is one of the three or four most popular foods in existence, and as versatile as any single food can be. The Chinese had noodles; the Italians perfected pasta. In one form or another it has gone the rounds of most of the major Eastern and Western countries. Nothing takes more readily to seasonings and flavourings, and it can be anything from a first course or main dish, with a sauce, to a salad, a soup, or a dessert. Nowadays, with the aid of an electric or hand-operated pasta machine, it's easy to make your own pasta fresh, dry it briefly, and cook it right away – fresh pasta takes only a few minutes to cook, much less than the commercial, dried type. You can also, in some towns, buy pasta from shops that make it fresh. There are many, many brands of dried pasta, and you should shop around until you find one to your liking – the imported Italian pasta is usually the best.

   In dried pastas, we have the various round, straight ones, starting with the very small spaghettini, which can be used generally with any of the spaghetti sauces, from the simplest of all, which is just melted butter and grated cheese (see page 47). Then you have a larger spaghetti and macaroni of various sizes and shapes, from the small elbow macaroni to larger, straight macaroni to the huge ziti. Pasta comes in dozens of other shapes; some are like little seashells (conchiglie) or butterflies (farfalle). The cooking time for dried pastas varies according to shape and size. Naturally, the thin spaghettini cooks faster than the large macaroni and the small seashells faster than the large ones. This is something you gauge from the package directions and your own experience and preference – whether you like your pasta cooked to the traditional Italian *al dente* stage, still firm to the bite, or cooked to a mushy paste. Pasta should always be cooked in a large pot in ample amounts of salted water kept at a rolling boil throughout the cooking period (see page 47). After 6 minutes, taste often until it reaches the degree of doneness you prefer. Drain at once, if you wish, you may rinse the pasta with hot or cold water and then with hot water again. If you are going to serve the pasta on individual plates, toss it with a spoonful or two of oil first so it doesn't stick together, then add the sauce. However, I have come to like the modern Italian way of saucing pasta (see page 47), in which the cooked pasta is marinated in the hot sauce for 2 or 3 minutes and tossed well with 2 forks so that it becomes imbued with the flavours. Pasta is usually served with grated Parmesan, Romano, or asiago cheese, save for seafood pastas and one or two others that are best without it – though that, too, is a matter of personal taste.

PEACHES The sweet, tender, and perishable peaches that used to abound in our markets have been almost ruined by modern growing and shipping practices. Now peaches may look beautiful, but they are hard-hearted under the skin. Naturally, try to find soft-fleshed ones. Take advantage of the two to three weeks when local tree-ripened peaches may be found. Early white peaches, if you can find them, are pure nectar. Simply chill and slice; eat with sugar and cream. The later, golden-fleshed peaches are good this way, too, or with a raspberry purée (see page 327). They are superb in ice cream (see page 350), and for preserves or tarts. Peaches may be grilled (see page 128), baked, or poached (see page 64) with the addition of a little lemon or vanilla for flavouring, and make a great dessert. Poaching is a good way to treat hard peaches. For certain cooked dishes, such as roast duck with peaches (see page 95), a firm tinned variety may replace the fresh.

PEARS Like peaches, pears for the market are picked too green and are artificially ripened. They never approach the lusciousness of tree-ripened fruit. If you find pears that are soft and ripe to the touch, rush them home and eat them at once. The Bartlett or Williams pear, bell-shaped and yellow, is the earliest, on the market from July to November. At its best, it has an indescribable perfume and wonderful flavour and texture and is delicious eaten raw or poached. Later come the Conference, brown or russet colour with a tapering neck; the large Comice, yellow or greeny-yellow, splashed with red; and the brown Winter Nelis, all artificially ripened. However, all these pears poach extremely well (see page 64), and most of them bake well. Baked pears are usually not peeled, just halved, cored and baked with brown sugar and a clove or two for about an hour in a 170°C (325°F, gas mark 3) oven. The result, when cloaked in double cream, is pretty spectacular. Pears make interesting tarts and fritters (see page 211), and are good sautéed (see page 201). They are very friendly to cheese – Roquefort, Brie, Camembert, and practically all of the fine cheeses are good companions for pears.

PEAS

Green peas. When buying fresh green peas in the market, break open a pod. The pods should be juicy, crisp and bright green, and the peas inside small, green and tender. Avoid peas that are large, pale and starchy, with old, dry-looking pods. To cook, shell and boil briefly in salted water to cover, just until tender (time depends on size and age), then toss with butter. Or braise with lettuce leaves (see page 162). This is one vegetable that freezes well. Often frozen peas are better than fresh. Choose the tiny frozen peas and never follow the package directions or you will have stewed peas. Merely heat them through with butter to keep that nice crisp freshness.

Mangetout. Once a delicacy confined to Chinese restaurants, these edible-pod peas are becoming more generally available. Buy very young, when the pods are flat and the peas undeveloped. Test by breaking one. It should snap easily and have no strings down the sides. To cook, trim the ends and boil in salted water to cover for just a minute, until merely blanched, so they stay crisp. Drain and toss with butter. Or sauté sliced mushroom caps in butter, cut mangetout into julienne strips, and toss with the mushrooms for less than a minute, until they turn bright green. Add more butter, season with salt and pepper, and serve. They may also be cut into julienne, tossed quickly in butter, and added to lamb or beef stew at the last minute, as a garnish. Frozen mangetout are passable, but they lack the delicious crispness of the fresh.

PEPPER   Pepper is a funny spice, really three spices in one, each with a different flavour. Peppercorns are the berries of the tropical *Piper nigrum* vine and no relation to the vegetable, capsicum pepper.

Black peppercorns. The dried berries – the ones we use most generally. They are sold whole, to be ground in a pepper mill, or cracked or ground by spice companies. As with other spices, best ground fresh.

White peppercorns. The black peppercorns minus the wrinkled black outer layer – and minus much of the flavour. Some people feel it is more refined to use white pepper in a white sauce or dish so that you don't have black specks. To me white pepper is unpleasant, acrid, and lacking in flavour. Forget niceties – who cares if there are a few flecks of black in a white sauce? It's the taste that counts.

Green peppercorns. The fresh immature berries, imported preserved in brine or frozen, are soft in texture, with an extremely pungent and exciting flavour, totally different from dried peppercorns. They have been on the market less than 15 years and are our newest flavour. Very perishable, they should be used quickly, made into green-pepper butter and frozen, or put into a small jar, covered with water, and frozen. Use crushed green peppercorns in sauces and butter to serve with meat, poultry and fish, as a replacement for crushed black peppercorns in such dishes as grilled peppered duckling (see page 115) or steak *au poivre* (see page 167). **Cayenne pepper** is not ground from peppercorns but from the capsicum pepper (see next page).

PEPPERS

Sweet or bell peppers. Members of the capsicum family, come in green, red and yellow. The red and yellow peppers are ripe versions of the green. Look for firm, shapely peppers without soft or discoloured spots or wrinkled skins. Remove stem end, seeds and white ribs, and slice into strips or rings, or chop, for salads, sautés, cooked dishes. Personally, I feel that if peppers are to be served cooked, they should be grilled until the thin, indigestible skin chars and can be scraped off (see page 126). Grilled peppers make a magnificent vegetable dish if cut into wide strips and sautéed lightly in olive oil with garlic and a drop or two of vinegar. Peppers lend themselves admirably to stuffing. Remove stem end and seeds and parboil for 10 minutes to soften the skin, then stuff and bake.

Pimientos. Another type of sweet red capsicum pepper, available skinned, cored, processed, and packed in jars or tins. Very mild in flavour. Use for colour in salads and as a garnish.

Hot chili peppers. There are many different varieties with varying degrees of heat. These are also members of the capsicum family. When preparing chilies for cooking, remove all the tiny seeds that hold the heat. Wash hands well after handling; the juice from chilies is highly irritating to the skin and eyes. **Tabasco** is a hot, pungent liquid pepper sauce made from small, fiery red Tabasco chilies packed into barrels, sealed with salt, aged three years, then mixed with vinegar and bottled. A most valuable product for cooking. Use as a substitute for cayenne pepper, in sauces such as hollandaise (see page 292), and in egg dishes. I always add a dash of Tabasco to scrambled eggs (see page 190).

PHEASANT   One of the finest game birds. There was a time when pheasant and other game were not considered to be edible until they had hung in the barn or a tree long enough to become quite green and odoriferous. They were then referred to as 'high', which they certainly were. We have, thank heavens, graduated from this barbaric custom. Pheasant must be cooked in such a way that the breast meat is kept moist, otherwise it becomes dry and unpalatable. For roast pheasant (see page 97), bacon or barding fat is usually draped over the breast as protection and lubrication. Young tender pheasant may be sautéed like chicken (see page 179). Older birds are best braised (see page 158).

PINEAPPLES   One of the western hemisphere's great food gifts to the world and long a symbol of hospitality. There are several varieties, from the very small sugar pineapples, about 10 to 15 cm. (4 to 6 inches) long, to the conical Brazilian pineapples (said to be the original fruit) that run 30 to 35 cm. (12 to 14 inches). To test for ripeness, lift the fruit to see if it is heavy with juice, press the skin at the bottom to see if it is soft, and smell it – there should be a full, fruity fragrance. Some say that if a centre frond pulls out easily the fruit is ripe. Avoid fruit that looks old or dry or has brown leaves. Large pineapples are a better buy, as there is more edible flesh. To peel a pineapple, slice off the bottom and leafy top and cut away the rind with a sharp knife, removing the little eyes with the knife point. Cut into fingers or crosswise slices and remove the core. Unless you are fortunate enough to get a fully ripened, sweet fruit, it will usually need sugaring to taste. Pineapple may be grilled (see page 128) and sautéed (see page 201), but to my mind it is best served raw and very cold, with some added flavour, such as a sprinkling of rum, kirsch, or framboise (white alcohol made from raspberries). For buffet presentation, cut off the top, remove the flesh with a small ball scoop, sugar it, and return to the shell, either alone or with other fruits, and chill before serving. Tinned pineapple is one of the more successful tinned fruits.

PLUMS   In the summer, plums are in season through July, August and September in at least ten to twelve different colours, shapes and flavours. The most common are the tender-skinned, yellow-fleshed red plums that must be eaten very ripe, or they are sour to the tongue. They are followed by the greengage, with greeny-yellow skin and yellow flesh, delicious to eat and excellent for tarts, pies, stewed plums and preserves. Then come the large yellow plums, good for eating raw, for baking, or for poaching, like pears and peaches, in a red-wine syrup or a plain syrup flavoured with liqueur. Greengage and yellow plums have a delicious sweetness.

POTATOES   It was once possible to have a pretty good working knowledge of the different varieties of potato and to choose the best for each cooking purpose. Now, with the standardization of agricultural produce, potatoes have become anonymous. We get simply – potatoes. There are two basic types, mealy and waxy. Waxy potatoes hold together better when boiled and sliced and are preferable for potato salad and sautéed potatoes (see page 196). Mealy potatoes are best for baking (see page 224) and roasting (see page 102), and are also good for boiling. Either type may be deep fried (see page 216).

New potatoes should be boiled or steamed whole. Do not peel. Scrub well, then cut a little belly band of skin from around the centre to keep it from bursting. Slightly undercook; it should be firm and crisp. Use for hot potato salad, as one of the accompanying vegetables for corned beef and cabbage (see page 24) and pot-au-feu (see page 30). Or cut into chunks, unpeeled, and deep-fry (see page 216). When buying potatoes, reject those that are soft, have wrinkled, scarred, or green-tinged skins (caused by exposure to the light), and sprouting eyes. Store in a cool, dry, well-ventilated cellar or cupboard away from the light.

To bake potatoes (see page 224), just scrub well and leave in their jackets. I like the skins crisp, so I don't rub them with fat, and I never, ever bake them in foil, which makes the skins soggy. To boil, either peel or leave the skins on (they hold together better for slicing), put into a deep saucepan with salted water to cover, put on the lid, and boil until tender when pierced with a knife, about 20 to 25 minutes, according to size and whether they are left whole or cut into pieces. After boiling, drain, return to the pan, and let dry out over low heat, covered, shaking the pan so they don't stick. To steam, put into an adjustable vegetable steamer in a deep pan with just enough water to come to the bottom of the steamer. Bring to a boil, cover and steam until tender – slightly longer than for boiling.

QUAIL Quail lend themselves to roasting, grilling like poussins, and sautéing. My favourite method is to remove the breasts and sauté them quickly (see page 180), using the less meaty legs and carcass for broth and soups. Whole roasted or grilled quail should be eaten with the fingers and, to my mind, they are not for company but for the family.

RABBIT I'm always astounded by people who say they don't like or have never eaten rabbit. They are to be pitied. I find this delicate, flavourful meat to be almost as useful as chicken. Commercially raised rabbits are available throughout the country, fresh and frozen. Fresh rabbits are usually sold skinned and cut up, if you so require. Or you may buy them whole and disjoint them yourself (see page 178). Frozen rabbits have been cut up and packaged. Young tender rabbits may be sautéed like chicken (see page 178). Older rabbits and wild rabbits are better braised or stewed.

RASPBERRIES Perhaps the most luscious and, in some ways, the most glamorous of all the fruits. No other berry comes close to them in flavour, and raspberry jam is probably the most popular of all preserves. Apart from jam-making, it would be a crime to cook raspberries. Eat them raw, with or without sugar, with cream or *crème fraîche*, flavoured with a little liqueur, if you like. Use them whole in little raspberry tarts. Purée them for raspberry fool (see page 327) or to spoon as a sauce over other fruits, such as strawberries, peaches and pineapples.

RHUBARB Long before supermarkets existed, rhubarb was the first fruit of the spring season, and a tonic, too, in the form of the rhubarb and soda given to children as a blood purifier. Nowadays the light-pink forced rhubarb appears on the market in December and lasts through the spring. It is milder in flavour than the later, dark-red field-grown or garden rhubarb, with its coarse leaves and tart taste. Botanically a vegetable, but always used as a fruit, rhubarb is fragile and needs very little cooking, but a good deal of sweetening. Only the red stalks are used; the leaves contain oxalic acid and should not be eaten. Buy crisp, firm, tender stalks, wash, trim off leaves and base, and cut them into 8-cm (3-inch) lengths. Blanch in boiling water for 1 minute, then drop into a simple syrup and poach until just tender. Or place in a casserole or baking dish with sugar to taste and perhaps a little grated orange rind, cover, and bake in a 180°C (350°F, gas mark 4) oven for 12 to 15 minutes. The fault with most rhubarb is that, overcooked to a stringy pulp, it is not the firm, interesting fruit it can and should be. Rhubarb makes excellent pies (in the old days, it was known in America as pie plant). Poached, puréed, and mixed with double cream, it becomes a delicious rhubarb fool.

RICE   Probably the most universally used of all the starches, yielding only to the potato. Rice comes in two versions, long grain and short grain, and various types, and may be bought both loose and packaged. I like to use **long-grain rice** for boiling (see page 50), pilafs, and most recipes where rice is needed, such as stuffings, salads (see page 52), casseroles (see page 278), the Spanish paella and *arroz con pollo*, and for egg-lemon soup (see page 300). **Short-grain rice** is better for puddings. **Parboiled rice** works well steamed (see page 51), according to the directions on the package. **Brown rice**, unpolished rice with merely the husk removed, is treated like long-grain rice but will take longer to cook – 40 to 50 minutes. **Arborio or Italian short-grain rice** with a plump starchy grain is the classic rice for risotto (see page 51), although I find long-grain rice works almost as well, if carefully cooked. One of the very few rices that still needs washing and soaking is the Indian **Basmati rice,** used in Indian cooking and also for Middle Eastern dishes such as *chello*. Rice expands considerably in cooking – one cup of raw rice will swell to three cups when cooked.

SALT   Salt, which comes from salt flats formed by evaporated sea water and from land deposits of rock or crystalline salt, has always been considered to be the most basic and necessary of all seasonings. Salt is one of the oldest known methods of preserving or curing meats and fish, especially beef, ham and cod. Salt is used to 'cook' the Scandinavian cured salmon called *gravad laks* (see page 324). There are several kinds of salt on the market, of different strengths and types.

Ordinary table salt. Often mixed with magnesium or sodium carbonate to make it flow more easily, table salt is fine and quite intense in flavour. Use it with care.

Coarse salt. Coarser in texture and less salty in flavour, I consider this preferable for both cooking and the table. It is pure salt, with no additives.

Malden salt. This and other sea salts have large crystals and are usually ground in a salt mill. They are expensive and are mostly used as table salt.

Ice-cream salt or rock salt. Used in ice-cream freezers or as a bed on which oysters on the half shell are grilled or roasted (see page 129), has the coarsest crystals.

SAUSAGES   A favourite subject of mine. I adore them, especially with sauerkraut (see page 38). There are hundreds of varieties of sausage, but the following are some you find most often in supermarkets and butchers' shops. If you can shop around in ethnic markets, you'll find many more.

Black pudding. A black sausage, known in French as **boudin noir** or in German as **blutwurst**, made with pigs' blood, meal and coarse pieces of pork. Traditionally grilled and served with potatoes and applesauce. There is also a dried, ready-to-eat blood sausage inlaid with pieces of tongue and fat, usually sliced and served cold.

Bockwurst. A German veal sausage, flavoured with chives. Poach (see page 38) or grill (see page 117). Serve with mashed potatoes or sauerkraut, or for breakfast with scrambled eggs.

Bologna. The most common of the ready-to-eat sausages, served cold and thinly sliced.

Bratwurst. A veal and pork or pork sausage, rather bland, with a herby flavour, popular in German and Swiss cuisine. Readily available and delicious grilled and served with sauerkraut or sautéed onions. **Weisswurst** is very similar.

Chorizo. A sausage of coarsely cut pork coloured with paprika, slightly piquant, and much used in Spanish dishes. Can be bought fresh or dried. May be poached, sautéed, or grilled. Available in some supermarkets and delicatessens, imported from Spain.

Cotechino. A large Italian sausage that should be poached before using.

Frankfurters. America's beloved hot dogs. The best are made from beef, the lesser quality from a variety of meats and innards. Their flavour ranges from very bland to very spicy. Look for all-beef frankfurters. Heat through in water, or grill. **Knockwurst** are similar but thicker and heavier. Again, the all-beef are best.

Kielbasa. A large, highly seasoned Polish sausage. Sold as long sausages or as rings. Some are fresh and should be poached or grilled; other types are dried and can be eaten cold, or heated.

Mortadella. An enormous dried sausage, similar to bologna but larded with fat pork. Should be sliced very thin. Sometimes served wrapped around a breadstick, as an hors d'oeuvre.

Pork sausages. The familiar link sausages or sausage meat we buy or make. May be finely or coarsely chopped with varied seasonings, mostly sage, but also thyme, garlic, coriander, chives and anise. Sauté or grill sausages. Form sausage meat into flat cakes and sauté gently until cooked through and crisp on the outside.

Salami. There are a dozen different varieties of salami, from the very dry Italian Genoa salami containing peppercorns and garlic to salamis seasoned with paprika and other spices. Taste and decide which of the many are for you. May be bought sliced, but I prefer to buy a piece and slice my own.

SHELLFISH

Crabs. Grey-brown when alive, brownish-red when cooked, crabs are sometimes sold live, but usually boiled by the fishmonger. Medium-sized ($1\frac{1}{2}$ kg. or 3 lb.) crabs are best.

Lobsters. Lobsters are sold both live and cooked, dark blue when alive, scarlet when boiled. They vary in size from ½ kg. (1 pound) or less, up to giants of 12 to 14 kg. (25 to 30 pounds). Smaller lobsters are better eating. The average ½ to 1 kg. lobster, boiled or grilled, is considered a serving for 1. For cooking, buy only live lobsters. Have the fish merchant lift one so you can see how active it is. There are dozens of ways to prepare lobster but, to me, the simplest and by far the best is boiling (see page 42). Serve hot with melted butter or cold with mayonnaise. Fresh or frozen lobster meat, though horrendously expensive, goes quite a long way in salads, seafood combinations, lobster *au gratin* (see page 129) and other cooked dishes. Canned lobster is not bad, but the taste is not the same as the fresh.

Mussels. A delicious bivalve with a tapering bluish-black shell. Mussels must be carefully cleaned (see directions on page 45). They are usually sold by the quart (a quart will serve 2) and range in size from about 4 cm. (1½ inches) to almost 15 cm. (6 inches) long. Small ones are the choicest. May be eaten raw but are more usually steamed in water or white wine until the shells open and served in their lovely broth, or used in shellfish stews and paella. Eat from the shell or remove and use in soup (see page 45), salads, and as a cold hors d'oeuvre with rémoulade sauce. They're a tremendously addictive delicacy.

Oysters. Luxury class shellfish, usually eaten raw, but may also be cooked. Fresh raw oysters are very perishable and should be eaten right away. To serve raw, open the shells with an oyster knife (or have the fishmonger do it for you), loosen the oyster from its lower shell, and serve it that way – resting on the half shell. Count on at least half a dozen raw oysters per person, or about 3 dl. (½ pint) shelled oysters, if they are to be cooked. Oysters may be grilled (see page 129), baked or scalloped (see page 273), fried, added to steak and kidney pie (see page 254), or simmered in soups and stews just until the edges curl – they must never be overcooked.

Prawns and Shrimps. These crustaceans come in all sizes, from the tiny shrimp, perfect for salads, shrimp cocktail, or potted shrimp, to the medium-sized grey-shelled prawn and the large pale pink Dublin Bay prawn. I find the medium size best for most general cooking, such as sautéing and frying (see page 207), for casseroles and other dishes, and for eating cold as appetizers or in salads. Dublin Bay prawns are fine for grilling (see page 124). One pound of prawns or shrimps serves two as a main course. You can buy raw prawns in the shell, cooked prawns in the shell or shelled, and quick-frozen prawns both raw and cooked. Most ready-cooked prawns are so overdone they are mushy and tasteless (and tinned are not worth buying). If possible, buy fresh raw prawns and cook them yourself. There's no need to remove the black vein from raw or cooked prawns, except for aesthetic reasons. To do so, cut the shell along the back with sharp-pointed scissors, and remove the vein. The prawns are then easier to shell, before or after cooking. Serve cold prawns as an appetizer with lemon, mayonnaise, or rémoulade sauce.

SPICES   There are two important things to remember about spices. 1. Buy in small quantities only as needed and don't buy every spice you see. 2. Don't keep spices too long. The principal spices you need for general cooking, apart from peppercorns, which are discussed on page 393, are **cloves, cinnamon, ginger** (see page 370) and **nutmeg.** Also useful to have on hand are **anise seed, allspice, caraway seed** and **mace.** Commercially ground spices deteriorate very quickly and lose their brightness, bouquet and pungency. I grind most of my spices as I need them, using a small electric coffee mill that I keep just for that purpose. It even grinds cinnamon bark. Spices may be ground in a mortar and pestle, but it is an arduous job and the results are never as even and fine. If you don't want to grind spices, buy them ground, in small amounts, from a spice store (many sell by mail) and discard them when they lose their freshness. Nutmeg should always be bought whole and freshly grated; the little tin nutmeg grater of classic design costs very little. Spices are for use, not for show. Keep them away from heat and light, in the dark of a kitchen cupboard, not in pretty jars on open shelves.

SQUAB   Young domesticated pigeons, weighing about 350 to 450 g. (¾ to 1 pound). Usually bought cleaned and ready for the oven. The meat is darkish and flavourful. Squab may be roasted like poussins (see page 87). I like to stuff them with fresh herbs, garlic and a tiny onion and roast them in a baking dish with bacon over the breasts for 40 to 45 minutes at 200°C (400°F, gas mark 6). Or they may be split down the back, flattened with a blow of the fist, and grilled on both sides, like chicken. Squab, like quail, should be regarded as finger food. They are ideal birds for picnics if roasted or grilled the day before.

SQUID   Squid belong to the family of molluscs, but have no outer shell, only a thin bladelike bone inside the tubular body. With their greyish skin, beady eyes, and long tentacles, squid look like smaller, elongated octopuses, which may be the reason they are unfairly shunned. Most people don't like the look of them, don't know how to prepare them, and seem to be afraid to try them – a great pity, for the flesh is delicious if not overcooked. Squid need careful cleaning and should be skinned before cooking. Remove the head and pull out the pulpy intestines. Remove the thin, transparent, bladelike bone, leaving the tubular body in one piece. If the recipe calls for the tentacles, which are just below the eyes, cut them off and reserve them. Also reserve the sac of inky fluid if this is needed; otherwise discard it. Peel off the thin greyish skin covering the outside of the body. The cleaned body may be stuffed and braised, sliced and sautéed, cooked in rice with its own black ink, cut into rings, floured and deep-fried, along with the tentacles, or used in a fish stew or paella.

STRAWBERRIES   Strawberries were once a great seasonal delight. Now we can get them all the year round, but unfortunately some are bred more for beauty than for taste. One has to be careful about buying, especially in the winter. Don't let your eyes fool your palate. Snitching and tasting one is kind of hard to do in today's markets, but you *can* feel and smell the berries. They should feel ripe but not mushy, and have a good fragrance. Be sure to check the box to make sure there are no rotten ones hidden on the bottom. Wild strawberries, tiny and deliciously sweet, may be picked in the summer all over the country, but are seldom seen in markets. Eaten with cream, with raspberry purée (see page 326), or in strawberries Romanov (see page 326), 450 g. (1 pound) of strawberries will serve two. Or stretch them in a tart (see page 248), *sorbet* (see page 351), or ice cream (see page 349).

SUET   Suet, or beef kidney fat, finely chopped, makes an interesting and different pastry for meat pies and turnovers, and it is a necessity for beefsteak and kidney pudding (see page 35). If rendered until melted in a heavy frying pan, it adds great flavour to a steak sautéed in the French manner. Rendered suet or rendered beef fat trimmed from steak are marvellous for chips or fried potatoes.

SWEDES See Turnips.

SWEET POTATOES   An elongated tuber with an orange or reddish skin, resembling a potato, but not as thick. Bake (about 1 hour) or boil (30 to 40 minutes until tender) in the jacket, like potatoes. May be mashed or puréed and used in casseroles, as a tart filling, sliced and sautéed, or peeled, cut into strips and deep-fried like chips.

TOMATOES   One of the most versatile and popular of all fruits. Use only firm, ripe tomatoes for grilling (see page 125), sautéing, or tomato salads. For cooking, tomatoes should be peeled and seeded. Drop in boiling water for half a minute to loosen the skin. Cut out core at stem end, peel, cut in half crosswise, and squeeze in your fist to force out the seeds. Or quarter and scoop out the seeds with your finger. Unless tomatoes are fully ripe, tinned peeled Italian plum tomatoes or solid-pack tomatoes are a better buy for cooking. Other tinned forms of tomato are tomato purée, often used as part of the liquid in braised dishes, and concentrated tomato paste, used to intensify tomato flavour in dishes such as tomato sauce (see page 49).

TURKEY   What used to be the great Christmas treat is now available throughout the year. Turkeys nowadays are bred to grow firmer, larger breasts, much to the dismay of those who prefer the dark meat. Fortunately, one may buy turkey in parts, fresh or frozen, so dark-meat lovers can feast on legs and thighs. Turkey breasts of varying sizes are an excellent buy, as they are practically solid meat. Roast them or use for a variety of dishes such as turkey salad, turkey tonnato and escalopes of turkey (sliced thin, like veal scaloppine). Except at Christmas it is difficult, although not impossible, to find fresh-killed, hand-plucked turkeys. Although they are more expensive, I happen to feel that they are superior enough to the frozen birds to warrant the higher price. While whole turkeys are most often roasted (see page 88), they may also be braised or poached. They vary in size from very small, around $2\frac{1}{2}$ kg. (5 pounds), up to 14 and 16 kg. (30 and 35 pounds). Buy according to how much you and your family like turkey, for there are bound to be leftovers and it's silly to buy more than you can use. A $3\frac{1}{2}$-kg. (8-pound) turkey will serve 4, with ample leftovers; a $4\frac{1}{2}$-kg. (10-pound) will serve 6, with leftovers; and a $5\frac{1}{2}$- to $6\frac{1}{2}$-kg. (12- to 14-pound) will serve 8 to 10.

TURNIPS There are two types of turnips in our markets, the small early purple-topped white ones and the huge yellow swedes, available all winter. White turnips are at their best when young and very small, about egg size. Peel, slice and cook in boiling salted water to cover until just tender. Combine with carrots or celery, or purée and mix with puréed carrot. Also good braised, or parboiled and sautéed (see page 193). Use turnips as an accompanying vegetable for boiled corned beef and cabbage (see page 24), in oxtail ragout (see page 150), or in the *mirepoix* for braised meats. When buying swedes, look for the small or medium size. Large ones are often pithy and spongy. Peel, cut into pieces, steam, or boil in salted water to cover until tender. Mash with plenty of butter and freshly ground pepper. Mashed swedes are extremely good with mushroom duxelles (see page 386) swirled into them, excellent baked in a casserole with eggs, crumbs and onions. I also like to cut white turnips and swedes into julienne strips, blanch them, and sauté with julienne strips of broccoli stalks (see three-vegetable sauté, page 200).

VANILLA Probably the most popular and widely used flavouring for cakes, cookies, puddings, custards and creams such as *crème anglaise* (see page 290), ice cream (see pages 348 and 349), poached peaches (see page 350), and other desserts. Use only vanilla bean or pure vanilla essence, made from vanilla beans soaked in alcohol. Artificial vanilla, known as vanillin, has only the smell and not the rich taste of the real thing. The thin, long, dark-brown vanilla bean, though expensive, will give you a lot of mileage. Put into a jar of sugar, vanilla beans aromatize the sugar and give it a permanent delicate flavour. For a fine homemade vanilla essence, slit 4 or 5 beans, put into a small bottle of cognac or vodka, and after 2 weeks, it's ready to use. Or slit $2\frac{1}{2}$ cm. (1 inch) of vanilla bean and scrape the tiny, flavourful black seeds into custard, an ice-cream mixture, or a cake or pudding batter. The finest, moist vanilla beans, almost overpowering in flavour, are sold in bulk by bakers' supply houses.

VINEGAR   In salad-making, remember the old adage, 'A spendthrift for oil, a miser for vinegar.' Vinegar should never overpower. The recent vogue in French cooking for chicken, rabbit and game birds with a vinegar sauce is, to my palate, more fashionable than delicious. Traditionally, in many Western and Oriental countries, vinegar and sugar are combined in sweet-and-sour dishes, such as sauerbraten and sweet-and-sour pork. And, of course, vinegar and sugar go together in pickling. Vinegar alone is for vinaigrette sauce and salad dressings, marinades and court bouillon, and a touch is essential in mayonnaise (see page 294). If you can beg or borrow a 'mother', the natural yeast culture that, put into leftover wine, turns it into vinegar, it is easy to make your own. Otherwise, buy the best wine vinegar you can, either white or red. Should you want a tarragon or basil flavour, steep fresh herbs in the vinegar for a week or two. For general cooking purposes, use wine or cider vinegar. For salads, use wine vinegar, rice wine vinegar, sherry vinegar, fruit vinegars, herb-flavoured vinegars. For pickling and preserving, use cider vinegar or distilled white vinegar.

YAMS   The yam is most often seen in West Indian markets. The flesh is white or yellow and the texture rather like a potato. Boil or bake in the jacket, like potatoes. Peel, slice and dress with butter, or purée.

YEAST   Sold commercially in two forms: dried yeast in packages and tins, and fresh yeast in cakes. Both are equally efficient. Dried yeast is stocked by every supermarket, but in many communities fresh yeast is hard to find. One may have to beg a large piece of it from a friendly baker. Cake yeast will keep for several months if you cut it into small pieces (enough for one batch of bread at a time), wrap it tightly in foil or plastic wrap, and store it in the freezer. Just remove as needed and place in warm water to get it working (the foaming and swelling proves the yeast is still active). Dried yeast dissolves best in lukewarm water 45°C (110° to 115°F) with the addition of a tiny bit of sugar to reactivate it faster. Fresh yeast, on the other hand, must not be put in water over 35°C (95°F), or the delicate organism that causes fermentation and makes the bread rise will be killed. The best way to make sure the water is the right temperature is to test it with a thermometer, but soon you will get the feel for the appropriate temperature when you simply test it on your wrist.

Carving

Carving a Standing Rib Roast

With small sharp knife cut along rib bones, holding roast steady with fork.

Slice with sharp slicing knife toward the ribs. Slice thin for English cut, thick for American.

Transfer slices with knife and fork to serving plate or platter.

Carving a Turkey

With fork to balance, remove leg and thigh at joint.

Slice section from the drumstick and the thigh on separate board or platter.

With sharp, pointed knife remove wing at joint.

continued

With fork to balance
and sharp carving knife,
cut medium-thin,
long slices of meat.

When meat has been sliced
away, turn bird
and proceed with otherside
in the same manner.

Carving a Leg of Lamb

Place lamb with shank
bone on carving board.
Secure with fork, and with
slicing knife cut diagonal
slice to the bone.

Continue carving
medium-thin slices.
You may cut additional
slices to the left and right.

When necessary, turn
leg over and proceed with
cushion on the other side.

Carving a Goose

Place the goose on carving board or platter and, with fork to balance, remove leg and thigh with sharp, pointed slicing knife. Remove wing.

Cut meat from legs and thighs.

Cut 1 or 2 slices across the neck end of bird.

Starting from breast bone slice parallel slices of breast and loosen by cutting along the bone.

Repeat on opposite side and cut with a smaller pointed knife.

Index
. . . .

allspice, 400
almonds, 387
  amandine sauce, 187
  blanched, 23–4, 387
  and Brussels sprouts, 194
anchovy fillets
  and celery hearts vinaigrette, 310
  in garlic and oil sauce, 48
  and hearts of palm vinaigrette, 310
  hollandaise, 294
  white bean and tuna salad, 316
anise seed, 400
apples, kinds, 357
  braised, with red cabbage, 361
  with braised pheasant, 158
  fritters, 211
  and prune stuffing, 93, 94
  rings, sautéed, 166; flambéed, 166
    fried; 201; glazed, 201
  sauce, 65
  tart, Swiss, 247–8
apricots, 357
  fritters, 211
  preserves: glaze for savarin, 266–8
    ice cream, ice-tray, 350
  soufflé, 241
arrowroot: as thickener, 283–4, 292
artichokes (globe artichokes), 357,
    to buy, 357, to remove choke, 357
  boiled, 60, 357
  canned, vinaigrette, 310
  poached à la Grecque, 62–3
asiago, 363
asparagus, 357–8
  boiled, 59–60, 357
  canned, 358; vinaigrette, 310
  omelet, 193
  sautéed, 166
aubergine, 358; to draw out excess
    water, 358
  French fried, 215–16
  grilled, 125, 126; with Parmesan
    cheese, 126
  poached, à la Grecque, 62–3

  ratatouille, 153
  stuffed, 274–5
avgolemono, soupa, 300–301
avocados, 358, to buy, 317, 358, to
    prepare, 314, to prevent
    discolouring, 317, 358, to ripen,
    358
  guacamole, 317–18, variations, 318
  puréed, as thickener, 300
  salad: with greens, 306–7; onion and
    grapefruit (or orange), 315;
    onion and tomato, 313–14
  soup, chilled, 341; and butter-
    milk, 320

bacon, 382
  blanched, 24
  and dandelion greens, sautéed,
    372
  omelet, 193
baking, 221–4, 226
  equipment, 14, 15, 17–18
  parchment or wax paper, 20, 262
  See also pans
baking powder, 222, 223
baking soda, 222, 223, 358
bananas, 358–9
  crêpes directoire, 231
  flambéed, à l'Archestrate, 201
  grilled, 128; ice cream, 348
  sautéed, 166
basil, 372–3
bass
  sea, baked, 278–9
batter, 203, 204
  beer, 207–8
  cake, mixing by hand, 10, 263–6
  crêpes, 227
  fritters, fruit, 210–11
  fritto misto, 208–9
  onion rings, 210
  prawn, 207–8
batter bread, 261
Bavarian cream, orange, 338–9

Bavarian cream (contd.)
génoise filled with, 268
bay leaf, 373
beans, 359
  baked, 223
  boiled, 359
  Breton beans, 58–9
  cannellini, 310, 316
  to cook, 58, 359
  dried, 58, 359
  lentil casserole, 276
  salad, 59; with salmon, 316; with
    sardines, 316; with tomato,
    cucumber, and green pepper,
    82; in tomato shells, 316; with
    tuna, 316; with tuna, anchovies,
    and olives, 316
  soaking, 359
  vinaigrette, 310; with
    tomatoes, 81
beans, broad, 359
  boiled, 359
  vinaigrette, 310
beans, French, 359; to buy, 359
  boiled, 59–60, 359
  beans, green, *see* beans, French
  poached, à la Grecque, 62–3
  sautéed, 166, 193, 359
  vinaigrette, 310, 359
beans, kidney
  canned, vinaigrette, 310
beans, white, 58, 359
Béarnaise sauce, 294
béchamel sauce, 282, 285–6
  to thicken or thin, 286
  variations, 287–8
beef, 376; to buy, 376; cuts
    (illustrated), 377–9; grades, 376
  boeuf à la mode, 133–4, 146–7
  bourguignon, 155, 170–71, 284
  braised, 134, 146–7, 376; with
    wine and brandy, 148
  brisket, 146, 379
  broth, *see* stock or broth *below*
  carpaccio, 304, 323
  chili con carne, Jeanne Owen's, 150
  corned, *see* corned beef
  devilled bones, 290
  estouffat de Noël, 149
  filet mignon, 378

filet, raw, marinated, 322–3
goulash, Viennese, 149
hamburger, 378; grilled, 110;
  sautéed, 169–70
heart, 378
kebabs, 118–19
kidneys, 379
liver, 379; *bourguignon*, 170–71
London grill, 110; teriyaki
  marinade, 110, 111
oxtail, 379; ragout, 150–51
pot-au-feu, 30–33
pot roast, French-style, 133–4,
  146–7
roast, 69, 70, 75–7, fillet
  (tenderloin), 77–8, 378; low-
  temperature method, 75, 77; pre-
  searing method, 75–6; rib, to
  carve, 75, 405; rib, cold, 77
salad, 147
sausages, 398
shashlik, 119–20
steak, 378; to buy, 107–8, doneness,
  testing for, 108–9
steak, grilled, 107–9; charcoal-
  grilled, 109
steak, flank, grilled, 107, 110
steak, sirloin, 378; to carve, 109
steak, Swiss, 137–8
steak and kidney pie, 254–5
steak and kidney pudding, 35
steak *au poivre*, 167–9
steak tartare, 303, 304, 321–2
stock or broth, 26, 27, 32–3; brown
  sauce, 288–9; caramel colouring,
  33, 288–9; to clarify, 32; *glace
  de viande*, 23, 32
Stroganoff, 164
suet, *see* suet
Swiss steak, 137–8
testicles, broiled or sautéed, 379
tongue, 377
tripe, 379; *à la mode de Caen*, 223
zrazys Nelson, 171
beefsteak and kidney pie, 254–5
beefsteak and kidney pudding, 35
beer
  batter, 207–8
  in braising liquid, 134
beetroot, 359

baked, 359
boiled, 359
canned, vinaigrette, 310
greens, boiled, 371–2
salad, with greens, 307, 359, 371–2
beignets soufflés, 204, 217–18
Belgian endive, *see* endive
beurre manié, 282, 283, 286, 288, 289
bicarbonate of soda, *see* baking soda
biscuit crumbs
    as breading, 213
    homemade, 274
    scalloped oysters, 273–4
black pudding, 284, 383, 397–8
blackberries, 359
blanching, 22, 23–4
blender, 15–16
blutwurst, 284, 383, 397–8
bockwurst, 385, 388
boeuf à la mode, 133–4, 146–7
boeuf bourguignon, 155, 284; liver,
    170–71
boiling, 21–4
bologna, 398
Bordelaise sauce, 289–90
boudin noir, 284, 383, 397–8
bouquet garni, 373
brains
    calves', 384; *fritto misto*, 208–9
    lambs', 379–80
    pork, 381
braising, 105, 133–6
    liquids, 134
    mirepoix, 134–5, 140, 143
bratwurst, 385, 388
Brazil nuts, 387
bread, 222, 223, 257–62; pans, 14, 17
    batter bread, 261
    chapon, in salad, 305
    cornbread, 261–2
    croutons, 318–19; in omelet, 193; in
        salad, 313; in soup, 318–19
    crumbs: as breading, 175–7, 203,
        204, 205, 211–16; as thickener,
        284
    dough, 257; flour, 257, 258,
        369–70; kneading, 259;
        risings, 258; yeast, 257,
        258, 403
    sauce, 284, 299

toast, 105
white, basic, 258–60
breading
    cornmeal, 213, 365
    crumbs, 175–7, 203, 204, 205,
        211–16
Breton beans, 58–9
broad beans, *see* beans, broad
broccoli, 360; to buy, 360
    flowerets: boiled, 360; poached,
        à la Grecque, 62–3
    fritto misto, 208–9
    omelet, 193
    sautéed, 193; stems, 360; three-
        vegetable, 200
broccoli rabe, 360
broth
    beef, 26, 27, 32
    in braising liquid, 134
    chicken, 26, 28–9; double, 28–9
    to clarify, 29, 32
    oxtail, 151
    veal, 26, 27, 30, 139, 141
brown butter, 198
brown sauce, 282, 283, 284
    basic, 288–9; caramel colouring, 33,
        288–9; *glace de viande*, 32
    quick, 289
    variations, 289–90
Brussels sprouts, 360
    sautéed, 194; with almonds, 194;
        with chestnuts and bacon, 194
bulghur (cracked wheat), 316–17, 365
    kibbeh nayé, 304, 321
    pilaf, 53; with almonds, 53
        with mushrooms, 53
    tabbouleh, 316–17
butter, 360–61
    beurre manié, 282, 283, 286, 288,
        289
    brown, 198
    clarified, 189, 361
    cream frosting, 268, 269
    herb or flavoured, 109, 112–13, 374
    salt, 360
    unsalted (sweet), 360
buttermilk and avocado soup, cold,
    320

cabbage, 361

cabbage (contd.)
blanched, 23
boiled, 361
coleslaw, 311–12, 361; spicy, 312;
sweet-and-sour, 311–12
red, 361; braised, with apples, 361,
braised with chestnuts, 161
shredded, vinaigrette, 310
in salad, 306, 361
with sautéed pheasant, 179–80
savoy, 361
stuffed, 33–5, 361
vinaigrette, 310
See also sauerkraut
cakes, 262–3; doneness, testing for, 10;
mixing by hand, 9–10, 263–6;
pans and equipment, 17, 262
crumbs, as thickener, 284
flour, 263, 264, 369–70, to sift,
263, 264
génoise: with butter cream, 268–9;
with orange Bavarian cream,
338–9; with trifle, 339–40
1-2-3-4, 263–6
savarin with apricot glaze, 266–8
California gazpacho, 318–19
calves' brains, 384
fritto misto, 208–9
calves' feet, 134, 384
calves' liver, 385
fritto misto, 208–9
steaks, grilled, 116
calves' sweetbreads, *see* sweetbreads
cannellini (white beans), 310, 316
cannelloni, quick, 230
caper sauce, 288
caramel colouring, 33, 288–9
caraway seed, 400
carpaccio, 304, 323
carrots, 194, 361
boiled, 194, 361
and cucumber ring, with crabmeat,
341–2
poached, à la Grecque, 62–3
puréed, 61–2
roasted, 102
sautéed, 193; three-vegetable, 200;
Vichy, 194
vinaigrette, 310
carving, 72

beef: flank steak, 110; rib roast, 75,
405 (illustrated); sirloin steak, 109
duck, 96
goose, 409 (illustrated)
knife, 12
lamb, leg of, 408 (illustrated)
pork, roast loin of, 79
turkey, 406–7 (illustrated)
casseroles, 222, 223
cassis ice cream, 349
with créme de cassis: and peaches,
349; and raspberry pureé, 349
cauliflower, 361–2, to buy, 361–2
baked, with béchamel sauce and
cheese, 362
boiled, 362
flowerets: boiled, 362; poached, à
la Grecque, 62–3
fritto misto, 208–9
sautéed, 193, 195
vinaigrette, 310
cayenne pepper, 393, 394
celeriac, 362
puréed, 61
rémoulade, 310–11
vinaigrette, 310
celery, 362
boiled, 195
braised, 159–60, 362
hearts: braised, 159–60, 362;
poached, à la Grecque, 62–3;
vinaigrette, with anchovies, 310
and walnut ring, 275–6
in salad, 307
sautéed, 195–6
vinaigrette, 310
celery root, *see* celeriac
cereal crumbs: as breading, 213
chapon, 305
chartreuse, 135–6
Cheddar cheese, 362
cheese, 362–3; to keep, 362
coeur à la crème, 329
Gruyère cheese salad, 315
omelet, 193
quiche: Lorraine, 249–50; Swiss
onion, 251
Roquefort mousse with seafood
salad, 333–5
sauce, 287; mornay, 105, 287

in scrambled eggs, 190
soufflé, 233–5; spicy, 235
stuffed baked potato, 224–5
cherries, 363
chestnuts
and braised red cabbage, 161
and Brussels sprouts, 194
chicken, 83–4, 363–4; to bone, 175–6;
    to cut, 172–3; to cut backbone, 173
    doneness, testing for, 86, 111, 112,
    kinds, 363–4; to truss, 84–5
boiling fowl, 364
braised, 136
broth, see stock or broth below
Calandria, 156–7
consommé, 29
coq au vin, 155–6
creamed: in celery and pecan ring,
    275–6; in omelet, 193
crêpes, 229–30
fritto misto, 208–9
frying chickens, 364
grilled, 106, 107, 111
    with flavoured butter, 112–13
    marinade, 107; marinade,
    teriyaki, 107, 111–12
grilling chickens, 363–4
hash, in omelet, 193
hearts, grilled, 105
kebabs, 107
Kiev, 214
livers: grilled, 105; sautéed, 177–8
omelet, 193
panné, 175–7
poached, in double chicken broth,
    28–9; old-fashioned chicken and
    dumplings, 55
pot-au-feu, 23, 27, 30–33
poule au pot, 33–5
poussins, 364
    grilled, 112
    stuffed and roasted, 87–8
quiche, 250
roast, 69, 83–4; old-fashioned
    Sunday roast chicken with
    stuffing, 86–7; perfect, 84–6
    perfect, cold, 86
roasting chickens, 364
salad, in celery and walnut ring,
    275–6

sautéed, 165, 166–7; with
    Armagnac, 174–5; panné, 175–7
    with white wine and tarragon,
    172–4
stock or broth, 26, 28–9; double,
    28–9
chicory, 370–71
braised, 198
salad, 306, 307, 371
sautéed, with brown butter, 198
chili con carne, Jeanne Owen's,
    150
chili peppers, hot, 317, 394
chilling, 331–2
Chinese parsley, see coriander
chives, 373, 388, 390
butter, 113
chocolate, 364–5; to keep, 364–5;
    to melt, 364
roll, 239, 240
sauce, 255–7; custard, 292
soufflé, 239–40
chorizo, 398
Choron, sauce, 294
choux pastry, see pastry, choux
cilantro, see coriander
cima di vitello, 384
cinnamon, 400
clarifying
broth, 29, 32
butter, 189, 361
oil, 205
cloves, 400
cod, 368, 369
baked, 278–9
fillets, grilled, 120–21
salt cod, 368
steak, sauté Provençale, 187–8
coeur à la crème, 329
coffee custard sauce, 292
coffee granité, 352
coleslaw, 361
favourite, 311–12
spicy, 312
sweet-and-sour, 311–12
cookies, 270–72; kinds, 270
meringue kisses, 272
sand tarts, 271–2
Scotch shortbread, 270–71
coq au vin, 155–6

Corbitt, Helen: Roquefort mousse
    with seafood salad, 333–5
coriander (Chinese parsley; cilantro),
    373
corn, 365; to buy, 365
    on the cob, boiled, 59, 365
    sautéed, 193
    vinaigrette, 310
corn bread, 261–2
corned beef, 379
    boiled, and cabbage, 24–6
    hash ring, 277
cornflour: as thickener, 283–4, 292,
    331
cornmeal, 365
    as breading, 213, 365
    corn bread, 261–2
    mush, 54; fried, 54; sautéed, with
        game, 97, 98
    as thickening, 365
corn oil, 205, 388
    teriyaki marinade, 111–12
corn salad, 306, 371
cos lettuce, 306, 371
cotechino, 38, 398
    poached, with sauerkraut, 38–9
cottage cheese, 362
    quiche Lorraine, 249–50
courgettes
    blanched, 23
    fried, 204, 206–7
    fritto misto, 208–9
    gratin of greens, 273
    poached, à la Grecque, 62–3
    ratatouille, 153
    sautéed, 193, 199–200; three-
        vegetable, 200; with walnuts,
        199–200
    stuffed, 274
court bouillon
    for fish, 39; red wine, 343–4; white
        wine, 40
    for lamb breasts, 185
    for shellfish, 41–2
    vegetables à la Grecque, 62–3
crabs, 388; to clean, 200
    meat: creamed, in celery and walnut
        ring, 275–6; crêpes, 230; in
        cucumber and carrot ring, 341–2,
        sautéed, 189; seviche, 323–4;

spinach and seafood soup, cold,
    301–2
cracked wheat, see bulghur
cracker crumbs:
    homemade, 274
    scalloped oysters, 273–4
crayfish,
    à la nage, 41–2
cream, 365–6
    crème, fraîche, 301, 365–6
    See also soured cream
cream cheese, 363
    coeur à la crème, 329
    quiche Lorraine, 249–50
cream puff pastry (pâte à choux),
    217–18, 255–6
    beignets soufflés, 204, 217–18
    cream puffs with chocolate sauce,
        255–7
crème anglaise, see custard, sauce
crème brûlée, 105, 130–31
crème fraîche, 301, 365–6
crêpes, 226–31; pans and utensils,
    226–7
    batter, 227
    cannelloni, quick, 230
    chicken, 229–30
    crabmeat, 230
    directoire, 231
    fruit, flambé, 231
    ham, 230
    prawn, 230
    soufflés, 231
    turkey and mushrooms, 230
croquettes, 205, 211
    prawn and dill, 211–12
croutons, 318–19
    in omelet, 193
    in salad, 313
    in soup, 318–19
crumbs
    bread: as breading, 175–7, 203,
        204, 205, 211–16; sauce, 284,
        299; as thickener, 284
    cake, as thickener, 284
    cereal, as breading, 213
    cracker; home-made, 274; scalloped
        oysters, 273–4
cucumbers, 366; to remove excess
    water, 319, 342

blanched and sautéed, 366
and carrot ring with crabmeat,
    341–2
garnish, 336
and mushroom sauce, 171
poached, 366
salad, 308–9; in green salad, 307
and yogurt soup: Iranian, 319;
    Turkish, 319
Cumberland sauce, 82
currant jelly: glaze, 248
curry sauce, French, 287
custard, 223
crème brulée, 105, 130–31
sauce (crème anglais), 290–92;
    Bavarian cream, orange, 338–9;
    chocolate, 292; coffee, 292;
    génoise, 268; liqueur or spirits,
    210, 292; trifle, 339–40
cutting, 11–13

dandelion greens:
salad, 306, 371
sautéed, with bacon, 371, 372
devilled beef bones, 290
devilled breast of lamb, 185
devilled kidneys, 117
diable, sauce, 290
dicing, 13
dill, 373–4
in salad, 306, 374; mushroom, 308;
    tomato, 309
sauce, 288
doughnuts, 204–5
raised, 218–19
duck, 95, 366; doneness, testing
    for, 96, 114; frozen, 95, 366
braised, with beans, 157
grilled, 106; duckling, 114–15
    peppered, 115
roast, 95; and lentil casserole,
    276–7; with peaches, 95–6
wild, 366; grilled, teriyaki
    marinade, 107; roast, 98–9
dumplings, 55
and old-fashioned chicken, 55
duxelles, 386

eggs, 366–7; to freeze or store, 367; to
separate, 10, 233–4, 367; whites,
    10, 367; yolks, 367
hard-boiled, 24, 58
-lemon soup, 300–301
mollet, 24, 57
omelet, perfect, 191–3; fillings, 178,
    193
poached, 56–7
sauce, 288
scrambled, perfect, 190; additions
    to, 190; in spinach roll, 236
soft-boiled, 24, 56, 57
as thickener, 284, 331
electrical appliances, 15–16, 20
Emmenthaler, 363
endive, 371
salad, 306, 307, 371
equipment, cooking, 9–20
estouffat de Noël, 149

fat
barding, 77–8, 97, 98, 99, 381
frying, 205
goose, 93
lard and pig fat, 77, 82, 97, 98, 99,
    205, 375, 381
larding, 80, 381
suet, 35–6, 76, 77, 205, 401
fennel, 367
bulbs: braised, 159; poached, à la
    Grecque, 62–3
filberts (hazelnuts), 387
fish, 367–9; to buy, 367–8; cooking
    time, determination of, 40, 121,
    188, 213; doneness, testing for, 41,
    279; frozen, 106, 120, 186, 188
baked, 278–9; stuffed, 279
braised, 136; with mirepoix, 134
creamed, in omelet, 193
fillets, 188, 368, 369; baked, 279;
    fried, 213; grilled, 105, 106, 107,
    120–22; poached, with white wine
    sauce, 41; sautéed, 188
fried, 213
grilled, 105, 106, 107, 120–24,
    charcoal-grilled, 109; with
    fennel and flambéed, 367; kebabs,
    107, 118; marinade, 121–2
poached, with white wine sauce, 41
poached in court bouillon, 40; red

fish: poached (contd.)
wine, 343–4; white wine, 40
sautéed, 186–8, 388; meunière,
173, 186; Provençale, 187–8
seviche, 304, 323–4
steaks: baked, 279; baked, stuffed,
279; grilled, 121–2;
sautéed, 187–8
sushi and *sashimi*, 304
See also seafood; shellfish
flounder, 369
fillets, 369
flour, 369–70; to sift, 263, 264
beurre manié, 282, 283, 286,
288, 289
plain, 369
self-raising, 369–70
stone-ground, 370
strong (bread), 369
as thickener for sauces, 281–2,
283, 284
wholemeal and wheatmeal, 370
food processor, 15, 16
frankfurters, 398
freezing, 331–2
fritters
fruit, 210–11
soufflé (*beignets soufflés*), 204,
217–18
fritto misto, 204, 208–9
vegetables, 204
fruit, 325–9
citrus, to buy, 375–6, 390
crêpes, flambé, 231
fritters, 210–11
grilled, 127–8
poached, 63–4
sautéed, 201
soufflé, 241
frying, 163, 203–6
fats and oils, 205
pans and utensils, 205

game
braised, 133, 134, 135–6
grilled: kebabs, 118;
marinades, 107
game birds
braised, 133, 134; with mirepoix,
134, 135; with vegetables

(*chartreuse*), 135–6
grilled, 106, 107; marinade, 107
roast, 69, 96–9
garlic, 389–90; to buy, 389; to peel,
10, 389–90
in salad, 305
sauces: Greek, 298–9; Greek,
variations, 299; and oil, 48; oil
and anchovies, 48
sautéing with, 390
vinaigrette sauce, 305
gazpacho, California, 318–19
génoise
with butter cream, 268–9
with orange Bavarian cream, 338–9
with trifle, 339–40
ginger, 370, 400
ice cream, 349
glace de viande, 23, 32
gnocchi, 54–5
potato and semolina, 55–6
goose, 92, 370; to carve, 409; doneness, testing for, 94; frozen, 92;
to truss, 84–5
fat, 93
roast, with prune and apple
stuffing, 93–4
goulash, Viennese, 149
Grand Marnier soufflé, 237–9
granité, 350–51
coffee, 352
lemon, 351
grapefruit: to peel segments, 315
grilled, 127
salad, with avocado and onion, 315
and sherry jelly, 345
gratin of greens, 273
gravad laks, 304, 324–5
greaseproof paper, 20, 262
Greek garlic sauce, 298–9
variations, 299
greens (for cooking), 371–2
boiled, 59–60
gratin, 273
greens (for salads), 304–7, 370–71
mixing with hands, 10, 307
gremolata, 154
grilling, 103–7
pans, 15, 17, 106
groundnut oil, 205, 388

Gruyère cheese, 363
  quiche, Swiss onion, 251
  salad, 315
guacamole, 317–18
  variations, 318

haddock, 368, 369
  baked, 278
  fillets, 368, 369; broiled, 120–21
  smoked, 368
halibut, 368
  steaks: grilled, 121–2; sautéed,
    187; sauté Provençale, 187–8
ham, 382, to remove excess salt by
    blanching, 24; to remove excess
    salt by soaking, 81
  baked, 80–81; glazed, 81–2;
    glazed, cold, 82
  country, 81
  crêpes, 230
  fresh, 382; kebabs, 118; marbelized,
    80–81
  grilled steaks, 115
  mousse, cold, 336
  omelet, 193
  picnic, 383
  quiche Lorraine, 250
  sautéed, 166
  in scrambled eggs, 190
  in spinach roll, 236
  and veal pâté, 345–7
hamburger, 378
  grilled, 110
  sautéed, 169–70
hash
  chicken, in omelet, 193
  corned beef ring, 277
hazelnuts (filberts), 387
headcheese, 381
  mock, see jellied veal
health salad, 314–15
hearts
  beef, 378
  chicken, grilled, 105
  lamb, 381
  pork, 382
  veal, 385
herbs, 372–5; to buy, 372; to keep,
    372; ratio of dried to fresh, 372;
    steeping, 24

bouquet garni, 373
butter, 109, 112–13, 374
  marinade, 107
  omelet, 193
  rice, 51
  scrambled eggs, 190
  vinaigrette sauce, 306
hollandaise sauce, 105, 284, 292–4
  with anchovies, 294
  with mustard, 294
  with tomato paste (sauce Choron), 294
  variations, 294
horseradish, 375
  sauce, 287

ice cream, 332, 347
  apricot, ice-tray, 351
  banana, 348
  cassis, 349
  ginger, 349
  lemon, 349
  peach, 350
  strawberry, 349
  vanilla: basic, 348–9; French,
    349–50
ices, see granité; sherbet
Iranian cucumber and yogurt soup,
    319
Irish stew, 135, 152
Italian link sausages, grilled, 117
  and lentil casserole, 276–7

jellied veal, 30, 342–3
jelly
  currant, glaze, 248
  sherry and grapefruit, 345
Jerusalem artichokes, 375
julienne, how to, 12

kale, 372
kebabs, 107, 118
  beef shashlik, 119–20
  marinades, 107, 110, 111–12
  shish kebab, 118–19
Kenwood mixer, 15–16
kibbeh nayé, 304, 321
kidney beans, see beans, kidney
kidneys
  grilled, 106–7
  lamb, 380; beefsteak and kidney

kidneys: lamb (contd.)
    pudding, 35; sautéed, in
      omelet, 193
    pork, 382–3
    sautéed, 164
    veal, 384; beefsteak and kidney pie,
      254–5; beefsteak and kidney
      pudding, 35; grilled, 117; to
      clean, 254; devilled, 117; flambé,
      182; *fritto misto*, 208–9
kielbasa, 38, 398
    poached, with sauerkraut, 38
knives, 10–14, 16
    care of, 10
    to sharpen, 14
knockwurst, 398
    and lentil casserole, 276
kohlrabi, 375

lamb, 379–81; cuts, 380–81; doneness,
    testing for, 116
    aubergine stuffed with, 274–5
    brains, 379–80
    braised, 152; shanks, and lentil
      casserole, 276; shoulder, with
      ratatouille, 153
    breast, 381; devilled, 185
    chops, 380; grilled, 106, 115–116
    grilled, 104, 106, 107;
      marinades, 107
    hearts, 381
    kibbeh nayé, 304, 321
    kidneys, 380; beefsteak and kidney
      pudding, 35; sautéed, in
      omelet, 193
    leg, 381; to carve, 408; roast, 72–5;
      baker's style, 74–5
    liver, 381
    roast, 70, 71; leg, 72–5; leg, baker's
      style, 74–5
    shish kebab, 118–9
    stew, Irish, 135, 152
    sweetbreads, *see* sweetbreads
    tongues, 380
lard, 205, 375
larding, 80, 381
leeks, 389; to clean, 389
    poached, à la Grecque, 62–3
lemons, 375–6
    granité, 351

ice cream, 349
    mousse, frozen, 335
lentil casserole, 276–7
lettuce: kinds, 370–71
    blanched, 23
    braised, 160
    in salad, 306–7, 370, 371
    in stuffing, 370
    See also chicory
limes, 376
liqueur custard sauce, 210, 292
liquidizer, 15–16
liver
    beef, 379; *bourguignon*, 170–71
    grilled, 106–7
    calves', 385; *fritto misto*, 208–9;
      steaks, grilled, 116
    chicken: grilled, 105; sautéed, 177–8
    lamb, 381
    pork, 383
    sautéed, 164
lobster, 399; to buy, 42–3
    à la nage, 41–2
    au gratin, 129–30
    boiled, 42–3
    creamed, in celery and pecan ring,
      275–6
    in cucumber and carrot ring, 341–2
    spinach and seafood soup, cold,
      301–2
London broil, 110–11
Lyonnaise potatoes, 197

mace, 400
madeira
    puréed parsnips with, 62
    sauce, 290
Magimix, 15–16
mandarins, 376
marinades, 107
    braising, 140
    grilling, 107, 118, 119, 120,
      121–2, 124
    roast venison, 100
    teriyaki, 107, 110, 111–12
mayonnaise, 284, 294–8; to prevent
    curdling, 284, 295, 296, 367
    mustard, 297
    skordalia, 298–9
    smoked salmon, for cold roast veal, 298

sour cream, 297
tomato, 297
tuna, for cold roast veal, 297–8
variations, 296–8
measuring equipment, 18
meat, 376–85
barding, 77–8, 97, 98, 99, 381
basting, 69–70, 106–7
boiled, 21, 22–3, 24
braised, 105, 107, 133–4, 135, 136
grilled, 104–7
cooled or chilled, 332
cuts, 367–85
doneness, testing for, with fingertips, 9, 10, 71
freezing, 377
frozen, 71–2, 106, 377
larding, 80, 381
marinades, *see* marinades
pâte, 332, 345–7
minced, 377
roast, 67–72; spit-roasting, 68, 71,
135
salted, blanching, 24
sautéed, 105, 164–5
stock, *see* stock
uncooked, to keep, 377
See also carving; game
meat thermometer, 19, 70–71
melons, 385; to keep, 385
cantaloupe, 328–9, 385
Charentais, 385
honeydew, 328–9, 385
Ogen, 328–9, 385
watermelon, 385; drunken, 329
with port, 328–9
meringue cookies, 270
meringue kisses, 272
mincing, 13
mint, 374
sauce, 74
mirepoix, 134–5
puréed, as sauce, 135
veal: braised shoulder, 140; stuffed
breast, 142
mixer, 15, 16, 20
mixing equipment, 18
mornay sauce, 106, 105, 287
mortadella, 398
moulds, 17–18, 232, 333–4

mousse, 333
ham, cold, 336
lemon, frozen, 335
Roquefort, with seafood salad,
333–5
mousseline sauce, 294
mozzarella, 363
mushrooms, 385–6
blanched, 23
caps, poached, à la Grecque, 62–3
creamed, in celery and pecan ring,
275–6
crêpes, with turkey, 230
and cucumber sauce, 171
dried, 386
omelet, 193, 308
grilled, 125
paste (duxelles), 386
salad, 307, 308
sautéed, 193, 386; with turnips,
196
in scrambled eggs, 190, 308
soup, cream of, 300
in tomato sauce, 49
mussels, 399; to clean, 45
soup, 45
mustard, 386
hollandaise, 294
mayonnaise, 297
sauce, 287; sweet, 324–5
vinaigrette sauce, 305–6

nectarines, 386
New England boiled dinner, 24–6
nutmeg, 400
nuts, 386–8; to buy, 386–7; to keep,
387
roll, 240
as thickener, 284, 298

oils, 205, 388; to clarify and purify,
205; to keep, 305
vinaigrette sauce, 304–5
olive oil, 388; to keep, 305, 388
marinades, 121–2; red wine, 100,
119, 120; teriyaki, 111; vermouth
and herbs, 107; white wine, 124
vinaigrette sauce, 304–5
omelet, perfect, 191–3
fillings, 178, 193

1-2-3-4 cake, 263–6
onions, 388–90; to keep, 388
  French fried rings, 204, 210
  omelet, 193
  pearl or pickling, 389
  quiche, Swiss, 251
  red or Italian, 389; avocado and
    grapefruit (or orange) salad,
    315; avocado and tomato salad,
    313–14
  in salad, 307; with oranges, 99,
    390
  sautéed, 166, 193; with cheese,
    166; with wine, 166
  soup, *au gratin*, 43–4
  spring onions, 389; poached, à la
    Grecque, 62–3; in scrambled
    eggs, 190
  stuffed, 274
  vinaigrette, 310
  white, large (Bermuda), 388
  white, small, 389; to peel, 79, 389
    poached, à la Grecque, 62–3
  yellow globe (Spanish), 388
    braised, 162; French fried, 210
  See also chives; garlic; leeks;
    shallots
oranges, 390; to buy, 390; to peel
  segments, 315
  Bavarian cream, 338–9
  frosting and filling for 1-2-3-4 cake,
    264, 266
  génoise, 268
  mandarins, 376
  marmalade soufflé, 241
  salad: with onion, 99, 390; with
    onion and avocado, 315
  sauce, for duck, 290
  sugared, 328
  temple, 376
Owen, Jeanne
  chicken sautés, 166–7
  chili con carne, 150
oxtail, 379
  braised, 150
  broth, 151
  ragout, 150–51
oysters, 399
  Casino, 129
  sauce, 48–9

  scalloped, 273–4

palm, hearts of
  vinaigrette, 310; with anchovies
    and potato, 310
pan-fried, *see* sautéing
pans, 14, 16–17
  crêpe, 226–7
  custard sauce, 290
  frying, 205
  grilling, 14, 17, 106
  omelet, 191
  roasting, 69
  sautéing, 163–4
  white sauce, 285–6
papayas (pawpaw), 390
paprika, 390–91; to keep, 390
  Hungarian, 149, 390
  Spanish, 390
parboiling, *see* blanching
parchment, cooking or kitchen, 20,
  262
Parmesan (Parmigiana), 363
  mornay sauce, 105, 287
parsley, 374
  butter, 112–13, 374
  fried, 213
  rice, pungent, 51
  sauce, 288
parsley, Chinese, *see* coriander
parsnips, 391
  puréed, with madeira, 62
pasta, 391–2; to buy, 46, 391
  with butter and cheese (*al burro*),
    47; and cream, 47
  cheese for, 47, 392
  to cook, 22, 46–7, 391
pasta sauces: to serve, 47, 391–2
  garlic and oil (*aglio olio*), 48;
    with anchovies, 48
  mornay, 287
  oyster, 48–9
  tomato, 49; with mushrooms, 49;
    with sausage, 49
pastry, 223, 242
  choux (*pâte à choux*; cream puff),
    242, 255–63; *beignets soufflés*,
    204, 217–18; cream puffs with
    chocolate sauce, 255–7
  puff, simple, 242, 251–4

shortcrust, 242
suet, 35–6
tart, rich (*pâte brisée*), 242–7;
    apple, Swiss, 247; strawberry,
    simple, 248
pâté: containers for, 345–6; cooling
    and chilling, 332
veal and ham, 345–7
pâte à choux, 242, 255–6
beignets soufflés, 204, 217–18
cream puffs with chocolate sauce,
    255–7
pâte brisée, 242–7
apple tart, Swiss, 247
strawberry tart, simple, 248
pawpaw, *see* papayas
peaches, 392; to peel, 326; to ripen,
    326
blanched, 23–4
grilled, 128
ice cream, 350
poached, 64, 392
puréed, soufflé, 241
with raspberry purée, 327
with roast duck, 95–6
sugared, 326–7
peanuts, 387
pears, 392; kinds, 392
baked, 392
fritters, 211
poached in red wine, 64
sautéed, 166, 201
peas, green, 392–3
boiled, 59, 392
braised, with lettuce, 162
soup, chilled minted, 340
peas, mangetout, 60, 393
pepper, 393; freshly ground, 305,
    393
black peppercorns, 305, 393
green peppercorns, 393
grilled peppered duckling, 115
steak au poivre, 167–9
white peppercorns, 393
pepper, cayenne, 393, 394
peppers, 393–4
chili, hot, 317, 394
pimientos, 394
sweet or bell (green, red, yellow),
    393–4; blanched, 23; green, in

salad, 307; green, sautéed, 193;
    green, stuffed, 274; grilled, 126–7;
    to remove skins, 126–7;
    vinaigrette, 310
Périgueux sauce, 290
pheasant, 97, 394; doneness, testing
    for, 97–8
roast, 97–8
sautéed: with cabbage, 179–80;
    with cabbage and juniper
    berries, 180
wild, braised, 158
pigeon, *see* squab
pilaf, bulghur, 53
with almonds, 53
with mushrooms, 53
pimientos, 394
pineapple, 394–5; to buy, 394;
    ripeness, testing for, 394
flambé, 128
fritters, 211
grilled, 128
with raspberries, 328
sautéed, 166, 201
pine nuts, 387
and rice, 51
stuffed aubergine, 274–5
piquante sauce, 290
pistachio nuts, 387–8
plaice: grilled fillets, 120–21
plums, 395
poaching, 23
polenta, 54
fried, 54
pommes paille, 217
pork, 78, 381; cuts, 79, 381–3
brains, 381
chops, 381–2; braised, with sauer-
    kraut, 154–5; browned, and
    lentil casserole, 276; Niçoise,
    184–5; sautéed, 164–5
fat, 381; barding, 77–8, 97, 98, 99,
    381; lard, 205, 375; larding,
    80, 381
ham, *see* ham
headcheese, 381
heart, 382
hocks, 383; braised, Italian
    style, 154
kidneys, 382–3

pork (contd.)
liver, 383
loin, 79, 382; kebabs, 118; roast,
79–80, 382; roast, with fennel, 367
pigs' ears, 381
pigs' trotters, 383; boeuf à la mode,
146–7; in braising liquid, 134;
estouffat de Noël, 149
rind: in braising liquid, 134;
estouffat de Noël, 149
roast, 70; fresh ham, marbelized,
80–81; loin, 79–80, 382; loin,
with fennel, 367
salt pork, 24, 382
sausage, 383, 398; see also sausages
shoulder, 383
spareribs, 381, 382; roasted, 83
tenderloin (fillet), 382; braised,
and lentil casserole, 154–5
tongue, 381
potatoes, 395–6; to buy, 395; to keep,
395; kinds, 395
Anna, 225–6
baked, 224–6, 395; with
crumbled bacon, 224; with sour
cream and chives, 224; stuffed,
224–5
boiled, 23, 26, 395
chips, Saratoga, 205
French fried, 204; perfect, 216–17
fried, 203, 205, 217
gnocchi, and semolina, 55–6
Lyonnaise, 197
puréed, 61
roasted, 102
sautéed, 171, 193, 196–7
shoestring, 217
steamed, 395–6
straw (pommes paille), 217
as thickener, 284
pot-au-feu, 23, 27, 30–33
pot roast, French-style, 133–4,
146–7
pots, 14, 16–17
poule au pot, 33–5
poultry
boiled, 21
braised, 133; with mirepoix, 134,
135
grilled, 104, 106–7;

charcoal-grilled, 109; kebabs,
118; marinades, 107, 111–12
cooled or chilled, 332
roast, 69–70
to truss, 84–5
See also carving
prawns, 399–400; to clean, 399–400
à la nage, 41–2
creamed, in celery and walnut
ring, 275–6
crêpes, 230
in cucumber and carrot ring,
341–2
and dill croquettes, 211–12
fried, 207–8
spinach and seafood soup, cold,
301–2
pressure cooker, 26
prunes
and apple stuffing, 93, 94
soufflé, 241
puff pastry, cream, see cream puff
pastry
puff pastry, simple, 242, 251–4

quail, 396
sautéed, 180–81; breasts, with
white wine, 181
quiche, 223, 248–9
chicken, 250
Lorraine, classic, 249–50; with
cheese, 250; with ham, 250
onion, Swiss, 251
pastry shell, 242–7, 248–9
spinach, 250–51
turkey, 250

rabbit, 396
sautéed, with tarragon, 178–9
ragout, oxtail, 150–51
raspberries, 396
fool, 327–8
with pineapple, 328
purée, 326, 327; soufflé, 241
sugared, 327
ratatouille, 153
red snapper
baked, 278–9
poached, 40
seviche, 324

steak, sauté Provençale, 187–8
reduction of liquids, 23
red wine
  coq au vin, 155–6
  estouffat de Noël, 149
  marinades, 100, 119, 120
  pears poached in, 64
  salmon poached in red wine aspic,
    cold, 343–4
  vinegar, 305, 403
rémoulade
  celery root, 310–11, 362
  sauce, 297
rhubarb, 396–7
rhubarb chard, 371
rice, 49–50, 397
  arborio (Italian), 50, 397
  Basmati, 397
  boiled, 22; old-fashioned, 50
  brown, 49–50, 397
  flour, as thickener, 284
  long-grain, 49, 50, 397
  long-grain, parboiled, 49, 50,
    397; steamed, 50–51; steamed,
    variations, 51
  risotto, 50, 51–2; Villa d'Este, 52
  salad, 52–3
  short-grain, 50, 397
  and turkey casserole, 278
ricotta, 362
risotto, 50, 51–2
  Villa d'Este, 52
roasting, 67–72
  basting, 69–70
  pans, 69
  spit-roasting, 68, 71, 135
  temperature, 69, 70–71; meat
    thermometer, 19, 70–71
rocket, 306, 307, 371
Roquefort mousse with seafood salad,
  333–5
rosemary, 374
  butter, 109, 112–13
roux, 281–2
  thickened sauces, 285–90
Russian dressing, 297
Russian salad in tomato shells, 344

safflower oil, 388
saffron rice, 51

sage, 374
salad dressings, *see* sauces and
  dressings
salade Niçoise, 312–13
  variations, 313
salads
  avocado, onion, and grapefruit (or
    orange), 315
  beef, cold, 147
  cabbage, 306, 361
  celery root rémoulade, 310–311
  chapon, 305
  chicken, in celery and walnut ring,
    275–6
  coleslaw, 311–12, 361; spicy, 312;
    sweet-and-sour, 311–12
  composed, 312
  croutons, 313
  cucumber, 308–9
  greens, 304–7, 370–71; additions to,
    307; mixing with hands, 10, 307
  Gruyère cheese, 315
  health, 314–15
  mushroom, 307, 308
  Niçoise, 312–13; variations, 313
  orange and onion, 99, 390
  rice, 52–3
  Russian, in tomato shells, 344
  seafood, 335; in celery and walnut
    ring, 275–6
  spinach, 143, 306–7
  tomato, 309; with onion and
    avocado, 313–14; stuffed with
    Russian salad, 344; stuffed with
    white bean salad, 316;
    variations, 309
  vegetables vinaigrette, 307–10
  white bean, 59; and salmon, 316;
    and sardines, 316; with tomato,
    cucumber, and green pepper, 82;
    in tomato shells, 316; and tuna,
    316; tuna and anchovies, 316;
    vinaigrette, 310
salami, 398
salmon, 368–9
  gravad laks, 304, 324–5
  grilled fillets, 120–21
  poached, 40; cold, in red wine
    aspic, 343–4
  smoked, 369; mayonnaise for cold

salmon: smoked (contd.)
    roast veal, 298; risotto Villa
      d'Este, 52; in scrambled eggs, 190
  steak, sautéed, 187; Provençale,
    187–8
  tartare, 304
  and white bean salad, 316
salt, 397
sand tarts, 271–2
sardines: in white bean salad, 316
sauces and dressings:
  amandine, 187
  bananas à l'Archestrate, 201
  Béarnaise, 294
  béchamel, 282, 285–6; variations,
    287–8
  Bordelaise, 289–90
  bread, 284, 299
  brown, 282, 283, 284; basic,
    288–9; caramel colouring, 33,
    288–9; *glace de viande*, 17, 32;
    quick, 289
  caper, 288
  cheese, 287
  chocolate, 255–7; custard, 292
  Choron, 294
  coffee custard, 292
  crème fraîche, 301, 365–6
  cucumber and mushroom, 171
  Cumberland, 82
  curry, French, 287
  custard (crème anglaise), 290–92;
    chocolate, 292; coffee, 292;
    liqueur or spirits, 210, 292
  diable, 290
  dill, 288
  egg, 288
  garlic, Greek, 298–9; variations,
    299
  garlic and oil (*aglio olio*), 48;
    with anchovies, 48
  guacamole, 317–18; variations, 318
  hollandaise, 105, 284, 292–4;
    anchovy, 294; mustard 294;
    tomato, 294
  horseradish, 287
  madeira, 290
  mayonnaise, 284, 294–8, 367;
    mustard, 297; smoked salmon,
    298; sour cream, 297; tomato,

    297; tuna, 297–8; variations,
    296–8
  mint, 74
  mousseline, 294
  mustard, 287; hollandaise, 294;
    mayonnaise, 297; sweet, 324–5
  orange, 290
  oyster, 48–9
  parsley, 288
  pasta, to serve, 47, 391–2
  Périgueux, 290
  piquante, 290
  raspberry purée, 326, 327
  rémoulade, 297
  Russian dressing, 297
  skordalia, 298–9; variations, 299
  smoked salmon mayonnaise, 298
  soured cream: and lemon juice, 309;
    mayonnaise, 297
  suprême, 287
  tarragon, 287
  tartare, 297
  thickeners and liaisons, 281–5
  Thousand Island dressing, 297
  tomato: hollandaise, 294
    mayonnaise, 297; for pasta, 49,
    for pasta, with mushrooms, 49;
    for pasta, with sausage, 49; for
    veal chops Niçoise, 144
  tuna mayonnaise, 297
  velouté, 287; with chicken broth,
    98
  verte, 296–7
  vinaigrette: basic, 304–5; garlic,
    305; herbs, 306; mustard, 305–6
  white: basic, 282, 285–6;
    variations, 287–8
  white wine, for fish, 41, 287
  yogurt and lemon juice, 309
sauerkraut
  braised, 161
  with braised pork chops, 154–5
  with sausage, 38–9
sausages, 397–8; kinds of, 397–8
  grilled, 117
  and lentil casserole, 276–7
  poached, 38; with sauerkraut, 38–9
  See also individual kinds
sautéing, 105, 163–7, 203
  clarified butter, 189, 361

meunière, 164
pans, 163–4
savarin with apricot glaze, 266–8
scallops
broiled, 105, 107, 123–4
seviche, 323–4
Scotch shortbread, 270–71
sea bass: baked, 278–9
seafood
salad, 335; in celery and walnut
ring, 275–6
and spinach soup, cold, 301–2
See also fish; shellfish
semolina and potato gnocchi, 55–6
seviche, 304, 323–4
variations, 324
shallots, 389
pungent parsleyed rice, 51
shashlik, beef, 119–20
shellfish, 398–400
à la nage, 41–2
grilled, marinade, 107, 124
poached, 39
salad, 335; in celery and walnut
ring, 275–6
seviche, 304, 323–4
spinach and seafood soup, cold,
301–2
See also individual kinds
sherbet (sorbet), 332, 350–51
strawberry, 351
sherry and grapefruit jelly, 345
shish kebab, 118–19
shoestring potatoes, 217
shortbread, Scotch, 270–71
shrimps, 399–400; to clean, 399–400
creamed, in celery and pecan ring,
275–6
simmering, 23
skewer cooking, see kebabs
skordalia, 298–9
variations, 299
slicing, 11
smelt: fried, 213
snapper, red, see red snapper
sole
fillets, 369; grilled, 120–21; seviche,
323–4
sautéed, 186
sorbet, see sherbet

sorrel: salad, 306–7
soufflé fritters, see beignets soufflés
soufflés, 222, 231–3; dishes or moulds,
232
apricot, 241
cheese, 233–5; spicy, 235
chocolate, 239–40; roll, 239, 240
crêpes, 231
fruit, puréed, 241
glacé, 337–8; Benedictine, 337–8
coffee-flavoured liqueur, 338
Grand Marnier, 237–9
nut roll, 240
orange marmalade, 241
prune, 241
soups: thickeners and liaisons, 299–300
avgolemono, 300–301
avocado and buttermilk, cold, 320
beef broth, 26, 27, 32
chicken broth, 26, 28–9; double,
28–9
chicken consommé, 29
croutons, 318–19
cucumber and yogurt: Iranian,
319; Turkish, 319
egg-lemon, 300–301
gazpacho, California, 318–19
mushroom, cream of, 300
mussel, 45
onion, au gratin, 43–4
oxtail broth, 151
pea, chilled minted, 340
spinach and seafood, cold, 301–2
tomato, quick iced, 320
veal broth, 26, 27, 30, 139, 141
vegetable, four-day, 44–5
soured cream, 365
and lemon juice dressing, 309
mayonnaise, 297
soyabean oil, 388
spaghetti
with garlic and oil (aglio olio),
48; and anchovies, 48
oyster sauce, 48–9
spareribs, 381, 382
roasted, 83
spices, 400
to buy and keep, 400
spinach, 372; to clean, 372
boiled, 372

spinach (contd.)
    gratin of greens, 273
    omelet, 193
    puréed, with watercress, 372
    quiche, 250–51
    roll, 236–7
    salad, 143, 306–7
    sautéed, 197
    and seafood soup, cold, 301–2
    wilted, 60
squab (pigeon), 400
squid, 400–401
    to clean, 400
steeping, 24
stew, Irish, 135, 152
stock, 26–8, 134; to clarify, 29, 32
    beef, 26, 27, 32–3
    chicken, 26, 28–9
    oxtail, 151
    veal, 26, 27, 30, 139, 141
    vegetable, 27–8
strawberries, 401; to buy, 401
    coeur à la crème, 329
    ice cream, 349
    puréed, soufflé, 241
    with raspberry purée, 326
    Romanov, 326
    sorbet, 351
    tart, simple, 248
straw potatoes, 217
stuffing
    chicken, roast, 86–7; poussins,
        roast, 87–8
    goose, roast, prune and apple, 93–4
    turkey, roast: bread, 89–90; meat,
        89, 90
    veal: birds western style, 144–6;
        braised stuffed breast, 141–3
suet, 35–6, 76, 77, 205, 401
    barding, 77–8
    pastry, 35–6
sunflower oil, 388
suprême sauce, 287
swedes, 402
    three vegetable sauté: with carrots
        and courgettes, 200; with turnips
        and broccoli, 200
sweetbreads
    braised, 136; with mirepoix, 135
    calves', 381, 385
    creamed, in celery and walnut ring,
        275–6
    fritto misto, 208–9
    lambs', 381
    sautéed, 164; with ham, 183–4
sweet potatoes, 401
Swiss apple tarts, 247–8
Swiss chard, 371
    boiled, 60, 371
    gratin of greens, 273
    sautéed, 371
Swiss onion quiche, 251
Swiss steak, 137–8

Tabasco, 394
tabbouleh, 316–17
tangelos, 376
tangerines, 376
tarragon, 374–5
    butter, 112–13
    chicken, sautéed with white wine,
        172–4
    rabbit, sautéed, 178–9
    sauce, 287
tartare
    salmon, 304
    sauce, 297
    steak, 303, 304, 321–2
tarts: lining mould or pan, 232
    apple, Swiss, 247–8
    pastry (pâte brisée), 242–7
    strawberry, simple, 248
temple oranges, 376
teriyaki marinade, 107, 111–12
    chicken, grilled, 111–12
    flank steak, grilled, 110
terrine, 345–6
testicles
    beef, grilled or sautéed, 379
thermometer, meat, 19, 70–71
thickeners and liaisons, 281–5
    arrowroot, 283–4, 292
    avocado, puréed, 300
    for béchamel sauce, 286
    beurre manié, 282, 283, 286,
        288, 289
    cornmeal, 365
    cornflour, 283–4, 292, 331
    crumbs, bread or cake, 284
    eggs, 284, 331

flour, 281–2, 283, 284
  nuts, 284, 298
  potatoes, 284
Thousand Island dressing, 297
thyme, 375
  butter, 109
tins, 14, 17, 20
  bread, 14, 17
  cake, 14, 17, 262
  cookie, 17, 270
  pastry, 17, 245–6
  quiche, 17, 248
toast, 105
tomatoes, 401; to peel, 309; to peel
    and seed, 401
  blanched, 23
  grilled, 125–6
  hollandaise, 294
  mayonnaise, 297
  omelet, 193
  purée, in braising liquid, 134
  salad, 309; with onion and
    avocado, 313–14; variations, 309
  sauce, for pasta, 49; with
    mushrooms, 49; with sausage, 49
  sauce, for veal chops Niçoise, 144
  soup, quick iced, 320
  stuffed, 274; with Russian salad,
    344; with white bean salad, 316
  vinaigrette, 309
  and white beans vinaigrette, 81
tongue
  beef, 377
  lambs', 380
  pork, 381
  veal, 384
trifle, 339–40
  génoise, 268–9
tripe, 379
  à la mode de Caen, 223
trout, 369
  au bleu, 369
  sautéed, 186–7; amandine, 187;
    with herbs, 187
tuna
  mayonnaise, for cold roast veal,
    297–8
  and white bean salad, 316; with
    anchovies, 316
turkey, 88–9, 401–2; to carve, 406–7;

doneness, testing for, 91, 92; to
  truss, 84–5
  casserole, with rice, 278
  crêpes, with mushrooms, 230
  frozen, 402
  quiche, 250
  roast, 69, 70, 88, 402; without
    stuffing, 69, 70, 91–2; with two
    stuffings, 89–91
Turkish cucumber and yogurt soup,
  319
turnips, 402
  blanched, 23
  glazed, 198
  and mushrooms, sautéed, 196
  sautéed, 193; three-vegetable, 200
  See also swedes

vanilla, 402
  extract, homemade, 402
  ice cream: basic, 348–9; basic,
    variations, 348–9; French,
    349–50; French, variations,
    349–50
veal, 383–5; cuts, 384–5
  aspic, 30
  birds western style, 144–6
  braised, 138; breast, stuffed, 141–3;
    breast, stuffed, cold, 143;
    shoulder or leg, 139–41
  broth, see stock or broth below
  chops, 384; Niçoise, 144
  and ham pâté, 345–7
  hearts, 385
  jellied, 30, 342–3
  kebabs, 118
  kidneys, 384; beefsteak and kidney
    pie, 254–5; beefsteak and kidney
    pudding, 35; to clean, 254;
    devilled, 117; flambé, 182; fritto
    misto, 208–9; grilled, 117
  knuckle, 384; in braising liquid,
    134
  roast, 69; cold, with smoked
    salmon mayonnaise, 298; cold,
    with tuna mayonnaise, 297–8
  sausage, 385, 398
  sautéed, 181–2
  scallops (scaloppine), 164, 384;
    fines herbes, 181–2; fritto misto,

veal: scallops (contd.)
208–9
stock or broth, 26, 27, 30, 139, 141
tongue, 384
vitello tonnato, short-cut, 298
Wiener schnitzel, 215; with egg
and anchovies, 215
vegetables
blanched, 22, 23–4
boiled, 22, 59–60
braised, 135–6
fritto misto, 204; with meat,
208–9
kebabs, 107, 118, 119–20
grilled, 125
mirepoix, 134–5
omelet, 193
poached, à la Grecque, 62–3
purée, basic, 60–61
roasted, 102
sautéed, 166, 193; three-vegetable,
200
soup, four-day, 44–5
stock, 27–8
stuffed, 274
vinaigrette, 307–10
See also salads
velouté sauce, 287
with chicken broth, 98
venison, 99–100
marinade, 100
roast, 100–102; haunch, 101–2;
rack, 100–101
verte, sauce, 296–7
Viennese goulash, 149
vinaigrette sauce
basic, 304–5
garlic, 305
herbs, 306
mustard, 305–6
vegetables, 307–10
vinegar, 403
wine vinegar, 305, 403
vitello tonnato, short-cut, 298

walnuts, 388
aubergine, stuffed, 274–5
courgettes, sautéed, 199–200
watercress, 371
omelet, 193
puréed, with spinach, 372
salad, 307, 371
watermelon, drunken, 329
weisswurst, 398
wheat, cracked, *see* bulghur
white sauce, basic, 282, 285–6
to thicken or thin, 286
variations, 287–8
white wine
court bouillon: for fish, 40; for
shellfish, 41–2
marinade, 124
quail sautéed in, 181
sauce, for fish, 41, 287
vinegar, 305, 403
whiting
fried, 213
grilled fillets, 120–21
Wiener schnitzel, 215
with egg and anchovies, 215
wine
in braising liquid, 134
marinades, 100, 119, 120, 124
vinegar, 305, 403
See also red wine; white wine

yams, 403
yeast, 222–3, 403; fresh, to keep, 403;
to reactivate, 258–9, 403
bread, 258–9
yogurt
and cucumber soup: Iranian, 319;
Turkish, 319
and lemon juice dressing, 309
Yorkshire pudding, 75

zrazys Nelson, 171

MORE ABOUT PENGUINS
AND PELICANS

For further information about books available from Penguins please write to Dept EP, Penguin Books Ltd, Harmondsworth, Middlesex UB7 0DA.

In the U.S.A.: For a complete list of books available from Penguins in the United States write to Dept CS, Penguin Books, 625 Madison Avenue, New York, New York 10022.

In Canada: For a complete list of books available from Penguins in Canada write to Penguin Books Canada Ltd, 2801 John Street, Markham, Ontario L3R 1B4.

In Australia: For a complete list of books available from Penguins in Australia write to the Marketing Department, Penguin Books Australia Ltd, P.O. Box 257, Ringwood, Victoria 3134.

In New Zealand: For a complete list of books available from Penguins in New Zealand write to the Marketing Department, Penguin Books (N.Z.) Ltd, P.O. Box 4019, Auckland 10.